CARLOS CHÁVEZ AND HIS WORLD

CARLOS CHÁVEZ
AND HIS WORLD

EDITED BY LEONORA SAAVEDRA

PRINCETON UNIVERSITY PRESS
PRINCETON AND OXFORD

Published by Princeton University Press, 41 William Street,
Princeton, New Jersey 08540
In the United Kingdom: Princeton University Press,
6 Oxford Street, Woodstock, Oxfordshire OX20 1TW
press.princeton.edu

For permissions/credits, see pages xviii

Library of Congress Control Number: 2015937552

Cloth ISBN: 978-0-691-16947-7
Paper ISBN: 978-0-691-16948-4

British Library Cataloging-in-Publication Data is available

This publication has been produced by the Bard College Publications Office:
Mary Smith, Director
Irene Zedlacher, Project Director
Karen Walker Spencer, Designer
Emily Hart, Cover Design
Text edited by Paul De Angelis and Erin Clermont
Music typeset by Don Giller

This publication has been underwritten in part by grants from Roger and Helen Alcaly
and Furthermore, a program of the J. M. Kaplan Fund

Printed on acid-free paper. ∞

Printed in the United States of America.

1 3 5 7 9 10 8 6 4 2

To Robert L. Parker
A Gloria Carmona

Contents

Preface

Carlos Chávez was the most powerful Mexican artist of the twentieth century. Not necessarily the best (who could determine that?) or even the best known, but undoubtedly the most powerful. Chávez's cultural agitation—for indigenous music, for modernism, for a place for Mexican music in the world, and for a Mexican culture widely supported by the state—started early, in the years of the Revolution (1910–1921). But it acquired full visibility when, in 1928, he founded the Orquesta Sinfónica de México (OSM), setting the organizational and musical standards for orchestral activity in Mexico. Drawing from both private and state funds as well as a substantial ticket income, Chávez managed to keep his orchestra afloat for twenty-one years until 1949, when he dissolved it and regrouped its members as the state-funded Orquesta Sinfónica Nacional. Chávez, Silvestre Revueltas (his assistant conductor in the early years), and the OSM offered a platform for Mexican composers of three generations, including those that came immediately before and after their own, to create new music and to try it out before an increasingly musically educated albeit bellicose and demanding audience. In the 1930s and '40s the newspapers gave ample coverage, including photographs, to the fashionable Friday concerts, frequented by the famous and the wealthy. On Sundays, though, the audience was made up of blue-collar workers and students with tickets at discounted prices. One of Chávez's goals was to form an audience for art music—old and new—and he pursued it further by offering free concerts to children and workers in collaboration with trade unions, and touring the country extensively with his orchestra.

Chávez's innovative programming of twentieth-century music polarized audiences and critics. Although politics and music were enmeshed with one another and all kinds of topics, both petty and lofty, were debated, for over two decades music was at the center of public opinion and social life in an unprecedented fashion. Subject to debate were questions such as how modern or modernist Mexican music should be, and how it was to represent Mexico, a particularly compelling issue in the 1920s and '30s. Chávez's answers were unequivocal: Mexican music should be very modern, finding its rightful place within the evolution (my choice of word here is deliberate) of Western art music, and it should represent Mexico in whichever way it might—or even not at all.

In his own music, Chávez sought to imagine, invent, and propose as adequate to his audiences and fellow musicians specific musical representations—iconic and indexical topoi—of pre-Columbian and contemporary indigenous musics, which in the early twentieth century were commonly but mistakenly considered to be one and the same. In pieces such as *Los cuatro soles*, *Xochipilli*, and *Sinfonía india*, Chávez constructed the indigenous as simple but not simple-minded, innocent but not gullible, pure, sober, laconic, reserved, and powerful. In works such as the *Sinfonía de Antígona* and *Daughter of Colchis* (which Martha Graham titled *Dark Meadow*), he used similar musical means to construct a different antiquity: the Greek. In the 1920s and '30s, his style allowed him to be national while being modernist, objective, and anti-Romantic: he could write primitivist music alongside machine-music. But from his early works to his late ones, whether representational or abstract, we find in Chávez's stylistic preferences a remarkable consistency that stems from what Yolanda Moreno Rivas called an "ethical willfulness." His instrumental colors are bright and well defined, his textures polyphonic, his melodies diatonic and modal or pentatonic, his dissonances piercing, his forms innovative but solid, and his rhythm surprisingly complex yet based on simple rhythmic figures. Chávez's music is powerful and stubborn. It doesn't always enchant, but it most often persuades; it can be harsh and emotionally restrained, and yet when Chávez chose to indulge in lyricism, he showed he could write a beautiful melody. As the composer's beloved friend, Aaron Copland, used to say: his music takes more than one listening.

Although Chávez spoke often in favor of modernism, he did not advocate nationalism as a style (but rather as a political position), and his agenda was clear: to play as much Mexican music, and as many times, as possible. The best, the truest Mexican music, he believed, would eventually emerge from this process. For the same reasons, he taught little aesthetics and did not care much for style in his teaching of composition, focusing instead on encouraging experimentation and on developing the students' technique along the same lines he had earlier taught himself to compose: with attention to scales and collections of pitches, motivic work, instrumental color, texture and counterpoint, and the resultant vertical structures. Two separate generations of composers passed through his studio, one in the 1930s and another in the 1960s (when Chávez taught with Julián Orbón). Among these can be counted some of the best composers of the mid- and late twentieth century, including José Pablo Moncayo in the first group, and Eduardo Mata and Mario Lavista in the second. At the same time, Chávez opened numerous spaces for the performance of new Mexican music: the aforementioned OSM, beginning in the late 1920s, the music series at the Conservatorio Nacional de Música and at the Departamento de Bellas Artes in the early 1930s, the Instituto Nacional de Bellas Artes (INBA) from its founding in 1947, and finally at the Colegio Nacional in the 1950s and '60s, where as an inaugural member he again worked on audience formation and consciously left behind the model of the composer–intellectual as the mover and shaker of Mexican music.

Chávez did not only create spaces for music. As director of the Departamento de Bellas Artes in 1933–34, he was behind the promotion of dance, photography, filmmaking, and theater created within "an ethics of social justice," as he stated in an administrative document of the time. The political winds soon shifted away from him, however, and he stayed away from governmental positions for over a decade. But after having been invited to serve as the cultural advisor in Miguel Alemán's presidential campaign in 1946, Chávez designed and founded the Instituto Nacional de Bellas Artes (INBA), Mexico's most important cultural institution within the fine arts until the recent advent of the Consejo Nacional para la Cultura y las Artes (CONACULTA) in 1988. INBA began operations on 1 January 1947, eventually grouping all state-sponsored art schools, music performing organizations, dance companies, theatres, and museums within a ministry of culture of sorts. Indeed, with INBA's by-laws Chávez institutionalized the protection of Mexican art as one of the duties of the state. Yet INBA was not to be an organ merely for the preservation and presentation of art, but also for its steady creation. The propulsive nature of INBA at its inception was clearly captured in Chávez's own words: "If experimentation is not to be carried out, then nothing should be carried out."

From his position at the head of INBA, Chávez devised numerous projects for which he called on some of the brightest minds in Mexican culture. Outstanding among them was the impulse he gave to Mexican dance. Drawing inspiration from the Ballets Russes, he brought together composers, artists, and choreographers, such as Mexican-American José Limón, for the production of new Mexican ballets, an initiative spearheaded by his life-long friend, painter, and anthropologist Miguel Covarrubias. Chávez and Covarrubias had been partners in art since their twenties, when they concocted fabulous and ambitious ballets and pantomimes to be produced on the stages of New York, where they both lived for a few years. Although these early projects came to nothing, they paved the way for later joint enterprises. But Covarrubias was not the only Mexican artist to whom Chávez was close. From an early age he also participated in joint intellectual and artistic projects with writers such as Carlos Pellicer, Xavier Villaurrutia, and Salvador Novo, and painters such as Diego Rivera and Agustín Lazo. These activities included literary magazines, experimental theater, ballets (such as *Horsepower*, with Rivera, which did come to fruition in Philadelphia in 1932), recordings and performances, and, of course, the musical setting of Mexican poetry.

Chávez had a complex and fascinating relationship with political power. He occupied governmental administrative positions three times in his life. These did not always end happily. From 1929 to 1934 he served in the Ministry of Education, first as director of the Conservatorio Nacional de Música and then briefly, as noted, as director of the Departamento de Bellas Artes. Yet he resigned from the latter post after barely a year when his mentor, the socialist Minister of Education Narciso Bassols, was forced out of office. Chávez served out his entire term as the founding director of INBA during Alemán's presidency, from 1947 to 1952, but when at the request of President Luis Echeverría he returned to head that institution in 1973, thereby taking charge of music in Mexico once more, he lasted barely a few months before he was ousted by the musicians themselves and their trade unions.

For most of his life, however, Chávez managed to be close to political power even while he was not a part of it. Commanding substantial fees as a composer writing on commission from institutions abroad and as a conductor with an international career, he was able to remain personally independent from government. Although the OSM was often the focus of political contention in regard to Chávez's programming and choice of guest conductors (or lack thereof), it operated on a mixture of private, local, and federal funding, and its legal standing prevented it from being taken over by the state—despite the many public campaigns favoring exactly that. But the state saw no advantage in taking over responsibility for an orchestra that brought prestige to Mexico and worked perfectly well without its intervention: Chávez delivered.

However, Chávez's relations with other artists did not always go well. Disagreements and fights, personal and public, were often prompted by the clash of larger-than-life personalities and/or political differences. Chávez's energy and strong will were the stuff of legend. He could be authoritarian, even when very young. He did not think of art and arts administration as a democracy. He called to work with him only those people in whom he believed, and he brushed aside and left behind many others who eventually resented him: his ideas, the changes he implemented, the preference shown to him by the state regardless of the particular administration, and the way in which he shaped Mexican culture. In Mexico a black legend developed around him which cannot be dispelled until its ingredients—true and false—are sorted out.

Chávez often took refuge from the turmoil of his Mexican life by going to New York: first as a penniless, aspiring composer in Greenwich Village, then as a conductor, established composer, and arts administrator at the Barbizon Plaza Hotel—he used the hotel's stationary to scribble down drafts for countless projects—and finally living in his own apartment near Lincoln Center. Working with Edgard Varèse, his mentor in the fight for modernism, and the Composers' Guild, and later with Aaron Copland, Henry Cowell, and the personalities associated with the League of Composers and its journal, *Modern Music*, Chávez established himself as an integral part of the burgeoning modern music scene of the 1920s. And he developed a deep appreciation for African-American music. While remaining firmly rooted in New York, he later expanded his reach to the West Coast, its institutions and its composers—Cowell, John Cage, Lou Harrison. While at the helm of OSM, and once his own social mobility allowed him to have homes in both Mexico City and on the Pacific Coast in Acapulco, he provided friends such as Copland, Colin McPhee, Virgil Thomson, and Leonard Bernstein with numerous "Mexico summers": spaces where they could relax, create, or, in the case of Copland's *Short Symphony* and McPhee's *Tabu-Tabuhan*, listen to the premiere of their works with the OSM. And whereas he never wielded in the United States the power he had in Mexico, he was not without it, and he was often consulted by institutions such as the Guggenheim Foundation or asked by governmental and cultural organizations to facilitate projects in Mexico. As I wrote elsewhere, Chávez had a love affair with the United States and with everything it meant for him: modernity, power, efficiency, opportunity, warm friendships, and a home away from home.

As busy, productive, complex, and fascinating a life as I have painted here (and perhaps precisely on account of that), Chávez is still largely unknown to us. And so are his work and worlds. The composer's international reputation rests on a few Indianist works, and even so his iconic Aztec ballets have not been performed in over half a century. The Fourth, Fifth, and Sixth symphonies (commissioned, respectively, by the Louisville Orchestra, the Koussevitzky Foundation, and the New York Philharmonic) are unknown, as are his late orchestral pieces *Elatio* and *Discovery* (also U.S. commissions) and the *Soli III* for solo instruments and orchestra (commissioned by Germany's Südwestrundfunk). And pianists remain largely ignorant of his magnificent piano music.

Chávez's repertoire as a conductor was impressively vast, yet his conducting career also remains unexplored. His relationship to the politically and financially powerful is little understood, although that has not stopped many in Mexico from condemning him for it. Nor do we yet have a full appreciation of his work at the helm of INBA, an institution crucial for Mexican culture. His enormous correspondence with personalities in Europe, the United States, and Latin America is unknown to non-Spanish-speaking readers. And we still need to come to grips with the changes in his political ideas over the years, from his Marxist-inspired projects and writings of the 1930s to his political allegiance to the United States during the Cold War. The list of things we do not know about Chávez could go on for pages.

This volume aims to fill some of those lacunae. Christina Taylor Gibson gives us a new and more complex vision of an aspect of the composer's career we thought we knew well: Chávez's connections to the New York new music scene, which she examines through the lens of *Modern Music*. Howard Pollack expands our perspective on Chávez's friendship with Aaron Copland by considering the latter's relationship with Silvestre Revueltas and asking intriguing questions for us to ponder about their mutual influences. Stephanie N. Stallings opens a new area in Chávez's U.S. connections by exploring his affinities to and differences with Henry Cowell's ideas on music, non-Western cultures, and the future of music, as she also initiates the exploration of Chávez's understanding of African-American culture. Ricardo Miranda and Roberto Kolb-Neuhaus cement our knowledge of Chávez in Mexico. Miranda analyzes stylistic trends in three generations of outstanding Mexican composers whose works were programmed by Chávez, but who remain largely unknown outside of Mexico. Kolb-Neuhaus moves away from the lack of objectivity that had plagued much earlier scholarly research on the intense personal and professional relationship between Chávez and Revueltas, reframing it as a productive and thought-provoking compositional dialogue.

The second part of the volume offers closer views of Chávez and his works. In a brilliant technical analysis that leaves us wanting to know more, Amy Bauer tackles some of the more esoteric of his compositions, the late *Soli* and *Inventions*. We experience the same effect after reading Luisa Vilar-Payá's incursion into the piano music, in which she persuasively argues for Chávez's interest in the autonomy of the musical work. David Brodbeck provides insight into the composition of one of Chávez's most challenging works, the Violin Concerto, using previously unknown correspondence and other documentary evidence to offer a privileged view into the world of conductors and the musical marketplace in the

United States. My own essay offers a historically contextualized reading of Chávez's representation of the indigenous in music.

Chávez's greater world, the one he shared with painters, writers, photographers, and foreign "pilgrims" to Mexico, is the subject of the third section of the volume. Helen Delpar and James Krippner bring to bear on Chávez their expertise on binational cultural exchanges between Mexico and the United States. Krippner highlights the role of Chávez's friendship and support in the work of photographer and filmmaker Paul Strand in Mexico, while Delpar places Chávez within the context of the United States vogue for all things Mexican during the 1920s and '30s. Ana Alonso-Minutti takes us to the 1950s with a perceptive account of Chávez's role as a composer-intellectual within the prestigious Colegio Nacional. Susana González Aktories and Antonio Saborit explore the relationships between Chávez and other Mexican artists of his generation. González Aktories focuses on the members of the literary group Los Contemporános, who were among Chávez's oldest friends, and offers us a nuanced reading of the composer's settings of poetry by Pellicer and Villaurrutia. Saborit uses accounts by such eyewitnesses as poet José Juan Tablada and anthropologist and author Anita Brenner to reconstruct for us a riotous chronicle of the friendship, joint projects, and lively social life shared by Chávez and Miguel "El Chamaco" Covarrubias within Mexico City's and New York's artistic milieus. The more famous but nevertheless unexplored relationship between Chávez and his friends Diego Rivera, David Alfaro Siqueiros, and Rufino Tamayo is here represented by Anna Indych-López's insightful analysis of their portraits of the composer. Finally, Leon Botstein brings the volume to a close with a brilliant and thought-provoking essay that situates Chávez within the broader context of Mexican culture and politics of the twentieth century, while reflecting on his place within Western art music.

All the contributors to this volume are superb scholars; many are also personal friends and scholarly accomplices. To speak of Chávez and his world is really to speak of Chávez and his many worlds. As editor of this volume, I have tried to cover as many of them as possible, and I have limited authors to fewer words than their topics deserved. This was a merciless request, but all graciously complied. Needless to say, we hardly managed to cover enough. The result is nevertheless an extraordinary collection of tantalizing morsels, tempting glimpses of a plethora of opportunities for further research into Chávez and his many worlds.

Acknowledgments

My special gratitude and admiration go to Leon Botstein for bravely choosing to devote this year's Bard Music Festival to Carlos Chávez, a difficult but important composer, a fascinating and controversial historical figure, and yet virtually unknown to audiences in the United States. What Eugene Ormandy once said of Chávez could be said as well of Leon Botstein: "He's a fighter!" Profound thanks are also due to Christopher Gibbs for his enthusiasm, openness, and patience; I realize I must have put him in a difficult position from time to time, but he was never anything but a joy to work with. Thanks as well go to Irene Zedlacher, the magician behind the scenes, and to the members of the very professional Bard team. A previous editor in this wonderful series once proposed that as soon as cloning editors becomes possible we should begin with Paul De Angelis. I second the motion. Paul possesses superb editorial skills and diplomatic abilities, for which I am deeply grateful. I also wish to express my thanks to Don Giller, Erin Clermont, and the rest of the editorial team, as well as to our capable translator Rebecca Levi. I owe a further debt of gratitude to two of my colleagues at the University of California, Riverside—to Byron Adams, for his warm support within the program committee, and above all to Walter Clark, who graciously allowed me to be fully in charge of this project, which for me was such a pleasure.

I am deeply grateful to the superb binational team of scholars who contributed to this book, including my husband, David Brodbeck, now a fellow *chavista*. I know I pushed most of them outside their comfort zones, both scholarly and personally. I truly appreciate their professionalism, and am moved by their loyalty and friendship.

Many primary sources went into the making of this book, and I would like to acknowledge Bob Kosovsky and the staff of the New York Public Library for the Performing Arts, where Chávez's music manuscripts are located, and the staff of the Archivo General de la Nación in Mexico City, which holds the rest of his estate. Finally, I wish to acknowledge Chávez's heirs, Anita Prieto and Jana Angulo, for their interest in the project. The book is dedicated to Robert L. Parker and Gloria Carmona, deans of Chávez scholarship.

Permissions and Credits

Music Sales Company, G. Schirmer, Associated Music Publishers, Inc., has graciously given its permission to reprint musical excerpts from the following copyrighted works by Carlos Chávez:

Energía © Copyright 1968 (Renewed) by Carlanita Music Co. Used in Example 1 in "Chávez, *Modern Music*, and the New York Scene" by Christina Taylor Gibson.

Sinfonía india © Copyright 1950 (Renewed) by G. Schirmer Inc. Used in Example 2 in "Chávez, *Modern Music*, and the New York Scene" by Christina Taylor Gibson, and in Example 7b in "Carlos Chávez and the Myth of the Aztec Renaissance" by Leonora Saavvedra

"North Carolina Blues" © Copyright 1961 (Renewed) by Carlanita Music Co. Used in Example 1 in "The Pan/American Modernisms of Carlos Chávez and Henry Cowell" by Stephanie N. Stallings.

Cantos © Copyright 1933 (Renewed) by Carlanita Music Co. Used in Examples 3 and 4 in "Carlos Chávez and Silvestre Revueltas: Retracing an Ignored Dialogue" by Roberto Kolb-Neuhaus.

"Solo," from Seven Pieces for Piano © Copyright 1936 (Renewed) by Carlanita Music Co. Used in Examples 2 and 3 in "Chavez and the Autonomy of the Musical Work: The Piano Music" by Luisa Vilar-Payá.

Third Sonata © Copyright 1972 (Renewed) by Carlanita Music Co. Used in Examples 4a, 4b, and 5 in "Chavez and the Autonomy of the Musical Work: The Piano Music" by Luisa Vilar-Payá.

Ten Preludes, Ten Modal Preludes © Copyright 1940 (Renewed) by G. Schirmer, Inc. Used in Examples 6, 7, 8, and 9 in "Chavez and the Autonomy of the Musical Work: The Piano Music" by Luisa Vilar-Payá.

Five Caprichos © Copyright 1983 (Renewed) G. Schirmer, Inc. Used in Example 10 in "Chavez and the Autonomy of the Musical Work: The Piano Music" by Luisa Vilar-Payá.

El fuego nuevo © Copyright 1925 (Renewed) by Carlanita Music Co. Used in Examples 1a, 1b, 2a, and 2b in "Carlos Chávez and the Myth of the Aztec Renaissance" by Leonora Saavvedra.

Los cuatro soles © Copyright 1925 (Renewed) by Carlanita Music Co. Used in Examples 3, 4, 5, and 6 in "Carlos Chávez and the Myth of the Aztec Renaissance" by Leonora Saavvedra.

Violin Concerto © Copyright 1964 (Renewed) by Carlanita Music Co. Used in Examples 1a and 1b in "Music and the Marketplace: On the Backstory of Carlos Chávez's Violin Concerto" by David Brodbeck.

Music Sales Company, G. Schirmer, Associated Music Publishers, Inc., has graciously given its permission to reprint musical excerpts from Colin McPhee's *Tabu-Tabuhan* © Copyright 1960 (Renewed) by Associated Music Publishers, Inc. (BMI). Used in Example 3 in "Chávez, *Modern Music*, and the New York Scene" by Christina Taylor Gibson.

Hal Leonard Corporation has graciously given its permission to reprint musical excerpts from the following copyrighted works by Silvestre Revueltas:

Colorines © Copyright 1966 Southern Music Publishing Company. Used in Examples 2 and 3 in "Carlos Chávez and Silvestre Revueltas: Retracing an Ignored Dialogue" by Roberto Kolb-Neuhaus.

"Heroic Prelude" from *Two Little Serious Pieces* © Copyright 1957 Southern Music Publishing Company. Used in Example 5 in "Carlos Chávez and Silvestre Revueltas: Retracing an Ignored Dialogue" by Roberto Kolb-Neuhaus.

Boosey & Hawkes and Music Sales Company, G. Schirmer, Associated Music Publishers have graciously given its permission to reprint musical excerpts from the following copyrighted works by Carlos Chávez:

Sonatina for Piano © Copyright 1924 (Renewed) by Carlanita Music Co. Used in Example 1 in "Chavez and the Autonomy of the Musical Work: The Piano Music" by Luisa Vilar-Payá.

Invención © Copyright 1962 (Renewed) by Carlanita Music Co. Used in Example 1 in "Non-Repetition and Personal Style in the *Inventions* and *Solis*" by Amy Bauer.

Invention II © Copyright 1965 (Renewed) by Carlanita Music Co. Used in Examples 2 and 3 in "Non-Repetition and Personal Style in the *Inventions* and *Solis*" by Amy Bauer.

Invention III © Copyright 1969 (Renewed) by Carlanita Music Co. Used in Example 4 in "Non-Repetition and Personal Style in the *Inventions* and *Solis*" by Amy Bauer.

Soli II © Copyright 1963 (Renewed) by Carlanita Music Co. Used in Examples 5 and 6 in "Non-Repetition and Personal Style in the *Inventions* and *Solis*" by Amy Bauer.

Soli IV © Copyright 1976 (Renewed) by Carlanita Music Co. Used in Example 7 in "Non-Repetition and Personal Style in the *Inventions* and *Solis*" by Amy Bauer.

Also, the following copyright holders have graciously granted permission to reprint or reproduce the following copyrighted material:

The Estate of Julián Orbón © Copyright 1982 for "Carlos Chávez's Symphonies" by Julián Orbón.

Aperture Foundation for photograph by Paul Strand used as Figure 1 (p. 225) in "Carlos Chávez and Paul Strand," by James Krippner.

The Permissions Company, Inc., on behalf of Copper Canyon Press, for Eliot Weinberger's English translations of poetry by Xavier Villaurrutia used in "The Literary Affinities and Poetic Friendships of Carlos Chávez," by Susana González Aktories.

Centro de Información-Fototeca de El Colegio Nacional for the photograph of its founding members, Figure 1 (p. 275) in "The Composer as Intellectual: Carlos Chávez and El Colegio Nacional," by Ana Alonso-Minutti.

Banco de México Diego Rivera Frida Kahlo Museum Trust, Mexico, D.F. / Artists Rights Society (ARS), New York, for the portraits of Chávez by Diego Rivera, reproduced as Figure 1 (p. 297) and Figure 4 (p. 301) in "Portraits of Carlos Chávez: Testimonies of Collaboration," by Anna Indych-López.

Art Resource, NY, and María Elena Rico Covarrubias for the portrait of Chávez by Miguel Covarrubias, reproduced as Figure 2 (p. 298) in "Portraits of Carlos Chávez: Testimonies of Collaboration," by Anna Indych-López.

National Portrait Gallery, Smithsonian Institution / Art Resource, NY, and María Elena Rico Covarrubias for *Lightning Conductors* by Miguel Covarrubias, reproduced as Figure 3 (p. 299) in "Portraits of Carlos Chávez: Testimonies of Collaboration," by Anna Indych-López.

Museo de Arte Moderno, Mexico City, INBA-Conaculta. © Instituto Nacional de Bellas Artes y Literatura, 2015, for the portrait of Chávez by David Alfaro Siqueiros, reproduced as Figure 5 (p. 302) in "Portraits of Carlos Chávez: Testimonies of Collaboration," by Anna Indych-López.

Yana Angulo and Chávez family and © Tamayo Heirs/Mexico/Licensed by VAGA, New York, NY, for the portrait of Chávez by Rufino Tamayo reproduced as Figure 6 (p. 303) in "Portraits of Carlos Chávez: Testimonies of Collaboration," by Anna Indych-López.

Tamayo Heirs/Mexico for *Cosmic Terror* by Rufino Tamayo, Figure 1 (p. 309) in

“The Modernist Invention of Mexico: Carlos Chávez, the Mexican Revolution, and the Cultural Politics of Music,” by Leon Botstein. Art © Tamayo Heirs/Mexico. Licensed by VAGA, New York, NY.

Tamayo Heirs/Mexico and The Museum of Modern Art for *Girl Attacked by a Strange Bird* by Rufino Tamayo, Figure 2 (p. 310) in “The Modernist Invention of Mexico: Carlos Chávez, the Mexican Revolution, and the Cultural Politics of Music,” by Leon Botstein. Digital image © The Museum of Modern Art. Licensed by SCALA / Art Resource, NY. Art © Tamayo Heirs/Mexico/Licensed by VAGA, New York, NY.

The author and publishers have made every effort to trace holders of copyright. They much regret if any inadvertent omissions have been made.

CARLOS CHÁVEZ AND HIS WORLD

PART I

Chávez's Musical World

Chávez, *Modern Music,* and the New York Scene

CHRISTINA TAYLOR GIBSON

> No other musical magazine of our century can possibly have the place in history, either as monument or as source material, that "Modern Music" already occupied, because no other magazine and no book has told the musical story of its time so completely, so authoritatively, so straight from the field of battle and from the creative laboratory. Its twenty-three volumes are history written by the men who made it.
>
> —Virgil Thomson, *New York Herald Tribune*, 12 January 1947

As Virgil Thomson noted in his obituary for *Modern Music,* which ran from 1924 through 1946, the magazine served as the central chronicle of the New York new-music scene during the years it was in existence.[1] Although technically the house organ of the League of Composers, it was the only publication of its kind—none of the other new-music organizations produced a periodical—and, like many "little magazines" of the early twentieth century, its small circulation belied its influence. Its editor and manager during the entire run was Minna Lederman, who used her considerable personal and intellectual resources to shape the publication. Intended as a critic's gateway into contemporary music, the articles it published were not of a highly technical nature, yet most of the participating authors were themselves composers intent on sharing their worldview. In this way the publication served as a central text for both new-music participants and its would-be observers. If, as Benedict Anderson suggests, communities are often "imagined" in the pages of periodicals, then *Modern Music* offers the most detailed available map of New York musical modernists' identity.[2]

Carlos Chávez's views and music figure prominently in the magazine. During *Modern Music*'s run he was an integral part of the New York new-music scene, first as a young ultra-modernist and then as an established composer-conductor with a transnational career. Chávez's self-concept as a modernist can be traced in *Modern Music*'s pages, beginning with his article "Technique and Inner Form,"[3] which places the composer in an intellectual music avant-garde, and continuing through the very last issue of the magazine, in which Salvador Moreno published an encomium to the Orquesta Sinfónica de México's (OSM) performance of new music in Mexico. More importantly, *Modern Music* situates Chávez within the new-music community scene of New York, revealing his alliances, status, and identity within the group. In other words, it conveys key information about the politics governing the performance and reception of his music, especially as it pertains to his U.S. career and legacy.

Methodology

Although scholars have long recognized that Chávez's reception in the United States was inextricably intertwined with politics—both of the small-scale interpersonal variety and that of large populations tied together by virtue of race, nationality, or status—here I apply a network-derived analysis that is deeply indebted to approaches found in several recent ethnomusicological texts. Perhaps most pertinent is Ingrid Monson's book on jazz improvisation in New York, *Saying Something*. Like her, I examine "the interactive shaping of social networks and communities that accompany musical participation" while recognizing that "participation" may take a very different form when the musical practice is less "interactive" in its performance practice.[4]

Chávez's experience in the New York modernist music community during the years in question, 1927–46, varied; in part it was dependent on his own understanding of the culture's strictures and his navigation of them to better his status. The community was also in flux and responsive to outside forces. Chávez's network in New York was extensive, and it would not be possible to document the entirety of it in a short essay. Instead, I seek new insight into the ways in which friendships with men like Henry Cowell, Colin McPhee, and Aaron Copland affected his work for and with *Modern Music,* as well as his access and influence within the New York music community.[5]

Chávez's Modernisms in *Modern Music*

Modern Music arose out of a nascent but vibrant new-music culture in New York City. By the year of its first publication, 1923, sectors of the city had fallen under the spell of Leo Ornstein and Edgard Varèse. *Pro-Musica*, the International Composers' Guild, and the League of Composers presented contemporary music with much attention in the local press.[6] But, as Minna Lederman describes it, critics were inclined toward sensational objections rather than genuine engagement with the music; the League conceived of the magazine as a response and a literary charm campaign. In this respect, they met with near instant success: "The immediate target was the press, whose critics at once fell in love with the *Review*. Not only W. J. Henderson (*New York Sun*), Lawrence Gilman (*New York Tribune*), and Olin Downes (*New York Times*) but reporters all across the country hailed our journal."[7]

Over the next few years the community around the magazine expanded, so that when Chávez was living in New York (1926–28), its intended public included the new-music community of the city, their counterparts on the West Coast, and those within that circle of influence, including critics, scholars, intellectuals, and artists in other fields.[8] They drew this diverse and attentive readership by offering something that no other periodical had with such regularity: straightforward analysis of contemporary music written by composers active in the scene.

It was in this guise that Chávez's name first appeared in the publication. In an article titled "New Terms for New Music," Henry Cowell referred to the composer's *Energía* as an example of "contrapuntal polytonality."[9] To illustrate his point, he provided half of measure 19 from the first movement of the work (see Example 1) and explained that "'contrapuntal polytonality' can be formed by setting more widely related keys against each other in such fashion that each one will stand out independently." Thus, though none of the keys are firmly established, the viola part approaches G-sharp/C-sharp major, the cello line C major, and the bass A major. There is also a two-against-three motion between the viola/bass and the cello, which contributes to the sense of independence among the lines. Unseen in the example, but apparent in the complete score, are the multiple levels of "contrapuntal polytonality," made stark by the idiosyncratic instrumentation: piccolo, flute, bassoon, horn (F), trumpet (B-flat), bass trombone, viola, cello, and double bass. Surrounding measure 19, each group of instruments has a different melodic and harmonic identity. Chávez notes that the brass should play "neither softer nor louder than winds and strings," emphasizing equity among the parts. Such a technique is not sustained throughout the movement; it is followed by several measures in which the winds and strings trade melody while the brass is confined to brief interjections and moments of unison or tonal harmony that offer respite from the rigorous dissonance found elsewhere.

Example 1. Carlos Chávez, *Energía*, mm. 19–23.

Readers unfamiliar with Chávez and his work would have had little context to evaluate the composer's use of "contrapuntal polytonality." Cowell provided no information beyond the one-measure example and basic definition cited above. For those who had heard Chávez's music performed or seen the scores he was lending to and playing for friends in the New York music community, the reference would have resonated. Absent knowledge of the *Energía* score, which had not yet been performed in public in New York, *Modern Music* connoisseurs would have been familiar with the fourth movement of *H.P.* (*Horsepower* or *Caballos de vapor*), *Otros tres exágonos,* the three sonatinas, and the Third Sonata, all of which had been

Example 1. Continued

performed in the city over the past few years.[10] These scores are similar to *Energía* in their use of machine imitations, creative approaches to timbre, and, most relevant here, employment of dissonance and counterpoint. Indeed, both the piece and Cowell's analytic approach to it were apt representatives of Chávez's desired aesthetic and image at the time.

The portrayal of Chávez as an experimenter was supported by the composer's article printed just a few pages later in the magazine. Titled "Technique and Inner Form," the essay proposes an entirely new approach to composition pedagogy; it suggests that composition schools should stop asking students to adopt the styles and techniques of the past, even as practice exercises.[11] Instead, they should focus on new approaches so that the music is more likely to reflect the time, place, and personality of the composer. In primitive societies, Chávez wrote, "The young were taught the

Example 1. Continued

musical elements, to set their problems (which were almost always of a magical nature), and to solve them." Today, he argued, a different approach was called for: "Let him see the elements of the problem . . . but let him in no way be taught to solve the problem. The known devices and rules for solution lead to results that are too much alike, and therefore useless."

The article reflected Chávez's self-taught approach, and it suggested the reforms he was trying to make as head of the Mexican National Conservatory, a post he held from 1928 until 1933, and again for a few months in 1934. Several years later Chávez refined these ideas in another article for *Modern Music,* "Revolt in Mexico":

> We no longer believe that music is beautiful because it contains unique and absolute truths according to unique and

> quite immutable laws. We believe that technic is the concrete means of artistic expression, and that consequently each example of authentic music implies its own particular technic. No type of music is *the* music, and there is no absolute truth containing the whole truth of all music.[12]

The modernist stance of "Technique and Inner Form" and "Revolt in Mexico" characterized Chávez's writings for *Modern Music*. He was particularly concerned with the practical, systemic obstacles to the creation and performance of new music. In the articles quoted above, his primary concern was pedagogy; in "The Function of the Concert"[13] and "Music for the Radio,"[14] he turned his attention toward avenues for performance of new music. The first of these articles is concerned with patronage and the implications of the contemporary economics of music making. Although he concluded that "the concert has lent itself to increasing the importance of the performer at the cost of the composer," he believed the situation was reversible: "The big symphony societies, the university, school, and college departments of music, and all the concert-giving societies in general music realize that they should round out the musical organization assigned to them by once more making the encouragements of creation the nucleus of their functions."[15]

Although Chávez does not refer to his professional life in "The Function of the Concert," it is clear that his role as both a composer and performer informed his views. His most influential platform for reforming musical life was not through composing, but in his position as conductor and musical director of the Orquesta Sinfónica de México, from 1928 to 1946. Under his guidance, the OSM developed a repertoire with a great degree of modernism and nationalism.[16] In recognition of this feat, Virgil Thomson reprinted several OSM programs in the *New York Herald Tribune*. By studying that concert repertoire next to a set of New York Philharmonic programs from the same year (to which Thomson was surely making an implicit comparison), one can see the relatively large amount of time and space accorded new and American works at the OSM (Table 1). Although other U.S. symphony orchestras like the Boston Symphony Orchestra and the Philadelphia Orchestra were more adventurous in their programming, none superseded the modernism and nationalism found in the OSM programs.[17]

"Music for the Radio" explores the utility of radio as a medium to reinvigorate contemporary musical life. Once again, Chávez's advice to composers is of a practical nature: "Since the process of transmission is dependent primarily on the microphone, it seems inevitable that music written for the radio ought to be planned with that basic consideration."

Table 1. Seven Concert Programs from the 1938–39 Season

New York Philharmonic Programs selected from John Erskine, *Philharmonic-Symphony Society of New York*	**OSM Concert Programs reprinted in *New York Herald Tribune***
Weber, Overture to *Der Freischütz* Sibelius, *The Swan of Tuonela* and *The Return of Lemminkäinen* Stravinsky, *The Firebird* Mozart, Adagio and Fugue for Strings Beethoven, Symphony No. 5	Bach, Suite No. 3 Poulenc, Concerto for Two Pianos Debussy, *Iberia* Shostakovich, Symphony No. 1
Reznicek, Overture to *Donna Diana* Elgar, Viola Concerto (arr. Lional Tertis, Cello Concerto, Op. 85) Respighi, *The Fountains of Rome* Tchaikovsky, Symphony No. 4	Cherubini, Overture to *Anacreon* Mozart, Piano Concerto in G Major Stravinsky, *Rite of Spring* Debussy, *La mer*
Schubert, Dances for Strings Debussy, Preludes and Entr'actes from *Pélleas et Mélisande*, Acts 1, 2, and 4 Sibelius, Violin Concerto in D Minor, Op. 47 Wagner, Overture to *Tannhäuser*	C. P. E. Bach, Symphony in F Major J. S. Bach, Suite No. 1 J. Ch. Bach, Symphony in B-flat Vivaldi-Bach, Concerto for Four Pianos Buxtehude-Chávez, Chaconne
Beethoven, Overture to *Coriolanus* Bach, Violin Concerto in A Minor Schumann, Symphony No. 1 Franck, *Le chasseur maudit* Lalo, Violin Concerto in F Minor, Op. 20	Ravel, *Mother Goose* Berlioz, *Symphonie fantastique* Debussy, *Prelude to Afternoon of a Faun* Ravel, *Pavane for a Dead Infanta* Ravel, *Daphnis and Chloe* Suite No. 2
Sanders, Little Symphony No. 1 in G Schumann, Piano Concerto in A Minor, Op. 54 Brahms, Symphony No. 4	Huizar, Symphony No. 3 Bloch, Suite for Viola and Orchestra Mendelssohn, Violin Concerto in E Minor Prokofiev, *Scythian* Suite
Handel, Concerto Grosso for Strings in G Minor, No. 6, Op. 6 Mozart, Piano Concerto in A Major (K. 488) Falla, *Nights in the Gardens of Spain* Strauss, Overture to *Der Zigeunerbaron*	Beethoven, *Egmont* Overture Boccherini, Cello Concerto in B-flat Berezowsky, Violin Concerto Sibelius, Symphony No. 1
Stravinsky, Suite from *Pulcinella* Beethoven, Piano Concerto in C major, Op. 15 Franck, Symphony in D Minor	Mozart, *Les petits riens* Bach, Concerto in D Minor for Two Violins Stravinsky, *Apollon musagète* Chávez, *Sinfonía de Antígona* Chávez, *Sinfonía india*

He goes on to enumerate the various approaches to amplifying an ensemble and ways in which composers might use the process to create new sonic experiences. As in "The Function of the Concert," Chávez expresses optimism about the future of music for radio: "Up to now no compositions have appeared which even begin to use the specific instrumental resources of electrical transmission. Surely, sooner or later, such music must come."[18]

By 1940, the year he wrote "Music for the Radio," the relationship between modernism and modern technology had absorbed Chávez for almost fifteen years. First seen in the mechanical sonic environment evoked in works like *Energía*, it also motivated tours of the Bell Laboratories in New Jersey in 1932, a series of articles for the Mexican newspaper *El Universal* that same year, and his first published book, *Toward a New Music: Music and Electricity* (1937).[19] Although Chávez wrote an entire chapter on radio in *Music and Electricity*, that piece dealt with the new realities of employment and dissemination in a technological age. By examining the best methods for composing for the medium in "Music for Radio," he extended the implications in his earlier writings.

According to correspondence with Lederman, there was a more immediate inspiration for the *Modern Music* article. In May 1938, Chávez sent a telegram to her, ostensibly referring to an earlier conversation: "I am experimenting writing for radio. I think it is better to write article later."[20] A year later they revisited the topic: "As a matter of fact, what I want to say in the proposed article will be more or less the result of my experiences in writing my Harp Concerto for Radio, in which I will be working in the course of this year."[21]

The experiment of the Harp Concerto was not successful—at least the composition was not preserved in Chávez's files, and there is no trace of it in his catalogue—but his exploration of the topic was timely. In the 1930s and '40s classical composers were being commissioned to write for radio, resulting in several works composed especially with the medium in mind. Chávez's own *Sinfonía india* (1935) had been written at the invitation of William Paley, the president of Columbia Broadcasting System (CBS). Of particular influence was Deems Taylor's series of commissions for CBS radio, which produced William Grant Still's *Lenox Avenue*, Aaron Copland's *Music for Radio*, Roy Harris's *Time Suite*, and Louis Gruenberg's *Green Mansions*, all written and performed in 1937.[22]

All four of Chávez's articles for *Modern Music* situate the composer as an innovator, with practical solutions to some of the most entrenched problems plaguing modern composers. In every case Chávez agitated for reforms that might further the creation, performance, and acceptance of new music. His solutions were rooted in his own experiences working to change musical life in Mexico. It is probably true, as several authors claim, that Chávez used knowledge gained during his New York trips in the 1920s to create the foundation for a modernist music scene in Mexico City.[23] But it is equally true that during the 1930s and '40s

Chávez regarded his accomplishments in Mexico City as a model for his colleagues in the United States, and many of them, including Thomson, agreed with such an analysis.

Criticism, Connections, and Aesthetic Intersections

As Chávez became more closely identified with Mexican musical life and cultural identity, writers and reviewers for *Modern Music* could hardly avoid analyzing aspects of "Mexicanness" in his music and career. Unlike the profiles and reviews in the popular press, however, the *Modern Music* community was most concerned about Chávez's avant-gardism; that is, the marriage of nationalism and modernism absorbed these writers, not the exotic *mexicanidad* so readily profiled elsewhere. Such attributes were first praised in 1928 by Aaron Copland in the pages of *The New Republic* and Paul Rosenfeld in his book *By Way of Art*.[24] Yet, before 1932, none of Chávez's overtly nationalist works had been performed in the United States. While building the OSM and serving as head of the National Conservatory, Chávez continued to pursue opportunities to premiere works in the States, particularly his nationalist ballets. When he asked Copland for help, the composer responded:

> Why don't you write to Minna Lederman to ask her to do the publicity you need? I doubt if she will refuse if you ask her personally. Or possibly, someone like Miss [Anita] Brenner could do the actual work and Minna could advise how, where and when to send it out. Or possibly, you could have all the material written and typed in Mexico City and Minna could send it out for you up here.[25]

In his reply Chávez expressed interest in the idea, but there is no evidence that Lederman became his publicist in a formal capacity. She did demonstrate investment in his career, however, when Chávez returned to the United States in 1932 to promote the performance of his ballet *H.P.* The performance featured costume and stage designs by Diego Rivera, and was to be executed by Leopold Stokowski and the Philadelphia Orchestra.[26] In a letter written about two months before the premiere, Lederman fretted about the upcoming issue:

> It is unfortunate that you won't be here before the first of March. Paul Rosenfeld, as I wrote you, will write an article

> about you and, moreover, it is important that he have an opportunity of looking over any new music you have. . . . You see this is for the March issue which is to come out about a week and a half before the performance of your ballet. This will give the newspapers and other magazines an opportunity to quote from Paul's article after it appears in our magazine and in time to add publicity to your ballet.[27]

For various reasons, including his own health and Chávez's busy schedule, Rosenfeld was unable to complete the article in time for the March–April issue alluded to above. Two of Rivera's sketches were included, one featuring the coconut costume and another the stage design for the second scene. In the same issue, Marc Blitzstein reviewed a performance of *Energía* in a concert under the auspices of the Pan American Association of Composers. The next issue, May–June 1932, included a sizable profile by Rosenfeld as well as a review of the *H.P.* production by Blitzstein.

In his review of *Energía*, Blitzstein noted that the music "undergoes no development, almost no change. It would be hard to imagine music fresher, more candid and engaging than that of Chávez; but either he has not yet found a form which will enable him to grow, or it is not the sort of music which is meant to grow."[28] *H.P.* certainly provided a change in aesthetic, if not the type of growth for which Blitzstein searched. The work's synopsis deals with interactions between the North and South with the hard-edged modernism found in *Energía* representing the North and a folk music–infused lyricism representing the South. Blitzstein observed that this approach also proved problematic for the composer: "Since Chávez's music is hard, not soft, literal, brutal and unperfumed, we were offered the paradox of a 'Southern' composer dealing most successfully with the 'Northern' aspects of his theme."[29]

Although *H.P.* was Chávez's first public venture in a more accessible, nationalist direction, it was *Sinfonía india,* his second orchestral work performed in the United States, that ensured the composer's place in U.S. musical life. This time, rather than using folk music to represent the "Southern," the composer turned toward native music and an ancient past, aligning himself with the primitivism made famous by Stravinsky in *Rite of Spring* and subsequently found in so many works of the period. *Sinfonía india* premiered on CBS radio in 1936 in a program of Mexican music constructed and led by Chávez. Collectively the program—which included nationalist Indianist works by his students and protégés, and suggested a new direction for the

Example 2. Carlos Chávez, *Sinfonía india*, mm. 34–42, entrance of Mexican percussion in measure 37.

public face of Mexican music—appeared to impress traditionalists and modernists alike. Canadian composer Colin McPhee reviewed the performance for *Modern Music,* and his prose is nothing short of breathless:

> One feels on hearing this music first of all a primitive energy that has nothing of the exotic but is a clear and forceful expression of racial vitality both useful and healthy. . . .

Example 2. Continued

> There are no tricks in the workmanship—no preoccupations with "problems." It races along like a runner happy in his strength and with energy to spare in the end. We need such music as we need fresh air and exercise.[30]

Much of McPhee's description of *Sinfonía india* could easily apply to his own orchestral masterpiece, *Tabu-Tabuhan,* which was composed

Example 3. Colin McPhee, *Tabu-Tabuhan*, mm. 147–56, entrance of gamelan-like instruments (reduced score).

later the same year. Both are large-scale symphonic works that draw on non-Western traditions—ancient Mexico in the case of Chávez and contemporary Bali in the case of McPhee—and are simultaneously suffused with a modernist musical language. These basic similarities place both compositions in a larger complex of non-Western modernisms found in works by Stravinsky, Bartók, and Varèse, among others, and it is likely that

Example 3. Continued

both men were subject to a variety of influences. Yet the convergences in approach found in *Sinfonía india* and *Tabu-Tabuhan* extend more deeply than those found with other composers, providing a musical documentation of the cross-influence possible within the *Modern Music* network.

The most obvious similarities relate to the instrumentation, structure, and texture of the compositions. Both works are written for an enlarged

Example 3. Continued

symphony orchestra with a small ensemble of foreign instruments embedded therein. The smaller groups are largely percussive. Chávez calls for drums and rattles, requesting Native American instruments where possible. McPhee uses a six-person battery of percussionists playing marimba, xylophone, drums, and cymbals; within the composition the percussion often plays with the two pianos to evoke the sound and texture of the Balinese gamelan. McPhee subtitled his work "Toccata for Orchestra and 2 Pianos," and Chávez referred to his as a "symphony," but both use elements of the concerto grosso in their treatment of the sub-ensembles. For example, in *Sinfonía india* the entrance of the Mexican percussion in measure 37 is analogous to the first solo portion of a concerto grosso. The full orchestral sound quiets, highlighting the smaller group, with a "continuo" of clarinet and bass, gradually morphing into a "tutti" at rehearsal number 9 (see Example 2). The entry of the Balinese elements in *Tabu-Tabuhan* is much more subtle, but there are long stretches of alternation also recalling concerti grossi, with the pianos serving as a kind of Balinese-inspired continuo (see Example 3).

Most of McPhee's Balinese melodies are taken from the composer's own transcriptions of gamelan works and contain the musical characteristics familiar to that genre, including a narrow range of melodic motion, usually only four or five notes, syncopated rhythm, and frequent ostinati. The additive texture, particularly in the first movement, recalls the field recordings of gamelan performance. Such attributes conveniently bridge the divide between the Western styles McPhee admired—classical, jazz, and Latin American popular music—and the music of Bali that he wished to exhibit. They also suited European expectations of the "exotic," making the work part of a larger body of twentieth-century symphonic music to evoke the primitive. In this way, *Tabu-Tabuhan* was closely linked to *Sinfonía india,* in which Chávez also used transcribed melodies, pentatonicism, and ostinati.

Although both the source material and the approaches used to recontextualize it are very different, one suspects that the connections between the two works and the techniques used in them were not lost on Chávez. That is why in his article "Revolt in Mexico," Chávez argued that modernism could and should be pan-ethnic, as long as it was also highly individualistic: "The music of Bach and Palestrina is beautiful—and so is that of a Chinese, Mexican, or Balinese musician. They are different, however, and the difference is one of complexion of technic. If a Mexican musician uses Bach's technic, he is selling his birthright for a mess of pseudo-Bach."[31] It might seem odd that Chávez listed Bali alongside China and Mexico, but interest in Bali was very much in the air at the time: we find it realized in Margaret Mead's scholarly writings and Miguel

Covarrubias's drawings and writings, as well as a host of travelogues.[32] Covarrubias was a close friend of both Chávez and McPhee; surely he shared his experiences and field research. In addition, recordings of gamelan were among the first "world music" to be widely distributed and were part of Henry Cowell's collection, which he shared with Chávez.[33] But the most avid advocate for Balinese music in the New York community was McPhee. During the 1930s, McPhee shared his knowledge, often playing his transcriptions for friends in New York.[34] Such performances must have influenced Chávez, who was in the midst of his "Aztec" period and was searching for a way to make modernist primitivism appealing to Mexican audiences.[35]

McPhee's transcriptions impressed Chávez sufficiently to motivate an invitation to Mexico. As McPhee later recalled:

> It was in the mid-1930s, back in New York for a year, that I suddenly had the idea, partly suggested by Carlos Chávez, of writing an orchestral work utilizing material I had collected in Bali. "Come to Mexico City," he said, "write it, and I will play it with the orchestra."[36]

As a result, McPhee spent what his wife, Jane, termed a "Mexico summer" at the San Angel Inn, outside Mexico City; and it was during that period that he composed *Tabu-Tabuhan*.[37] The summer concluded with a premiere performance by Chávez and the OSM, only months after the composer had presented his own *Sinfonía india*. For critics and subscription audiences in Mexico, the *Tabu-Tabuhan* premiere may have served as a subtle reminder that the primitivism in Chávez's works was connected to trends within the larger cosmopolitan modernist community; it was certainly part of Chávez's efforts to connect the avant-gardism of the OSM with that of the United States and Europe.

In the years that followed, McPhee became Chávez's greatest advocate in the pages of *Modern Music*. Although Chávez's music and career were examined in articles by others, his name appears most frequently in articles by McPhee, who wrote many of the "Scores and Records" columns for *Modern Music* between 1939 and 1944, and several reviews of live music in 1936 and 1937. The music represented in these reviews is wide-ranging in both aesthetic and genre; it includes an examination of a performance of the *Sinfonía de Antígona*, the score of the lesser-known Ten Preludes, and the recordings released for the Museum of Modern Art exhibit *Twenty Centuries of Mexican Art*, for which Chávez organized a series of concerts. *Antígona* is a large, abstract orchestral work, Ten

Preludes a Baroque-influenced exercise in technical brilliance, and the MoMA exhibit ranks among Chávez's most nationalist enterprises. For McPhee, though, the works were united by a stylistic approach. The "vitality" and "energy" noted in *Sinfonía india* are observed repeatedly. For example, in his review of Ten Preludes, McPhee writes of "the intensity . . . the determined drive toward the objective of the piece."[38] In every case he is impressed, observing that "Chávez has complete mastery of his medium."[39]

McPhee was not the only *Modern Music* writer to find Chávez's works inspirational. In addition to the expected reverence from Copland[40] and Rosenfeld,[41] there is a review by Donald Fuller of Chávez's Piano Concerto, which proclaims the work "one of considerable mastery . . . as mature and powerful an expression as I have heard from Chávez."[42] Particularly notable are reviews of Chávez's conducting appearances by John Cage and Elliott Carter. Both observed Chávez's skill at making new works come alive for an audience; for example Cage wrote, "The impression made was direct and vital. The rest of the music we have heard recently is weak and doesn't reach far enough to even touch."[43] Carter also explores the links between the music of Mozart, Debussy, Ravel, Falla, Stravinsky, and Chávez's own aesthetic, leading to a detailed examination of his style. In direct opposition to the popular favorites *H.P.* and *Sinfonía india,* which became standard works on programs Chávez conducted in the United States, Carter lists as his favorites *Antígona, Tierra mojada, Spirals,* and the Sonatina for Violin and Piano. These are celebrated not for their "Mexicanness" or primitivism, but because they are "conceived in a new idiom"; that is, they are ultra-modern.[44]

Not every *Modern Music* critic's praise was unqualified, and two concerns arise repeatedly. The first is particularly apparent in the early reviews and is best summarized by Israel Citkowitz's statement that the rhythm in the Third Sonata "gets out of [Chávez's] grip and proceeds to chug-chug all over the keyboard."[45] That is, here as elsewhere Chávez had allowed his thirst for experimentation to outpace his ability, preferring imperfection over predictability. The second issue is addressed in Copland's review of Seven Pieces for Piano: "One despairs in a single paragraph of making music like this accessible to those who have no taste for it."[46] Rather than mourning or celebrating the presence of Mexicanness in the work, Copland is far more concerned that it might not find an audience.

Chávez and Power in the New York Modernist Community

By the 1940s, Chávez's influence in Mexican cultural life was palpable, and his wielding of it famously tyrannical. In an essay Ricardo Pérez Monfort wondered if during that era the composer-conductor was a "*caudillo o cacique cultural*"—in that construction Chávez's musical dictatorship remained unquestioned.[47] One would not use the same language to describe his reputation in the United States. Without an official post, directorship of a major symphony orchestra, or the ear of politicians, Chávez could not possibly exert the same force on musical life. Furthermore, as a Mexican operating in the States, he occupied an insider/outsider status, as others have noted.[48] Yet what becomes apparent in the pages of *Modern Music* is that Chávez did possess and wield a different type of power within the New York new-music community during the late 1930s and early '40s, partly because he was able to use his position within Mexico to fortify friendships and connections beyond its borders.

The exchange with McPhee described above is just one example of the largesse Chávez was capable of showing. Reports of his generosity are found in many of the biographies and memoirs of his contemporaries. Copland made several extended visits to Mexico, the first in 1932 and several subsequently, including a trip in 1936 during McPhee's "Mexico summer." Stokowski telegraphed a few days ahead of his arrival in 1930 and was able to lead the OSM in a performance.[49] Paul Strand spent months traveling around Mexico, finding work through Chávez's recommendation.[50] Chávez was among Mabel Dodge Luhan's most important contacts when she visited Mexico, as documented in her memoir, "Whirling Through Mexico."[51] Within his circle of friends and associates in the United States, Chávez became well known for his willingness to introduce U.S. artists, intellectuals, and friends to Mexico. The correspondence files in the Archivo General de la Nación (AGN) contain many requests for Chávez's help, including those from Martha Graham and Marsden Hartley.[52] When visiting, U.S. friends invariably attended performances of the OSM, where they were able to witness not just the modernism and nationalism in the programming, but also the focus on U.S. music.[53] One of the very first works the orchestra performed was John Alden Carpenter's *Skyscrapers*; over the next several years, they would feature compositions by William Grant Still, Henry Cowell, Roy Harris, Virgil Thomson, and Aaron Copland.[54]

In the pages of *Modern Music,* the strength of Chávez's influence was apparent in the occasional reports about musical life in Mexico, particularly during the last decade of publication. When Lederman decided to run a regular column about music in the Americas titled "Inter-American Review," she turned toward Chávez for help: "Don't you want to write us a letter from Mexico telling how musical life is effected [*sic*] by the war?"[55]

Although he agreed to do so, he was unable to provide *Modern Music* with an article for the magazine. In a letter dated 4 January 1943, Chávez describes the problem: "There was a lot of ground to cover and many connected subjects to deal with. . . . I have now twelve typewritten pages, but it is still only a first draft. As I see it now, in its definite form the article will have around 25 pages."[56]

On 19 January, Lederman replied, declining the article because of its length (pieces for *Modern Music* did not exceed 2,700 words).[57] Chávez was not asked to contribute to the column again; indeed, *Modern Music* did not print another article by him.[58] The search for "Inter-American Review" columnists continued. Two days after writing to Chávez, Lederman wrote Copland in desperation, "Having embarked on a Latin-American section now I'd like to be able to fill it."[59] Copland's ideas included Salvador Moreno, "a young composer in the Chávez camp."[60] Moreno first contributed a short article for the March–April 1945 issue; not surprisingly, it included a long section on Chávez and the OSM prefaced with the statement "The Symphony Orchestra of Mexico continues to be the most important factor in the musical life of the Republic."[61]

The theme continued in a similar piece Moreno wrote for the last issue of the magazine:

> During the past season of seventeen concerts, more than forty works by moderns and contemporaries were presented—a really extraordinary number for any orchestra in the world—and of these more than twenty were played for the first time in Mexico. The presence of three great contemporary composers, Stravinsky, Milhaud and Hindemith, as guest conductors in programs mainly of their own works, made this an exceptional season. . . . The zeal of Carlos Chávez in encouraging symphonic activity is at last bearing fruit in the whole republic.[62]

Thus Moreno posits that Chávez created a critical node in Mexico City within a cosmopolitan modernist network. The Mexico City node drew from the musical culture of Europe, augmented that inheritance with homegrown music, and radiated outward from the capital to Mexico's other urban centers. Although unstated in the article—but implied in its language and publication in *Modern Music*—Chávez's Mexico City was also threaded to New York, by more than New World identity. Both locations were modernist scenes strengthened by attention diverted from war-ravaged Europe. Moreover, Chávez's multidimensional modernist impulses were amplified in both cities. In New York he felt an affinity to avant-gardists like Cowell, Varèse, and Copland, and a sense of community in the *Modern Music* circle, but in Mexico City he was able to effect changes in musical life that made widespread acceptance of modernism seem possible.

Conclusion

Minna Lederman and *Modern Music* were at the center of a modernist culture in New York connecting contemporary composers to one another, to music critics, and to modernists around the world by creating a forum in which they could express their understanding of new music and the mechanics that supported it. An examination of Chávez's participation in the publication confirms the composer's centrality to New York musical modernism and refines our understanding of the cosmopolitan, transnational relationship between the musical communities of Mexico City and New York as mediated by both the composer and his friends in New York. The importance of Chávez's role is not only demonstrated by the frequency with which he wrote and was written about in the publication, but also by the substance of that material. That is, even in negative or mixed reviews, such as those by Blitzstein, his music was regarded as part of a serious experiment in new music.

Chávez's articles for *Modern Music* reveal his belief in the publication as a mechanism to ignite change within the music community of New York, and he saw his experiences in Mexico as informative. His own prose is subtle about making this connection, but others, like Thomson in the *Herald Tribune* and Moreno in *Modern Music,* emphasized more directly the rare adventurousness in Chávez's programming and reform agenda. Such articles suggest that Mexico City should be considered alongside New York as having formed part of a nascent international modernist scene.

The material illuminating Chávez and *Modern Music* also establishes that the composer and the musical life he cultivated in Mexico were as critical in developing the careers of others as New York was in shaping Chávez's career. The evidence dismantles any view of knowledge flow as unidirectional. Chávez's efforts to create a performance platform for modernist, American orchestral music were widely admired and envied; composers and new music enthusiasts in the United States wished to emulate him and his orchestra. Not only are his articles for *Modern Music* practical and informative, but his music compositions and patronage inspired fellow composers, including Colin McPhee. Chávez's ideas about modernism, like those of Lederman, Cowell, Rosenfeld, and Copland, shaped the development of music in New York, inspiring composers and critics to reimagine the possibilities for new music. In this way he was not an exotic Mexican, but a cosmopolitan modernist whose contributions to the New York modern music scene were integral to the development of music and identity there.

NOTES

1. Virgil Thomson, "Closing Activities," Box 1, *Modern Music* Archive, Performing Arts Reading Room, Library of Congress.

2. Benedict Anderson, *Imagined Communities: Reflections on the Origin and Spread of Nationalism* (New York: Verso, 2006). The idea pervades the book, but is introduced in Chapter 3, "The Origins of National Consciousness," 37–46.

3. Carlos Chávez, "Technique and Inner Form," *Modern Music* 5/4 (May–June 1927): 28–31. (Henceforth *MM*.)

4. Ingrid Monson, *Saying Something: Jazz Improvisation and Interaction* (Chicago: University of Chicago Press, 1996), 2. Other texts informing my approach include Julian Gerstin, "Reputation in a Musical Scene: The Everyday Context of Connections Between Music, Identity, and Politics," *Ethnomusicology* 42/3 (Fall 1998): 385–414; and Benjamin Brinner, *Knowing Music, Making Music: Javanese Gamelan and the Theory of Musical Competence and Interaction* (Chicago: University of Chicago Press, 1995). Although a large body of literature in popular music studies examines "scenes," I have found the methods in the works cited above to be more applicable here.

5. I am deeply indebted to scholars who study Chávez and New York. The works I have relied on most include Leonora Saavedra, "Carlos Chávez y la construcción de una alteridad estratégica," in *Diálogo de resplandores: Carlos Chávez y Silvestre Revueltas,* ed. Yael Bitrán and Ricardo Miranda (Mexico City: INBA/CONACULTA, 2002), 125–36; also Saavedra's "Of Selves and Others: Historiography, Ideology, and the Politics of Modern Mexican Music" (PhD diss., University of Pittsburgh, 2001); Robert L. Parker, *Carlos Chávez: Mexico's Modern-Day Orpheus* (Boston: Twayne, 1983); also Parker's "Carlos Chávez and the Ballet: A Study in Persistence," *Choreography and Dance* 3–4 (1994): 81–88; and "Carlos Chávez y la música para el cine," *Heterofonía* 17/1 (January–March 1984): 13; Carol A. Hess, *Representing the Good Neighbor: Music, Difference, and the Pan American Dream* (Oxford: Oxford University Press, 2013); Antonio Saborit, "Mexican Gaities: Chávez en la Babilonia de hierro," in *Diálogo de resplandores,* 139–48; Stephanie N. Stallings, "Collective Difference: The Pan-American Association of Composers and Pan-American Ideology in Music, 1925–1945" (PhD diss., Florida State University, 2009).

The foundational scholars in this area are Robert Parker, Roberto García Morillo, and Robert Stevenson. Their thinking is strongly connected to those more interested in Chávez's work and legacy in Mexico, such as Gloria Carmona, Yolanda Moreno Rivas, and José Antonio Alcaraz. There are too many texts by Carmona to list here; the most useful for this study are Carlos Chávez, *Escritos periodísticos (1916–1939),* ed. Gloria Carmona (Mexico City: El Colegio Nacional, 1997); and Carlos Chávez, *Epistolario selecto,* ed. Gloria Carmona (Mexico City: Fondo de Cultura Económica, 1989). The relevant work by Moreno Rivas is *Rostros del nacionalismo en la música mexicana: Un ensayo de interpretación* (Mexico City: Fondo de Cultura Económica, 1989); and that of Alcaraz is *Carlos Chávez: Un constante renacer* (Mexico City: INBA/CENIDIM, 1996).

I also draw on the scholarship of those who examine music in New York, particularly Carol Oja, who has closely studied *Modern Music,* the League of Composers, and the people who functioned within such organizations. Other pertinent works are Michael Meckna, "Copland, Sessions, and *Modern Music*: The Rise of the Composer-Critic in America," *American Music* 3/2 (Summer 1985): 198–204; David Metzer, "The League of Composers: The Initial Years," *American Music* 15/1 (Spring 1997): 45–69; "'New Music of New Ears': The International Composers' Guild," *Journal of the American Musicological Society* 36/2 (Summer 1983): 266–86; Carol Oja, ed., *Stravinsky in* Modern Music *(1924–1946)* (New York: Da Capo Press, 1982); and Carol Oja, *Making Music Modern* (Oxford University Press, 2000).

6. Oja, *Making Music Modern,* 11–58; Michael Broyles and Denise Von Glahn, *Leo Ornstein: Modernist Dilemmas, Personal Choices* (Bloomington: Indiana University Press, 2007), 85–146.

7. Minna Lederman, *The Life and Death of a Small Magazine (*Modern Music, *1924–1946)* (New York: Institute for Studies in American Music, Brooklyn College, 1983), 4.

8. Ibid., 9.

9. Henry Cowell, "New Terms for New Music," *MM* 5/4 (May–June 1928): 21–27.

10. *Otros tres exágonos* was performed under the auspices of the International Composers' Guild (ICG) on 8 February 1925. The fourth movement of *H.P.* premiered under the auspices of the ICG 28 November 1926. The sonatinas and Chávez's Sonata III had been performed at the first Copland-Sessions concert, 22 April 1928.

11. Chávez, "Technique and Inner Form," 28–31.

12. Carlos Chávez, "Revolt in Mexico," *MM* 13/3 (March–April 1936): 35–40.

13. Carlos Chávez, "The Function of the Concert," *MM* 15/2 (January–February 1938): 71–75.

14. Carlos Chávez, "Music for the Radio," *MM* 17/2 (January–February 1940): 89–92.

15. Chávez, "The Function of the Concert," 71–75.

16. See Francisco Agea, ed., *21 Años de la Orquesta Sinfónica de México, 1928–1948* (México: Orquesta Sinfónica de Mexico, 1948).

17. In Table 1 I have listed the works performed by the New York Philharmonic for the 1939 season. These programs and others may be found in John Erskine, *The Philharmonic-Symphony Society of New York: Its First Hundred Years* (New York: Macmillan, 1943). The article may be found under "Mexican Programs," *New York Herald Tribune,* 16 March 1941. In that article, as in Table 1, Thomson lists a Symphony in B-flat by "H. Ch. Bach." I suspect this is a misprint; it should read J. Ch. Bach, or Johann Christian Bach, in which case the piece identified would most likely be the Fourth Symphony from Op. 6 or one of the two B-flat symphonies from Op. 9.

18. Chávez, "Music for the Radio," 89–92.

19. Carlos Chávez, *Toward a New Music: Music and Electricity* (New York: W. W. Norton, 1937).

20. Chávez to Lederman, 3 May 1938, Fondo Carlos Chávez, Archivo General de la Nación (henceforth AGN).

21. Chávez to Lederman, 23 March 1939, AGN.

22. Akihiro Taniguchi, "Music for the Microphone: Network Broadcasts and the Creation of American Compositions in the Golden Age of Radio" (PhD diss., University of Florida, 2003); Margaret Susan Key, "Sweet Melody over Silent Wave: Depression-Era Radio and the American Composer" (PhD diss., University of Maryland, 1995).

23. Robert Parker and Leonora Saavedra have commented on New York's early influence, and Carol Oja, in *Making Music Modern,* implies as much with her comment that "New York became Paris for this young man from Mexico City" (278). Robert L. Parker, "Carlos Chávez and the Ballet," 81–88; Leonora Saavedra, "Carlos Chávez y la construcción de una alteridad estratégica," 125–136 and "Of Selves and Others."

24. Aaron Copland, "Carlos Chávez—Mexican Composer," *The New Republic,* 2 May 1928, 322–23; Rosenfeld, "The Americanism of Carlos Chávez," in *By Way of Art: Criticisms of Music, Literature, Painting, Sculpture, and the Dance* (New York: Coward McCann, 1928).

25. Copland to Chávez, 31 October 1928, Copland Collection, Library of Congress.

26. For a more detailed analysis, see Christina Taylor Gibson, "The Reception of Carlos Chávez's *Horsepower*: A Pan-American Communication Failure," *American Music* 30/2 (Summer 2012): 157–93.

27. Lederman to Chávez, 2 February 1932, AGN.

28. Marc Blitzstein, "Premieres and Experiments," *MM* 10/3 (March–April 1932): 124.

29. Marc Blitzstein, "Music and Theatre—1932," *MM* 10/4 (May–June 1932): 164–66.

30. Colin McPhee, "Forecast and Review: New York—January, February 1936," *MM* 13/3 (March–April 1936): 42–43.

31. Chávez, "Revolt in Mexico," 36.

32. Hickman Powell, *The Last Paradise* (New York: J. Cape and H. Smith, 1930); Hendrik De Leeuw and Alexander King, *Crossroads of the Java Sea* (New York: J. Cape and H. Smith, 1931); Gregory Bateson, Margaret Mead, and D. Carleton Gajdusek, *Balinese Character: A Photographic Analysis* (New York Academy of Sciences, 1942); Miguel Covarrubias, *Island of Bali* (New York: Alfred A. Knopf, 1937).

33. Many letters were exchanged about recordings of world music. For example, Cowell to Chávez, 11 September 1932; and Cowell to Chávez, 17 February 1933, AGN.

34. A description of McPhee's activities in New York can be found in Carol Oja, *Colin McPhee: Composer in Two Worlds* (Washington, DC: Smithsonian Institution Press, 1990), 94–101.

35. Saavedra, "Of Selves and Others," 301–16.

36. Oja, *Colin McPhee,* 101.

37. Ibid., 99–102.

38. Colin McPhee "Scores and Records," *MM* 17/ 3 (March–April 1940): 179–81.

39. Colin McPhee, "New York's Spring Season," *MM* 13/4 (May–June 1936): 39–42.

40. Aaron Copland, "The Composer in America, 1923–1933," *MM* 10/2 (January–February 1933): 87–92.

41. Paul Rosenfeld, "The Newest American Composers," *MM* 15/3 (March–April 1938): 153–59.

42. Donald Fuller, "Americans to the Fore—New York, 1941–42," *MM* 19/2 (January–February 1942): 110–11.

43. John Cage, "Chávez and the Chicago Drouth," *MM* 19/3 (March–April 1942): 185–86.

44. Elliott Carter, "Late Winter, New York, 1937," *MM* 14/3 (March–April 1937): 147–54.

45. Israel Citkowitz, "Winter Music, New York, 1933," *MM* 10/3 (March–April 1933): 155–57.

46. Aaron Copland, "Scores and Records," *MM* 14/2 (January–February 1937): 98–101.

47. Both are loaded terms for Mexicans. A *caudillo* is a forceful, charismatic, sometimes violent leader, and often one who overstays his time in power. A *cacique* is an overlord or petty tyrant, often found in rural spaces. Ricardo Pérez Monfort, "Carlos Chávez en los años cuarenta: Caudillo o cacique cultural," in Bitrán and Miranda, *Diálogo de resplandores,* 182–92.

48. Saavedra, Parker, Stallings, and Hess have examined aspects of this dynamic, although much of their work focuses on the intense negotiations of Chávez's early career, ca. 1924–36.

49. Parker, "Carlos Chávez and the Ballet," 81–88; Oliver Daniels, *Stokowski: A Counterpoint of View* (New York: Dodd, Mead, 1982), 278.

50. Parker, "Carlos Chávez y la música para el cine," 13.

51. "Whirling Through Mexico," Mabel Dodge Luhan Papers, Beineke Library, Yale University.

52. Letter of introduction by Claire Reis for Martha Graham sent to Chávez, 19 May 1932, AGN; Marsden Hartley to Chávez, n.d. (1932), AGN.

53. Agea, *21 Años de la OSM,* 43-69.

54. Ibid.

55. Lederman to Chávez, 6 October 1942, AGN. The casual, friendly nature of the inquiry is reflected in much of their correspondence, which continues until the end of Chávez's life and inspired Lederman to make her own trip to Mexico in the 1960s.

56. Chávez to Lederman, 4 January 1943, AGN.

57. Lederman to Chávez, 19 January 1943, AGN.

58. Chávez to Lederman, 11 January 1946, AGN. Chávez later contributed to a volume of Stravinsky essays, also edited by Lederman and published after the magazine folded.

59. It had been Copland's idea to publish the column, thus the constant dialogue with him. Lederman to Copland, 22 January 1943, Modern Music Collection, Library of Congress.

60. Copland to Lederman, 6 October 1944 (posted from Tepoztlan, Morelos, Mexico), Modern Music Collection, Library of Congress.

61. Salvador Moreno, "Inter-American Reviews: Mexico," *MM* 22/3 (March–April 1945): 191–92.

62. Salvador Moreno, "Inter-American Reviews: Big Three in Mexico," *MM* 23/4 (Fall 1946): 304–5.

The Pan/American Modernisms of Carlos Chávez and Henry Cowell

STEPHANIE N. STALLINGS

The fifty-year friendship and professional relationship between Carlos Chávez and Aaron Copland has been well documented.[1] Often overlooked, however, is Chávez's relationship with Henry Cowell, another American modernist active in New York in the 1920s. Though they were not close friends, their working relationship between 1928 and 1940 provides privileged insights into several issues of significance to the historicization of Chávez's early career. This essay builds on recent work by Leonora Saavedra and Alejandro Madrid, who have rewritten Chávez's participation in certain avant-garde movements in the 1920s.[2]

As Chávez's music gained performances and positive critical attention in New York, Edgard Varèse, Cowell, and others recognized a fellow ultramodernist in dissonant works such as the Sonatina for Violin and Piano (1924) and *Otros tres exágonos* (1924). In late 1927, Varèse founded the Pan-American Association of Composers (PAAC), fully expecting Chávez's participation and help in defining Pan-American music as experimental and ultramodern.[3] In truth, Chávez would have been a valuable collaborator, but the launch of his career in Mexico in 1928 curtailed his involvement.

Although the theme of inter-American musical activity runs through Chávez's and Cowell's correspondence and mutual activities, they had different ideas about how to promote the best new American music and, indeed, what values were to be included in the concept of musical Americanism. The two composers also shared interests: the future of modernist music and its growing affinity with scientism, and the exploration and development of non-Western musical concepts and instruments in their own compositions and in their respective classrooms. They shared the distinction of introducing to the Americas some of the first seminars in non-Western musics, Chávez in his post at the Conservatorio Nacional in Mexico City and Cowell at the New School for Social Research in New York. Both composers were also prolific writers, publishing not only scores of articles for general audiences but also theoretical monographs proposing strikingly compatible forward-looking visions on the future of modern music.

Near Misses: Two American Moderns in 1920s New York

Chávez visited Europe in the winter of 1922 and the United States from December 1923 to March 1924, and again from September 1926 to June 1928. Several of his compositions from these years, including "Polígonos" for piano (1923), *Otros tres exágonos*, and the Sonatina for Violin and Piano reflected an awareness of modernist composition from Europe and the United States. During his visit to New York, Chávez's fellow Mexican José Juan Tablada introduced him to Varèse, the founder of New York's premiere modern music performance society, the International Composers' Guild. Chávez returned to Mexico and began to organize concerts of contemporary music at the Escuela Nacional Preparatoria. He programmed works never before heard in Mexico, including compositions by Satie, Schoenberg, Stravinsky, Varèse, Honegger, Milhaud, and Poulenc.

From May to December 1923, Cowell embarked on his first European tour as a pianist-composer, giving performances in Berlin, Vienna, Paris, and London. Upon his return he gave a concert at Carnegie Hall's main auditorium on 4 February 1924, where he proudly introduced New York to his notorious pianistic novelty, the tone cluster.[4] Chávez was in New York at that time, but no extant account suggests he attended Cowell's concert or met him personally. In early 1925 Cowell began a working relationship with Varèse, and in March headed home to California, where he started a new venture that had been seeded by Varèse's request that he organize a branch of the Guild in San Francisco.[5] On 22 October 1925, the New Music Society of California held its inaugural concert in Los Angeles, with Varèse's *Octandre* on the program.[6] Chávez also programmed *Octandre* on one of his new music concerts in Mexico City in December that same year. Chávez's friendship with Cowell began during his second sojourn in New York, from 1926 to 1928.

Pan-Americanism and the PAAC

Ascribing a utopian quality to the Americas, Varèse cultivated relationships with a number of Latin American artists and composers, many of whom were members of the Guild.[7] After the Guild's dissolution in 1927, the idea to link composers in the Americas in a new society must have seemed like a logical one, with U.S. newspapers touting the need for Pan-American cultural cooperation.[8] Varèse then founded the PAAC, which included both Chávez and Cowell. The performance of a movement from Chávez's ballet *H.P.* (*Horsepower* or *Caballos de vapor)* on a Guild concert in 1926 may have contributed to the momentum. It is easy to imagine *H.P.*, with its blending of modernist and Mexican elements and its theme of interaction between the industrial North and the fertile South, as the closest anyone had yet come to the creation of a Pan-American style.[9]

Varèse began organizing the PAAC as early as July 1927. He wrote to Chávez of a trip he was planning: "You know that my presence in Mexico and the pleasure I would experience on knowing your magical country, would be a powerful aid to our cause. . . . On my return I will talk about several projects I think will have good success and in which you would be involved."[10] Chávez communicated Varèse's new plans to his colleague Silvestre Revueltas, who responded, "My sincere thanks to Varèse. . . . I am enchanted by the idea of the Concert Society, and of course I accept."[11]

Listing Chávez and Revueltas as incorporating members, the Pan-American Association was announced in both the New York and the *Los Angeles Times* on 18 March 1928. In June Chávez returned to Mexico to accept a position as director of the newly formed Orquesta Sinfónica de México (OSM). In December he was also appointed director of the Conservatorio Nacional. His new positions may have limited his involvement in PAAC activities, but other factors may have contributed as well. The initial lack of organization, funding, and critical attention to the PAAC between 1928 and 1930 may have diminished Chávez's interest. The very term "Pan-Americanism," originating in a U.S.-based frame of reference, held the assumption that there existed Americas distinct from each other, an idea Chávez resisted if not outright rejected in favor of the more inclusive concept of "Americanism," referring to the entire continent. Finally, his virtual non-participation in the PAAC while maintaining individual relationships with many U.S. composers, including Cowell, provides evidence of his skill in negotiating multiple factions of the U.S. modern music scene.

Chávez's relationship with Cowell intensified in early 1928. Some insight into their early common activities in New York can be gained through Cowell's frequent letters to his father and stepmother. Though these reports often read as more aspirational than strictly factual, they suggest there was initial excitement surrounding the Pan-American project. In February, Cowell wrote that Chávez "wants me to come to Mexico City . . . to play my concert with orchestra. . . . Varèse is organizing all the best known moderns here into a 'Pan-American' composer's society. C. C. Birchard . . . will publish a new magazine to be its mouthpiece in English and Spanish."[12] A few weeks later, Cowell wrote to his stepmother that "[Miguel] Covarrubias, the cartoonist, drew me yesterday for an article which Chávez is writing about me for a leading Mexican magazine."[13]

In 1928, Cowell published Chávez's Sonatina for Violin and Piano in *New Music Quarterly*, the publishing arm of his New Music Society. New Music was Cowell's preferred method of supporting composers he thought had great potential.[14] In March, Cowell wrote again to his father: "Anything we do for Chávez [in New Music] will come back to us in Mexican connections; he is to play my Symphonietta [*sic*] with his orchestra in Mexico City, and my Concerto later [and] promises to arrange for solo recitals there for me."[15] Cowell hoped that promotion of his Mexican colleague's music would pay dividends in terms of promoting his own works—just the type of reciprocal relationships the PAAC had said it hoped to establish.[16] In July he dutifully reported to Chávez about the Sonatina's publication in *New Music Quarterly* and his article in *Aesthete* magazine.[17] In June Cowell had published a four-page article in *Pro-Musica Quarterly* describing Chávez's music as "particularly clean-cut, crystalline, straightforward, and with an impelling rhythm."[18] Probably sensing Chávez's new preoccupation with establishing the OSM, Cowell wrote on August 7: "Please do not disapear [*sic*] entirely from the face of the earth,"[19] the first of many entreaties for cooperation. He requested the scores for Chávez's "Fox" for pianist Richard Buhlig to play on a New Music concert in San Francisco[20] and *Energía* to build a PAAC chamber concert around it. In exchange, Cowell sent "the little trio I promised you for performance in New York next year."[21]

Varèse moved to Paris in October 1928, leaving Cowell in charge of PAAC activity. Although Chávez did not have a prominent role in the PAAC, his music was celebrated on its concerts from the very beginning. On 12 March 1929, Stephanie Schehatowitsch played his Sonatina for Piano as well as "36" in the first PAAC concert in New York. The concert was designed to showcase new music from Latin American composers, several of whom had had their works performed in concerts of the Guild and the League of Composers.[22] Pieces by Heitor Villa-Lobos, Cuban composers Alejandro García Caturla and Amadeo Roldán, and Guatemalan pianist Raúl Paniagua completed the program. Later the PAAC programmed Chávez's *Energía* for four concerts in Europe: in

Paris in June 1931; and three times in 1932—in New York in February, in Berlin in March, and in Budapest in April. They also programmed the Sonatina for Violin in Vienna in a chamber program conducted by Anton Webern.

However well meaning Cowell's desire to be inclusive, the undercurrent of exoticism and discovery in the programming strategy reads today as a bit tone deaf. We might wonder how Chávez felt about being represented on a program with composers whose only connection to each other was the state of being viewed as peripheral to New York's modern music scene, when several of them had long been an integral part of it. Several European reviewers of PAAC concerts in fact noted a distinction between Chávez (described by French critic Paul le Flem as "one who does not linger in shady, floral groves to pitch his tent") and other Latin American composers more "sensitive to the suggestions of folklore."[23]

The year 1932 marked the beginning of a period of increased recognition for Chávez in the United States. On 31 March, the Philadelphia Orchestra and the Philadelphia Grand Opera mounted a production of *H.P.*, choreographed by Catherine Littlefield and featuring sets and costumes by Diego Rivera. Christina Taylor Gibson has analyzed the critical reception of the ballet and pointed out the ways in which it failed to live up to the promise of Pan-American cooperation touted by the press leading up to the event.[24] Following the ballet's abstract program notes and a "dogged search for 'Mexican-ness'" in Chávez's works, advance publicity ignored the complexity inherent in the work's depictions of "North" and "South" and instead presented a simple narrative of an industrious United States and a primitive Latin America. The result was a confused audience and mixed reviews.[25] Nevertheless, as Taylor Gibson also points out, the ballet's production raised Chávez's profile in the United States. That year Cowell thought more could be done to promote inter-American musical exchange. He returned to the idea of the Pan-American music journal and asked Chávez to send some ideas for it.[26] With mixed reviews of his Pan-American–themed ballet *H.P.* coming in, Chávez preferred "to postpone the idea of the Pan American journal for next year, so that we have time to think it over carefully."[27] The following year, in February, it was Chávez who picked up the conversation on the journal, writing, "I wish I could go to New York and [work] out together the idea of the Panamerican Journal."[28] With renewed enthusiasm, Cowell started making plans and speaking with interested parties.[29] Varèse, however, returned to New York in August 1933 and shortly thereafter resumed control of the PAAC, shutting Cowell out of the decision-making process.[30]

Non-Western Musics

The search for knowledge about so-called primitive musics from around the globe coincided with (and was greatly informed by) modernist composers' quest for new musical materials to renew their aesthetics. Cowell is now well known for his enthusiasm for non-Western musics, but Chávez certainly shared his interest. During the six years he held the directorship of the Conservatorio Nacional (1928–34) he began several projects to collect indigenous folk musics of Mexico and the world. To that purpose, he founded three research academies at the Conservatory, including the Academia de Investigación de la Música Popular, which would carry out fieldwork to collect and transcribe Mexican folk and popular traditions; the Academia de Historia y Bibliografía to collect a bibliography on art music and on the musics of Asia and Africa; and the Academia de Investigación de Nuevas Posibilidades Musicales, which was to establish forward-looking theories by critically studying the musical scales of the world and the instruments on which they were played.[31]

Cowell, too, was interested in gathering information on world musics. In December 1930, he applied for a John Simon Guggenheim Memorial Foundation Fellowship to study in Berlin, listing Chávez as a reference. Chávez's recommendation endorsed Cowell's proposed study, which was "indeed of high interest . . . Cowell will benefit immensely by getting directly in touch with musical culture of diverse countries and epochs, thus obtaining a wider notion of human expressions."[32] Thanks to recommendations from Chávez and twenty-two other composers, musicologists, and critics, Cowell won the fellowship. Just before Cowell's second trip to Berlin, Chávez requested recordings of "primitive folk music" and asked if Cowell would hand-select records during his stay in Berlin to create a collection.[33] Cowell agreed, having already been commissioned to form a similar collection for the New School. He delivered the promised records to Chávez in February 1933.

Cowell returned to New York with a broader understanding of the applicability of various world musics to modern musical composition. His new purpose was to "draw on those materials common to the music of all the peoples of the world to build a new music particularly related to our own century."[34] Cowell's transethnicism, which he viewed as a new universalism, reflected a desire to combat the spread of French neoclassicism in modern music—something he called "easy to compose, easy to understand, [and] easy to forget"—and to espouse an American-based universalism.[35] Cowell would not apply his new understanding of universalist principles to his own compositions, however, until at least fall

1933, when he began teaching world music at the New School, in courses such as "Music Systems of the World," "Primitive and Folk Origins of Music," and "Theory and Practice of Rhythm." These classes introduced world musics and novel uses of rhythm and timbre to the young John Cage, among others, and in doing so helped inaugurate music written for ensembles of percussion instruments, which demonstrated vast potential for expressing a multiplicity of transethnic styles and aesthetics. Cowell likely began composing his first work for percussion ensemble while teaching "Music Systems of the World." *Ostinato Pianissimo,* completed in 1934, represents Cowell's attempt to synthesize and distill world music elements in percussion works. Non-Western percussion instruments appear in it: Afro-Cuban bongos and *güiro*, as well as Indian *jalatarang* (rice bowls) and gongs, but Cowell broadened their timbral possibilities by calling for them to be played in uncharacteristic ways.[36]

Meanwhile, Mexican government-sponsored archaeological research on pre-Columbian cultures and artifacts yielded Daniel Castañeda and Vicente Mendoza's work on pre-Hispanic percussion instruments, *Instrumental precortesiano* (1933). This 280-page volume published by the Mexican National Museum of Archaeology, History, and Ethnography included hundreds of photographs, architecturally detailed drawings, and explanations of the origins of percussion instruments in Mexico, such as the varied types of *teponaztli, huéhuetl,* and *timbal*, as well as estimates of their accompanying rhythms.[37] Between 1931 and 1934 Chávez held a series of composition seminars at the Conservatorio Nacional, the purpose of which was to give young Mexican composers "a living comprehension of the musical tradition of their own country."[38] Seminarians included *Instrumental precortesiano* co-author Mendoza, Daniel Ayala, Blas Galindo, and Silvestre Revueltas. Chávez and Cowell were, therefore, among the very first to teach non-Western music in an academic setting in America. One goal of Chávez's seminars was to explore ways to incorporate indigenous instruments, mostly percussion, into Mexican orchestral music. In a 1936 article in *Modern Music*, Chávez explained that the seminars resulted in a group of instruments they called the Mexican Orchestra, "a specially balanced ensemble of conventional instruments with the addition of *huéhuetls, teponaxtles, chirimías,* and various kinds of water-drums [and] rasps."[39] Chávez wrote *Cantos de México* for this orchestra in 1933. At that time, however, none of the seminarians composed for an all-percussion ensemble. Chávez himself would not do so until 1942, when John Cage commissioned his Toccata for Percussion.

The Future of Modern Music

Chávez and Cowell shared many concerns about the state of modern American composition, which emerge in their respective writings. Chávez wrote about 225 newspaper articles focused primarily on nationalism, musical life, and institutions in Mexico, but his publications for U.S. audiences tended to focus on theoretical concerns.[40] Similarly, Cowell produced journalistic writings for a general audience throughout his career, and he wrote a number of theoretical articles and books. Chávez and Cowell both struggled with what they perceived as the limitations of their inherited musical materials and training. They each historicized their musical present by examining the music of contemporary indigenous peoples and drew on teleological explanations for modern advances in order to advocate effectively for the incorporation of new and experimental music.

In his article "The Two Persons," Chávez explored the limitations of music as an art form existing only in time, "extinguished and gone forever at the exact moment of its creation."[41] He discussed the failures of Western notation to record the elements of a musical work as it is conceived in the mind of a composer, a theme he would address again in *Toward a New Music: Music and Electricity* (1937),[42] and one Cowell also treated in "Our Inadequate Notation" (1927). Notation as it exists, wrote Cowell, can give "bare details of the pitch and rhythm of conventional modes, but little else. Quarter steps, exact slides and involved cross-rhythms cannot accurately be notated."[43] Not surprisingly, Cowell was elated to read in "The Two Persons" that Chávez also considered Western notation one of several critical impasses in modern music. Cowell called the article "a masterpiece. It clearly puts forth one of the most vital and least understood subjects in musical art. . . . I wish to talk to you of music as in time or space—I believe it to be in both!"[44] As far as we know, Chávez did not entertain the last hypothesis, which Cowell would explore years later in his experiments with music for modern dance.

Chávez and Cowell both tackled a problem felt by many composers of their generation: they saw themselves as the heirs of centuries of musical tradition, yet their music was often misunderstood by critics and audiences. Chávez begins *Toward a New Music* by claiming, "The great masters were not ahead of their time—their public was behind it."[45] The social evolutionism sparked by Herbert Spencer's ideas on natural selection, Oswald Spengler's rise and decline of societies, Auguste Comte, and Marx and Engels (who argued that evolutionist theory mirrored their views on progress within societies) pervaded the sociological thought of the period.[46] Chávez attempted to validate modern music by placing it in a historical lineage and emphasizing the scientific basis of art. Just as there are scientific advances such as central heating, electric lighting, and skyscrapers, he argued, there is progress inherent in artistic activity: "History and physics will well explain the artistic phenomena of today. Only by their study may we obtain a much-needed perspective on the present."[47] With this argument Chávez primed readers for his later discussion of the possibilities of electrical sound production and reproduction.

Evincing comparable social thought, Cowell's writings similarly conflate teleological scientism and artistic development. This is especially true of *New Musical Resources* (1930), the publication of which Chávez facilitated by introducing it to Alfred A. Knopf.[48] "With a more accurate knowledge of acoustics," Cowell wrote, "we have begun to perceive that acceptance or rejection [of intervals] has not been haphazard."[49] Thus began Cowell's theory of musical relativity, in which "rhythm and tone . . . are definitely related through overtone ratios."[50] Cowell's interest in developing an overarching theory of music grounded in acoustics "came about at first through wishing to explain . . . why certain materials I felt impelled to use in composition . . . have genuine scientific and logical foundation."[51] Since theosophy and philosophies of intuitiveness, not formal training, directed Cowell's early education and experiments with tone clusters at the piano, here he attempted to simultaneously legitimize and historicize those experiments by finding a theory to encompass them all, proving that "modern music is not proceeding blindly."[52]

Herein lies the main point of divergence between the two composers' writings on new musical resources and their uses. Cowell believed that composers were at an impasse in musical development because they lacked sufficient instrument technology to progress any further. His response to the challenge at that time was to examine which other musical elements, particularly the rhythms and timbres of non-Western musics, could be mined for future innovations. Chávez, on the other hand, seemingly unhampered in his musical expression, nevertheless found in electrical instruments a wealth of new technological developments that were capable of producing an infinite variety of new sounds and allowed the vision of the composer to be made permanent so that it was no longer subjected to the vagaries of the performer as interpreter.

Likewise, the two men dealt differently with what they perceived as the limits of musical notation. Cowell asserted that modern notation was not graphically correct, and that if a composer desired a new effect and left it to the performer, "any of a hundred different ones may be produced."[53] Chávez agreed: "Several performances, taken from identical writings, are always different performances."[54] Cowell's answer was to experiment with new graphical devices adapted to suit modern compositional choices. His piano piece *Fabric* (1917), for example, exhibited a contrapuntal texture of three simultaneous rhythms. In order to facilitate reading the multiple rhythmic relationships, Cowell devised a system of notating new subdivisions of the whole note, all indicated using differently shaped noteheads. By 1927, he realized that non-Western musics also resisted accurate transcription using Western notation, pointing out that "printed examples of Indian music . . . if sung purely as written . . . become conventional tunes."[55] On this point, too, Chávez agreed: "The constant small irregularities in time and tempo in folk music cannot be captured in notation with complete fidelity."[56] Cowell's solution remained rooted in proposing new ways for notes to appear graphically in the score. Similarly, Chávez in 1929 had called for "a system of marks on paper that can exactly represent all and every one of the properties of the sound called for [and] a way of indicating the procedure of performances with which to work out these properties with absolute precision . . . independent of an interpreter."[57] By 1936, however, he had given up that hope: "It would probably not be wrong to say that occidental musical writing in reality lacks the possibility of future development."[58] His proposed solution lay instead in "the act of permanently recording musical conceptions" through the use of new sound reproduction technologies such as the player piano.[59]

Cowell was concerned with the player piano insofar as it offered one possible solution to the limitations of notation discussed above. "The only notation," he wrote, "that must of necessity be graphically correct, since it produces the sound itself, is the holes in a player piano roll."[60] Chávez, for his part, considered a broader role for the reproducing piano, that of "spreading music without the necessity of wide specialization in it as a profession, or of depending on performers not always at hand, or requiring a remuneration or compensation for their professional services."[61] Chávez's aspiration was to cultivate audiences for high-quality art music—a project that could be assisted by reproducing instruments. The real advantage offered by the perforated roll, however, was "the possibility of a music not limited by the anatomic capacity of two or four however dextrous [*sic*] hands."[62] Composers desiring to use the player piano, such as, later, Conlon Nancarrow, may have found encouragement not only in Cowell's *New Musical Resources* but also in Chávez's more detailed outline of the possibilities of such instruments: "the only means for achieving music of fixed values unaltered during successive performances. . . . Only then will a fixed music exist, and the musical creator, like the sculptor and painter, give actual permanence to his conceptions."[63]

Chávez was clearly invested in the theoretical possibilities of electronically produced music, but he did not explore those possibilities in his own works until his 1968 ballet *Pirámide* for SATB chorus, orchestra, and tape. *H.P.*, which he composed while researching *Toward a New Music*, has a mechanical theme, driving rhythms, and purposely harsh dissonances, which might have made it an opportune work in which to experiment with electronic timbres. But the early version of the theremin, which was the only electronic instrument at that time that could have been incorporated into an orchestra, had, he said, "various major inconveniences. One is the difficulty of fixing the pitch . . . another is the inevitable *portamento* between a sound and the one following it. . . . A third is that the 'attack' is always imperfect and awkward."[64] The theremin did not provide the absolute control over sound that Chávez desired of technology.

Cowell, uncomfortable following the path that led to eliminating the performer's will from music making, instead experimented throughout the 1930s and 1940s with methods to maintain the integrity of his intentions while allowing performers more interpretive liberty.[65] His earlier claim in a letter to Chávez that he believed music to exist "in space as well as time" informed his efforts in collaborations with modern dancers, who were occupied with developing choreography to pre-composed music. In developing his work *Synchrony* for Martha Graham in 1930, Cowell proposed a solution he believed would treat both art forms equally, which was to create a contrapuntal relationship in which the music climaxes while the dance movements are subdued, and vice versa—a compelling idea theoretically but one that did not work well in practice. *Synchrony* was never performed as a dance work, but Chávez programmed a concert version with the OSM in December 1932.

Chávez as American Modernist

Notably absent from the PAAC repertoire and mission was an acknowledgment of the African American contribution to modern music, a thread Chávez included in his concept of Americanism. Unlike Cowell, Varèse, and others in their New York circle, he appreciated jazz. He collected Art Tatum records and frequented jazz establishments in Harlem with his friends Colin McPhee and Miguel Covarrubias. Though recognizably jazzy idioms never formed a thread in Chávez's compositional persona, he showed an early interest in incorporating jazz-themed elements in his modernist piano works *Foxtrot* (1925), "Fox" (1928), and "Blues" (1928). He programmed a performance of John Alden Carpenter's *Skyscraper Suite* for the first season of the OSM in 1928, followed closely by Aaron Copland's *Music for the Theatre*. The significance of white U.S. composers using black music was not lost on Mexican critics. Salomón Kahan noted that in Copland's music, "Jazz, that primitive musical form by means of which the oppressed blacks took their revenge on the North American majority, imposing on them their musical way of intuiting and feeling, has been purified, ennobled and elevated to symphonic dignity."[66] Nor was Chávez indifferent to the plight of African Americans in the United States. As its nascent civil rights movement gained momentum he composed "North Carolina Blues" (1942), a song incorporating elements of jazz set to a poem by Mexican poet Xavier Villaurrutia about the lynching of black citizens in the Jim Crow South.[67]

Villaurrutia (1903–1950) found initial success among Mexico City's modern literary circles in the early 1920s.[68] In 1928 he co-founded the Mexican literary magazine *Contemporáneos*, in which his translations of Langston Hughes's "I, Too," "Poem," and "Suicide Note" from *The Weary Blues* (1926) and his "Prayer" from *Fine Clothes to the Jew* (1927) appeared in the fall of 1931.[69] "North Carolina Blues" appeared in Villaurrutia's collection *Nostalgia de la muerte* (Nostalgia of death) in 1938. Its repeated refrain, "En North Carolina," vaguely recalls the spiritual-inspired repetitions in Hughes's poems "Fire" and "Moan," though "North Carolina Blues" does not contain the AAB form of the blues poems from *Fine Clothes to the Jew*, with which Villaurrutia was familiar, nor does the poem exhibit Hughes's fine-tuned rhythmic sense.[70] Each occurrence of the refrain "En North Carolina" interrupts what little rhythmic flow is present in the preceding stanza; thus, though a lyrical take on the harsh realities of being a person of color in the Jim Crow South, "North Carolina Blues" is not a "jazz poem" (see Example 1).

In his setting Chávez evokes a blues style without incorporating its harmonic or melodic idioms, much as he did in the earlier piano works "Blues" and "Fox." The piano accompaniment in D minor maintains constant forward motion throughout, creating a strong feeling of restlessness. The vocal line in the A section contains interval patterns that resemble (but do not actually comprise) a blues scale in B-flat, accompanied by a lumbering piano reminiscent of a funeral march in D minor. The B section, which forms a curiously early emotional climax to the poem, gruesomely portrays the hanging of a black man:

Meciendo el tronco vertical	Rocking his vertical torso
desde las plantas de los pies	from the soles of his feet
hasta las palmas de las manos	to the palms of his hands
el hombre es árbol otra vez	the man is tree again.[71]

Example 1. "North Carolina Blues," mm. 16–27.

To highlight the grotesque dance of death Chávez employed habanera (mm. 18–21) and cinquillo (mm. 22–25) patterns in the piano, building harmonic and rhythmic forward movement toward a climax in measure 25. As if in answer to the horrified listener's question, "Where could such a thing happen?" the full refrain returns immediately: "En North Carolina."

The lynching of blacks was an appalling reality of African American life in the southern United States well into the twentieth century. The placement of the lynching at the beginning of "North Carolina Blues," however, suggests that what is depicted in later verses, the subjugation of blacks under Jim Crow laws, is also unconscionable (and perhaps dangerous to any darker-skinned Latin Americans who travel there). Though the song has remained a neglected work in Chávez's oeuvre, it asserted a measure of solidarity with the vibrant African American artistic communities he encountered in Harlem rather than with the official narrative of Pan-Americanism that largely promoted the interests of U.S. capital in Latin America. It suggested possibilities for a version of musical Americanism that addressed rather than ignored the challenges of race, class, and empire.

Following the anti-lynching theme of "North Carolina Blues," Chávez programmed William Grant Still's cantata *And They Lynched Him on a Tree* (1940), set to a text by U.S. poet Katherine Chapin Biddle, for an OSM concert in 1944. During the first half of the twentieth century more than two hundred anti-lynching bills were introduced in the U.S. Congress. The House of Representatives passed three of them, including one while Still was composing the piece in January 1940, but it, like the others, failed to pass the Senate. Biddle's graphic vision of the work included a "white chorus" to depict a lynch mob, a "Negro chorus" to discover and bemoan the lynching, a male narrator, and a small orchestra.[72] Chávez saw to the text's translation into Spanish for the OSM performance, which he sent to Still and Biddle for their revision. The narrator at the concert was poet Carlos Pellicer, a close friend and associate of both Chávez and Villaurrutia.

Eschewing a U.S.-led musical Pan-Americanism that positioned him with other Latin American composers whose works were often described as picturesque and evoking local color, Chávez focused his compositional efforts on the inherently modern. But Chávez's modernism was compatible with progressive, transnational ideals. Continued research into his participation in an Americanism that took into consideration the political role of the composer and artist, as well as a shared struggle for economic and racial justice, will further challenge readings that accept him unambiguously as a Mexican nationalist unconcerned with artistic development outside his own country. Especially fertile soil is found in the connections between Latin American and African American artists and composers in the early twentieth century, many of whom have already been charted by visual art and literary scholars.[73] Several historians have addressed the members of these groups' shared adoption of socialist principles in the face of racial and economic oppression.[74] Chávez, like Charles Seeger in the United States, concerned himself with applying Marxist social theory to the role of the composer in the early 1930s.[75]

Thus Chávez and Cowell, though both steeped in progressive artistic and social thought and espousing compatible visions of the future of modernist music, represented contesting views of Americanism in an era of increasing interaction between the United States and Latin America. Both saw possibilities for solving aesthetic crises in modern music by developing a distinctly American modernism that included the methodical exploration of world music styles and an informed assimilation of selected transethnic musical materials. The solution of technical challenges, too, provided a rich source for both composers' imaginations, as they proposed compatible visions of the future of concert music that involved developing electrical sound technologies. Cowell was not concerned with composing overtly political works in the 1930s, and though he clearly desired closer cooperation between American composers of all stripes, his nonconformist, all-inclusive vision was read by some of his U.S. contemporaries as a lack of seriousness and a refusal to choose a compositional camp. Chávez, on the other hand, courted politics both when it suited his artistic vision and when it served his sophisticated recasting of U.S. Pan-American discourse. Many of the warm professional interactions between Chávez and Cowell, though not indicative of a close personal relationship, offer us privileged insights into a dimension of Chávez's early career in which he was dedicated to furthering his own vision of a modernist musical America.

NOTES

1. See, for example, Robert L. Parker, "Copland and Chávez: Brothers in Arms," *American Music* 5/4 (1987): 433–44; and Howard Pollack's essay in this volume.

2. Leonora Saavedra, "Carlos Chávez's Polysemic Style: Constructing the National, Seeking the Cosmopolitan," *Journal of the American Musicological Society* 68/1 (2015): 99–150; Alejandro L. Madrid, *Sounds of the Modern Nation: Music, Culture, and Ideas in Post-Revolutionary Mexico* (Philadelphia: Temple University Press, 2008).

3. See Stephanie N. Stallings, "Collective Difference: The Pan-American Association of Composers and Pan-American Ideology in Music, 1925–1945" (PhD diss., Florida State

University, 2009); and Deane Root, "The Pan-American Association of Composers, 1928–1934," *Yearbook for Inter-American Music Research* 8 (1972): 49–70.

4. Though Cowell emerged as the primary figure in promoting tone clusters and claimed to have used them in his piano works as early as 1913, Leo Ornstein treated the piano similarly and had won recognition for his startling performances in New York starting in 1915. See Michael Broyles and Denise Von Glahn, *Leo Ornstein: Modernist Dilemmas, Personal Choices* (Bloomington: Indiana University Press, 2007); and Carol Oja, *Making Music Modern* (New York: Oxford University Press, 2000), 11–24.

5. Joel Sachs, *Henry Cowell: A Man Made of Music* (New York: Oxford University Press, 2012), 131.

6. On the New Music Society, see Rita Mead, *Henry Cowell's New Music 1925–1936: The Society, the Music Editions, and the Recordings* (Ann Arbor, MI: UMI Research Press, 1981).

7. These included poet José Juan Tablada, and composers Enrico Fabini from Uruguay, and Acario Cotapos from Chile.

8. The *New York Times* covered the February 1928 Pan-American Congress in Havana, which included discussions of closer cooperation in the form of mutual scientific, health, and cultural societies.

9. Sidney Robertson Cowell attributed the idea of the PAAC to Chávez, though she was also biased against Varèse for perceived slights against her husband: "[Henry] said Carlos brought the idea to him." Interview transcript with SRC, Henry Cowell Papers, JPB 00-03, Music Division, New York Library for the Performing Arts (henceforth NYPL).

10. Varèse to Chávez, 20 July 1927, Fondo Carlos Chávez, Archivo General de la Nación (henceforth AGN). Original in French; Spanish translation in Gloria Carmona, *Epistolario selecto de Carlos Chávez* (México City: Fondo de Cultura Económica, 1989), 78–79. All translations from *Epistolario* are mine.

11. Revueltas to Chávez, n.d., 1927, AGN; Carmona, *Epistolario selecto*, 83.

12. Henry Cowell to Harry Cowell, 2 February 1928, Cowell Papers, NYPL.

13. Henry Cowell to Olive Cowell, 23 February 1928, Cowell Papers, NYPL. As of this writing, I have not been able to locate the drawing.

14. Cowell's dedication to promoting and publishing Charles Ives's music, for example, has had especially far-reaching consequences for its reception.

15. None of these plans came to pass. Cowell never visited Mexico.

16. On Cowell's promotion of Latin American composers, see Rita Mead, "Latin American Accents in *New Music*," *Latin American Music Review* 3/2 (1982): 207–28.

17. Cowell to Chávez, 10 July 1928. All correspondence between Chávez and Cowell cited in this essay can be found at Fondo Carlos Chávez, AGN. Copies courtesy of the editors.

18. Henry Cowell, "Carlos Chávez," *Pro Musica Quarterly* 6/4 (June 1928): 19–23.

19. Cowell to Chávez, 7 August 1928, AGN.

20. Buhlig performed Sonatina for Piano in the New Music Society concert on 24 October 1928 ("by request," according to the program). Mead, *Henry Cowell's New Music*, 102.

21. Cowell to Chávez, 28 August 1928, AGN. Chávez made tentative plans to return to New York in 1929 to present a series of chamber concerts. Whether these were intended to be PAAC concerts is unclear; they never happened.

22. In 1923 Clare R. Reis, along with several Guild members disenchanted with Varèse's authoritarian hand, formed a new concert society, the League of Composers. See Oja, *Making Music Modern*, 217–19.

23. Paul Le Flem, "Le deuxième concert de musique américaine," *Comoedia*, 15 June 1931.

24. Christina Taylor Gibson, "The Reception of Carlos Chávez's *Horsepower*: A Pan-American Communication Failure," *American Music* 30/2 (2012): 157–93. Carol Hess's

Representing the Good Neighbor: Music, Difference, and the Pan American Dream (New York: Oxford University Press, 2013), which also discusses *H.P.*, came too late to my attention to be discussed here.

25. Taylor Gibson, "The Reception of Carlos Chávez's *Horsepower*," 173.

26. Cowell to Chávez, 20 April 1932, AGN.

27. Chávez to Cowell, 29 April 1932, AGN.

28. Chávez to Cowell, 13 February 1933, AGN.

29. Cowell to Chávez, 7 April 1933, AGN.

30. Cowell mentioned the journal again in October 1934, this time in connection with Charles Seeger. See Leonora Saavedra, "The American Composer in the 1930s: The Social Thought of Seeger and Chávez," in *Understanding Charles Seeger, Pioneer in American Musicology*, ed. Bell Yung and Helen Rees (Urbana: University of Illinois Press, 1999), 57–59.

31. Leonora Saavedra, "Of Selves and Others: Historiography, Ideology, and the Politics of Modern Mexican Music" (PhD diss., University of Pittsburgh, 2001), 231–32.

32. Chávez to Henry Allen Moe, 17 December 1930, AGN.

33. Chávez to Cowell, 23 May 1932, AGN.

34. Henry Cowell, "Towards Neo-Primitivism," *Modern Music* 10/3 (1932–33): 151.

35. Ibid., 150.

36. Amadeo Roldán had already composed his *Rítmicas V* and *VI* for percussion (1930), which shared the distinction with Varèse's *Ionisation* (1929–31) of being the first all-percussion works in Western music.

37. Castañeda and Mendoza were invited by Chávez to work at the Conservatorio Nacional and conducted research for this publication within the Academia de Música Mexicana.

38. Carlos Chávez, "Revolt in Mexico," *Modern Music* 13/3 (1936): 39.

39. Ibid.

40. See Leonora Saavedra, "Los escritos periodísticos de Carlos Chávez: Una fuente para la historia de la música en México," *Inter-American Music Review* 10 (1989): 77–91.

41. Carlos Chávez, "The Two Persons," *The Musical Quarterly* 15/2 (1929): 153–59.

42. Carlos Chávez, *Toward a New Music: Music and Electricity*, trans. Herbert Weinstock (New York: W. W. Norton, 1937).

43. Henry Cowell, "Our Inadequate Notation," *Modern Music* 4 (1927): 29.

44. Cowell to Chávez, n.d. [early 1929], AGN.

45. Chávez, *Toward a New Music*, 14.

46. Comte's law of three stages was particularly influential to Mexican intellectuals, including Chávez. It was widely believed that modernism represented the final "scientific" stage. See Leonora Saavedra, "Music, Evolutionism and National Identity in Mexico," paper read at the American Musicological Society's annual meeting, Seattle, 2004.

47. Chávez, *Toward a New Music*, 16.

48. Or so Cowell reported to his father in a letter dated 12 March 1928, Cowell Papers, NYPL. This could not be corroborated in the Chávez-Knopf correspondence at the Fondo Carlos Chávez, AGN.

49. "The Impasse of Modern Music," *Century* 114/6 (October 1927): 671.

50. Henry Cowell, *New Musical Resources* (New York: Alfred A. Knopf, 1930; 2d ed., Cambridge: Cambridge University Press, 1996), xi.

51. Ibid., xv.

52. Ibid., xii. On Cowell's theosophical upbringing, see Michael Hicks, *Henry Cowell: Bohemian* (Urbana: University of Illinois Press, 2002).

53. Cowell, "Our Inadequate Notation," 29.

54. Chávez, "The Two Persons," 155.

55. Cowell, "Our Inadequate Notation," 30.

56. Chávez, *Toward a New Music*, 58–59.

57. Chávez, "The Two Persons," 155.

58. Chávez, *Toward a New Music*, 36–37.

59. On the player piano as a formative music technology, see Timothy D. Taylor, "The Commodification of Music at the Dawn of the Era of 'Mechanical Music,'" *Ethnomusicology* 51/2 (2007): 281–305.

60. Cowell, "Our Inadequate Notation," 32.

61. Chávez, *Toward a New Music*, 45–46.

62. Ibid., 48–49.

63. Ibid., 62.

64. Ibid., 163.

65. Cowell's influence in this respect on John Cage, Lou Harrison, and his other students is well documented. See, for example, Leta Miller, "Henry Cowell and John Cage: Intersections and Influences, 1933–1941," *Journal of the American Musicological Society* 59/1 (2006): 47–112.

66. Salomón Kahan, "Impresiones musicales: Un genio de la música moderna," *El Universal Gráfico*, 5 September 1932, quoted and translated by Leonora Saavedra in "Revisiting Copland's Mexico," paper read at Indiana University, 21 October 2011.

67. Silvestre Revueltas had composed a song on an anti-lynching theme, "Canto de una muchacha negra," to Langston Hughes's poem "Song for a Dark Girl" in 1938.

68. On Villaurrutia, see Frank Dauster, *Xavier Villaurrutia* (New York: Twayne, 1971).

69. Xavier Villaurrutia, *Contemporáneos* 11 (September–October 1931): 157–59.

70. Blues poems in *Fine Clothes to the Jew* include "Lament Over Love" and "Bound No'th Blues."

71. My translation.

72. The work was premiered by the New York Philharmonic on 25 June 1940.

73. Deborah Cullen, "The Allure of Harlem: Correlations Between *Mexicanidad* and the New Negro Movements," in *Nexus New York: Latin/American Artists in the Modern Metropolis*, ed. Deborah Cullen (New York: El Museo del Barrio and Yale University Press, 2009), 126–51; Mary Kay Vaughn and Theodore Cohen, "Brown, Black and Blues: Miguel Covarrubias and Carlos Chávez in the United States and Mexico (1923–1953)," in *Open Borders to a Revolution: Culture, Politics, and Migration*, ed. Jaime Marroquín Arredondo, Adela Pineda Franco, and Magdalena Mieri (Washington, DC: Smithsonian Institution Scholarly Press, 2013).

74. Kate A. Baldwin, *Beyond the Color Line and the Iron Curtain: Reading Encounters between Black and Red, 1922–1963* (Durham, NC: Duke University Press, 2002).

75. See Saavedra, "The American Composer in the 1930s." Cowell expressed interest in composing proletarian music in a letter to Chávez of 12 October 1934, but he never did.

“*The heartbeat of an intense life*”: Mexican Music and Carlos Chávez’s Orquesta Sinfónica de México, 1928–1948

RICARDO MIRANDA

In 1948, Carlos Chávez claimed Mexico’s musical scene had experienced a “surprising degree of progress” when compared to the state of affairs twenty years earlier, at the outset of activities of the Orquesta Sinfónica de México (OSM).[1] Although such an accomplishment could not be credited entirely to the orchestra or its conductor, Mexican music had enjoyed during those two decades a prolific and unique period in which symphonic music flourished, as attested by the multiple premieres of a wide and interesting repertoire. A panorama of such activity not only reveals Chávez’s crucial role as catalyst and promoter of such music but puts into perspective the positive impact made by the orchestra. Although other composers and orchestras thrived at the time, it is clear that Chávez’s OSM was the strongest force when it came to promoting Mexican symphonic music.

Chávez had sent a clear message from the very beginning of his work as the OSM’s founder and conductor when he carefully considered who should be the first Mexican composer performed by the emerging orchestra. His correspondence of those years reveals that he asked major figures such as José Rolón and Manuel M. Ponce to send him symphonic scores that could be performed.[2] But at the inaugural concert of 2 September 1928, it fell to Rafael J. Tello to be the first national composer to be programmed, with his *Sonata trágica* for violin and orchestra, a choice that also allowed for a distinguished Mexican soloist and former conductor, José Rocabruna, to appear onstage. From then on, it was clear that Mexican composers would have an open space for their music to be performed by the new orchestra. This was a significant gesture, for though some of its musicians came from the ranks of the state-funded Orquesta del Conservatorio, the OSM was mostly a privately funded enterprise that gathered together musicians from diverse performing environments. And although the OSM received some funds and support from the government, these were not significant enough to compel it to adopt any specific policy regarding the promotion of Mexican composers. Perhaps this is why Chávez made a point of insisting, twenty years later, that one of the orchestra's greatest achievements had been the performance of ninety-three works written by thirty-three different Mexican composers. Indeed, leaving aside the exact census of works and composers performed, it is quite clear that no other Mexican orchestra, past or present, has managed to accomplish a similar feat.[3]

Three Generations of Composers

The orchestra's launching in 1928 coincided with two crucial factors that contributed to create a golden age of Mexican symphonic music: the chronological confluence of three generations of composers and a desire—embraced by most artists—to create a specifically Mexican repertoire. Three generations of composers are easily discerned by observing the orchestra's main period of activities, encompassing the twenty-one years from 1928 to 1948. The oldest generation (see Table 1) includes all composers born in the last quarter of the nineteenth century. Manuel M. Ponce, José Rolón, Rafael J. Tello, and Julián Carrillo were the most prominent figures of this generation, and during the initial stages their respective careers shared a few traits. Most were born outside Mexico City and received their most comprehensive musical training in Europe. Ponce went to Bologna in 1904 and in 1906 to Berlin, where he studied piano for one year with Martin Krause and met Ferruccio Busoni. Rolón found his way to Paris in 1904, where, in similar fashion, he studied piano under Moritz Moszkowski and composition and harmony under André Gedalge, before returning to Mexico in 1907. Carrillo, on the other hand, was unable to join any school or conservatory in France, where he had been sent to study on a grant by the Mexican government, but he was admitted to the Königliches Konservatorium der Musik in Leipzig, where he studied under Arthur Nikisch and Salomon Jadassohn. A talented violinist, he joined the ranks of the Gewandhaus Orchestra, an experience that may have driven him to ascend the podium of the Orquesta Sinfónica Nacional upon his return to Mexico.[4]

The second, better-known 1899 generation includes Chávez, Silvestre Revueltas, and Eduardo Hernández Moncada. Both Revueltas and Hernández Moncada collaborated with Chávez on different tasks,

Table 1. Mexican Composers Active During the Orquesta Sinfónica de México's 1928–48 Seasons

Timeline: 1880 · 1890 · 1900 · 1910 · 1920 · 1930 · 1940 · 1950 · 1960 · 1970 · 1980 · 1990

Orquesta Sinfónica de México	1928–48
Julián Carrillo, 1875–1965*	
José Rolón, 1876–1945	
Rafael Julio Tello, 1882–1946	
Manuel M. Ponce, 1882–1948	
Candelario Huízar, 1883–1970	
Antonio Gomezanda, 1894–1961*	
Carlos Chávez, 1899–1978	
Silvestre Revueltas, 1899–1940	
Eduardo Hernández Moncada, 1899–1995	
Daniel Ayala, 1906–1975	
Miguel Bernal Jiménez, 1910–1956	
Blas Galindo, 1910–1993	
José Pablo Moncayo, 1912–1958	
Salvador Contreras, 1912–1982	
Carlos Jiménez Mabarak, 1916–1994	

*Composer not performed by the OSM.

particularly as assistant conductors. However, as far as their compositional careers are concerned, their trajectories could not be more diverse: Revueltas's output can be read as a solid conglomerate of symphonic works written during the 1930s, though this creative impulse was abruptly interrupted by his untimely death in 1940. Hernández Moncada, on the other hand, made a late, albeit secure start in his compositional career, which meant that most of his important symphonic works can be dated after the premiere of his First Symphony, which Dimitri Mitropoulos conducted with the OSM in 1942. Prior to this date, Hernández Moncada had earned a reputation by preparing numerous orchestral arrangements and transcriptions for the orchestra's programs—music by composers such as Debussy, Bach, Mussorgsky, and Satie.

A third generation embraces composers born around 1910. The Grupo de los Cuatro, a name inspired by the French Les Six, included

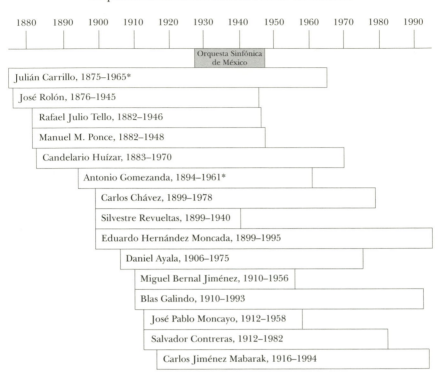

José Pablo Moncayo, Blas Galindo, Salvador Contreras, and Daniel Ayala, and made up the core of this generation. The Grupo de los Cuatro aimed to produce a style of music that, while not abandoning Mexicanist pieces, assimilated recent musical trends from composers such as Stravinsky, Milhaud, Poulenc, and Honegger, all of whom had received continual performances by the OSM.[5] To this list, one needs to add the names of Miguel Bernal Jiménez and Carlos Jiménez Mabarak, whose music held an important place within the Mexican musical scene of the time.

These three generations coincided in a common creative period during the 1930s and '40s. Ponce's and Rolón's mature years came with the flourishing of the 1899 generation, a time when the younger composers also made their first contributions to the Mexican symphonic repertoire. Nothing quite like it had taken place before in the history of Mexican music, nor has it since.

The common aim was to create a distinctly Mexican repertoire based on *the idea of a Mexican art music*. Practically every Mexican composer active during the first half of the twentieth century had a notion of what Mexican art music ought to be, and though these ideas varied in every instance, they gave birth to a considerable array of works, most of which were premiered by the OSM. Contemplating the vast output of Mexican music written at that time can be confusing due to the diverse aesthetic aims of the repertoire. This is hardly surprising, since the composers often conflated or changed aesthetic stances. Therefore, it is necessary to offer some definitions at this point, an exercise that should provide a guided tour of this vast and interesting repertoire, as well as clarify the perspectives of the composers.

The idea of creating a distinctly Mexican music arose during the nineteenth century. Works by Ricardo Castro (1864–1907), Julio Ituarte (1845–1905), and others fall under the influence of the Romantic *Charakterstück* as much as they aim to capture a Mexican character through the use of local popular songs.[6] But Ponce's groundbreaking lectures on the *canción mexicana*, delivered in 1913, provided a theoretical foundation for the new kind of nationalism that ensued.[7] For Ponce, it was in the *canciones mexicanas*—which he took to be traditional songs, mostly dating from the eighteenth and nineteenth centuries—that the national soul resided. He explained that these songs were influenced by Italian and Spanish vocal genres, which makes it appropriate to call them *canciones criollas*, a term that emphasizes their European origins.[8]

The first Mexicanist symphonic music, therefore, was centered on the principle of taking such *canciones* as a starting point for eventual thematic development within traditional Romantic genres. In this sense, Ponce's process of transformation is paradigmatic. He would, for instance, transcribe the melody of a *criollo* song such as "Si algún ser" from a live performance by a popular singer, and turn it directly into a salon arrangement for piano and voice. In this first version, Ponce always provided subtle harmonies and a fluent and delicate piano accompaniment.

In a second stage, the arrangement was orchestrated and the melody developed and enriched by further harmonic intricacies. As such, "Si algún ser" is found again as the third of Ponce's *Instantáneas mexicanas*, a symphonic suite that Chávez premiered with the OSM in July 1947. The late date of composition reveals that the idea of using traditional melodies as the thematic material of nationalist compositions held sway long after 1911, when Ponce published his first arrangements of *canciones mexicanas*. In fact, this nationalist technique was used by most composers, regardless of their background or generation. Chávez himself provided an exuberant orchestration of "La sandunga," a traditional song from Oaxaca, in the midst of his ballet *H.P.* (*Horsepower* or *Caballos de vapor*) (1926–32),[9] and the crude sound of the typical northern *tambora* (large drum) is likewise heard in Candelario Huízar's *Pueblerinas*, a symphonic poem written and premiered by the OSM in 1931. Other composers noteworthy for their use of *canciones criollas* include Bernal Jiménez,[10] Antonio Gomezanda,[11] and Moncayo, whose emblematic *Huapango* (1941) along with Galindo's *Sones de mariachi* (1941) became the Mexican symphonic pieces most often performed.

Earlier, in 1927, *El festín de los enanos*, a symphonic scherzo by José Rolón, had been unanimously awarded first place in a national competition organized by the First National Congress of Music, held in Mexico City in 1926. The competition encouraged the use of *canciones criollas* as the thematic material of symphonic writing. Rolón's *El festín* was inspired by a children's story written by Jalisco-born poet Alfonso Gutiérrez Hermosillo, similar to the way that Goethe's ballad *Der Zauberlehrling* inspired Paul Dukas's *L'apprenti sorcier*. Striking and novel for the Mexican repertoire was Rolón's use of three popular melodies—"Los enanos," "El payo," and "Señor Don Simón"—within the framework of a piece based on *ostinati* and daring harmonies, full of ninth chords and other blunt chromatic sonorities. Indeed, when he replied to Chávez's request for music that could be performed at the OSM's inaugural concert, Rolón considered this piece to be the most suitable. The piece was not chosen, as it had been repeatedly performed during 1928 after winning the competition. It nevertheless received multiple performances by the OSM during 1929, 1935 (with Ernest Ansermet conducting), and 1937.[12]

The notion of collecting folk music is linked to nineteenth-century European Romanticism, and Mexican composers born in the nineteenth century and educated in the Romantic repertoire were naturally prone to write their first works in such a style. A representative group of Romantic symphonic pieces written by Mexican composers would include Carrrillo's suite *Los naranjos* and his First Symphony, together with José Rolón's *Obertura de concierto* (1920) and his Symphony in E Minor (1924). To these pieces we should add works by Tello and Ponce, particularly Tello's *Sonata trágica* and Ponce's exuberant and virtuosic Piano Concerto, premiered in 1912, with the composer as soloist and Carrillo conducting. Even as late as 1934, Ponce wrote a Romantic symphonic piece, *Poema elegiaco*, moved by the recent death of his close friend the poet Luis G. Urbina. As the music dies out, one can almost hear, amid sonorities not unlike those of Mahler or Delius, the last strands of Mexican Romanticism.

Mexican Modernism

Mexican musicians gradually abandoned the use of a Romantic style in favor of modernism. Crucial to defining Mexican modernism is the impact Igor Stravinsky's music had on many Mexican composers of the time. Even when his music was not very well known, his name was synonymous with the avant-garde and a point of reference whenever aesthetic discussions took place. Ponce, for instance, praised Stravinsky's neoclassicist aesthetic, which he had followed in works such as the Violin Sonata and chamber music of the 1930s. Revueltas, on the other hand, scorned his critics when they pointed out that Stravinsky was an obvious influence on *Planos* (premiered by the OSM in 1934).[13] It is therefore not surprising that Stravinsky was one of the most performed composers during the twenty-one years of the OSM. Indeed, Stravinsky himself was invited to conduct his music in concerts held in 1940 and 1946. Before that Chávez had been preparing the ground not only for the appreciation of Stravinsky's music, but also that of other composers hitherto unheard in Mexico, such as Bartók, Milhaud, Poulenc, and Shostakovich.

There can be no doubt that the performance of these contemporary, ultra-modern musical celebrities (to quote terms then commonly found in the Mexican press) made it possible for Mexican composers to venture into more complex and advanced writing without exposing their music to severe criticism. Nevertheless, some of Chávez's opponents, such as Estanislao Mejía, condemned this trend, accusing Chávez's scores of being "obscure and incomprehensible."[14] "Modernism," ventured

Mejía in the same article, "had as its main source of inspiration the music of Debussy, Stravinsky, Dukas, and others." This declaration cannot be read as anything but a challenge to Ponce—who since 1912 had championed Debussy's music in Mexico, as well as Dukas's—and Chávez, Stravinsky's Mexican advocate *par excellence*. In fact, the only Mexican composers to have studied with any of these European composers were Ponce and Rolón, who in the late 1920s and '30s studied with Dukas and Nadia Boulanger in Paris. These studies, as well as their contact with the music of composers such as Edgard Varèse, Florent Schmitt, Stravinsky, and even Arnold Schoenberg—whose acquaintance Ponce and Rolón made at Boulanger's—explains why they wrote or revised some of their most significant modernist works after their Parisian sojourns. In describing Chávez's Piano Concerto, written in 1938, Otto Mayer Serra—a Catalonian musicologist trained in Berlin and in exile in Mexico due to his support of the Spanish Republic—had heard how "substances of folk origin became transformed into original material."[15] Regardless of whether that phrase does justice to Chávez's Concerto, it shows accurately that in the 1920s and '30s Mexican composers concerned themselves more with technique and formal discourse, and less with the invocation of Ponce's national soul, which by then not even Ponce seemed to care much about.

Although made up of a rich, complex, and widely varied group of pieces, we can discern particular trends within Mexican modernism. One is the idea of composing Mexicanist music using *canciones criollas*, though coupled with a specific program and written in a modernist style. Strikingly, such pieces can almost be reduced to a single program: *el pueblo* (the people). The idea of composing music evoking different Mexican scenarios representing the people took hold at different moments in many important compositions. In chronological order, these include Rolón's *Zapotlán* (1929), Huízar's *Pueblerinas* (1931), Bernal Jiménez's *Noche en Morelia* (1941), Ponce's *Ferial* (1941), as well as two later examples, Moncayo's *Tierra de temporal* (1949) and Gomezanda's *Lagos* (1956).[16] All have in common an evocation of local towns, such as Bernal's Morelia, Rolón's Zapotlán, or Gomezanda's Lagos de Moreno, coupled with a musical discourse that seems to abandon, bar by bar, the Romanticism of previous symphonic works. In their quest for a faithful representation of local sounds, some composers re-created the actual tuning of guitars by local players before a *serenata (Zapotlán,* second movement, "Gallo romántico") or the characteristic music of the barrel organ typical of the ice-cream vendors found in Mexican plazas. This is precisely what we hear—in an almost spectral piano solo that never returns—in the middle of Bernal's *Noche en Morelia*.

But it is in Ponce's *Ferial* where we can best appreciate the essential nature of this group of pieces. Ponce's town is not a precise geographical location but a prototypical *pueblo* (village) in whose plaza the local patron saint is celebrated. Ponce pairs representative social groups with particular musical identities (that is, a tune with a personal kind of orchestration or timbre), which at the beginning are heard in succession: the organ music from inside the church, the subtle roar of worshipers praying aloud, the monotonous tune of a street musician asking for money, the music from the merry-go-round, a tune sung by someone in love ("Cuiden su vida," a favorite *criollo* song of Ponce's), the perfunctory sound of a local band, the earthy tunes that accompany the ancient dances performed by the *huehuenches*[17] in the church's atrium, and last but not least, the explosions of fireworks and the overpowering toll of church bells. In the second part of the piece, Ponce succeeds in accommodating all of these unequal musical motives within a dazzling and brilliant counterpoint, which then moves toward an apotheosic climax. Every Mexican citizen, past or present, from north or south, from the coast or the high mountains, knows what a local fiesta is about; hence the particular appeal of such a piece, in which Ponce's work reached one of its most technically accomplished and mature moments.

An altogether different notion of what constituted Mexican music emerged from the combination of two political ideas widely disseminated by the Mexican government after the Revolution. The emerging regime claimed to have overthrown the bourgeoisie in order to promote social justice, and in this sense made a central tenet of its program the providing of land and financial security to the lowest classes, particularly to those living in the countryside. Among them, the indigenous populations had been notoriously exploited by the old regime. In addition, their ethnic music was believed to be descended from ancient, pre-Hispanic music, and the new regime now wanted to exalt Mexico's pre-Hispanic past. The combination of these two ideas gave birth to another current within Mexican musical modernism, one that aimed to capture the musical values of indigenous music and reconstruct pre-Hispanic sound. Of course, it is not possible to recover pre-Hispanic music because historical or archeological sources are lacking. Chávez, however, led composers such as Luis Sandi (1905–1996), Huízar, Vicente T. Mendoza (1894–1964), and María Teresa Prieto (1896–1982) in attempting to write in an archaic, pseudo pre-Hispanic language—one that was purely speculative in its intrinsic rhythmic, harmonic, and melodic elements. Chávez dedicated many essays and articles to the subject of Aztec music—which he considered morally superior to Western music—and never tired of praising its presumed qualities. In terms of cultural ideology, such a discourse seemed at the time logical and convenient; however, in terms of musical creation, it was quite clear that any claim to compose on the basis of pre-Hispanic musical elements was problematic. This may explain why Chávez turned to contemporary Indian music, a process he explained when introducing the first Mexican performance of his *Sinfonía india* (1935).[18]

Meanwhile, the conviction to write music with a pre-Hispanic flavor, whether imagined or based on ethnic sources, seemed to take hold of many other composers. Even Ponce, while in Paris, had fallen prey to the desire to write such music in his 1926 *Chant et danse des anciens mexicains* (revised 1933 and 1934).[19] Earlier, in 1925, Gomezanda had been asked to write a ballet score for Erwin Piscator's Berlin-based stage company. Its music, choreographed by Ruth Allerhand, was based on the Aztecs' "New Fire" ceremony. Gomezanda's *Xiuhtzitzquilo* premiered in Berlin in February 1928, just a few months before Chávez conducted the OSM's inaugural concert. The New Fire ceremony had also inspired a young Carlos Chávez to compose in 1921 his own ballet *El fuego nuevo*, which received only a concert performance, by the OSM, also in 1928. *Los cuatro soles*, a second ballet derived from Aztec mythology, a recurrent topic for Chávez, received a concert premiere by the OSM in 1930 and a fully staged performance in 1951.

It is clear that Chávez's interest in pre-Hispanic music left a mark upon younger, sometimes lesser-known composers whose works were also performed. To this group belong the forgotten scores of Francisco Domínguez's *El vaso de Dios*: *Ballet tlaxcalteca* (1930) and Prieto's symphonic poem *Chichén Itzá* (1944), as well as the better-known Second Symphony, *Oxpaniztli* (1936), by Huízar,[20] a piece whose name alludes to the autumnal ritual feast during which the Aztecs rendered homage to flowers and song, as embodied in their god Xochipilli. The elaborate titles of *Oxpanixtli*'s three movements clearly imply the narrative of a human sacrifice: I. Largo (Procession to deliver the chosen victim to the Temple); II. Adagio (Dance of birds and butterflies); III. Allegro (Masked dance after the sacrifice).[21]

Parallel interest in contemporary indigenous music also turned out to be productive. Works were created that used twentieth-century indigenous sources as substitutes for the *canciones criollas* employed earlier. Sometimes, as in the case of Mendoza's *Danza tarahumara*, perfomed by the OSM in 1930, the music was an orchestral arrangement of a local dance rather than a composition based on it. Ponce wrote a similar piece in the second of his *Instantáneas mexicanas* (1947), titled "Danza yaqui." But it was again Huízar who followed Chávez's suit in *Sinfonía india* with his Fourth Symphony ("Cora"), premiered by Mitropoulos and the OSM in 1942. This piece not only incorporated material from autochthonous Huichol and Cora music,[22] but called for the employment of indigenous percussion instruments, as did Chávez's *El fuego nuevo*. A year earlier, Luis Sandi, a close collaborator of Chávez's, had premiered *Norte: Tres movimientos sinfónicos sobre temas indígenas* (Three symphonic movements on indigenous themes, 1941), written in a similar vein.

Yet another current within modern Mexican symphonic music was that of producing a modernist discourse in which a Mexicanist sound was the result of abstraction and reduction rather than of quoting authentic or imagined musical materials. In this music, several elements—Revueltas's bandlike brass motives; Rolón's rhythmic motives, which condense the colliding accents found in mariachi *sones*; or Chávez's melodic pentatonicism, a scale he theoretically derived from the natural sounds of Aztec conch shells (*caracoles marinos*)[23]—offer the distinct impression of a Mexicanist sound, yet without necessarily resorting to quotation.

This kind of condensed Mexican modernism might be the most interesting and rich trend in the vast panorama of Mexican symphonic music during the twentieth century. Practically all of Revueltas's output can be placed in this category, from his widely known pieces like *Sensemayá* or *Redes* to the less well-known and yet wonderful *Colorines* and *Itinerarios*, which may easily lay claim to being his most accomplished works.[24] However, Revueltas's music was preceded by works of the 1920s in which modernism, understood as the combined employment of "rude" harmonies, as Rolón described them, and a complex and powerful polyrhythmic drive was a way to achieve intense and original expression. Perhaps Ponce, in his symphonic triptych *Chapultepec*, was the first to venture along this path, despite some Romantic gestures and the use of subtle programmatical references. A similar comment may very well apply to Chávez's own *Horsepower Suite* (*Sinfonía de baile*) (1931): aside from some *criollo* quotations and a program to be danced, most of its three-movements would easily fit into the same category.

A particularly acclaimed piece was Rolón's epic symphonic poem *Cuauhtémoc*. Chávez conducted its first performance in January 1930, the result of a composition competition launched by the OSM the previous year. *Cuauhtémoc* earned wide recognition, for not only did the jury, which included Chávez and Revueltas, praise the piece, but public and critics also expressed approval. For José Barros Sierra, it was "undoubtedly the masterwork of our contemporary music," a compliment repeated by Gerónimo Baqueiro Foster, Alfredo Domínguez, and other critics in Mexico City's main newspapers and journals.[25]

Cuauthémoc is an emblematic work and one of the most elaborate and ambitious pieces of Mexican modernism. And, because it was promoted by Chávez and the OSM as a result of the competition, it had a long critical impact in the following years. Composers such as Mejía and Arnulfo Miramontes, advocates of a more traditional, Romantic musical language, did not hesitate to criticize Rolón's music, condemning it in strong but groundless terms. Miramontes, for instance, would only say that "we do not like the rules emerging from Rolón's academy on the Avenida Insurgentes, which he imported from France . . . his *Cuauhtémoc* is full of awkwardness and harmonic incoherencies that asphyxiate the melody."[26] Such a bitter comment had been provoked by Rolón. After the OSM competition he won with *Cuauhtémoc*, dissenting artists led by Mejía launched a competition of their own. A jury, including Mejía, Tello, and Carrillo among others, awarded prizes to Miramontes and Alfonso de Elías. After attending the competition's awards concert, Rolón criticized the winning pieces in an article in which he praised the technical dexterity of his colleagues, but condemned their use of a "musical vocabulary dead for a long time."[27] Miramontes retaliated.

In musical terms and given its large scale, *Cuauthémoc* synthesizes many of the elements described heretofore. As its name implies, the piece is centered on the figure of the last Aztec emperor, whose epic defeat at the hands of the Spaniards is loosely evoked in its four movements. A short program, based on a historical sketch by Agustín Loera y Chávez, together with the descriptive titles of its movements, helps to define its atmosphere and content. The first movement, Andante, is described as a "procession and crowning" of the Aztec emperor. The second movement, in which Rolón employed an indigenous tune he collected in the area around his native town of Zapotlán, is an Agitato called "Heroic defense." The third movement, also an Andante, depicts Cuauthémoc's infamous torture by the Spaniards, followed without interruption by a "Hymn of glorification" marked *Allegro pomposo*. In the course of the third movement, Rolón employed verses alluding to Cuauhtémoc from *La suave patria* by celebrated Mexican poet Ramón López Velarde. However, the choir does not sing those well-known verses, but declaims them in the fashion of *Sprechgesang*. In the fourth movement, the choir does sing, but without text, in a clear allusion to Debussy's *La Mer*.

In addition to employing the already mentioned indigenous tune in the second movement, Rolón also notated some typical street cries of Mexico City, using them as melodic cells for the last movement. *Cuauhtémoc* is best described as a grand symphonic chiaroscuro that moves from its epic initial atmosphere in B minor to the desolation of the third movement—which he signaled with a daunting twelve-tone solo for the bassoon—that leads into a final, brilliant apotheosis in D major. With a nearly forty-minute running time, it is not surprising that critics such as Barros Sierra claimed to need "a second and further hearings" in order to fully evaluate the piece.[28] In 1935, Rolón composed another outstanding work with his Piano Concerto, in which polyrhythm and elaborate harmonies combine to create a piece "full of a thousand unheard-of combinations that give the piece a diversity and kaleidoscopic quality," as the Spanish musicologist Adolfo Salazar aptly put it.[29]

Younger generations gave Mexican modernism a touch of their own. In a desperate attempt to legitimize the Maya aspiration of his discourse and account for the lack of archeological musical findings, Ayala went so far as to propose that the Maya reliefs in Uxmal could be read as "frozen music" waiting to be deciphered.[30] Nevertheless, his *Tribu* (Tribe, 1935) makes imaginative use of developing rhythmic cells in which a primitivist, dynamic discourse is skillfully attained. Contreras, on the other hand, alluded to Mexico's Afro-Mexican roots only in the title of his best-known piece, *Danza negra* (Black dance, 1966), a late and most concentrated piece of Mexican modernism in which, once again, primitivism pervades.[31] Meanwhile, Moncayo's lighter textures, coupled with distinctive Mixolidian harmonies and a fine lyrical sense, mingle to create his distinctive style, evident in such fine pieces as *Bosques* (Woods, 1940) and *Cumbres* (Hilltops, 1941). Though these pieces had to wait until the 1950s to be performed, some of his later pieces were premiered by the OSM, such as his *Tres piezas para orquesta* (1947) and his Sinfonietta (1945).

Moncayo's only symphony was awarded the first prize in another OSM competition in 1944. This piece, given its traditional structure and overall conception, could be described as neoclassical, a category in which one could also place many other 1940s symphonic pieces—all premiered by the OSM—such as Hernández Moncada's First (1942) and Second (1943) symphonies, Jiménez Mabarak's First Symphony (1941), Huízar's First (1930) and Third (1938) symphonies, Prieto's Third Symphony (1946), Chávez's Concertos for Piano (1938) and Four Horns (1939), Bernal's "poem symphony" *Mexico* (1946), and Ponce's Violin Concerto (1943), the first performance of which was given by Henryk Szeryng under Chávez's baton. This piece was to generate a bitter exchange in the press, for Ponce was accused of insincerity by Jesús Bal y Gay, a Spanish refugee who, together with fellow exiles Rodolfo Halffter and Salazar, contributed to enlarge the scope and quality of music criticism in Mexico.[32] Bal y Gay implied that Ponce had adopted a more modern, abstract language, abandoning his lyrical, *criollo* song-inspired style. He failed to see that

Ponce's skillful treatment of his own famous *canción* "Estrellita" appears in disguised form throughout the entire piece.[33] To those accustomed to conceiving of Ponce's music as Romantic and evocative, this concerto did come as a surprise. In a sense, it was Ponce's swan song, as it was the last of his main works to be premiered in his lifetime. At the same time, the Violin Concerto showed how far he had gone stylistically at the end of his life.

Though many of the pieces mentioned bear a relation to the idea of composing specifically Mexican music, there were, needless to say, many other works in which a Mexican identity was not particularly relevant. From the beginning of their careers, composers such as Ponce and Rolón, but also younger ones like Chávez or Revueltas, often set aside their Mexicanist intentions in favor of a personal, cosmopolitan expression. This trait can best be appreciated in their concert songs and their solo and chamber works. A representative example is Ponce's *Tres romanzas* (on texts by Mikhail Lermontov), premiered by the OSM in 1935 in a benefit concert to raise funds for a statue of Debussy in Paris.[34] On the other hand, a significant manifestation of what can be termed abstract modernism in Mexico had been Carrillo's *Preludio a Colón* (Prelude to Columbus, 1925), a piece for soprano and chamber ensemble composed entirely in microtones. In developing microtonalism, Carrillo played a pioneering role alongside composers such as Alois Hába, Ivan Vishnegradsky, and Georgy Rimsky-Korsakov, while producing some of the most original and avant-garde Mexican music of the 1920s and '30s. Carrillo enjoyed a successful if polemical career of his own, but neither his Romantic nor his microtonal works were ever performed by the OSM.[35]

The OSM performed other Mexican works written in a modern, abstract language. Indeed, Chávez himself played a crucial role in writing music that was concerned more with formal procedures and less with identity and a Mexicanist point of view. Chávez's *Sinfonía de Antígona* (1933) is an early example of such a tendency.[36] The shift between a Mexicanist position and a more abstract, formal one is best exemplified by two works by Chávez. In 1940 he wrote *Xochipilli-Macuilxóchitl*, a piece for percussion and wind ensemble he later described as "an imagined Aztec music." By 1942, Mexican agendas withdrawn, the OSM performed his Toccata for percussion ensemble, in which he mainly concerned himself with rhythmical and structural inner procedures. This same opposition can be found in other composers, such as the young José Pomar, who wrote a *Huapango* performed by the OSM in 1931. If the rhythmic drive proper to *huapangos* and *sones* from the Gulf Coast was the prominent element of this piece, his *Preludio y fuga rítmicos* (1932) for percussion, harp, and woodwind ensemble explores formal rhythmic procedures per se, with no local or Mexican origin claimed for musical content.[37] Although toward the end of 1948 the writing of abstract modernist works was, so to speak, one stylistic possibility among many for the OSM, for composers like Chávez and Carrillo, this trend would acquire a particular relevance in the following years, as reflected in their theoretical writings and in the more abstract nature of their respective aesthetics.

Chávez's role in the creation and flourishing of Mexican symphonic music must not be underestimated. If, from a historical perspective, it might seem unfortunate that he chose not to perform music by Carrillo and Gomezanda, two of the most important composers of the time, that same perspective allows us to conceive of the period 1928–48 as the halcyon days of Mexican music. It was a time like no other, when new works by different composers were always being premiered, days when high-quality music criticism thrived in journals and newspapers, and a time that witnessed, no doubt, the emergence of some of the masterworks of Mexican music.

NOTES

1. Carlos Chávez, "Prólogo," in *21 Años de la Orquesta Sinfónica de México 1928–1948* (Mexico City: OSM, 1949), 9–14.

2. For discussion of the programming for the early OSM, see the following correspondence of 1928: Chávez to Rolón, Mexico, 20 July and 30 October; Tello to Chávez, Mexico, 23 July; Chávez to Ponce, Mexico, 20 July and 17 August; and Rolón to Chávez, Paris, 9 October. Thanks are due to Leonora Saavedra for calling my attention to these and other materials at the Fondo Carlos Chávez, Archivo General de la Nación. The dates for Mexican composers discussed in this essay are given in Table 1.

3. The main source for a balance of works premiered by the OSM is *21 Años de la Orquesta*, prepared by Francisco Agea and printed by the orchestra. Despite minor inaccuracies, this publication offers a fair view of the orchestra's task during those two decades.

4. Carrillo conducted the Orquesta Sinfónica Nacional from 1921 to 1929. According to Otto Mayer Serra, in *Música y músicos de Latinoamérica* (Mexico: Atlante, 1947), during that period the orchestra took its first tour of the country with Arthur Rubinstein as soloist and performed music by Mexican composers such as Ponce, Rolón, Antonio Gomezanda, Juan León Mariscal, and, needless to say, Carrillo (2:709–10).

5. The members of Grupo de los Cuatro were Chávez's composition students during the early 1930s.

6. Representative works of the nineteenth-century piano repertoire are Castro's *Aires nacionales mexicanos* and Ituarte's *Ecos de México*, both of which employ folk themes cast in Lisztian virtuoso writing.

7. Ponce's main essay on the *canción* is "La Canción mexicana," *Revista de revistas* (Mexico City), 21 December 1913. See Leonora Saavedra, "Manuel M. Ponce y la canción mexicana," *Heterofonía* 142 (2010): 155–82.

8. *Criollo* refers to any person born in the New World of European parents. Alejo Carpentier first called attention to the importance of this term and its origin as applied to

Latin American music in "América Latina en la confluencia de sus coordenadas históricas y su repercusión en la música," in *América Latina en su música*, ed. Isabel Aretz (Mexico City: Siglo XXI, 1980), 7–19. I will use *canción criolla* instead of *mexicana* in this essay.

9. The ballet was first performed in concert version by the OSM in 1931. Chávez later made a ballet suite, *Sinfonía de baile*.

10. On Bernal Jiménez, see Yolanda Moreno Rivas, *Rostros del nacionalismo en la música mexicana* (Mexico City: Fondo de Cultura Económica, 1989), 234–38.

11. On Gomezanda, see Jorge Velazco, "Antonio Gomezanda y el nacionalismo romántico mexicano," *Latin American Music Review* 12 (Spring–Summer, 1991): 65–73.

12. See Ricardo Miranda, *El sonido de lo propio: José Rolón y su música* (Mexico City: CONACULTA, 2007).

13. "Opinions were divided," wrote Revueltas after the critical appraisal of *Planos*, and "some thought it was Stravinsky's; goodness knows what Stravinsky would have thought. As two pianos and gongs were used, chords at the beginning and end resemble the final chords of *Les noces*; however, they are neither the same notes nor the same intervals, which is probably why they resemble each other more so." See Silvestre Revueltas, "Planos," in *Silvestre Revueltas por él mismo*, ed. Rosaura Revueltas (México: Era, 1989), 212. For Ponce, Stravinsky's neoclassicism was a "well-understood return to classicism in which many musical virtues are to be found which were wrongly dismissed by romanticism." See "Manuel M. Ponce, notable músico mexicano, nos habla sobre el arte de su Patria: Strawinsky y la música moderna," *El Debate* (Montevideo), 21 September, 1941. The equation of Stravinsky with modernism weighed heavily on other musicians. This translation and others in this essay are mine.

14. Estanislao Mejía, "Modernismo en música," *El Universal*, Mexico City, 4 July 1934.

15. Otto Mayer Serra, *The Present State of Music in Mexico* (Washington, DC: Organization of American States, 1960), 41.

16. The symphonic poems of Huizar, Bernal, and Ponce were premiered by the OSM. Rolón's *Zapotlán* was first performed in 1929 by the short-lived Orquesta Sinfónica de Mexicanos with Revueltas conducting, and Moncayo's *Tierra de temporal* was first performed by the OSM's successor, the Orquesta Sinfónica Nacional. Moncayo's score won a first prize at a composition competition held to mark Chopin's centenary; the jury was presided over by Chávez.

17. *Huehuenches* are indigenous dancers. Ponce had seen them perform in the atrium of a church in San Juan Teotihuacán.

18. Roberto García Morillo, *Carlos Chávez: Vida y obra* (Mexico City: Fondo de Cultura Económica, 1960), 89, reproduces a comment by Chávez on indigenous music. Chávez gathered most of his thoughts and speculations on pre-Hispanic music in "La música," in *México y la cultura* (Mexico City: Secretaría de Educación Pública, 1946), 473–503.

19. See Leonora Saavedra, "Manuel M. Ponce's Chapultepec and the Conflicted Representations of a Contested Space," *The Musical Quarterly* 92 (2009): 279–328.

20. On Huízar, see Micaela Huízar, *El surco de un artífice* (Mexico City: CENIDIM, 2004); and José Antonio Alcaraz, *En la más honda música de selva* (Mexico City: CONACULTA, 1998), 64–59.

21. As mentioned in the program notes of its first performance, it had been Huízar's intention to write a ballet, much in the manner of Stravinsky's *Rite of Spring*.

22. The Cora and Huichol are inhabitants of Jalisco and Nayarit, in western Mexico.

23. Chávez, "La música," 487–89.

24. Some of Revueltas's best-known pieces, such as the suites for *La noche de los mayas* and *Redes*, were not put together by the composer. These suites were derived from film scores Revueltas wrote for the eponymous motion pictures and arranged by conductors such as José Yves Limantour and Erich Kleiber. On Revueltas's film music, see Eduardo Contreras Soto, *Silvestre Revueltas en escena y en pantalla* (Mexico City: INBA-INAH, 2012).

25. José Barros Sierra, "Crónicas musicales," *El Universal* (Mexico City), 10 January 1930; Gerónimo Baqueiro Foster, "El quinto concierto de la Orquesta Sinfónica," *El Universal*, 11 January 1930.

26. Miramontes refers to Rolón's private academy of music in Avenida de los Insurgentes, Mexico City. On *Cuauthémoc*, see Miranda, *El sonido de lo propio*, 145–76.

27. José Rolón, "A propósito de un concurso de música nacionalista," in Miranda, *El sonido de lo propio*, 75.

28. José Barros Sierra, "Crónicas musicales," *El Universal* (Mexico City), 10 January 1930.

29. Adolfo Salazar, "Concierto para piano y orquesta de José Rolón," program notes for the Orquesta Sinfónica de Guadalajara's 1961 season, in Miranda, *El sonido de lo propio*, 201–3.

30. Daniel Ayala, "La música maya aborigen," *Cultura musical* 10 (August 1937): 18–21.

31. On Contreras, see Aurelio Tello, *Salvador Contreras: Vida y obra* (Mexico City: CENIDIM, 1987).

32. Jesús Bal y Gay, "Resumen de la temporada sinfónica," *El Universal* (Mexico City), 9 September 1943.

33. See Jorge Barrón, "National Anthem: Manuel Ponce's Violin Concerto," *The Strad* 108/1281 (January 1997): 48–55.

34. See Ricardo Miranda, *Manuel M. Ponce: Ensayo sobre su vida y su obra.* (Mexico City: CONACULTA, 1998), 65.

35. The only Mexican microtonal piece performed by the OSM was Rafael Adame's Concertino for Cello and Orchestra, in 1939. Adame had been a pupil of Carrillo. In the early 1920s, Carrillo and Chávez had an unfortunate encounter that prompted mutual rejection, both personal and musical.

36. It is no coincidence that *Sinfonía de Antígona* was the piece that awakened Mejía's cries against modernism.

37. On Pomar, see Emilio Casco Centeno, "Análisis de la sonatina para piano de José Pomar," *Heterofonía* 134–35 (2006): 109–28.

Carlos Chávez's Symphonies

JULIÁN ORBÓN
TRANSLATED, INTRODUCED, AND ANNOTATED BY
LEONORA SAAVEDRA

The symphony and its many technical and generic implications were at the core of Carlos Chávez's thought as a composer, pedagogue, and eternal student of compositional techniques. We know of two early attempts, a symphony written while Chávez was still in his teens, between 1915 and 1918, and the *Sinfonía de la patria* (1923), the first performance of which was canceled on the day before it was scheduled to be heard. None of these works has ever been performed, and the manuscript of the *Sinfonía de la patria* has only recently been recovered.[1]

Chávez wrote six symphonies as a fully formed composer, beginning with two composed during the 1930s. The *Sinfonía de Antígona* (1933) was fashioned from incidental music written for a production of Sophocles's *Antigone* in Jean Cocteau's version that was directed by Celestino Gorostiza. Chávez led the premiere in Mexico City on 15 December 1933 with his Orquesta Sinfónica de México. In this work Chávez rehearses his own abstract and austere style to represent both Greek antiquity and the intensity of Antigone's tragedy. In *Sinfonía india* (1935), written in New York and premiered by Chávez at William Paley's invitation on the CBS radio network on 23 January 1936, the composer chose rather to represent Mexico's indigenous cultures, as implied by the work's title. This successful, innovative synthesis of traditional symphonic principles and primitivist elements is one of the rare instances in which Chávez used melodies collected by music scholars from indigenous Cora, Huichol, and Seri cultures.

Fifteen years later, Chávez began a period of concentration on the symphony. In 1950 he undertook the composition of his Third Symphony (1950–54), commissioned by Clare Booth Luce in memory of her daughter Ann Clare Brokaw, and premiered on 11 December 1954 at the First Festival of Latin American Music in Caracas, Venezuela. This intense, rather somber work stands in decided contrast with the sunnier, more tonal and Mexicanist Fourth Symphony (1954), aptly nicknamed "Romántica," which was commissioned and premiered by the Louisville Symphony Orchestra, with Chávez conducting, on 11 February 1953. While he was still at work on the Third Symphony, Chávez turned to composing a symphony for strings only, the Fifth (1953), in which periods of intense activity coexist with moments of stasis and timbral exploration. The Fifth Symphony was composed on a commission by the Serge Koussevitzky Foundation and premiered by the Los Angeles Chamber Orchestra on 1 December 1953. Finally, in 1961, while he was teaching composition to a new generation of Mexican composers, Chávez began his Sixth Symphony, modeled in many respects upon Brahms's Fourth. Composed for the 1962 opening of the Philharmonic Hall at Lincoln Center, this work was finally premiered by Leonard Bernstein and the New York Philharmonic Orchestra on 7 May 1964.

The lecture by Spanish-Cuban composer Julián Orbón (b. Avilés, Spain, 1925; d. New York, 1991) reproduced here was first published as liner notes for the 1982 recording of Chávez's six symphonies by Eduardo Mata and the London Symphony Orchestra.[2] These notes were followed by a detailed analysis of each of the symphonies, which we do not include.[3] Orbón's text provides a fine introduction to the general characteristics of Chávez's style. More importantly, it emphasizes the significance of these works for Spanish and Spanish-American music.

Orbón directly addresses the general anxiety, common to all Romance language–speaking composers with regard to the symphony, that most prestigious of instrumental genres—a genre whose paradigmatic embodiments were created by German-speaking composers and constitute the core of the Western art music canon of the late nineteenth and early twentieth centuries. Orbón then advances a theory that is both essentializing and thought-provoking. Historically and temperamentally, he notes, the form of thematic transformation natural to the Spanish-speaking world is variation, which sheds new light on melody. In contrast, writing developmental forms requires a specific temperamental disposition—let us call it the Romantic—as well as a willingness to reason through thematic development and motivic transformation. This is acquired by the Spanish-speaking composer, in Orbón's view, only by the deliberate study of symphonic and other masterpieces in developmental form. Chávez's natural disposition and enormous willpower, Orbón seems to say, led him to produce six symphonies of universal value and significance. And in the end, Chávez's preoccupation with the Romantic individuation of form and predilection for motivic work is what allows us to understand much of his music.

Orbón also addresses the issue of nationalism in Chávez's work, a vexing one as understood by the 1970s, especially when viewed narrowly, and searches for a way to absolve Chávez from its sin. Finally acknowledging the evident absence of any pre-Columbian music that could be absorbed into Chávez's Mexicanist compositions, Orbón turns to the composer's historical moment, one of intense and fundamental transformation of social and cultural structures. It is the post-revolutionary impulse to seek historical justice for the past that informs Chávez's oeuvre, Orbón argues, rather than any real pre-Columbian music. And here Orbón advances another theory, or rather, a definition: Nationalism is but the regional expression of permanent and universal values such as we find in the symbolic and mythical thinking of pre-Columbian cultures.

Few people were as well situated to understand Chávez's compositional thought as Orbón, a Spanish-Cuban composer who belonged in the 1940s to Cuba's Grupo Renovación. As Chávez's assistant professor from 1960 to 1963 at the *taller de composición* (composition workshop) of the Conservatorio Nacional de Música in Mexico City, Orbón was able to watch Chávez think and teach.[4] As the author himself notes, the two men continued to have endless exchanges on music over the many years of their friendship, first in Mexico and later in New York, where Orbón resided and Chávez spent long stretches of time each year.

The Symphonies of Carlos Chávez

In the pages dedicated to me in *Music in Cuba*, Alejo Carpentier refers to a comment I made regarding the absence of great symphonic forms, of symphonies in short, in Spanish music:

> The musician who succeeds in being a Spanish Brahms with a language responding to our sensibility today will have found the clue to the problem. Neoclassicism is often the refuge of those who want to avoid the risky but necessary adventure of lyricism.[5]

The first edition of Carpentier's book dates to 1946; the aforementioned conversation must have occurred in 1944. Indeed, in those years, many of us who were first embarking upon our creative work took Stravinsky's *Musical Poetics* as our guiding text, and *Pulcinella* and *A Soldier's Tale*, together with Prokoviev's Classical Symphony or the Scarlatti-inspired last movement of de Falla's Hapsichord Concerto, as models of economy of means and formal simplicity, in brief, of classical order. We were intent on rejecting the expansion of the symphonic form of the second half of the nineteenth century, from Brahms to Mahler.

But very soon I began to wonder if in the nature of such rejection was something that went beyond the submission to a style that dominated European music for two decades and whose influence remained steady even longer in Spanish America. Could it be that symphonic forms are a means of expression foreign to our specific creative being?

A creator is a synthesis of the collective and the individual, of history and intimacy, even of the space around us: the depths, as Juan Ramón Jiménez[6] used to say, the depths that things and humans carry in their true being. Maybe, then, the conditions were not ready in those depths of ours to allow us to conceive of sonata form and its symphonic manifestation. In order to arrive at such a conclusion it seemed necessary to investigate which musical form belongs, with the most evident legitimacy, to our historical reality. The answer is not difficult: during the sixteenth century, that extraordinary period of nascent harmonic structures, of tonal transitions and embryonic forms, Spain gave birth to instrumental variation.

It is needless to insist, of course, on the capital importance of this event for the future course of European music. It is true that there were previous examples, such as *My Lady Carey's Dompe*,[7] but these are but rudimentary approximations. The first set of variations that makes use of the techniques that constitute the very essence of the form appeared in the *Delfín de música para vihuela*, by Luis de Narváez (1538). It was followed by Alonso Mudarra's and Enríquez de Valderrábano's music, and by the expressive and technical fulfillment of the form achieved by Antonio de Cabezón in his *Diferencias sobre "El canto del caballero."* Regarding the *basso ostinato* type of variation, we find the germ of a *passacaglia* in Diego de Ortíz's *Tratado de glosas* (1553).* Variation is, therefore, the form that emerges most naturally from our musical past.

We need now to approach the technique as employed by the masters of the period in question. For our purposes, it is enough to observe that of the many resources employed in the art of variation, ornamentation is at the core of the sixteenth-century Spanish masters' conception of the

*An extensive consideration of these issues is found in the masterful study by Robert U. Nelson, *The Technique of Variation: A Study of Instrumental Variation from Cabezón to Max Reger* (Berkeley and Los Angeles: University of California Press, 1948).

form. Ornamentation can adopt diverse functions, from decorative figuration to a polyphonic contrapuntal structure such as we find in *El canto del caballero*. The taste for ornamentation that we perceive in all types of instrumental Spanish music of the sixteenth century seems natural if we consider that it is precisely in ornamental splendor that Spain left the imprint of the most original manifestations of her genius. It is found in the variation of matter itself, teeming with forms, of the Baroque, *churrigueresco*, and *barroco de Indias,*[8] and in the variation of reality, bathed in new light, such as there is in the metaphorical ornamentation of Góngora's poetry.

Just as we find ornament at the base of variation, the principal element at the core of sonata form—in its development section—is the motive. The division of a theme into motives, and the intuition of the constructive potential of fragmentation, necessitates a type of musical thought different from that which we have observed in instrumental variation. The issue now is a dialectical attitude, a logic of becoming, in a way, a "system"; that is why sonata form and its symphonic expression achieves its highest fulfillment in the musical thought of the great German masters. We can arrive, in a very general sense, at the following conclusion: ornamentation sheds light on a theme, while motivic work reasons through it. And it is such reasoning, turned into creative impulse, that confers to the motive the incessant possibility of giving rise to a temporal order such as we observe in the great symphonic development sections and in *Tristan*. It is the music of reason that animates so many pages of Hegel's *Phenomenology of Spirit* or Heidegger's *Being and Time*.

We find ourselves in the following situation: of those two possible attitudes with regard to a theme that we have described above, the first one seems to be more natural to us; the second we must take on through knowledge of the examples that we find in the great masters of musical form.

This appears to be the obstacle standing in the way of symphonic form in the Spanish-American world. Of all great musicians in our culture, only Heitor Villa-Lobos, by virtue of that disproportionate amount of energy that prompted him to try his hand at all musical genres, composed a symphony; that is, until Carlos Chávez in 1933 wrote *Antígona*.

Chávez's clear awareness of the issues discussed in these pages was evident to those of us who were fortunate enough to know him intimately. I was able to grasp the essence of his main ideas on creation and pedagogy through many years of unforgettable dialogues. Of all possible approaches to a score, Chávez favored motivic analysis. This was a true obsession for him. His scores of Beethoven's symphonies and quartets, of Brahms's symphonies, were literally covered with markings showing, with tenacious attention to detail, the motivic uses of the thematic materials. There were not even two notes for which he did not try to find a logical derivation from one of the motives previously introduced. His conception of form was radically organic, anatomic, a term he in fact used in one of his writings on formal analysis.

Chávez's preoccupation with motivic work is crucial for our understanding not only of the symphonies but of his oeuvre as a whole. A very moving anecdote can help illuminate his passion for the nature of a theme and its potential. A few weeks before his death, as I was commenting on the prodigious eighteenth variation of Rachmaninoff's *Rhapsody on a Theme by Paganini*, and on how a melody of great lyric strength was the result of the inversion of a theme actually far removed from all lyricism, Chávez, using strength that he extracted only from his incomparable willpower, took the trouble to write down Paganini's theme and its inversion, in order to verify "by himself" the rigor in the new disposition of the intervals.

Inversion, even within a canon, is one of the contrapuntal resources most often used by Chávez. In the Fifth and Sixth symphonies, in the Violin Concerto, there are extraordinary examples of his expertise in this technique, and of its employment, never accidental but always organic, only at crucial moments in the formal structure. Given the nature of Chávez's music—dependent to a great extent upon linear formations in motion of which harmony is often a result—motives acquire central importance. This characteristic favors enormously his sense of symphonic form. There followed in his music a proliferation of motives, emerging from each other in continuous juxtaposition as he searched for an asymmetrical music based on the principle of non-repetition, a search that culminated eventually in the *Invención* for piano.

Otherwise, the most specific traits of Chávez's music are all found in his symphonies. Since this is an issue that has been examined enough in critical studies of his work, I will briefly describe some of the basic elements of his style. He uses modalism frequently, a kind of modalism that is linear rather than harmonic. It is interesting that despite his constant use of some melodic designs that originate in the modes, his harmony does not appear to derive from them.

The construction of chords based on stacked fourths, or the use of parallel fifths and octaves, is a common procedure that he often maintains through extensive passages and even throughout an entire work, as in *Sinfonía antígona*. This does not mean we cannot find harmonies based on triads: the Sixth Symphony offers abundant examples of them, such as in the radiant tonal affirmation that is at the base of the first theme, and the first inversion triad that supports the beginning of the second thematic idea. It is nevertheless true that Chávez favors the fourth as the generating harmonic interval, which in a way systematizes the frequent occurrence of dissonance.

He frequently uses the semitone so insistently that it acquires the character of a magical invocation, as in *Sinfonía antígona*, and in certain closing periods, such as the coda of the Sixth Symphony. Sometimes it also becomes a defining element of the thematic structure, as seen in the *passacaglia* that closes this work. Robert Stevenson's observations regarding certain rhythmic formations typical of Chávez is particularly accurate:

> As far as rhythms are concerned, his pieces set a certain basic unit and stick to it. If the basic figure is an eighth, running eighths will continue throughout the entire piece or section of a piece. If the basic figure is sixteenths, running sixteenths will continue.*

Rapid and extensive successions of triplets appear often as motoric impulse, especially during development sections, in counterpoint to the themes and their motivic development. Orchestration is one of the main achievements of Chávez's style: anything that might evoke a traditional approach is, if possible, avoided. The individuation of timbres and their fusion into other timbres help create unusual textures: trombones, tubas, and double basses acquire *concertante* prominence alongside the woodwinds and the quartet of strings. Tuttis generate sonic blocks of implacable power, in chords literally "torn off the orchestra," as Alejo Carpentier mentions in relation to the Third Symphony.[9] Chávez's writing for strings tends to highlight the autonomy of the parts, demanding of each of them passages situated at the limits of their technical possibilities, or else uniting them in instrumental/harmonic textures of absolute novelty, as with the use of harmonics in the slow tempo of the Fifth Symphony.

These are, in an extremely compact summary, of course, some of the most readily apparent constructive elements in Chávez's work. Let us now examine the background, those depths mentioned by Juan Ramón Jiménez—which in this case are the depths of the historic background—to better understand the man and the work.

The beginning of Chávez's musical life coincides with one of those moments in which Spanish America became conscious of its historical and

*Robert M. Stevenson, *Music in Mexico* (New York: Thomas Y. Crowell, 1952), 245.

social reality. These are the years of the Mexican Revolution.[10] The originality of the Mexican Revolution consisted in its seeking of social justice for the future while demanding historical justice toward the past. It is a revolution that returns to myths, that resurrects the gods. The past, which as an immense horizon of suspended historical time springs back to life in the revolutionary upheaval, is that of the great pre-Hispanic cultures.

In my own testimony in the pages of the *Homenaje Nacional a Carlos Chávez*, published by the Instituto Nacional de Bellas Artes, I wrote, referring to the Revolution:

> I think we can well situate that period within what [José] Lezama [Lima] called the "imaginary eras." In those essential years [Alfonso] Reyes went to the origins of the language in his edition of the *Cantar del Cid*; [José] Vasconcelos set the final destiny of the race; the remote gods seemed to become incarnate, by the thousands, in the hieratic peons of the great muralists; the old combative romances of the borderlands sprang back to life in the *corridos* of the Revolution and, taking it all in, on a mysterious threshold, as if at the center of that hallucinated time appeared Emiliano Zapata.[11]

That rediscovery of the primordial cultures and those times are present in the music of Carlos Chávez. Melodic lines advancing on implacable marches, stone-like harmonic formations, instrumental textures that convey a ritual character onto the simplest melody—all those are sonic constants that we find from *El fuego nuevo* to *Pirámide*.[12] And all that within a classic objectivity, such as is manifested in the sacred space of Teotihuacán.[13]

Carlos Chávez felt no affinity for what the term "nationalism" implies; and indeed, nationalism, understood as a school of composition, has little to do with Chávez's approach to the historical and spiritual reality of his country. The term is generally applied to the use, either more or less extensively, of certain folklore that would allow the identification of a national character. There is no need to insist on the limitations that such an understanding of the term can impose.

In the same way that a magic/religious conscience creates a series of myths or sacred figures such as Quetzalcóatl, Osiris, Viracocha, or Melchizedek,[14] the spirit of the people, what the Germans call *Volksgeist*, gives birth to a series of equally common aesthetic values that can make us feel intensely the musical emotions present in a Romanian or Hungarian dance, in the ballads of the mountains of Kentucky, in a Spanish *petenera*, a Russian liturgical chant, or a *son* from Veracruz. Grasping these expressions of the spirit of the people evidently demands a delicate intuition from the listener, a specific disposition of a person's sensitivity that is, on the other hand, equally necessary to understand a poem by Eliot, Góngora, or Mallarmé.

We might try, for now, to advance the following definition: the immersion into the spirit of the people as the source of a culture allows the individual creator to interpret such culture by reinventing it. This process includes analogies and parallelisms with other cultures; thus the interpretation achieves the sort of transcendence that renders visible the quality that we call universal. The myths, local characters, and historical events of Ireland are the point of departure for the construction of those literary monuments *Ulysses* and *Finnegan's Wake*. Furthermore, a simple neighborhood ballad was the original cell that Joyce expanded into the protean energy and the infinite complexities of that masterwork.

In Bartók's string quartets, for example, many intervallic dispositions, scalar systems, metric groupings, and resulting harmonies originate in certain typical traits of Hungarian, Bulgarian, and Romanian folk music, among others. But within Bartók's creative individuality, these elements form objective structures, merging into a technique that can be assimilated by a composer of any nationality because the musical essence so achieved is just as universally valid as that which we find in Beethoven's string quartets.

Carlos Chávez partakes of this process. The difference with Bartók is that Bartók had at hand a practically unlimited amount of folk material, as shown by his many volumes of transcriptions of popular music. In approaching pre-Hispanic music, Chávez found himself with a very slight number of authentic examples; therefore his task was much more that of reinventing than of assimilating. Chávez imagines or "imaginates" pre-Cortesian music; a few melodic designs, some percussive formulas, the survival or description of some instruments, scarce living testimonies heard during his time in Tlaxcala, are enough for him to invent music in which the documentary circumstance is obscured, transformed into Carlos Chávez's personal language, from which an objective and universal technique has already emerged. This universality resides in those aspects called (narrowly, in my opinion) "indigenist" in Chávez's work. The term, in its most common meaning, makes one think immediately of local limitations, tinted with exoticism, that take away any validity or objectivity from the works so conceived.

Now, the great Mesoamerican classic cultures and their fusion into the Mexica[15] syncretism inaugurate one of the major mythic creations of history. Some of the clues regarding their magical and religious thinking, such as the burnt water, the duality of the bird-snake, the conception of the king-priest, are summits of symbolic thinking. All this is part of Chávez's emotional and intellectual constitution, and places him within a superior, transcendent, and universal world that is a source of myths. In any case, we are dealing with the same "indigenism" that made Wagner search for the generating impulse of the tetralogy in the *Niebelungenlied* or else in the Nordic theogonies. We thus arrive at the following definition of nationalism, one that implies an inversion of its habitual meaning: assuming the intrinsic quality of the work, nationalism is but the regional expression of permanent and universal values.

The two lines of the Spanish musical tradition—the very cultured one that stems from the composers for vihuela, Cabezón and [Tomás Luis de] Victoria, and goes through Manuel de Falla, and the popular and equally cultured one that is integrated into the different types of Spanish-American mestizo music[16]—do not appear to be determining influences on the formation of Chávez's musical language. Nevertheless, with regard to the first of the lines, the use as motoric impulse of triplets and sixteenth notes that often ornament a theme or its motivic transformations has a venerable antecedent in the technique of the Spanish masters of the sixteenth century. Of the second line, we of course find examples in Chávez's music, but, leaving aside literal quotations such as the "Sandunga" in *H.P.*, Chávez imposes a certain abstraction onto popular themes, eliminating topical features and retaining a core of designs that he then incorporates into his language.

We cannot expect from Chávez the kind of folkloric treatment that we perceive in Galindo's *Sones de mariachi* or Moncayo's *Huapango*, which form the bone marrow of Revueltas's style to a substantial degree.[17] In these composers' music, the harmonic, metric, and instrumental conditions of popular music are taken to a superior speculative realm where they, nevertheless, remain. We are dealing here with some sort of illumination of the primary material achieved through the orchestration, the harmony, the rhythmic transformations—all this creates a poetic image, provokes an epiphany in which the secrets of those musics of the people are newly revealed. This happens, above all, in Revueltas's music. Chávez aims to appropriate internal structures rather than to feel an immediate seduction; there is more energy than contemplation in his attitude. Of course, both visions are equally legitimate, and there are superb examples of both in Debussy, de Falla, and Bartók.

Chávez's passion for formal structure necessarily drove him to its superior form of expression. Let us now turn to his own ideas on the symphony:

> In order for Beethoven to achieve the great depth of the Ninth Symphony he needed to be able to first conceive the particular structure of that great work. Without a doubt, form for this reason is not, and must not be, a formula. While the first symphonists in the eighteenth century, not yet artists but artisans, and even the transitional masters such as Haydn and Mozart, wrote symphonies by the dozen, all cut with the same mold, Beethoven, the first great master of form, wrote only nine symphonies, achieving great progress between each of them. Of all the constitutive elements of music, form must be the most characteristic not only of every composer, but of every work.[18]

Chávez here radically accepts Romantic individualism. This is a rather understandable decision for a composer approaching symphonic form. The individuation of the formal structure is the process that takes place in the great symphonic century: an imperious expansive sequence that remains uninterrupted from Beethoven to Mahler.

Romanticism introduces a unique orchestral pathos: a longing substance, a symphonic impulse that breathes already in those themes that erupt radiantly and that, at the same time, seem to have been already "there," sounding forever. This is what happens with the initial theme of Robert Schumann's Third Symphony, in the immense opening of Brahms's Fourth, or in the absolute determination with which Beethoven's Eighth Symphony commences. Such Romantic condition, such Romantic lineage, seems to exist prior to the symphonic impulse.

Now, did Chávez possess the Romantic condition? Many times his music is seen as the antipode of Romanticism, born of the most radical experiences of the twentieth century. However, like all great artists Chávez was able to assimilate the paradoxical. And it is certain that the symphonic/Romantic impulse had always been in him. Let us observe Manuel M. Ponce's testimony in a 1921 article on Chávez:

> The most outstanding aspect of Chávez's music is its aspiration to modernism and originality, which is perfectly justified in such a young man, and Chávez is still very young, despite his serious and even melancholy demeanor. He has talent. He

> is under the double influence of Schumann's and Chopin's Romanticism and of modernism, which attracts him with its air of novelty and exoticism.[19]

Let us emphasize two names within Ponce's fine appreciation, Schumann and Chopin, and especially an adjective: melancholy. Young Chávez showed one of the surest marks of a Romantic sensibility: melancholy. And he also preserved his enthusiasm for Romantic music; a portrait of Chopin, whom he greatly admired, was in his studio in the Lomas de Chapultepec neighborhood, and when he moved to New York in his last years, the portrait moved with him to his new apartment, where he used to show it, saying: "It is the only authentic [portrait] and it has nothing to do with the idealized versions that are so well known."

The preoccupation with the individuation of form entails a type of subjectivity that fills formal structure with emotional content. And lyric emotion is also present in Chávez's music. It would be enough to cite his songs, full of expressive substance—the way he can situate himself, for example, in the melancholy atmosphere of the blues, in his masterful version of this genre on a text by Villaurrutia—to realize the presence of such lyricism.[20] But we also find it in other works, culminating, for me, in an extraordinary moment in the Largo of the Violin Concerto, in the soloist's recitative-like improvisation over an immutable pulse in the first violins and a pedal point in the cellos and basses: one of the highest instances of lyric tension I know of in the literature for this instrument.

If we think about form animated by a lyric essence, then we are practically invoking Brahms. And the analysis of Brahms's work was one of Chávez's constant inclinations. Chávez studied the four symphonies, the piano concertos and the Double Concerto, exhibiting great meticulousness in his harmonic and motivic investigation, on which he insisted with absolute fervor (it is peculiar—and we must note—that Bruckner and Mahler were never among Chávez's favorite composers). He subjected the development sections of Brahms's symphonies to rigorous examination; the formal periods, the motivic relations, the orchestration were not only a matter for personal study but also part of the curriculum in the composition workshop[21] in which I had the privilege of participating, and which concluded with long sessions dedicated to studying the renovation in the technique of variation of a *basso continuo*, such as we find in the *passacaglia* or *chaconne* of Brahms's Fourth Symphony.

In 1944, the need for symphonic formal expression in our music as viewed by Alejo Carpentier was on its way to being fulfilled; the *Antígona* and *India* symphonies had already been composed. Nevertheless, a few years would still be needed until Carlos Chávez, in a memorable process of continuous refinement, perfected a language that, culminating in the Sixth Symphony, placed him among the great symphonists of the twentieth century.

NOTES

1. On the fate of *Sinfonía de la Patria,* see Leonora Saavedra, "Of Selves and Others: Historiography, Ideology, and the Politics of Modern Mexican Music" (PhD diss., University of Pittsburgh, 2001), 122–25; and Julián Carrillo, *Testimonio de una vida* (San Luis Potosí: Comité Organizador "San Luis 400," 1992), 172.

2. Julián Orbón, liner notes to *Chávez: The Complete Symphonies,* London Symphony Orchestra, cond. Eduardo Mata, originally released by Peerless (1982), then as VoxBox, 2-CDs, 5061 (1992). The liner notes are in Spanish.

3. Other important texts on Chávez's symphonies include Jesús Bal y Gay, "La 'Sinfonía de Antígona' de Carlos Chávez," *Nuestra Música* 5/17 (1950): 5–17; Robert L. Parker, *Carlos Chávez: Mexico's Modern-Day Orpheus* (Boston: Twayne, 1983), 67–83; and Roberto García Morillo, *Carlos Chávez: Vida y obra* (Mexico City: Fondo de Cultura Económica, 1960), 73–78, 88–95, 152–170.

4. As part of their training at the workshop, young composers were asked to write pieces, including symphonies, closely modeled upon Classical and Romantic compositions in aspects such as form or harmony and even style. Chávez's close modeling of his Sixth Symphony on Brahms's Fourth is, no doubt, testimony to his excitement over this pedagogical technique

5. Alejo Carpentier (1904–1980) was a Cuban writer, composer, and musicologist. See Alejo Carpentier, *La música en Cuba* (Mexico City: Fondo de Cultura Económica, 1946), 259; English version: *Music in Cuba* (Minneapolis: University of Minnesota Press, 2001).

6. Juan Ramón Jiménez (1881–1958), Spanish poet, received the Nobel Prize in Literature in 1956.

7. Anonymous English composition, ca. 1520.

8. *Churrigueresco* and *barroco de Indias* are lavish, highly ornamented Baroque architectural styles of the the late seventeenth and early eighteenth centuries. *Barroco de Indias* refers specifically to New World styles in poetry and architecture, closely related to the emergence of a *criollo* (Spanish-American) conscience.

9. Alejo Carpentier, "La *Sinfonía Núm: 3* de Carlos Chávez," *El Nacional* (Caracas), 18 December 1954, as quoted in Roberto García Morillo, *Carlos Chávez: Vida y obra*, 157.

10. The Mexican Revolution began in 1910 and ended in 1921.

11. Julián Orbón, "Testimonios" in *Homenaje Nacional a Carlos Chávez* (Mexico City: INBA, 1974), 14. José Lezama Lima (1910–1976) was a prominent Cuban writer. The Mexican writer Alfonso Reyes (1889–1959) published a prose version of the *Cantar de mío Cid* (*The Lay of the Cid*, ca. 1200), the oldest Spanish epic poem, in 1919. José Vasconcelos (1882–1959), Mexican philosopher, coined the term "cosmic race" to speak of the peoples of Spanish America. Emiliano Zapata (1879–1919) was a peasant military leader of the Mexican Revolution who acquired mythic proportions in post-revolutionary times.

12. *El fuego nuevo* (1921) and *Pirámide* (1968) are ballets composed by Chávez on pre-Columbian topics.

13. Teotihuacán is the name of the pre-Columbian city and ceremonial center located in the Valley of Mexico.

14. Mythic figures in the Toltec, Egyptian, pre-Incan, and Hebrew cultures.

15. The Mexica people are also called Aztecs.

16. Mestizo, of mixed race and culture.

17. Blas Galindo (1910–1993) and José Pablo Moncayo (1912–1958) were Chávez's composition students. Silvestre Revueltas (1899–1940) was his contemporary and friend.

18. Source of this quotation not located.

19. Manuel M. Ponce, "Carlos Chávez Ramírez, pianista y compositor," *Arte y labor: Organo de la Unión Filarmónica de México* 2/16 (1921): 7. Manuel M. Ponce (1882–1948) had been Chávez's piano teacher and was a composer in his own right.

20. Orbón is referring to Chávez's song "North Carolina Blues" (1942) for voice and piano, a setting of a poem addressing the plight of African Americans in the southern United States, written by Xavier Villaurrutia, Langston Hughes's translator into Spanish.

21. Chávez's composition studio was at the Conservatorio Nacional de Música from 1960 to 1965.

Carlos Chávez and Silvestre Revueltas: Retracing an Ignored Dialogue

ROBERTO KOLB-NEUHAUS

More often than not, the life and work of Silvestre Revueltas has been narrated by stressing the contrast, and even conflict, with Carlos Chávez. Yet there was a time when a strong friendship and artistic partnership bound them together. In 1928 Chávez invited Revueltas to return to Mexico as a violin teacher and conductor of the school orchestra at the Conservatorio Nacional de Música, as well as assistant conductor of the Orquesta Sinfónica de México (OSM), which Chávez had recently founded. At the time, Revueltas was residing in the southern United States, where he worked as a violinist and silent-film orchestra conductor. Unlike Chávez, who fully embraced composition early in his life, Revueltas focused mainly on a career as a violinist, composing only on the side. In his capacity as a perfomer he briefly collaborated with Chávez in 1925, in a concert of modern music organized by the latter in Mexico, and it appears that, however brief this encounter, it was sufficient to lay the groundwork for a friendship marked by emotional and intellectual closeness.

The friendship can be inferred from the intimate familiarity that emanates from the letters they wrote to each other after their first collaboration, now preserved by Revueltas's daughter Eugenia and in the Chávez collection at the Archivo General de la Nación. Only a close relationship, for example, would allow one of them to criticize the other's compositions.[1] This Chávez does in a letter to Revueltas of 11 March 1927, confidently complaining about the latter's "Wagnerian" attitude in *Elegía* or about the title given to another piece, *Batik* (ca. 1926), "una cosa *tan bien* con un nombre tan mal" (such a *good thing* with such a bad title).[2] In return, Revueltas confided to Chávez his discomfort about this piece: "The damn *Batik*, which I didn't like because I felt that it should have been scored for different instruments."[3] Revealingly, Chávez's letter to Revueltas not only expresses his intense desire to meet with him again but ends suggestively by asking, "¿Cuándo tendremos nuestra orquesta?" (When will we have our orchestra?).

Revueltas seems to have been on Chávez's mind all during his quest to found a new orchestra in Mexico, so his letter of invitation in December of 1928 comes as no surprise. In 1971, in a lecture at El Colegio Nacional, Chávez would recall the happy coincidence of the creation of the OSM and Revueltas's desire to return to Mexico: "It was all for the best: as teacher at the Conservatory, Silvestre would contribute the good violin school that we so urgently needed; he would get himself trained as a conductor acting as my assistant; he would offer useful knowledge to the string sections of the orchestra, and he would be a great collaborator in the tireless struggle I had embarked on against the mediocrity, conservatism, and vulgarity dominant in Mexico at the time."[4]

The two composers' friendship only seems to have deepened upon Revueltas's return to Mexico, judging by joint projects that imply a relationship of closeness, not only on a professional level but on an intellectual and personal one as well. This particularly fertile relation lasted until 1935, when a series of circumstances led to a lasting estrangement, manifest at first in the separation of their professional paths but, arguably, also in the growing breach between their aesthetic and political goals.[5] Two issues may lie behind the estrangement: in 1934 Revueltas was appointed to compose the music for the film *Redes* (*The Wave*, originally *Pescados*), a project developed by Paul Strand and Chávez, who had intended to write the score.[6] A year later, Estanislao Mejía, Chávez's political enemy and head of the Conservatorio Nacional de Música, created a federally subsidized symphony orchestra to compete with Chávez's privately funded OSM. Revueltas, at the time assistant conductor of the OSM, accepted the invitation to lead the competing Orquesta Sinfónica Nacional, without first informing Chávez.[7] Although the parting of ways never led to a confrontation between the two men, verbal or otherwise, public reception in those years thrived on emphasizing their difference (mostly constructed), as their mythified selves effectively served as flagships of conflicting political and cultural interest groups. Eurocentric and conservative composers as well as post-revolutionary nationalists, who (wrongly) believed they were represented by Revueltas's music and persona, were on one side, and cosmopolitan modernists perceived by the latter group as elitist and anti-national, and presumably embodied by Chávez as composer and cultural administrator, were on the other.

Although Mexico's social and cultural structure changed considerably over the decades following Revueltas's death in 1940, it can be argued that the figures of both Chávez and Revueltas continued to serve as symbols of similar antagonistic cultural discourses. Perhaps for this reason, more often than not, reception in Mexico focused not on their music, but on mythical historicizations of their respective biographies.

Robert Parker's and Yolanda Moreno's pioneering writings in the 1980s and the centenary of these composers' birth in 1999 are largely responsible for bringing about an increased, and above all lasting, interest in the artists in the United States and Mexico, transcending the biographical to include discussions of their music.[8] In the case of Revueltas, the discussion has tended to leave behind the emotional character of the panegyric that predominated earlier in favor of more substantive aesthetic discussions.[9] The variety and depth of Chávez's musical contributions are only now starting to be recognized in their fullest dimension.

Professional Collaboration

Direct correlations of the two men's joint professional activities, as well as their political and aesthetic views, however, remain extremely scarce.[10] This seems odd, to say the least, considering the close working relationship between the two composers from 1930 to 1934, and, as I shall argue here, the basic kinship of cultural and political purposes regardless of differing aesthetic stances. Perhaps the above-mentioned tendency to appropriate their biographies for purposes of controversy unrelated to their musical work is responsible for the lack of attention paid to positive links that stand out, even at a first glance. Thus the purpose of this text is to explore some of these apparent links, clearing the way for further inquiries into what seems to have been an intense and fruitful dialogue between the two composers.

What was the nature of Chávez and Revueltas's early collaboration? From Revueltas's arrival in Mexico in 1929 and until 1934, they worked closely together, as can be inferred from their intensely collaborative work in the Orquesta Sinfónica de México and the Conservatorio Nacional de Música. Communications related to the management of the OSM speak of a fluent exchange, although it was clearly Chávez who bore the brunt of the overwhelming administrative responsibilities. Their joint undertakings are very unusual for a principal conductor and his assistant, and therefore doubly significant: they shared the baton during concerts, conducted each other's premieres, wrote program notes for each other, and jointly organized many of the activities of the orchestra. This kind of collaboration would usually be expected from equals in rank, which they were not. And yet, the hierarchy seems not to have affected their basic alliance, both aesthetic and political, an agreement strong enough not to stand in the way of the free development and manifestation of individual stances regarding shared concerns and issues. (Indeed, it could be argued that Chávez's well-documented need to be in control and

Revueltas's reluctance to assume any kind of administrative role were complementary and made this collaboration possible.)

The dialogue that can be inferred from their collaboration and common projects clearly situates them on the same side of the barricades that separated a Mexican modernist avant-garde from the local Eurocentric conservatives. The resonance between them is corroborated by Revueltas himself in a declaration, written in 1937 during the Civil War in Republican Spain, where he had participated in the Second Congress of Antifascist Artists and Writers (fall of 1937). This text, "Panorama musical de México," published in Mexico City's *El Nacional* in January 1938, seems all the more significant, since it was written at a time when both composers had somewhat clumsily disassociated their professional careers.[11] In his review of musical life in Mexico since his return, Revueltas establishes at the outset his appreciation for Chávez, the "musician of iron—this is what I called him while we were working together"; he was the man who "organized the activity and musical production of Mexico." He includes Chávez and himself among those who were intent on destroying traditionalists: "We were a small group, sharing the same impulse and a goodly amount of destructive energy." Their common target was well defined: "Our new and good-humored impetus fought against the ancestral apathy and the cavernous obscurity of academic musicians. It washed, cleansed, and swept the old Conservatory, which was crumbling with tradition, woodworms, and glorious sadness." He vindicated the modernist programming of Chávez's orchestra, which introduced a wide range of then little-known composers, such as Stravinsky, Debussy, Honegger, Milhaud, and Varèse. He dwelt on the protests of the conservatives: "The reaction was strong, and we met the encouraging hissing, stamping, insults, and aggressive indignation of the lazy and idle audience and the usual critics." Even the existence of two competing orchestras, presumably a principal cause of their estrangement, is vindicated by Revueltas in collaborative terms: "There are two symphony orchestras in Mexico: the Mexican, under Chávez's direction, and the National, led by me. Both pursue the same path and the same longing for improvement. The work of these two orchestras has stimulated musical creation."

The sincerity of these statements seems corroborated by a previous statement, published by Revueltas as part of his 1933 polemic with critic Salomón Kahan, who aggressively denounced Chávez's betrayal of national values for flirting with north-of-the-border modernities. Kahan contrasted him with Revueltas, whom he considered an example of a Romantic composer truly rooted in the Mexican self, and for that reason could be forgiven an occasional "modernistic excess." Revueltas joins sides with Chávez, and, making use of his characteristic irony, lashes out at Kahan:

> Mr. Kahan has found my path. . . . He has discovered recesses of my spirit that were unknown to me; his sharp psychologist's eye has shed light upon the unlit intricacies of my soul and has shown it in its naked truth to the audiences. . . . I have always loved people with a strong and upright spirit; who know nothing of the easy paths so well liked by the mental idleness of the majorities. It is for this reason that those "modernists" Mr. Kahan despises are my friends. Among these "modernists" is Aaron Copland with whom I share the same ideology. Aaron Copland recognizes and admires the prolific work of Carlos Chávez. *Cuauhnáhuac, Colorines, Janitzio*, etc. would never have seen the light of day if it hadn't been for the incentive from and encouraging energy of Carlos Chávez.[12]

Testimonies to Chávez and Revueltas's dialogue and shared militancy such as this one are scarce, due to Revueltas's reluctance to verbalize his thoughts on music, especially in his early years as a professional composer, which are precisely those that united his pursuits with those of Chávez. Whereas Chávez projected an academic persona, continually publishing texts, giving lectures, and sponsoring research, Revueltas appears to have chosen the role of an avant-garde provocateur and political activist, mostly turning his back on academic performance and discourse.

During the years of Chávez and Revueltas's intense collaboration, only Chávez regularly published his thoughts in journals and newspapers, in Mexico and in the United States. Revueltas published only three texts in 1933, all in a satirical and sarcastic vein, attacking the foes so clearly defined later in his article, "Panorama de la música en México."[13] Little can be inferred from these texts about his music. Chávez, in contrast, wrote profusely and competently about music.[14] The topics he touched upon in his articles are reflected in his music in different ways. More interesting, these same topics also echoed in the music Revueltas wrote at the time, suggesting an as yet unexplored *musical* dialogue: the local modernists' need for a redefinition of the relation between high and popular art; the struggle to modernize the Conservatory (Revueltas wrote his most provocative and experimental pieces for the school orchestra); the challenge of creating a musically expressed local identity in the context of a universal modernity and in opposition to the preceding Eurocentric discourse; the devising of musical strategies that could communicate political messages in post-revolutionary

Mexico; and the search for modernist innovation. It therefore seems desirable to explore this dialogue in the two composers' music, in addition to looking for it indirectly, in epistolary and other verbal exchanges. Some manifestations of such a musical dialogue will be suggested here.

Common Foes

Coincidences of creative stance seem to emerge even before we speak of a concrete collaboration between the two composers. While Revueltas was in the United States as a violinist during the 1920s, his composing centered on two interests that would persist throughout his life and be correlated in different ways in his works: the search for modernist innovation and the need to express in his music his strong political beliefs. In Revueltas's vision these two goals were irreconcilable with a then-dominant trend: nationalist concerns, which, judging by various statements and the satirical rhetoric in some of his compositions, seem to be associated with a reactionary traditionalism or with essentialisms that both he and Chávez opposed.[15] This third creative vein, a negative stance of satirical anti-nationalism, seems strategically opposed to his positive quest for modernist and political innovation.[16]

The first drive, modernism, can be seen early on in *Batik* and in an unnamed sequel, a composition in four movements for twelve instruments presumably started in San Antonio and finished upon Revueltas's return to Mexico. It can later be found in the four String Quartets (1930, '31, and '32), *Tres piezas para violín y piano* (1932), *Toccata (sin fuga)* (1933), and *Planos (Danza geométrica)* (1934). His political passion is inscribed in two pieces for violin and piano that introduce the lasting subject of many later compositions, that is, the street dweller, either peasant or proletarian: *Tierra pa' las macetas* (Potting Soil, 1924?) is a *pregón* (vendor's cry) turned melody, and *El afilador* (The Knife-sharpener, 1924) resorts to word painting, representing the turning of the sharpening stone by means of an ostinato.[17] Revueltas's sound gestures, such as the *pregón*, the pan flute melodies of the knife-sharpeners, or whistled codes to represent the peasant-proletarian soundscape of the street constitute a fundamental semantic subject in many of his early works. The political subject is encountered throughout Revueltas's works in the musical personae of peasants, the homeless, street protesters, revolutionary fighters, soldiers seen as fellow proletarians, black slaves, prisoners, and exploited fishermen, represented both in instrumental and vocal music, and notably in scores composed for cinema, ballet, and political satire.

Just as in the case of contemporary painters David Alfaro Siqueiros, José Clemente Orozco, and Antonio Ruiz, or photographer Manuel Álvarez Bravo, Revueltas's interest lies in the people's social condition rather than in their representation as Mexicans. This issue appears to lie at the heart of his intentions when, back in Mexico, he decided to set aside his violin in favor of composition and conducting. Significantly, Revueltas borrowed two popular *sones* of the time as subjects in his first composition after returning to Mexico, *Pequeña pieza para orquesta* (1929), which possibly was never performed in his lifetime.[18] The parodic intent of this mock nationalist composition becomes obvious soon enough. The piece plays with the idea of false starts, interrupting the main theme four times, each time starting over from scratch. When the piece finally reaches its climax, the theme is undermined by the second *son*, set against it in strident harmonic and metric incongruence, ending right there, in total discord. This strategy, the rhetorical distortion of conventional symbols as a way to attack the dominant expressions of nationalism, would be found varyingly expressed in better-known future compositions. It is evident in the opening movement of the second quartet, satirically titled *Magueyes* (1932) after a popular melody. Ironically described by the composer as a "Mexican sketch" without being "folkloric, nor serious, nor transcendent," it continuously restates the borrowed tune, only to distort it time after time. In the same fashion, the fast movements of *Janitzio* (1933–36) state a long list of folk tunes, defined by Revueltas in his notes as "postcard music" and each disfigured immediately after enunciation.[19]

The banality of the representations of the Mexican that resulted from an all-encompassing nationalistic drive started in the 1920s and greatly bothered Mexican intellectuals, Chávez among them. He sought ways to counterattack this tendency, on the one hand composing music based on alternative symbols—for instance, a modernistic approach to the pre-Hispanic in *El fuego nuevo*, 1921[20]—but also, just as Revueltas did later on, resorting to an apparent satirization of nationalist prototypes. For instance, he chose what was probably the most conventional symbol of tradition, the Mexican folk dance known as the *jarabe*.[21] Assembling his own *Jarabe* on the basis of various well-known *jarabes*, Chávez proceeded to alter them chromatically upon repetition and immerse them in dense polyphonic contexts so as to, perhaps intentionally, weaken their effectiveness as recognizable symbols of the national. Although this composition can be interpreted in terms of a modern articulation of the local, it contains an element of irony comparable to Revueltas's openly declared satires.[22] Since Chávez's *Jarabe* remained unperformed, it is not very likely that Revueltas knew of it, but the coincidence between the strategies intended to alienate this kind of nationalist discourse is notorious and, as we shall see, not at all surprising.[23]

Some scores bear witness to this dialogue of allusion in a more direct way. One composition in particular, Chávez's *Cantos de México* (1933), was dedicated to Revueltas, and it appears not coincidental that in it Chávez, perhaps teasingly, emulates Revueltas's compositional topics and procedures. A year earlier, in the third movement of *Colorines* (1932), Revueltas composed music that appears to point directly at Chávez's contrapuntal diatonicism, a technique rarely, if at all, found in Revueltas's music. More intriguing, it contains in the external movements primitivist formulas such as proposed by Chávez in his ballets *El fuego nuevo* and *Los cuatro soles* (1925), premiered in concert versions soon after Revueltas's arrival in Mexico.[24] In conjunction with the stylistic hints to Chávez's linear modalism, this reference to Chávez's modernist Indianism appears to be a jovial representation of the dialogue itself. Are these mutual echoes merely coincidences or rather direct musical expressions of a perhaps teasing camaraderie?

Revueltas's Portrayal of Chávez

A simple listing of Revueltas's compositions in 1932, the year of *Colorines*'s composition, seems to confirm the composer's two main concerns at the time: experimentation with musical language in dialogue with other modernists (Satie, Stravinsky, Chávez himself) in *Three Pieces for Violin and Piano* in February, *Magueyes* in March, *Alcancías* (Piggybanks) in July; and the search for ever-new ways of embodying his political concerns, usually sacrificing the experimental urge to a point, in *El tecolote* (The Owl) in April and *Parián* in September. In its midst is *Colorines*, which tends to resist both categories. Its four movements comprise a collage of differing styles, the internal movements each "performing" Chávez and Stravinsky, the external ones themselves extreme collages of stylistic referents not meant to merge; on the contrary, in this multi-voiced construct any kind of thematic or stylistic prominence is avoided, as are the principles of organic form and the narrative.[25] It poses questions and possibilities, but no answers. Playfully, the composer challenges his listener with an equally inconclusive description of the piece's poetics, as described in his program notes:

> Screechy music, dislocated, according to some respectable opinions. With a little, or perhaps with a lot of imagination, others hear Romanticism in it. In any case it is of a

> prominently Mexican character. Ironic music, rude, tender, perhaps even a bit painful (to the ear?).[26]

As suggested, there are allusions to Chávez's primitivist works in the external collage movements of *Colorines*. Although this intertextual referent is not polyphonic, its melodic linearity is notorious, with a continuity derived from profuse sequential repetition such as in Chávez's primitivism. Also decidedly conventional in Chávez's primitivisms (and portrayed in its referent in *Colorines*), are the symmetry and simplicity of the meter, emphasized by a regular percussive pulse.[27] Such features can be observed in the following example, drawn from the opening movement of *Colorines*. To this style quotation, however, Revueltas adds his own satirical voice: it can be observed in mm. 24–30, where piccolo, E-flat clarinet and bassoon interrupt the exotic melody with fragmentary gestures drawn from street cries, pointing away decidedly from the past and to the (popular urban) present (see Example 1).

The decidedly atypical modalism found in *Colorines*' third movement—Lento, semplice—is a highly unambiguous representation of Chávez's polyphonic style (see Example 2). It leads us not so much to a specific composition of Chávez's but rather to the practices shared in a space about which precious little is known, but might explain this little homage: the *clase de composición* that Chávez started in 1931 at the Conservatory, which lasted until 1934.

Besides Revueltas, the composers who participated in this class belonged to a previous generation and had (like Revueltas) sufficient compositional experience not to be understood as students, thus it is very likely for this reason the class eventually took on the name *taller de composición* (composition workshop). The older composers included Vicente T. Mendoza (1894–1964) and Candelario Huízar (1883–1970). On the other hand, the workshop also included four would-be composers of the next generation, who decidedly were on the receiving end of Chávez's compositional instruction: Daniel Ayala (1908–1975), Blas Galindo (1910–1993), Salvador Contreras (1912–1982), and José Pablo Moncayo (1912–1958). Little is known about the dynamics of this odd transgenerational experiment, besides what Chávez transmitted retrospectively in an article published in *Modern Music* in 1936:

> All the students worked untiringly, writing melodies in all diatonic modes, in a melodic scale of twelve tones, and in all of the pentatonic scales. Hundreds of melodies were written, but not merely as exercises on paper. We had instruments

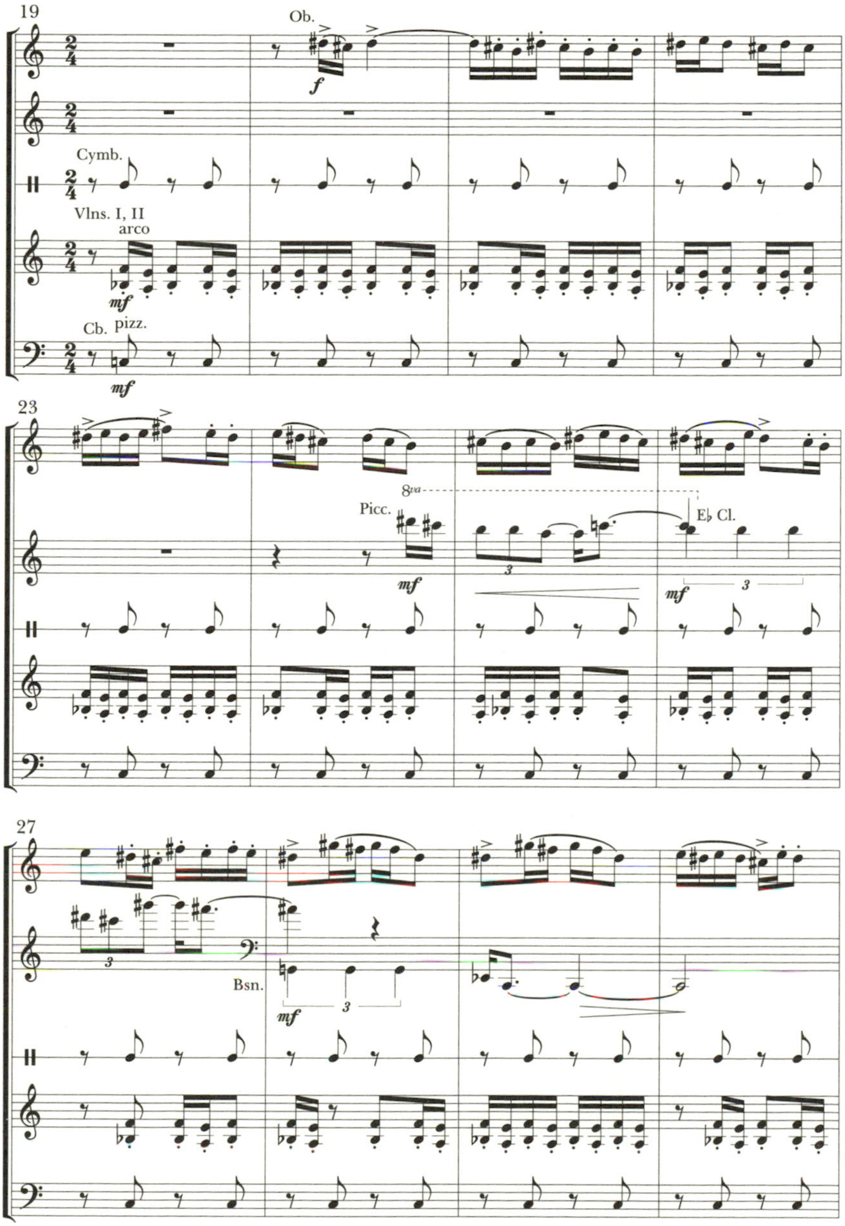

Example 1. Revueltas, *Colorines*, Moderato, mm. 19–30.

> in the classroom, and melodies were played on them, and found to be adequate or inadequate to the resources of the specific instruments. The result was . . . melodies with amazingly acute instrumental feeling.[28]

Chávez's article appears to describe what Revueltas embodied in his brief Lento, semplice. Also, Chávez clearly does not make any difference between the older and younger participants, classifying them all as his students. Indeed, Chávez repeatedly insisted on historicizing Revueltas as his student in different contexts, especially regarding reception in the United States. His words in this regard, however, contradict his actions: had Chávez not considered Revueltas a peer composer before they had even established a friendship, he would not have been instrumental in conveying his early compositions to Varèse and Cowell, or offered the Orquesta Sinfónica de México for the premiere of Revueltas's first large-scale symphonic projects *Cuauhnáhuac*, *Esquinas* (Corners), and *Ventanas* as early as 1931.

Chávez's "Portrayal" of Chávez and Revueltas

As suggested above, Chavez's *Cantos de México* is a musical portrayal of both composers. Divided, predictably, into two parts, the first is a self-portrait of the dedicator, Chávez; the second a portrait of the dedicatee, Revueltas. The first part appears to refer back to Chávez's early ballets, *El fuego nuevo* and *Los cuatro soles*. *Cantos* was written on the occasion of the first presentation of the Orquesta Mexicana, an ensemble made of instruments from pre-Conquest Mexico (percussion), and the colonized country (several types of guitars, lutes/vihuelas, popular harp, marimba, flute, trumpet, trombone, violin, among others), thus representing "the instrumental wealth of Mexico."[29]

Chávez was well aware that the roots of pre-Hispanic music, the "true Mexican music . . . are half-lost, half-destroyed. The conquest erased indigenous music and, in founding centers of a new culture, of a European culture, musical civilization implanted, imperfectly, a strange art" that was never truly naturalized.[30] The first part of *Cantos* appears to suggest an "imagined Aztec music," such as Chávez would write in *Xochipilli* (1940). It is, like much of his music at the time, composed in linear, contrapuntal ways, with no structural interest in harmony. A large percussion section is prominent here, and the music is non-thematic, with melodies developed improvisationally, as is the case in some indigenous music. The multiple voices are enunciated by differing instruments, clearly

Example 2. Revueltas, *Colorines*, Lento semplice, mm. 1–23.

suggesting the primitive instruments thus alluded to: mainly flutes and conch shells, above a basis of rhythmic percussion: *teponaxtle*, *huéhuetl*, Indian drum, rasp (*raspador*), rattle (*sonaja*), deer hoof (*pezuña de venado*), gong (see Example 3).

In articulating these melodies, Chávez uses a technique that in some ways echoes Revueltas: the voices are structurally irrelevant, improvisationally juxtaposed at unforeseeable times and with unforeseeable duration. The result is a music that recalls physical space and actors, musicians playing at the same time, but not together, a technique of representation that Revueltas had developed as a basic constructive principle

Example 2. continued

in *Esquinas* in 1931.[31] The constitutive elements are joined by a common, basic rhythmic pulse, congruence of color (melody assigned to the winds, rhythm to the percussion and plucked instruments), and pitch homogeneity, resulting in a cohesive texture that is quite easy on the ear.

The same principle of juxtaposition is continued in the second section, which draws again on invented music. But this time a brassy mestizo tune, such as usually associated with Revueltas, is foregrounded.[32] Not far into this section, we hear a second tune, aggressively interrupting the theme and thereafter disturbingly juxtaposed to yet another mock folk tune. The aggressive overlapping of musical signifiers is characteristic of

Example 3. Chávez, *Cantos de México*, Indianist self-reference, mm. 8–30.

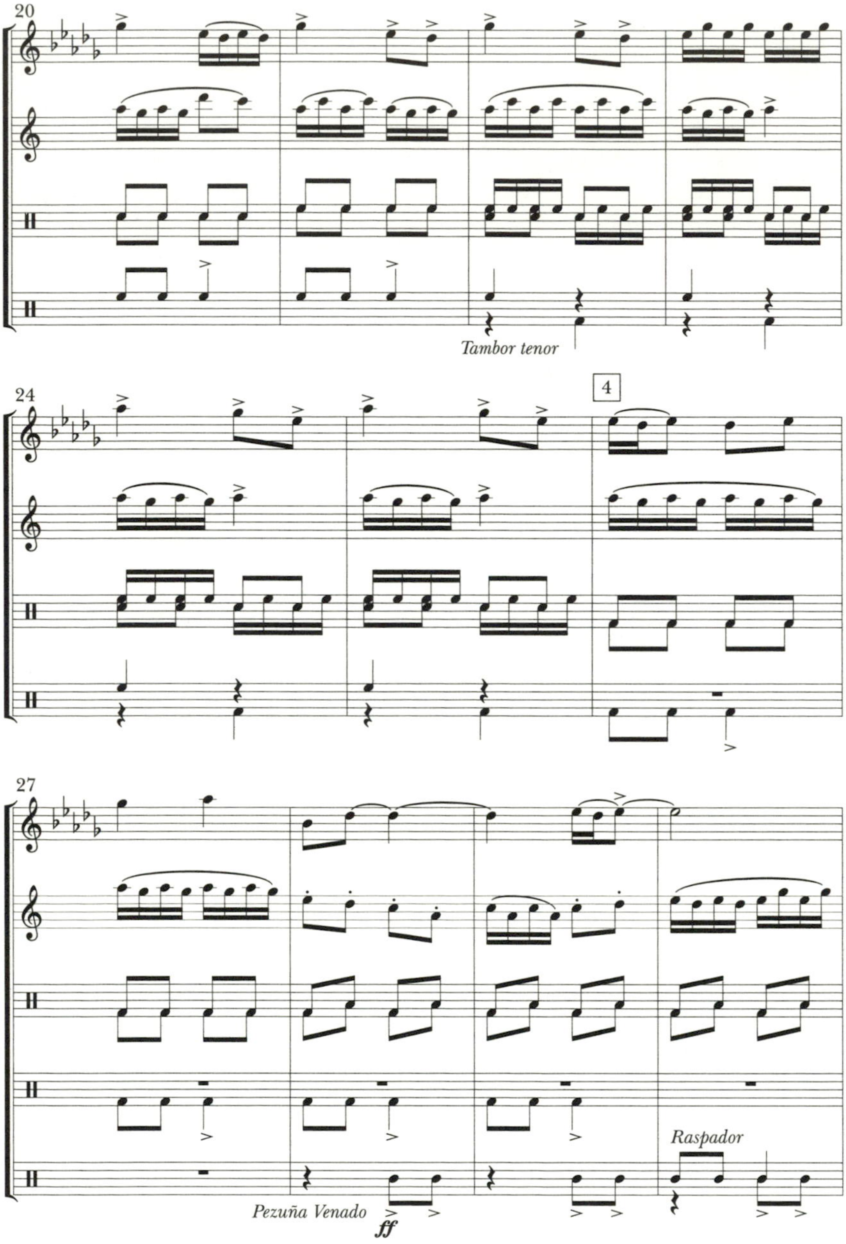

Example 3. continued

Example 4. Chávez, *Cantos de México*, mestizo juxtaposition à la Revueltas, mm. 102–16.

Revueltas, but not of Chávez. It is not meant to stress unity but rather diversity; not syncretism, but rather a noisy hybridity that by then had become Revueltas's trademark. Chávez's portrayal could hardly be more eloquent (see Example 4). Thus does Chávez render musically his dedication to Revueltas: compounded with the initial self-reference, the dialogue between the two composers is embodied musically in *Cantos*.

Two Views of Modernity

Striking parallels between Chávez's and Revueltas's compositions are not limited to the pieces discussed above. Chávez's *Soli I* (1933) is scored for the unusual combination of oboe, clarinet, trumpet, and bassoon, suggestively similar to Revueltas's *Three Little Serious Pieces* (*Tres piezas pequeñas serias*), scored for piccolo, oboe, clarinet, baritone sax, and trumpet. Revueltas's composition was left unfinished. As the surviving manuscript shows, *Three Little Serious Pieces* was intended as a three-movement composition, of which only the first movement and a section of the second were completed. Like many of Revueltas's scores, this one is surrounded by mystery: nothing is known about the actual date, the circumstances of its creation, or the reason it was left unfinished. The composer's autograph appears to have been taken out of the drawer in 1940, probably with a performance in mind, although no knowledge of such a performance exists.

Revueltas inserted the date of composition—"Mexico 1940"—at the end of the first movement and modified the order of the movements, thus beginning with the incomplete "Tempo de vals lento." This also led to the modification of the overall measure count, and perhaps later on to the title of the piece, which was eventually published in the United States, and still known today as *Two Little Serious Pieces*.

What interests us in this context, though, is the close relation *Three Little Serious Pieces* shows with *Soli I*, beyond the odd but very similar instrumentation. The aesthetic topics that concern this composition are stated in a handwritten text on the original title page, a text ignored in the published version. These are the very topics that occupied Chávez and Revueltas in the early 1930s: how to distinguish their music from past identity constructs embodied in the Romantic nationalism of their Eurocentric predecessors; how to create a new music that subscribes to post–Great War modernities, and at the same time devise strategies to distinguish it from that canon; whether or not to incorporate quoted or abstracted local signifiers in this quest, and if so, which signifiers to draw upon and how to use them.

These issues are satirically addressed in the three titles given by Revueltas to the proposed movements (unfortunately ignored in the published version): "Heroic Prelude," "Romantic Waltz," and "Pre-Hispanic Dance (Authentic)" (see Figure 2). Revueltas's humor is patent: a prelude is rarely heroic (and Revueltas's sounds anything but), a waltz tends always to be romantic, and the presumed "authenticity" of ancestral musical referents was of no interest to him, since he preferred present-day referents of a mestizo kind. Perhaps the three pieces were meant to express the "now" in Revueltas's view, since the "waltz" points back to Mexican salon music, and the pre-Hispanic even further back in time.

We will never know what Revueltas had in mind when he planned his "pre-Hispanic" fantasy, unless it was playfully intended as a hint at Chávez's two Indianist ballets, as was probably the case in his satires of primitivism in *Colorines* and *Cuauhnáhuac*. It is clear that the "Romantic Waltz" is a parody of artistocratic salon music, satirized through the use of a baritone saxophone in the bass part. Thus it establishes an ideological link with Chávez's rejection of Romantic nationalism. In turn, the "Heroic Prelude" seems to establish an exchange with Chávez's abstract modernism, one marked by contrast more than by coincidence: it is one of the most provocatively modernist pieces by Revueltas, showing no sign whatsoever of local cultural markers. If anything, it noisily and unexpectedly mingles fragmented signifiers of various markers of modernity, carefully avoiding their synthesis into a single, coherent discourse. Ostinati figures provide a necessary background texture, making possible a continuous temporal unfolding, but hardly disguise the fragmentation and discontinuity predominant in the foreground. The composer is adamant to stress the fragmentary, ephemeral unrelatedness of the brief, juxtaposed statements, assigning to each particular scales, rhythmic patterns, color, and location in the musical space. The irony behind Revueltas's description of this music as "heroic" becomes acutely evident in the grotesque gestures that dominate this musical discourse: extremely wide interval leaps, aggressive *frullati*, off-the-beat accents and sforzandi, and clashing harmonies (see Example 5).

What seems odd in this kind of writing is the apparent attitude of negation: a refusal to align with existing codes of modern art music or to develop what could be conceived as the pursuit of a personal style. Revueltas's musical discourse appears only to point to signifiers of a variety of musical modernities, without subscribing to them. This non-syncretic collage-style writing is closely associated with equivalent collage and montage experiments in the external movements of Revueltas's *Colorines*, and for this reason it can be assumed that *Three Little Serious Pieces* was written in tandem with that piece and in dialogue with Chávez's compositions at the time, rather than in 1940, when Revueltas's mindset was far removed from formal experimentation.

The "Heroic Prelude" may echo Chávez's modernist quest, but critically so, since it clearly avoids what is dear to him: the varying attempts at a modern-day *synthesis* achieved from within. No matter how many techniques Chávez resorted to—"mechanistic rhythmic unity, angular melodies, irregular metrics, linear textures, dissonant counterpoint, ostinati, polyrhythms, harmonies resulting from superimposed fifths, fourths, ninths, and sevenths"[33]—and behind these perhaps his most

Example 5. Revueltas, *Two Little Serious Pieces*, "Heroic Prelude," mm. 16–24.

revolutionary proposition, formulated later as the principle of non-repetition (according to Chávez, first used in *Soli I*),[34] his goal was always the development of a unitary, individual, and original voice that could distinguish him in the cosmopolitan, and particularly in the inter-American realm. If Revueltas's "Heroic Prelude" was indeed written in dialogue with Chávez, it could even be interpreted as a playful provocation, since, not unlike *Colorines*, it so adamantly insists on a discourse of non-continuity and heterogeneity, and systematically resorts to style quotation, indifferent to any concern for the development of a personal style. Probably we will never find out if this was the composer's intention.

Example 5. continued

In any case, *Three Little Serious Pieces* seems to speak directly to Chávez, this time not reverentially but instead as a provocative dialogue between two modernists. It manifests both what they have in common and what distinguishes the two. The comparison is useful, to a point even necessary, for the understanding of each other's stance regarding the ontology of musical composition in the situation of peripheral modernity they shared. After all, one must not forget that the two represented an extremely original Mexican avant-garde, a dual but ultimately single voice, with resonances in the inter-American realm that only now are starting to be recognized.

Chávez's and Revueltas's compositions of the 1920s and '30s clearly attest to a freedom of creative strategies, resulting in a multi-stylism that must be understood as the construction of identity as process, opposed to earlier Eurocentric concepts of identity as an essence to be discovered, vindicated, and built upon. They also reflect an understanding of Mexican society as a hybrid culture that would be violated if reduced to a single, arbitrary essence. In *El fuego nuevo* and *Los cuatro soles*, Chávez builds on a presumed essence, moved by the desire to construct a modern, local alterity within the canon of Western art music, as Leonora Saavedra has suggested.[35] In this respect, it is revealing that Chávez was at the same time composing music that did not build at all on local signifiers of past or present. The purpose of early experiments such as *Energía* (1925) and the six *Exágonos* (1923 and 1924), or compositions of the 1930s such as the Sonata for Four Horns, the first two movements of his second quartet, his *Soli I* and his *Spiral* (1934) for piano and violin, composed in the period of close collaboration with Revueltas, can be considered a comparable attempt to create an alterity within inter-American modernity, challenging dominant precepts of beauty with revolutionary concepts such as the principle of non-repetition—and thus achieving the specificity required within this canon-in-formation.

By recognizing the patterns of cultural colonialism and dependence, Chávez and Revueltas were able to break away from the relative sterility and enslaving stylistic imitation to which Eurocentric Mexican composers subjected themselves. This conscience of a post-colonial locus helped both Chávez and Revueltas establish conventional subjects, styles, and techniques not as an inherited tradition of a homegrown self but as an Other that can (and must) be freely and critically appropriated, rather than assumed and imitated, as their predecessors did. They shared the same conscience of locus, although in their desire to speak from within, they moved in different directions. Chávez was interested in appropriating and independently developing a prospectively inter-American, anti-European modern musical thought, focusing on proposals that would lend him an individual voice within this alternative canon. Revueltas tended to choose the avant-garde route that produces art by *attacking* art through irony, and therefore favored aggressive non-synchretic hybridity as well as satirical parody when dealing with modernity and essentialist nationalisms.

After 1935 Chávez's and Revueltas's creative goals and priorities would steadily grow apart. Revueltas became increasingly involved in political militancy, at first as a member of the LEAR (League of Revolutionary Artists and Writers), over which he would eventually preside in 1937. Revueltas identified passionately with the Republican cause in the Spanish Civil War, and this led him to a life-changing visit to Spain, also in 1937.

Revueltas's concept of modernity—change and progress in the arts linked to his political ideals—was now mostly sacrificed in the name of a socialist utopia as the nature and topics of his music began to echo this purpose. He lost some of his early spirit of provocation, satire, and irony, instead using music as a vehicle for an affirmative political message, a purpose better served by the use of relatively established conventions and straightforward linear structures and only a conservative use of modernistic techniques—methods such as one finds in *Sensemayá*.[36] Two works in particular, the film scores *Redes* (*The Wave*) and *Itinerario*, both destined to be performed as well in the concert hall, resort openly to a tonal Romantic narrative style and are notorious examples of Revueltas's affiliation with social realism.[37]

In retrospect, then, it is tempting to argue that the most uniquely "Revueltian" Revueltas, the composer of *Esquinas*, *Colorines*, *Alcancías*, *Magueyes*, *Janitzio*, *Música de feria*, and the *Little Serious Pieces*, among other scores, must be traced back to his early years as a professional composer, when he enjoyed freedom and stimulus for musical experimentation that he owed, no less, to Carlos Chávez.

NOTES

1. The online publication of Revueltas's digitized manuscripts is forthcoming, Biblioteca Digital Silvestre Revueltas, Coordinación de Colecciones Universitarias Digitales, UNAM.

2. Chávez to Revueltas, Fondo Carlos Chávez, Archivo General de la Nación, Mexico City (hereafter AGN). The score of *Elegía* is lost. All translations in this essay are my own in collaboration with Susana Kolb.

3. Revueltas used the Mexican swear word *pinche*. Revueltas to Chávez, Mobile, Alabama, n.d. [1927], AGN.

4. Chávez, "La música de México," 18 October 1971, typescript, AGN.

5. See Gloria Carmona, ed., *Epistolario selecto de Carlos Chávez* (México: Fondo de Cultura Economica, 1989), 16–17.

6. See James Krippner's essay on their relationship in this volume.

7. Since the 1990s some commentators have tried to go beyond the discourse of confrontation that dominated the earlier reception of Revueltas's music and life. See José Antonio Alcaráz, "El testimonio de Carlos Chávez sobre Silvestre Revueltas," *Carlos Chávez, un constante renacer* (Mexico: INBA/CENIDIM, 1996), 51–52; Roberto García Bonilla, "Mitos y realidades de Silvestre Revueltas," in *Visiones sonoras* (Mexico: Siglo XXI/CONACULTA, 2001), 17–34; Yael Bitrán and Ricardo Miranda, eds., introduction to *Diálogo de resplandores: Carlos Chávez y Silvestre Revueltas* (Mexico: INBA/CONACULTA, 2002).

8. See Yolanda Moreno Rivas, *Rostros del Nacionalismo en la música mexicana: Un ensayo de interpretación* (Mexico: UNAM, 1995); and Robert L. Parker, *Carlos Chávez: Mexico's Modern-Day Orpheus* (Boston: Twayne, 1983).

9. See, among others, Susana González Aktories and Roberto Kolb, *Sensemayá: Un juego de espejos entre música y poesía* (Mexico: JGH, 1997); Ricardo Zohn-Muldoon, "The Song of the Snake: Silvestre Revueltas's *Sensemayá*," *Latin American Music Review* 19 (Autumn–Winter, 1998): 133–59; Leonora Saavedra, "Of Selves and Others: Historiography, Ideology, and the Politics of Modern Mexican Music" (PhD diss., University of Pittsburgh, 2001); Luisa Vilar, "Innovación, espontaneidad y coherencia armónica en Silvestre Revueltas," in Bitrán and Miranda, *Diálogo de resplandores*, 31–46; Talía Jiménez Ramírez, "Los cuartetos de cuerdas de 1932: Estudio comparativo del Cuarteto No. 2 de Carlos Chávez y de Música de Feria de Silvestre Revueltas," in Bitrán and Miranda, *Diálogo de resplandores*, 47–67; Ricardo Miranda, "Del festín al alboroto: Forma y narrativa en *El renacuajo paseador* de Silvestre Revueltas," *Discanto* 1 (2005): 171–85; Susana González Aktories and Roberto Kolb, "*Sensemayá*, entre rito, palabra y sonido: Transposición intersemiótica y écfrasis como condiciones de una mitopoiesis literaria y musical," in *Entre artes, entre actos: Écfrasis e intermedialidad*, ed. Susana González Aktories and Irene Artigas (Mexico: UNAM, 2011), 293–316; Roberto Kolb-Neuhaus, *Contracanto: Una perspectiva semiótica de su obra temprana* (Mexico: UNAM, 2012).

10. See Jiménez Ramírez, "Los cuartetos de cuerdas de 1932."

11. Revueltas, "Panorama musical de México," in *Silvestre Revueltas por él mismo*, ed. Rosaura Revueltas and Philippe Chéron (Mexico: Era, 1989), 198–200.

12. Revueltas, "Contracanto," *El Universal* (Mexico City), 8 November 1933.

13. Revueltas, "En defensa y elogio de la crítica," "Contracanto," and "Coda," *El Universal*, 7 August, 8 November, and 29 December 1933.

14. Chávez's writings are collected in *Carlos Chávez, Escritos periodísticos (1916–1939)*, comp. and ed. Gloria Carmona (Mexico City: El Colegio Nacional, 1997). See also Leonora Saavedra, "Los escritos periodísticos de Carlos Chávez: Una fuente para la historia de la música en México," *Inter-American Music Review* 10 (1989): 77–91.

15. Kolb-Neuhaus, *Contracanto*, 249–95.

16. Compositions such as *Esquinas* (1931–33) show that Revueltas attempted to link musically the concepts of political and artistic innovation and progress. See ibid., 95–199.

17. See Robert L. Parker's introductions to *Batik* and *El afilador*, in *Silvestre Revueltas Edición Crítica*, general ed. Robert Kolb-Neuhaus (Mexico: UNAM, 2003).

18. The *son* (pl. *sones*) is a traditional rural musical genre with several regional variants, characterized by certain meters, often 6/8, certain melodic profiles, occasional hemiola, and polyphonic textures.

19. See Kolb-Neuhaus, *Contracanto*, 253.

20. On Chávez's Indianist music, see Leonora Saavedra's essay in this volume.

21. The *jarabe* is a rural dance genre made of short binary dances, dating from at least the early nineteenth century. Toward the end of Porfirio Diaz's dictatorship and especially after the Revolution, the *jarabe* was elevated to the category of national dance, featured publicly and taught to schoolchildren.

22. Leonora Saavedra, "Carlos Chávez's Polysemic Style: Constructing the National, Seeking the Cosmopolitan," *Journal of the American Musicological Society* 68/1 (2015): 99–150.

23. Revueltas often performed Chávez's 1924 Violin Sonatina, which has a similarly parodic treatment of a *son* melody. See Saavedra, "Carlos Chávez's Polysemic Style."

24. Chávez premiered *El fuego nuevo* in a concert version on 4 November 1928 and repeated it on 14 January 1930, when Revueltas would have heard it. *Los cuatro soles* was premiered on 22 July 1930.

25. For an extended analysis of *Colorines*, see Kolb, "Silvestre Revueltas vis-à-vis US Modernisms: A Dialogue of the Deaf?" *Latin American Music Review* (forthcoming, 2015).

26. Program notes for the Mexican premiere, 26 May 1932.

27. Saavedra, "Carlos Chávez's Polysemic Style."

28. Chávez, "Revolt in Mexico," *Modern Music* 13/3 (March–April 1936): 38.

29. Chávez, "La orquesta mexicana," *El Universal* (Mexico City), 3 November 1933. This article was included in the program notes for the concert.

30. Ibid.

31. See Roberto Kolb-Neuhaus, "'Dos por medio y cuatro por un real, mirando que el tiempo está fatal': El pregón en la semiosis musical de Silvestre Revueltas," *Tópicos del seminario* 19 (January–June 2008): 131–56.

32. *Mestizo* refers to a mixture of cultures, ethnicities, or races. Most Mexicans consider their culture a predominantly mestizo one.

33. Leonora Saavedra, "Carlos Chávez y la construcción de una alteridad estratégica," in Bitrán and Miranda, *Diálogo de resplandores*, 125–36.

34. Parker, *Carlos Chávez*, 47.

35. Saavedra, "Carlos Chávez y la construcción," 132. See also Saavedra, "Carlos Chávez's Polysemic Style."

36. See González Aktories and Kolb, "*Sensemayá*, entre rito."

37. Concerning *Redes*, see Roberto Kolb, "Silvestre Revueltas's *Redes*: Composing for Film or Filming for Music?" *Journal of Film Music* 2 (2009): 127– 44.

Aaron Copland, Carlos Chávez, and Silvestre Revueltas

HOWARD POLLACK

Aaron Copland and Carlos Chávez quickly became good friends after meeting each other in New York City in 1926.[1] Copland was twenty-five at the time, Chávez a year older. They had already achieved some notoriety among followers of new music, and had won several of the same friends, including the American music critic Paul Rosenfeld. But essentially they were at the start of their careers.[2]

Two years later, in 1928, Chávez became director of both the Mexico Symphony Orchestra and the National Conservatory, a remarkable dual appointment that afforded him considerable power and visibility, so much so that it left Copland, whose big successes awaited him by a good ten years, a bit astonished, not to mention "a little envious."[3] But both men still faced considerable struggles ahead, and their friendship, although conducted largely long distance, proved one of the things that consistently comforted and heartened them. "I'm sure you *must* know how dear you are to me in every way—how close I feel to you mentally and spiritually and musically," Copland wrote to Chávez in 1935. "You are always in my thoughts. . . . It is just in such times as these that friends like we are should encourage and sustain each other."[4] In 1946 Copland further told Chávez, "It has been almost twenty years since we met and I must tell you that I have known no other composer colleague who has given me a firmer support nor a more continued stimulus to my work." For his part, Chávez wrote Copland in 1933, "You are something of my own self, you mean for me understanding, you are with me in the real center of thought and creation," and again in 1951, "I always think of you no matter how long a time we do not hear from each other," and yet again in 1967, "You and I see things in the same light."[5]

They certainly championed each other's music with vigor. Chávez frequently conducted Copland's music in Mexico and around the world, including the first all-Copland orchestral concert in 1932. During his years with the Mexico Symphony Orchestra, he programmed one or another Copland work nearly every season, including, in 1934 and 1937 respectively, the world premieres of both the *Short Symphony*, which Copland dedicated to him, and *El Salón México*. Chávez continued to conduct old and new Copland works for decades. He also helped arrange working vacations for Copland in Mexico, including making his Acapulco home available in the summer of 1959.

Meanwhile Copland, who, with Roger Sessions, co-directed a landmark new-music concert series in New York from 1928 to 1931, programmed Chávez's music on no fewer than four of these Copland-Sessions Concerts, including the Three Sonatinas for various chamber combinations (1924) and the Third Sonata for piano (1928), which Chávez dedicated to Copland. Copland frequently performed the Piano Sonatina himself on various recitals, and persuaded Cos Cob to publish the work. After Copland assumed the directorship of the Yaddo Music Festival in the summers of 1932 and 1933, he once again programmed Chávez, this time the composer's "36" (1925) and "Unity" (1930). In later years, he helped Chávez procure a contract with Boosey & Hawkes as well as various commissions, performances, and guest-teaching appointments, including those at Tanglewood (1953) and the University of Buffalo (1958).

Copland's copious correspondence further evidenced his high regard for Chávez's music, as did the occasional published critical piece, including a 1928 article, "Carlos Chávez—Mexican Composer," which he subsequently revised for *Our New Music* (1941) and again for *The New Music* (1968).[6] What impressed Copland above all, perhaps, were the music's modern and non-European qualities, traits hardly distinguishable in his estimation. "His music is not a substitute for living but a manifestation of life," he wrote in 1928. "It exemplifies the complete overthrow of nineteenth-century Germanic ideals which tyrannized over music for more than a hundred years. It propounds no problems, no metaphysics." Copland thought Chávez's attempts at fashioning folk materials into "an art-form" even more successful than the comparable achievements of Falla and Bartók; and though admitting that a work like the Third Sonata presented "formidable difficulties to even the sympathetic listener," with familiarity, the music revealed itself to be "packed with meaning."

As early as the 1928 article, Copland discerned a crucial kinship between Chávez and the "ritualistic music of the Mexican Indian," speaking of the composer as "steeped in their [Indian] music long before he consciously thought of it as a basis for his work," and finding the ballet *The Four Suns* (*Los cuatro soles,* 1925) to possess "something of the monotony of the Indian dances themselves." In his revision of this essay for *Our New*

Music, he tempered such remarks, substituting the phrase "knew and admired their music" for "steeped in their music," and totally dispensed with the discussion of *The Four Suns* and its relation to the "monotony" of Indian dances. However, in other ways, he stressed what he took to be the Indian character of Chávez's music, changing the phrase "distinctly Mexican flavor" to "distinctive Indo-American doggedness," replacing "sun-filled, naïve, Latin soul" with "naïve, stolid, mestizo world," and describing Chávez's Sonata for Four Horns (1930) as "Mexican-Indian—stoic, stark, and somber, like an Orozco drawing." By this time, Copland had spent considerable time in Mexico, so this deepened sensitivity to the alleged Indian qualities of Chávez's music could be seen as reflecting his growing familiarity with Mexican music and culture in general. Moreover, Chávez's own intervening works, like *Sinfonía india* (1935) and the Ten Preludes for piano (1937), not to mention *Xochipilli: An Imagined Aztec Music* (1940), may well have helped make the relation of his music to Indian culture that much more palpable.

In his 1952 Harvard Norton Lectures, Copland once again emphasized the "imprint of the Indian personality" in Chávez's work. To such 1941 adjectives as "dogged," "stolid," "stoic," and "stark," he now added "deliberate," "sober," "lithic," and "earthy." "There are no frills, nothing extraneous," Copland told his Harvard audience. "It is like the bare wall of an adobe hut, which can be so expressive by virtue of its inexpressivity. . . . To me it possesses an Indian quality that is at the same time curiously contemporary in spirit. Sometimes it strikes me as the most truly contemporary music I know, not in the superficial sense, but in the sense that it comes closest to expressing the fundamental reality of modern man after he has been stripped of the accumulations of centuries of aesthetic experiences." Here, then, Copland explicitly made the connection—only implied in his earlier writings—between the contemporaneity and originality of Chávez's music and native Mexican culture.[7]

In his later years, Copland seems to have stayed most fond of Chávez's earlier scores, such as *Horsepower* (1926–32), the *Sinfonía de Antígona* (1933), and the *Sinfonía india*, which he conducted many times in the 1960s and 1970s. By contrast, he took more and more of Chávez's later music to task, commenting in a disapproving way about the stridency of this or that piece, or worse, "an increasingly didactic strain," as in the later symphonies. Copland often showed a predilection for the youthful work of his most admired contemporaries, so in that sense Chávez joined ranks in Copland's estimation with Sessions, Harris, Piston, and many others. But in any event, Copland remained steadfast in his conviction that Chávez represented "one of the first authentic signs of a New World with its own new music."[8]

Chávez held Copland's music in similarly deep esteem and for like reasons. In a 1929 program note to Copland's *Music for the Theatre* (1925), he spoke, for instance, of Copland's music as "genuinely American," adding, "Indeed, there is nothing tying him to tradition anymore. German transcendence is unknown to him. And if, upon analysis, some similitude between his music and the new music of the French were found, it would simply be the resemblance that exists between two new things."[9] At the aforementioned all-Copland concert in 1932, he spoke about Copland in much the same way as Copland described him, that is, as a composer of his time who reflected his distinctive world. Drawing analogies to Mozart and Bach, he in particular praised the Piano Variations (1930) as a work of "supreme intelligence, superior sensibility, and supreme culture."[10] Chávez apparently developed an even higher regard for Copland's challenging and somewhat recondite *Short Symphony* (1933), which Copland dedicated to Chávez. Describing the work's dialectical logic in 1934 as "simply unprecedented in the whole history of music," he still rated it some twenty years later as "one of the most beautiful and original works" of the twentieth century.[11] Other Copland works admired by Chávez included *Billy the Kid* (1938), the Piano Sonata (1939–41), and such later pieces as the Piano Fantasy (1952–57), *Connotations* (1962), and *Inscape* (1967).[12]

The strong attachment between Copland and Chávez involved fundamentally a certain resistance and solidarity in the face of European cultural domination. "European musicians are of the worst kind," wrote Chávez to Copland in 1931. "Conductors, pianists, violinists, singers and so on are 'prima donna' minded people—they are very important to themselves. We must change the situation, Aaron. We must not accept to be in the hands of foreign conductors and interpreters whose mind and heart (if they happen to have any) is [*sic*] far away of [*sic*] the spirit and culture of this new world." Answered Copland, "All you wrote about music in America awoke a responsive echo in my heart. I am through with Europe, Carlos, and I believe as you do, that our salvation must come from ourselves and that we must fight the foreign element in American music."[13]

Accordingly, Copland and Chávez found the differences between their music and that of European composers a source of mutual gratification. Discussing one of Chávez's works in 1933, Copland wrote, "The difference between our works and those of the Europeans was striking. Theirs were so smooth and refined—so very much within a particular tradition, and ours quite jagged and angular." And in 1934, Chávez wrote Copland, with respect to the *Short Symphony*, "Here is the real thing, here is our music, my music, the music of our time, of my taste, of my culture, here it is as a simple and natural fact of my own self, as everything belonging to oneself is simple and natural."[14] In short, Copland and Chávez strongly identified with each other—perhaps more deeply than with any other musical contemporary, a remarkable phenomenon considering their differences in background and temperament.

Copland's interest in Silvestre Revueltas, meanwhile, dated back to 1932, when, probably at Chávez's suggestion, he programmed Revueltas's Second String Quartet (1932) at the Yaddo Music Festival. "The Revueltas was very amusing," he wrote to Chávez after the performance. "It seemed like a little Mexican drama and I could easily imagine it being danced."[15] A few months later, on his first trip to Mexico, Copland and his companion Victor Kraft befriended Revueltas. Kraft—a young musician with strong leftist sympathies who later became a photographer—seemed especially taken with Revueltas and his music.[16] But Copland was impressed, too. In the fall of 1932 he recommended scores by both Chávez and Revueltas to Roger Sessions for possible inclusion on an International Society for Contemporary Music concert in Europe.[17] And in 1937, when Paul Strand's film *The Wave*, with a score by Revueltas, opened in New York, Copland took advantage of the occasion to write, for the *New York Times*, one of the earliest published accounts of Revueltas in English.

Noting that the larger New York concert-going public was already somewhat familiar with Chávez, thanks to his stints as conductor with the New York Philharmonic, this 1937 article opined that Revueltas deserved to be "equally well known, because he has already produced music which makes him a figure of importance in the general scheme of the modern musical movement. In certain respects, Revueltas is even more obviously the Mexican artist in his music than Chávez. He draws more directly on actual tunes that originated from popular Mexican music, and he composes organically tunes which are almost indistinguishable from the original folk material itself." Copland noted Revueltas's propensity for writing colorful tone poems and thought it only natural that the Mexican government would commission him to score what he called "Paul Strand's memorable film of Mexico," wondering whether the composer's "real future," along with, possibly, Shostakovich's, lay in the field of film music.[18]

Copland's piece for the *Times* also addressed in a characteristically evenhanded way what had become a controversial matter—in Mexico, at any rate—of Revueltas versus Chávez. "Speaking broadly, I should say that Revueltas's music has been more quickly appreciated in Mexico than that of Chávez," he wrote. "This may be due to the fact that its content is less intellectual and therefore can be more easily understood.

The music of Chávez is strong, stark and lacking in any exterior colorfulness; Revueltas's music, by comparison, is derived from the more usual everyday side of Mexican life. It is often highly spiced, like Mexican food itself. It is full of whims and sudden quirks of fancy and leaves one with a sense of the abundance and vitality of life." True to form, Copland hung photographs of Chávez *and* Revueltas on the wall of his Manhattan studio during these years.[19]

In *Our New Music*, published in 1941, one year after Revueltas's death, Copland once again compared the two Mexican composers, and though he reiterated his appreciation for both men's work, he now adopted a somewhat defensive tone on behalf of Chávez:

> It is paradoxical but true that in his own country Chávez is sometimes reproached for not being Mexican enough. This is usually said by way of contrast with the music of Silvestre Revueltas, whose untimely death robbed Mexican music of a very gifted composer. It was Chávez who induced his colleague Revueltas to write his earliest orchestral works and have their premieres with his orchestra. Revueltas was the spontaneously inspired type of composer, whose music was colorful, picturesque, and gay. Unfortunately, he never was able to break away from a certain dilettantism that makes his best work suffer from sketchy workmanship. Certain circles in Mexico are anxious to prove that by comparison with the natural spontaneity of Revueltas, Chávez's music is essentially cold and cerebral. But I see absolutely no need to choose here. It is not a question of Chávez or Revueltas, as at one time it was thought to be a question of Wagner or Brahms. We can have both men and their music for exactly what each is worth to us. In my own mind there is no doubt whatever that Chávez is the more mature musician in every way.[20]

A few years later, in 1944, Copland heard Chávez perform Revueltas's *Ventanas* (*Windows*, 1931), and informed his friend, composer Arthur Berger, that he found the work "amusing" but not very sound structurally. "He [Revueltas] was like a modern painter who throws marvellous daubs of color on canvas that practically takes your eye out, but it doesn't add up. Too bad—because he was a gifted guy."[21]

In his Norton Lectures, however, Copland dwelled exclusively on Revueltas's virtues and carefully avoided taking sides in the whole Chávez-Revueltas debate, writing instead, "It is illuminating to contrast the work of Chávez with that of his countryman, the late Silvestre Revueltas, whose vibrant, tangy scores sing of a more colorful, perhaps a more mestizo side of the Mexican character. Revueltas was a man of the people, with a wonderfully keen ear for the sounds of the people's music . . . . the pieces that he left us are crowded with an abundance and vitality—a Mexican abundance and vitality—that make them a pleasure to hear."[22]

After 1952, one loses track of any particular involvement in Revueltas on Copland's part. Although in his later years Copland conducted the music of the Mexicans Chávez and José Pablo Moncayo, he never seems to have performed any of Revueltas's scores. Nor did he discuss his friendship with Revueltas in his two-volume autobiography (1984, 1987), although while discussing the premiere of *El Salón México,* he recalled being relieved that Mexican listeners of the time regarded the piece "'as Mexican as the music of Revueltas,' which was like saying at that time, 'as American as the music of Gershwin.'"[23] This comment reminds us that Copland's assessment of Revueltas—the vibrant, accessible composer who captured the popular imagination of his country but whose work suffered from certain technical shortcomings—resembles his evaluation of Gershwin, and he possibly viewed Revueltas's relation to Chávez as somewhat comparable to that between Gershwin and himself.[24] But in other ways, at least from Copland's perspective, the analogy falls short; for instance, Copland would not likely have described Gershwin, as he does Revueltas, as a "composer who is thoroughly aware of the modern movement in music," and one, moreover, who was "a progressive soul in every sense of the word."[25]

As for the question of possible influence—reciprocal or otherwise—between Copland and his two esteemed Mexican contemporaries, that remains largely a matter of conjecture. All three composers had more or less attained their highly individual musical personalities at the time of their meeting. Still, especially in the case of Copland and Chávez, where one finds not only a lifelong involvement in each other's work but also a similar development—which might be summarized as evolving from the jazzy modernities of the 1920s to the more folkloric styles of the 1930s and 1940s to the twelve-tone or at least chromatic adventures of the 1950s and 1960s—one imagines some mutual influence.

This whole topic by and large has eluded systematic study, leaving many questions that await investigation. Did the severity of Chávez's music from the 1920s help point Copland in the direction of such austere works as the Piano Variations? Did Copland's *Short Symphony*, so admired by Chávez, have any influence on the latter's *Sinfonía india* (1935)? And did the *Sinfonía india*, in turn, leave its mark on Copland's

El Salón México, as Adriana Martínez Figueroa has suggested?[26] Is it mere coincidence that Chávez's *La paloma azul* (1939) employs a tune that Copland had quoted in *El Salón México*?[27] Or that Copland's *Canticle of Freedom* (1955) uses the same John Barbour text as found in Chávez's *A! Freedome* (1942)? Or that, as Joshua Rifkin has pointed out to the author, the finale of Chávez's Third Quartet (1943) anticipates the finale to Copland's Third Symphony (1944–46)? And what about the emergence of radical diatonicism in such scores from the late 1930s as Chávez's Ten Preludes (1937) and Copland's *From Sorcery to Science* (1939)? Or the striking correspondences between Copland's *Appalachian Spring* and Chávez's *La hija de Cólquide,* both written in 1943–44 for Martha Graham?

With regard to Revueltas, what influence might he have had especially on *El Salón México*, or even before that, on the *Short Symphony*? That Copland dedicated *El Salón México* to Victor Kraft seems suggestive, given the latter's attachment to Revueltas; and indeed, both Leonora Saavedra and Elizabeth Bergman Crist have discerned resemblances between Revueltas and this orchestral tribute to Mexico.[28] Saavedra's two unpublished papers on the subject remain particularly helpful in their specificity, as they cite a number of traits and signifiers in the Copland work possibly borrowed from Revueltas, including cadential descending thirds, harmonization of melodies in thirds and sixths, the use of collage and "layers of ostinati," and the pervasive presence of hemiola.[29] To what extent these features first found expression in Copland's music in the early 1930s, and to what extent they became part and parcel of his later work, remain, however, matters requiring more study. And how such traits overlap with and complement the apparent influence of Chávez on *El Salón México*—as observed by Figueroa and the present author—poses a question that needs to be addressed as well, as does the matter of Chávez's and Revueltas's influence, in this context, on each other.[30]

Even larger questions loom. If Copland had some significant debts to both Chávez and Revueltas, as appears the case, and perhaps they to him, can we speak of a Mexican-American tradition in the way that music historians refer to an Austro-German tradition or a Franco-Russian tradition? That is, do Mexican and U.S. twentieth-century composers inhabit a definable geocultural sphere? Clearly, more comparative work needs to be done in this area.

In one important way, at least, Copland showed himself apart from both Chávez and Reveultas: for all his responsiveness to the perceived Indian qualities of both composers' work—or, for that matter, of the Chilean composer Carlos Isamitt—he never seems to have involved himself in his own country's native culture. In his 1928 article about Chávez, he even stated, rather presumptively, "We cannot, like Chávez, borrow from a rich melodic source or lose ourselves in an ancient civilization."[31] And in 1929, he again asserted, "We have Indian songs. But what do the songs of the Indians mean to me?"[32] When the character of an Indian Girl, inspired by Pocahontas, turned up in one of Martha Graham's scenarios for *Appalachian Spring*, Copland firmly voiced his disapproval.[33] Moreover, in his Norton Lectures, he explicitly criticized America's Indianist movement of the early twentieth century: "It is understandable that the first Americans would have a sentimental attraction for our composers, especially at a time when the American composer himself was searching for some indigenous musical expression. But our composers were obviously incapable of identifying themselves sufficiently with such primitive source materials as to make these convincing when heard out of context."[34] He further argued, harkening back to ideas stated in 1928, that Indian "influence on serious music has been strongest in those countries where Indian culture was most highly developed and has been best preserved, such as Mexico and Peru."[35] In short, he believed that the absorption of the aboriginal vernacular among concert composers made more sense in Mexico than in the States because Mexican composers had access to a more developed Indian culture and could more fully identify with that culture.

Some recent scholars have suggested that Copland in fact owed more of a debt to America's Indianist movement than perhaps he realized or cared to admit, but such assertions still seem speculative.[36] Copland plausibly gleaned something from the Indianist movement by way of, say, Roy Harris, who had studied with Arthur Farwell; but any Indianist traits, such as they were, probably came more decisively through Chávez and Revueltas, or through the native musics that Copland heard in Mexico and later South America and that so impressed him. In his 1939 music appreciation text, *What to Listen for in Music*, he even quoted a "Mexican-Indian" tune found in Chávez's *Sinfonía india*, observing that the melody "uses repeated notes and unconventional intervals, with entirely refreshing effect."[37]

At the same time, Chávez and Revueltas arguably helped bring Copland closer to the idea of accommodating native folk traditions in the context of a modernist idiom. True, an increasing interest in folklore and folk music characterized many American composers in the 1930s. Moreover, Copland's so-called Americana works found some prefigurement in his earlier employment of traditional melodies, including the use of Eastern European Jewish melodies in his juvenilia and in his piano trio *Vitebsk* (1929), a matter often overlooked in these discussions. But

Copland's first trip to Mexico in 1932 seems to have been fairly decisive, nonetheless. One detects a renewed vigor and humor not only in *El Salón México* (begun in 1932 though not completed until 1936), but also in the *Short Symphony*, especially its last movement, which Copland composed in Mexico and which, he wrote to friends while working on it, "begins to sound rather Mexican to me."[38] The incorporation of Mexican elements gave Copland, who had already begun to embrace the different regions of his own country, a more fully American stylistic profile, something he quickly put to good use in *Billy the Kid* (1938), set in New Mexico, and *Rodeo* (1942), set in Texas. In addition, Chávez and Revueltas served Copland more generally as a model for his own sense of national and civic engagement. In sum, Mexico loomed large in terms of Copland's developing use of traditional American musics and, concomitantly, his evolving thoughts on music and society.

Notwithstanding a high regard for Heitor Villa-Lobos that dated back to his student years in Paris, Copland's interest in Mexico in turn seems to have led to a deeper appreciation of all Latin America, especially in the 1940s, as he traveled the length of the western hemisphere and began embracing the musics of Brazil, Cuba, and other countries.[39] This development, which raises the question not merely of a Mexican-American style but also a pan-American one,[40] gave substance to his own convictions, echoing those of his good friend, the writer Waldo Frank, that North Americans and Latin Americans had much to learn from one another.[41] Indeed, Copland not only counseled young Americans to travel to Latin America but also was instrumental in bringing many Latin Americans to the States, including Mexico's Blas Galindo and José Pablo Moncayo, Panama's Roque Cordero, Venezuela's Antonio Esteves, Argentina's Alberto Ginastera, Cuba's Julián Orbón, and Chile's Juan Orrego-Salas. For Copland, Chávez and Revueltas were more than good neighbors south of the border. They also helped clear a path to his own personal and artistic growth.

NOTES

1. This essay is a revised and expanded version of my article, "Más que buenos vecinos: La amistad de Aaron Copland con Carlos Chávez y Silvestre Revueltas," in *Diálogo de resplandores: Carlos Chávez y Silvestre Revueltas*, ed. Yael Bitrán and Ricardo Miranda (Mexico City: INBA/CONACULTA, 2002): 149–58. I would like to thank Leonora Saavedra, Eduardo Contreras Soto, and Gabriel Enrique Gómez-Sánchez for their help with this current version.

2. Robert L. Parker, "Copland and Chávez: Brothers-In-Arms," *American Music* 5/4 (1987): 433–44; Howard Pollack, *Aaron Copland: The Life and Work of an Uncommon Man* (New York: Henry Holt, 1999).

3. Elizabeth B. Crist and Wayne Shirley, *The Selected Correspondence of Aaron Copland* (New Haven: Yale University Press, 2006), 103.

4. Ibid., 110–11.

5. Adriana Martínez Figueroa, "Music and the Binational Imagination: The Musical Nationalisms of Mexico and the United States in the Context of the Binational Relationship, 1890–2009" (PhD diss., Eastman School of Music, 2009), 252; *Epistolario selecto de Carlos Chávez*, ed. Gloria Carmona (Mexico City: Fondo de Cultura Económica, 1989), 170, 184, 418, 976.

6. Copland-Chávez Correspondence, Copland Collection, Library of Congress; Aaron Copland, "Carlos Chávez—Mexican Composer," *The New Republic*, 2 May 1928, 322–23, repr. in *American Composers on American Music: A Symposium*, ed. Henry Cowell (New York: F. Ungar, 1962), 102–6, 202–11; Aaron Copland, *Our New Music* (New York: McGraw-Hill, 1941), 145–50; Aaron Copland, *The New Music* (New York: W. W. Norton, 1968), 145–50.

7. Aaron Copland, *Music and Imagination* (Cambridge: Harvard University Press, 1952), 91.

8. Pollack, *Aaron Copland*, 221; Copland, *The New Music*, 150.

9. Leonora Saavedra, "Revisiting Copland's Mexico," paper read at Indiana University, Bloomington, 21 October 2011, courtesy of the author.

10. Pollack, *Aaron Copland*, 221.

11. Ibid., 221–22.

12. *Epistolario*, 353, 542, 814, 928, 1017.

13. Pollack, *Aaron Copland*, 222.

14. Ibid., 222.

15. Crist and Shirley, *Selected Correspondence of Aaron Copland*, 92.

16. Pollack, *Aaron Copland*, 227.

17. Andrea Olmstead, ed., *The Correspondence of Roger Sessions* (Boston: Northeastern University Press, 1992), 190.

18. Aaron Copland, "Mexican Composer," *New York Times*, 9 May 1937.

19. Pollack, *Aaron Copland*, 94.

20. Copland, *Our New Music*, 209–10.

21. Pollack, *Aaron Copland*, 227.

22. Copland, *Music and Imagination*, 92.

23. Aaron Copland and Vivian Perlis, *Copland: 1900 Through 1942* (Boston: Faber and Faber, 1984), 247.

24. Pollack, *Aaron Copland*, 163–64.

25. Copland, "Mexican Composer."

26. Figueroa, "Music and the Binational Imagination," 254–61; Adriana Martínez Figueroa, "Aaron Copland and Carlos Chávez: A Friendship in Music" (BA thesis, University of Charleston, 1998), 58–59.

27. Robert L. Parker, *Carlos Chávez: Mexico's Modern-Day Orpheus* (Boston: Twayne, 1983), 117.

28. Saavedra, "Revisiting Copland's Mexico"; Elizabeth B. Crist, *Music for the Common Man: Aaron Copland During the Depression and War* (New York: Oxford University Press, 2005), 48.

29. Saavedra, "Revisiting Copland's Mexico"; Leonora Saavedra, "Of Dancing Halls and Music Festivals: Copland in Latin America," paper read at the American Musicological Society national meeting, Toronto, 4 November 2000, courtesy of the author.

30. Pollack, *Aaron Copland*, 302.

31. Copland, "Carlos Chávez," 323.

32. Pollack, *Aaron Copland*, 109.

33. Ibid., 394; Michael V. Pisani, "'I'm an Indian Too': Creating Native American Identities in Nineteenth- and Early Twentieth-Century Music," in *The Exotic in Western Music*, ed. Jonathan Bellman (Boston: Northeastern University Press, 1998), 256.

34. Copland, *Music and Imagination*, 91.

35. Ibid., 90.

36. Pisani, "'I'm an Indian Too,'" 256–57; Nina Perlove, "Inherited Sound Images: Native American Exoticism in Aaron Copland's *Duo for Flute and Piano*," *American Music* 18/5 (Spring 2000): 50–77.

37. Aaron Copland, *What to Listen for in Music* (1939; rev. ed., New York: McGraw, 1975), 44.

38. Pollack, *Aaron Copland*, 289.

39. See ibid., 228–33; Emily Abrams Ansari, "Aaron Copland and the Politics of Cultural Diplomacy," *Journal of the Society for American Music* 5 (2011): 335–64; Carol A. Hess, "Copland in Argentina: Pan-Americanist Politics, Folklore and the Crisis of Modern Music," *Journal of the American Musicological Society* 66/1 (Spring 2013): 191–250.

40. Scholars seem slow to take up such questions, but in the event, might profit from Stephanie N. Stallings's thesis, "Collective Difference: The Pan-American Association of Composers and Pan-American Ideology in Music, 1925–1945" (PhD diss., Florida State University, 2009).

41. Pollack, *Aaron Copland*, 104.

PART II

Biographical and Analytical Perspectives

Chávez and the Autonomy of the Musical Work: The Piano Music

LUISA VILAR-PAYÁ

Born in 1899 and, from an early age, a key player in the artistic and political arenas of Mexico, Carlos Chávez intensely lived and represented the acceleration of cultural change that characterized the onset of the twentieth century. His reception, nevertheless, typecasts him in ways that eclipse important aspects of his oeuvre. Chávez's determining, albeit controversial role in the development of Mexico's national culture in the 1930s and '40s has weighed heavily in the critical and historiographical response to his entire output. As a result, the aesthetic frame that supports his music has been all too often deemed fully exchangeable with the ideas believed to be behind the roles he played in the creation of post-revolutionary Mexican institutions. Quantitatively, this kind of approach left out most of his production. Qualitatively, it ignored aspects of structure and style that were at the core of his musical ideals. More balanced perspectives started to appear around the celebration of the one hundredth anniversary of his birth.[1] However, Chávez's interest in structural self-sufficiency remains an overlooked aspect of his compositional concerns.

Chávez wrote for the piano throughout his entire life—and did so abundantly. Hence, this corpus becomes an exemplary place to demonstrate his preoccupation with the autonomy of the musical work. Written within a span that covers almost six decades (1917–75) Chávez's piano music astounds for its diverse nature. Worth mentioning at the outset are a number of significant atonal avant-garde works that include his Third Sonata (1928), a twenty-minute long atonal *Invención* (1958), and *Five Caprichos* (1975). A set published under the title Seven Pieces for Piano represents a particularly relevant antecedent to those works; it comprises "Polygons" (1923), "Solo" (1926), "36" (1925), "Blues" (1928), "Fox" (1928), "Landscape" (1930), and "Unity" (1930).[2]

The melodic and harmonic treatment heard in a smaller group of short Mexicanist pieces underscores, even from a very early stage, his modernist inclinations: *Bendición* and *Noche: aguafuerte* (1920), *Xochimilco* Dance (ca. 1924), *La lorona* and *Danza de la pluma* (1943), and *Mañanas mexicanas* (1967). Meanwhile, the Fugues (1942) and the Ten Preludes (1937) explicitly testify to the contrapuntal flair and pedagogical commitment that characterizes a high percentage of Chávez's pianistic output. Concurrently, he wrote numerous pieces that explicitly dialogue with Viennese Classicism, as well as the virtuoso tradition of Chopin, Schumann, Liszt, Debussy, Ravel, Rachmaninoff, Bartók, and Prokofiev. Among these are the Four Nocturnes (1922), the Sonatina (1924), and the piano sonatas of 1917, 1919, 1960 and 1961. Likewise, his Three Etudes to Chopin (1949), *Left Hand Inversions of Five Chopin Etudes* (1950), Four New Etudes (1952), as well as his last Estudio, dedicated to Rubinstein (1973), represent Chávez's deep knowledge of the instrument and a particular fondness for density, polyphony, and rapid technical display. This characteristic is also shared by the avant-garde pieces mentioned above; after all, Chávez was himself an accomplished pianist.

Aside from the salient features that can be used to group together certain works, each piece of music embodies a constellation of imbricated references. These links between sound and cognition involve an ample assortment of signifiers, including those of Indian and mestizo music. However, recent scholarship has soundly questioned the ways in which Chávez's critical reception has dealt with such referents.[3] In addition, his multifaceted—indeed polyphonic—intellectual disposition requires a further expansion of the frameworks currently employed to study his music. Two doctoral dissertations illustrate this need. In 1982 Diane Nordyke strove to highlight any characteristics in the piano music that could signal Aztecness. At the same time, but not at the center of her discussion, she also remarked, "Despite his strong nationalistic bent, much of his music, especially the early and late compositions, has little relationship to musical nationalism."[4] More than two decades later, and referring to the Four New Etudes, Alejandro Barrañón assesses: "The fact that no obvious Indian elements are present in the late etudes—at least they are not perceived immediately by listeners—might explain the limited interest on these pieces by the majority of American critics."[5]

In this study I focus on Chávez's careful management of musical elements that support the perception of unity. His discourse as well as his music reveal an alignment with early twentieth-century modernism and the ideas of structural self-sufficiency, autonomy, and progress. Moreover, my approach demonstrates how Chávez's piano music displays a continuous, uninterrupted buildup of intertwined and symbiotic lines of thought, all linked to his concern with the development of the techniques of Western art music.

Autonomy and the Unity of the Musical Work

In 1927, the year before Chávez composed and performed his Third Sonata in New York, he published "Technique and Inner Form," his first article in *Modern Music*.[6] An earlier version was published in Mexico in 1924, the year he composed the Sonatina for piano.[7] I will argue here that the changes introduced in the English version of 1928 reflect the compositional development that occurs between the Sonatina and the Third Sonata. What remains from the 1924 version proves, first and foremost, that before the mid-1920s, Chávez was already involved in defending the autonomy and self-sufficiency of the work of music. Further, the additions and changes of 1928 solidify the composer's ideas, revealing his growing confidence and commitment to this line of thought.

Both versions of the article begin by insisting that form is inseparable from content. "External form unfolds from the center of a work of Art; the whole inner substance, when objectified, is nothing more than the external form."[8] The modernistic discourse against reference, agency, or against anything that would draw attention away from processes and materials themselves, prevails. In Chávez's words, "If we permit ourselves the liberty to read *between the lines* we may easily find just the opposite of what is in them."[9] Furthermore, reading between the lines "is like trying to put a fine scalpel between sense and technique—an operation which would enable us to believe that Stravinsky might express his meaning within the technique of Beethoven." In 1928—after having written the Third Sonata, an atonal work in which, as my analysis will show, a single harmonic kernel informs all structural junctures as well as the pitch-class content of different layers—Chávez insists obsessively on the ultimate correspondence between "internal substance" and tangible "external form." Not surprisingly, in this version he also equates the indivisibility of the internal and the external to the absolute values already present at the conception of a work:

> The means of objectifying works of art are tangible sounds, colors, metals, etc., and their attributes. The strength, the singular energy of these means lies precisely in the degree of perfection to which they develop all that is contained in

> the internal substance. Art is the result of converting internal substance into external form by tangible means; when this has been accomplished, *the internal form finally consists of nothing more or less than the external form. Such absolute values as a work of art possesses exist in the mind of the artist while he is still concerned with its conception*. Once externalized, the composition immediately takes on a relative value for the audience. Art is, in a sense, an agreement established between creator and spectator. A musical, pictorial or poetic work may affect one person profoundly and another not at all but everyone who listens to or looks at something that has been created establishes a relationship between himself and the object.
>
> However, the varying degrees of mutual understanding between spectator and author leave the work of art unaffected in respect to one matter, the interpenetration of its external and internal form.[10]

Only the penultimate sentence of this text appeared in the Spanish version, and it led to quite a different conclusion: "Sounds may affect one person profoundly and another little or not at all; the reason is that precision doesn't exist, and both the intellectual capacity and the means of intellectual communication are perfectly flexible."[11] In 1924, as shown here, Chávez dealt with polysemy and ambiguity, but in 1928 he avoided this discussion and proceeded to insist on the unity and autonomy of the cultural artifact. To interpret is to understand the structure that coalesces the physical and the intellectual; at the same time, the work of art remains "unaffected" by audience reception. Thus the English version of the article narrows the subject matter and aims to clarify the two perspectives most often used to promote autonomy, arguing for the artifact's logical and material indivisibility, and supporting the idea that structure equals meaning. "The unity of a work of art needs to be supplemented by no profound interpretations; it is all there in the lines, not between them, in the external form, which is the only natural embodiment of the form of the work at the center."[12] Part of this sentence also appeared in the Spanish version, but without the word *unity* and leading, once more, to a conclusion that attempted to explain why a single work of art may be subject to multiple readings. "Everything is in the lines; the lines, which are an external form, are also an internal form: they always imply a convention and there are many ways of interpreting them."[13]

In several articles published in 1924—after a first stay in New York that lasted for four months—Chávez used irony against interpretations based on extramusical references and opposed the extent to which a composer's biographical data was used to explain a specific piece.[14] The basic modernist tenets of the time are present in these articles, but the process of argumentation became more focused in *Interior y exterior*, and stronger still when he rewrote this article for its publication in *Modern Music* during his second stay in New York. As the following analyses will show, the music reaches higher levels of abstraction in the Third Sonata even though his interest in modernist musical trends was already there in his earlier Mexicanist pieces. Referring to his *canciones* for piano, Leonora Saavedra observes:

> Chávez, while following [Ponce's] model, included in his *canciones* elements that progressively revealed his own stylistic preferences for driving pulses, ostinati, discreet polyrhythm, non-contoured melodies, and developmental procedures. For example, he could add a moving, conjunct bass line establishing a steady, strong rhythmic pulse throughout a piece ("La Adelita/La cucaracha," 1915), lead the [middle] section of a *canción* into a development of its materials ("Adiós, adiós," 1919), or flatten the outline of the melody by reducing it to a handful of repeated pitches and pivotal intervals over a mildly dissonant ostinato ("Las margaritas," 1919).[15]

In addition to the elements Saavedra mentions here, the pieces written in the following decade show an increased preoccupation with conciseness and connectedness. The Sonatina and the Third Sonata represent a dramatic departure from the two previous and much longer piano sonatas. In the recordings made in 1999 by Chávez's friend, colleague, and disciple María Teresa Rodríguez, the *Sonata Fantasía* of 1917 takes thirty-four minutes, and the Second Sonata of 1919 more than twenty-seven minutes. In contrast, the Sonatina lasts less than five minutes and the Third Sonata of 1928 just over ten.[16] This turn to brevity is also perceivable in the Seven Pieces for Piano and goes hand in hand with the composer´s focus on autonomy and organicity.

Connectedness and Structure in the Sonatina and "Solo" from Seven Pieces for Piano

The Sonatina's internal division—Moderato, Andantino, Allegretto, Vivo, and Lento—loosely signals a multi-movement piece. The Lento rounds out the entire work, as it corresponds to the exact repetition of the initial Moderato, but with a different closure (mm. 23–25) and tempo marking (Moderato ♩= 84, Lento ♩ = 72). As a whole, the Sonatina displays the taste for continuous flow and taut organizational connectivity that characterizes much of Chávez's piano writing. Apart from a continuous quarter-note flow—in this case distinctly marked and accelerated by means of various descending triplets—the final Lento can be divided into four musical units that overlap at the head and tail (see Example 1).

With the juncture between the first two units, the distinct presence of the left hand's triplet makes the second unit sound like an extension of the previous. Likewise, at the end of the second unit, the last triplet of the left hand—as much as the melodic motion B_4–G_4, and the major seventh C_4–B_4 at the last beat of measure 12—anticipate the return, in measure 13, of a phrase that references the beginning of the Lento. Finally, the climax occurring in mm. 18–19, which also starts the piece's final gesture, ends up being shared between the third and fourth units; in the last eighth of measure 18 the left hand extends up to $A\sharp_4$ and then descends three octaves, until reaching the last note of the piece.

While harmonic and contrapuntal motions cross over each unit boundary, the extrapolation of specific collections of notes becomes a marker of autonomy or self-sufficiency. A basic example of this device can be seen when the middle voice that descends from F_4 to A_3 in mm. 5–7 returns in the bass line in augmentation in mm. 20–25.[17]

Chávez's fondness for uninterrupted dynamic and even rhythmic propulsion is also supported by his tempo markings: next to the Moderato and the Lento he indicates *sempre rigorosamente in tempo* and, on the first measure, he insists *tutto legato, la stessa intensità per tutte le voci*. These types of performance markings were common in the works of many composers of this period. They reflect a change in aesthetic interests, and are aimed to move performers away from the tradition of adding *rubato* or any other modification of tempo.[18] At the same time, Chávez's predilection for melodic and emotional flatness and incessant, even motion develops into a trademark as he wholeheartedly embraces a more modernist approach to the temporal unfolding of a piece. The importance he gives to dynamic markings as a substantial, almost independent, layer of construction can be seen in the manuscript copy of the Sonatina for cello and piano kept in the New York Public Library, where all the notes appear in green pencil, whereas almost all dynamic markings and ligatures are written in red.[19]

The compositional patterns heard in the Sonatina for piano turn ever more strategically audible as Chávez's harmonic language becomes increasingly complex and atonal. At the time of the Sonatina he had started

Example 1. Chávez, Sonatina, Lento.

composing the Seven Pieces for Piano. Written almost three years after the Sonatina, the second piece in the set, "Solo," exhibits some of the same compositional approaches, now employed in a more abstract and dissonant setting. It is a short, twenty-eight-measure piece that starts with a smooth melodic line. Nonetheless, though in the Sonatina the vertical dissonances are resolved (measure 13 beat 2, mm. 20 and 22 beats 2–3), in "Solo" they remain bare and insistent (mm. 6–9); also, "Solo"'s overtly pandiatonic beginning changes as the left hand extends its range downward to B$\flat_2$. This is the lowest pitch of the piece, a tritone away from the E that dominates the first half (Example 2). Conversely, the climax in the right hand occurs exactly in the middle, as the piece reaches its highest pitch in measure 14.

Example 2. Chávez, beginning of "Solo."

The final gesture reinstates the melodic line of measures 4–6. In addition, the last sonority comprises the (F_4–E_5) that started the piece and a D_4 that relates to the melodic goal stated in mm. 11–12 and 24–25 (Example 3).

Whereas the Lento of the Sonatina and "Solo" display Chávez's concern with formal interconnectivity and conciseness, the rest of the Seven

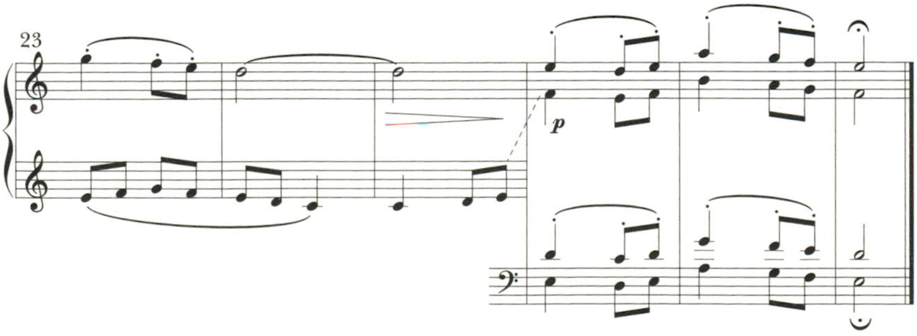

Example 3. Chávez, end of "Solo."

Pieces for Piano show the composer keeping pace with modernist trends: "Blues" and "Fox" explore harmonic cross-relations, syncopation, and last-beat accentuation. "Polygons," a piece of fifty measures, changes meter signature thirty-four times; "36" lasts forty-four measures and changes meter signature twenty-nine times. Unusual signatures such as 5/4, 7/4, 3/2, 2½/2, and 3½/2 recur in both "Polygons" and "36." Frequent metric changes, or the inclusion within a passage of a measure that adds a single beat (such as 1/4), become a constant feature of his music.

The Third Piano Sonata

Written during the composer's second long stay in New York (1926–28), the Third Sonata represents a significant moment of consolidation.[20] The first movement, Moderato, uses all the aforementioned compositional strategies and strives for a continuous flow, most of the time dovetailing the beginnings and endings of all structural units. Still, in dealing with a completely atonal language, and as a means of clarifying the role of some harmonic cells, Chávez differentiates the character of certain motives and phrases. Most important, the beginning of the piece becomes the seed of the entire movement. It includes a four-note cell, (F, F♯, G, C) in the right hand, which appears numerous times with identical pitch-class content and rhythmic profile (marked with rectangles in Example 4). Different transpositions of this kernel support the organization of the whole Moderato and illustrate Chávez's interest in organic structure.

The movement unfolds as a baroque binary form ABcA'B'. The most noticeable division happens between the end of B (measure 32) and the beginning of the codetta, which includes—a tritone away—material that was previously heard (compare mm. 6–7 to mm. 37–38). As for the first and second halves of the movement, the only difference between A sections occurs in the ways they connect with the B sections (mm. 19 and 58) and in measure 40, when the right hand plays its initial four-note motive an octave below. Section B (mm. 20–32), however, undergoes a number of important transformations its second time around (mm. 59–71).

The collection (E♭, E, F, B♭), a transposition of the right hand's initial four-note cell, informs the movement's lowest register (notes marked with arrows in Example 4). This transposition corresponds to a transformation of the kernel pivoted around F (Example 5), which explains the left hand's emphasis on F in mm. 27–32. Also, it supports the two most important changes that occur with the return of section B during the second half of the movement: the enharmonic D♯$_1$ in mm. 59–61, as well as the emphasis on B♭ at the end of the movement.

Another transposition of the same cell, now as (C, D♭, D, G), explains the right hand's arrivals: emphasis on C in measures 20–23; D♭ as the highest note of the melodic figure in mm. 37–38; emphasis on G in mm. 27–32 and mm. 59–62; and finally D at the end of the piece.

More than in previous pieces the overall character of the music is percussive. What remains most in one's memory is the repetition of rhythmic cells, as well as specific moments of arrival and their pitch-class content. All of this generates a type of plot that does not rely on melodic unfolding, as there are no themes or melodies in the traditional, classic sense. These characteristics, together with the movement's tight harmonic construction, represent a major breakthrough in the history of Mexican art music for the writing of autonomous, self-referential, atonal music.

The Idea of Non-Repetition

In the Ten Preludes of 1937, Chávez clearly experimented with structural balance and continuity, particularly in relation to an issue that became the focus of an entire generation of modernist composers: the role of repetition in music, and in art in general. As for the embodiment of this idea in a musical artifact, Chávez himself localizes it in a 1933 work, *Soli I* for oboe, clarinet, bassoon, and trumpet, written for the celebration of the tenth anniversary of the League of Composers in New York. In the notes made for the 1972 recordings of this work Chávez wrote retrospectively:

> The piece reflects various trends in my thinking of those days, with the jazzy, polyrhythmic inflections of the first movement, the very filtered "Mexican" tint of the fourth movement, and the altogether non-repe titive writing of the oboe in the third and the trumpet in the fourth, where the melody is unrolled in a constant process of renewal.[21]

These features are definitely present in his Ten Preludes. The alternation of triple and duple eighth notes that one can hear as related to the mestizo *jarabe* (a traditional Mexican folk dance), as well as the use of anhemitonic pentatonicism in the fifth prelude, serves as an example of that "filtered 'Mexican' tint" mentioned here by Chávez (Example 6). Pentatonicism was one of Chávez's signifiers of the Indian, but also one of the many collections with which he experimented as a modernist.[22] Meanwhile, the first prelude becomes a suitable place to analyze when the composer decides to repeat a musical idea, and when and how he resolves

Example 4a. Chávez, Third Sonata, Movement I, first half.

Example 4b. Chávez, Third Sonata, Movement I, second half.

C------G–F♯–F–E–E♭------B♭

Example 5. Chávez, Third Sonata, kernel pivot.

Example 6. Chávez, Prelude No. 5 from the Ten Modal Preludes (1937).

to transform it. This first prelude also illustrates how the "unrolling" of the melody in "a constant process of renewal" can occur in ways that resemble a type of mechanical movement, in this case, a rather subdued one.

Prelude No. 1 starts with the repetition of an idea that displays the characteristic melodic behavior of the modern E Phrygian mode. As it gradually descends from E_5 to A_4, the first phrase of the right hand emphasizes the cell [B_4, C_5, A_4]. In mm. 1–3 the phrase arrives at A_4, and in mm. 4–6 continues its descent to E_4 (Example 7). Concurrently, the left hand starts with the motive [E_3, F_4, D_4, E_4] and then continuously descends to E_2. The second time around, the left hand encounters the right hand in parallel octaves that arrive at E_3, E_4 in measure 6. At this point the descent is interrupted by a recall of the initial motive, now as [E_3, F_3, D_3, E_3], in the left hand. However, its extensions never coincide with the established pulse, or with the right hand's series of half notes that cross the bars 6–7 and 7–8. Though a more straightforward rhythmic comportment is briefly reestablished in mm. 9–11, a sense of displacement returns as the eighth-note rest in measure 12 delays the repetition of [E_6, B_5, D_6, A_5].

As seen in previous pieces, Prelude No. 1 displays Chávez's taste for continuous movement and interlocked phrases; it becomes almost impossible to mark the end of musical units without pointing out that a new one has already started.

Throughout the Ten Preludes Chávez fulfills this aesthetic ideal through a meticulous management of metrical, rhythmic, and harmonic matching and mismatching. In this kind of environment, exact repetition becomes as essential as variation. At the same time, motivic variation does not recall nineteenth-century Beethovenian schemes of development. Rather, it occurs as a twentieth-century version of Bachian *Fortspinnung*, where rhythmic and melodic cells keep reappearing in different contexts. The markings in Examples 7 and 8 show how the rhythmic cells that start the piece in the right hand reappear during the first thirty-one measures.

Example 7. Chávez, Prelude No. 1 from the Ten Preludes (1937), mm.1–12.

Both examples aim to highlight how these motives are linked (aligned and realigned) to the characteristic melodic third that permeates the entire prelude, and how they appear displaced (mm. 8–9, 26–27), shortened (measure 13), or changed at their beginnings or endings (mm. 11, 12, 24).

The clearest point of articulation in Prelude No. 1 occurs in measure 33, the start of a long climactic passage that ends in measure 57 and includes a slight change of tempo markings from *sostenuto pochissimo* (♩ = 80) to *poco più sostenuto* (♩ = 76) (Example 9). Rather than being primitivist music, as it might have been heard in the late 1930s, this passage seems to emulate the deferrals or displacements that occur when one hears clocklike mechanical motions that go at slightly different paces, but that at certain points do come together. During this long climactic buildup Chávez keeps recycling the same material, without repeating a single measure. Taking

Example 8. Chávez, excerpts from Prelude No. 1 from the Ten Preludes (1937).

measure 33 as point of reference, the changes are quite systematic: the F added as a second beat in measure 34, the D that divides the beat at the end of measure 35, the combination of both procedures in measure 36 (dividing the first beat instead of changing meter signature), and the displacement a third above in measure 37. Measures 38–42 display similar procedures but with the "wrong note" idea, as the compound octave held between both hands changes to a compound ninth. The octaves return in mm. 43–44 and the hemiola that occurs in mm. 45–46 adds interest but gets immediately reabsorbed into the continuous flow of the passage. The music is consistently organized in groupings of two measures, something that contributes to its clocklike character, and the use of high register and compound octave distances adds to this feeling.

This passage behaves as an abstraction or symbolic representation of mechanical motion. It was composed at a time when Chávez was also working on the publication of *Toward a New Music: Music and Electricity*, a book that from the beginning displays Chávez's fascination with the mechanical aspect of sound reproduction. As Gloria Carmona points out in her prologue to the 1997 reprint of the 1936 edition in Spanish, "The book reveals the composer's personal inquiries on the sound phenomenon itself and, more important, clarifies his aesthetic imperatives."[23] Are these imperatives represented in his writing of the piano preludes? The conception of the machine as an emblem of modernity and a musical predilection for continuous mechanistic flow are related. Rather than writing for pianola, as other composers of the time did, or imitating the sound of music boxes, carillons, and portable organettos with the piano, Chávez concentrates on the mechanical aspect itself. This is as true in the music as it is in the book, since he does not describe sound itself but focuses on how it is produced, and how the parts of the machine work together.

Chávez's Dialogue with European Mainstream Piano Writing

Non-repetition and originality play a central role in Chávez's compositional processes, in addition to being a leitmotif in his academic and journalistic writings. As relevant as this aspect becomes to the understanding of numerous passages of his works, including the overall structure of some pieces, a description of Chávez's piano music would not be adequate if it did not comment on how often and unabashedly his music tilted back toward mainstream European traditions. With the exception of the previously mentioned *Invención* of 1958, his modernistic *Mañanas mexicanas* of 1967, and the *Five*

Example 9. Chávez, Prelude No. 1 from the Ten Preludes (1937), mm. 33–55.

Caprichos of 1975, the works that he wrote after the two Fugues of 1942 carry on an overt dialogue with Viennese Classicism, or with the virtuoso piano textures of Schumann, Chopin, Liszt, Rachmaninoff, and Prokofiev.

Remarkably, Chávez did not hesitate to compose and include in his catalogue works that, for many ears, would seem to contradict his avant-garde trajectory. The most striking examples are found in the humoristic, kaleidoscopic approach to classic melodies, harmonies, and textures to be found in his Fifth Sonata (1960), or the explicit exercise in Mozartian style of the Sixth Sonata (1961) worked out with maximalist proportions.[24] Written only one year apart from each other, these sonatas could still be considered exceptions, but that is not the case for the Etudes to Chopin,[25] the five *Left Hand Inversions* (likewise based on Chopin), the Four New Etudes, and the *Estudio a Rubinstein*. Written at a later period in his life, these works also recall and continue some aspects of his Four Etudes of 1919–21 and the Nocturnes of 1922.

Chávez's own reflection on originality, written in 1945, seems to anticipate his last three decades of piano writing. It certainly helps to balance and better understand this element of his music:

> Artists are original only when they are able to accept influences. Not only do we accomplish higher artistic levels and originality when the influences are better assimilated, but also, when a larger number of influences have been integrated and incorporated.[26]

Alejandro Barrañón's doctoral dissertation analyzes Chávez's entire production of etudes. Apart from discussing how these pieces relate to Chopin and Debussy, Barrañón shows the ways in which Chávez incorporates the compositional techniques described in his Harvard Norton Lectures—among them, how radial symmetry (designs in which both hands often move in similar ways) contributes to the form and functions of the pieces. For Barrañón, "Chávez's compositional techniques are traditional in many respects, and yet his music sounds completely novel and fresh."[27]

It seems only natural that Chávez would write as many etudes as he did, and that they would be so idiomatic for the instrument. Not only do these pieces display his in-depth knowledge of the piano, but they belong fittingly to the tradition that interested Chávez the most: the writing of music in which repetition and variation interact in an atmosphere of non-stop propulsion and Baroque *Fortspinnung*. In this type of piece Bach is as much a model for Chopin as both composers are models for Chávez.

At the same time, the *Five Caprichos*, finished the year before he passed away, are completely avant-garde in nature. *Capricho* No. 4 displays a tripartite division marked Adagio ♩ = 40 (♪ = 80), Più mosso ♩ = 50, and Tempo Primo ♩ = 40. A total duration for the piece of 3'30" appears indicated in a Bartókian manner at the bottom of the last page (Example 10). Though not dodecaphonic or serial in the strict sense, the *Capricho* starts with a twelve-tone row identified in Example 10 as P_0, and ends with $P_{11,}$ its transposition a semitone below (mm. 50–58). The individual pitch classes that frame the row and its hexachordal and trichordal division appear emphasized during the piece, and serve as melodic and harmonic goals at all major points of articulation.

The central part of *Capricho* No. 4, Più mosso, is organized around (0, 4, 8) cycles, whereas the last section, Tempo primo, begins with a slow buildup based on cluster harmonies that culminates in measure 49 with a large chromatic tone cluster played with the flat of the right hand. Simultaneously, the left hand plays a *fortissimo* A_4, the same pitch-class that starts the first statement of the row at the beginning of the piece (Example 10). The harmonic content of the chord that immediately follows is identical to the first tetrachord of the series (measure 50). This tetrachord remains sustained by the pedal, while one hears, in strict order, the pitch-classes that conform P_{11}. This presentation of the row concludes with a $C\sharp_2$ that leads to the D_1 that ends the piece. It should be noted here that pitch-class D is the last member of P_0, the series that started the piece. Meanwhile C♯, the last pitch class of P_{11}, is also heard in measure 17 as the lowest note of the whole *Capricho*.

Once more, the formal layout of the *Capricho* illustrates how Chávez ensures that the structural outline of a piece remains audible in the foreground. In accordance with his own taste for ruthless musical continuity, he decides to obliterate rhythmically and melodically the completion of P_0 in measure 6 (mm. 7–8 in Example 10). In this *Capricho*, as in all the movements and pieces analyzed in this essay, and notwithstanding the ambiguities seeded during these works, elements of formal concordance and self-governance materialize at all major structural junctures. Such attention to the features of music that support the perception of unity lies at the core of Chávez's deep-rooted belief in the autonomy of the work of art. His commitment to the absolute indivisibility of technique and "inner form" as he described it in the 1920s and as he continued to sustain throughout his life, are present in his academic and journalistic writings as an intellectual testimony. Most important, he left his music as the ultimate proof of his beliefs and values.

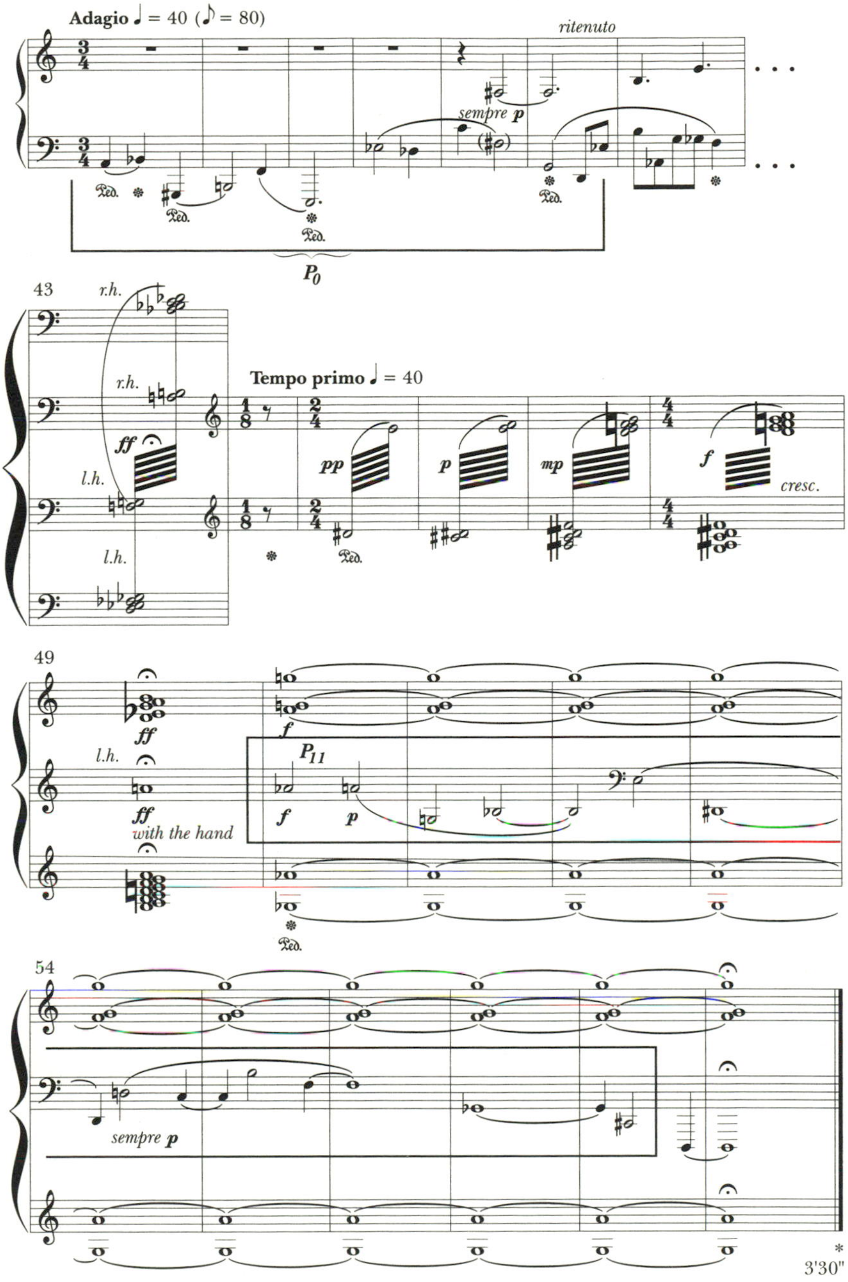

Example 10. Chávez, *Capricho* No. 4 of the *Five Caprichos* (1975), mm.1–7.

NOTES

1. See, for example, *Diálogo de resplandores: Carlos Chávez y Silvestre Revueltas*, ed. Yael Bitrán and Ricardo Miranda (Mexico City: INBA/CONACULTA, 2002); and Leonora Saavedra, "Of Selves and Others: Historiography, Ideology, and the Politics of Modern Mexican Music" (PhD diss., University of Pittsburgh, 2001).

2. The pieces were originally published by Henry Cowell in 1936 in *The New Music Quarterly*.

3. See, for example, Leonora Saavedra, "Carlos Chávez y la construcción de una alteridad estratégica," in Bitrán and Miranda, *Diálogo de resplandores*, 125–36; and Alejandro L. Madrid, *Sounds of the Modern Nation: Music, Culture, and Ideas in Post-Revolutionary Mexico* (Philadelphia: Temple University Press, 2008).

4. Diane Nordyke, "The Piano Works of Carlos Chávez" (PhD diss., Texas Tech University, 1982), 171.

5. Alejandro Augusto Barrañón Cedillo, "Carlos Chávez's Etudes for Piano" (DMA diss., University of Houston, 2006), 111.

6. Carlos Chávez, "Technique and Inner Form," *Modern Music* 5/4 (May–June 1927): 28–31.

7. Carlos Chávez, "Interior y exterior: Sexto editorial de música," *La Antorcha*, 6 December 1924, repr. in *Escritos periodísticos (1916–1939)*, ed. Gloria Carmona (Mexico City: El Colegio Nacional, 1997), 67–69.

8. Chávez, "Technique and Inner Form," 28.

9. Ibid., 28.

10. Ibid., 28–29, my emphasis.

11. Chávez, "Interior y exterior," 67. All translations in this article are mine.

12. Chávez, "Technique and Inner Form," 28.

13. Chávez, "Interior y exterior," 67.

14. See, for example, "Música y bellas artes: Tercer editorial de música," and "Querer es poder: Cuarto editorial de música," in Carmona, *Escritos periodísticos*, 41–47.

15. Leonora Saavedra, "Carlos Chávez's Polysemic Style: Constructing the National, Seeking the Cosmopolitan," *Journal of the American Musicological Society* 68/1 (2015): 106. The *canción mexicana* was a traditional, rural nineteenth-century Mexican genre. Chávez, Manuel M. Ponce, and many other composers arranged *canciones* for voice and piano in the 1920s.

16. *Carlos Chávez: Obra completa para piano, Edición conmemorativa del centenario 1899–1999*, María Teresa Rodríguez, piano (Mexico City: CONCULTA-INBA/BMG Entertainment, 1999).

17. In order to render visibility to Chávez's use of range, our examples expand beyond two staves. The piano works analyzed here are all published with the standard two-line staff for piano with the exception of the fourth *Capricho*, discussed at the end of this study.

18. I am grateful to pianist Geoffrey Burleson for his observations regarding the frequency and purposes of these markings.

19. New York Public Library for the Performing Arts.

20. On the Sonata, see also Carol J. Oja, *Making Music Modern: New York in the 1920s* (Oxford: Oxford University Press, 2000), 275–78.

21. Carlos Chávez, liner notes to *Soli I/ Soli II/ Soli IV*, Odyssey LP, Y31534 (1972).

22. See Leonora Saavedra, "Carlos Chávez's Polysemic Style" for a recent discussion of the roles of pentatonicism as well as the mestizo *jarabe* in Chávez's early music.

23. Gloria Carmona, "Prólogo," in Carlos Chávez, *Hacia una nueva música: Ensayo sobre música y electricidad*, ed. Gloria Carmona (Mexico City: Fondo de Cultura Económica,

1989), 11 (author's translation). English edition: *Toward a New Music*, trans. Herbert Weinstock (New York: W. W. Norton, 1937).

24. These two works were composed at a time when Chávez was instructing his students to write pieces based on the formal schemes of Mozart's piano sonatas. According to María Teresa Rodríguez, interviewed by Alejandro Barrañón: "Chávez demanded that his students write sonatas modeled according to Mozart's style, namely, with the same number of measures and the same thematic structure and key-plan. It was very interesting to listen to such different compositions, based on the same plan. Chávez learned composition as an autodidact by analyzing the works of the great masters, and he taught composition by the same method." Barrañón, "Carlos Chávez's Etudes for Piano," 129.

25. Commissioned by UNESCO for the one-hundredth anniversary of Chopin's death in 1949.

26. Carlos Chávez, "Rameau," *El Universal*, 24 March 1945, quoted and trans. by Barrañón, "Carlos Chávez's Etudes for Piano," 69.

27. Ibid., 125.

Carlos Chávez and the Myth of the Aztec Renaissance

LEONORA SAAVEDRA

In May 1940, Carlos Chávez wrote a short piece for wind and percussion instruments entitled *Xochipilli-Macuilxóchitl*. In the program for the premiere, given on 16 May at New York's Museum of Modern Art, the strange-looking title was followed by an explanation of sorts: "Music for pre-Conquest instruments (XVIth century)."[1] This new work opened a concert designed by Chávez to "give some conception of the historic development of music in Mexico."[2] The concert, repeated twice daily for two weeks, was conceived as a musical counterpart to the monumental art exhibition *Twenty Centuries of Mexican Art*, presented by Nelson A. Rockefeller, president of MoMA, with the combined support of both the museum and the Mexican government. In a press release dated 21 February 1940, MoMA promised the American public the opportunity "to see and study Mexico's art of today against the background of its cultural past." In particular, the exhibition was designed to "trace Mexico's culture through twenty centuries of its evolution," from "the greatness of its Pre-Columbian or Pre-Spanish periods" through "the splendors of the Colonial era," and on to "the strength and vigor of the Modern period," represented by works of the acclaimed muralists Diego Rivera, José Clemente Orozco, and David Alfaro Siqueiros—Chávez's contemporaries and friends. The organizers also made sure to include folk and popular art, since "they form so persistent and colorful a part of the life of the Mexican people."[3]

The agenda was thus set for Chávez and his concert, but designing a musical program that would approximate what the art exhibition promised to do was easier said than done. Chávez included two dances from his own modernist ballet *Los cuatro soles* as representative of the "strength and vigor" of modern Mexican music. A mass in the early Classical style by José María Aldana (1758–1810) filled the colonial slot. Chávez's associates, Luis Sandi and Gerónimo Baqueiro Foster, crafted a series of arrangements of melodies, used in genres such as the *son* and *corrido* as well as by contemporary Yaqui *indígenas,* to represent both folk music and the nineteenth and twentieth centuries.[4] The problem remained how to represent pre-Columbian music. And so Chávez composed *Xochipilli*.

In his introduction to the program notes, Chávez espoused the culturally omnivorous narrative of Mexican history produced by the political theory of *mestizaje* that had guided Mexican culture for four decades: "By the phrase 'Mexican music' we mean the Indian music of the ancient Mexicans; the music of Spanish or other origin implanted in Mexico, and, finally, the production in Mexico of a mixture of these elements." To this he appended a conception of contemporary indigenous culture that he shared with educators, anthropologists, and political leaders—in fact, some of the brightest minds of his time: "Indian music from the Conquest on remained static, while Spanish music has undergone constant evolution."[5]

In May 1940, as many times before, Chávez felt under pressure to affirm that "among the Aztecs, music achieved the marks of a true artistic culture."[6] Quoting Juan de Torquemada's sixteenth-century *Monarquía indiana* at length, he shared with his readers the astonishment of Spanish missionaries and soldiers regarding the complexity and precision of Aztec musical organization and music making. Relying on historical and organological evidence scholars had produced, Chávez set out to show that the Aztecs' pitch and scalar system was compatible with and comparable to those of other cultures of the world: "The Indians of our America discovered a natural scale, that of the so-called natural harmonics. This scale obeys a series of acoustic laws which are the basis of the musical system of the occident." Finally, through a series of perhaps questionable leaps in logic, he concluded that from this scale the Indians had "obtained their pentatonic scale without semitones."[7] Thus Chávez composed *Xochipilli*, for an ensemble comprising replicas of pre-Conquest wind and percussion instruments, using a system based entirely on anhemitonic pentatonic pitch collections.

When, many years later in 1964, Chávez published *Xochipilli*, he removed *Macuilxóchitl* and gave the piece a new subtitle: "An Imaginary Aztec Music." Wiser, more self-assured, and no longer under pressure to put Mexican music on the map of the great cultures of the world, Chávez painted in his introduction a more sober panorama of ancient musical culture. "We know very little or absolutely nothing about subjects such as the scale system, harmony, polyphony, and formal construction," he acknowledged, later adding a frank admission: "There are no melodies or rhythms that can be considered authentically pre-Cortesian; when I composed *Xochipilli* I couldn't have tried to quote anything directly. The melodies and rhythms in this piece are more than anything the result of my thoughts on topics of Mexican antiquity, and of my unlimited admiration for pre-Cortesian sculpture and painting."[8] In this manner, Chávez laid to rest once and for all the idea that his compositions embody authentic pre-Columbian music, or that the music of ancient Mexico can be recovered.

In the 1920s, Chávez had composed two ballets based on Aztec cosmogonic and cosmological beliefs, *El fuego nuevo* (1921) and *Los cuatro soles* (1925), along with many other compositions, many of a non-referential nature such as sonatas or symphonies.[9] In all these pieces, referential and non-referential alike, Chávez used a personal style he developed early in his life, one that lent itself to the representation of the ancient and primitive as well as of the modern and machine-like.[10] However, it was *El fuego nuevo* and *Los cuatro soles*, along with the idea, common in the critical reception of his music, that all his music invariably partook of an "Indian" element and even shows a personal "part-Indian" essence, that propelled him into the critical limelight in the mid-1920s.

Chávez had a genuine love of indigenous cultures and a true admiration for pre-Columbian ones. But he represented the Aztec or the Mexican indigenous in, and only in, the pieces in which he chose to do so, of which there are but a handful: *El fuego nuevo*, *Los cuatro soles*, *Sinfonía india* (1935), *Xochipilli,* and to some extent, *Pirámide* (1968).[11] Yet reconstructing pre-Columbian music, separating the indigenous from the European in contemporary indigenous music, and featuring it all in Western art music compositions was a difficult if not impossible task, fraught with inherent contradictions.

Chávez was a major historical agent in the creation of modern Mexico as it now imagines itself: a nation of mixed culture, heir to refined European traditions as well as to a glorious pre-Conquest past. What Chávez created was not pre-Columbian or indigenous music but high-art signifiers of it: symbolic representations with some basis in historically accurate evidence that, much more importantly, came to be recognized and adopted as symbols of the indigenous by many Mexicans. Therein lies the significance of his Indianist project. In the pages that follow I will, necessarily in an abridged fashion, situate Chávez within the large cultural and political transformations of which he was both an agent and a product, analyze the particular artistic shape of these signifiers, and briefly reflect upon the cultural work that they performed between 1920 and 1940.

Indígenas, Mestizos, and Indigenismo

When the Spaniards arrived in current Mexican territory in 1519, they found in the central and southern parts of the country a dense population with complex forms of political and social organization and native forms of art, science, and religion. Despite many commonalities, the population belonged to several different cultures and did not share a language, much less an identity. Many cultures were under Aztec domination and/or were the Aztecs' political antagonists. Having expelled from Spain all Muslim and Jewish inhabitants in 1492, the Spanish Crown now sought in America to convert all native peoples to Catholicism, and to keep all ethnicities—"races," they called them—not only unequal but strictly separate, legally and geographically. Despite the government's anti-miscegenation policy, these diverse social groups entered into contact with one another through service and trade. Over the three centuries of colonial domination a population of "half-breeds" grew to such an extent that in the eighteenth century an elaborate system of classification, the *castas*, was eventually put in place to survey and control it. People of mixed race were not often welcome by any of the three original ethnicities (European, indigenous, and African), and they lived in the cities, often begging and stealing. By the end of Spanish rule the mixed-race inhabitants were second in size only to the indígenas.[12]

The criollo population—American-born descendants of Spaniards—led the movement and war of independence against Spain (1810–21) and took the place of the Spaniards at the top of the social hierarchy in a politically and militarily unstable and culturally fragmented Mexico. A weak state and no formed nation emerged from independence. The population had been transformed into a free but economically and socially unequal body of newly minted citizens. With the Texas secession in the 1830s and war with the United States in the 1840s, Mexico had lost half of its territory by midcentury. After an encounter with the colonial designs of France's Napoleon III, which led to a short-lived Mexican Empire under the rule of Archduke Maximilian of Austria (1863–67), Mexico's political elites realized the urgent need to stabilize the country, modernize the economy, strengthen the state, and create a nation out of the country's inhabitants.

Laissez-faire liberalism was the economic doctrine adopted by the political elites, and the goal was to incorporate everybody, including the indigenous populations, into a capitalist economy of wage labor and small and big proprietors. At the same time, after the Reform War of the 1850s against the Catholic Church and the defeat of the French in 1867, the increasingly strong Mexican state sought to turn all Mexicans into members of a single polity, with no stronger allegiance to community, the (Catholic) Church, or the local boss than that to the nation-state. The indigenous populations, with their lack of Western education and ways of life, their ties to the land, their systems of beliefs and of economical and social relations inimical to capitalism, and their exclusive allegiance to their immediate community were thus regarded as an obstacle.[13]

The intellectual and political elites offered several explanations for the perceived reluctance, resistance, or inability of the indigenous peoples to incorporate capitalism and Western mores. These ranged from racist explanations, in line with the new pseudo-scientific European racial theories, to explanations that attributed the indígenas' "backward" state to centuries of exploitation and neglect. This latter position would become the predominant one after the Mexican Revolution of 1910–20. In the late nineteenth century, political elites utilized Spencerian theories of history and society, emphasizing survival of the fittest, to conclude that indigenous populations must cease to exist as such in order for Mexico to become a modern nation.[14] Forced and coerced loyalty to the state was often brutally imposed, as in the state wars against the Maya in Yucatán or the Yaqui in Sonora.

Interestingly, these same elites, who despite prevailing ideals of beauty and social refinement that insisted on the superiority of everything white, were increasingly mestizo, firmly rejected pseudo-scientific European and U.S.-American theories about the mixed races' degeneracy and inability to govern themselves. Such theories, of course, could and did provide an expedient rationale for colonialism and neocolonialism or, at the very least, foreign intervention in Mexico by the powerful nations of the time.[15] Asserting the legitimacy of the mixed race became a political agenda that sought to safeguard Mexico's sovereignty and provided the rationale for the social project of assimilating the indigenous populations. Intellectuals and politicians such as Justo Sierra and Andrés Molina Enríquez developed a theory of *mestizaje*, and the mestizo majority gradually became identified with the nation that was being created.[16]

In the last third of the nineteenth century, a period identified with the dictatorship of Porfirio Díaz—the Porfiriato—the state had neither the means nor the pressing need, or so it was thought, to massively incorporate the indígenas into the national culture. An elite nationalism began whose population targets were the criollo and mestizo social groups of the higher and developing middle classes, a population that did not necessarily recognize a mixed-ethnicity nation as their own, or the pre-Columbian past as their national past. Yet pre-Columbian cultures could give the new

Mexican nation continuity and long roots, as well as a past comparable to European classic cultures—provided that all connotations of savagery could be brushed aside. By the onset of the Revolution that overturned the Porfirian regime, important scholars such as Manuel Orozco y Berra and Alfredo Chavero had produced state-of-the art accounts of ancient Mexican history that culturally translated pre-Columbian civilizations for the educated classes.[17] Public architecture and sculpture had turned avenues and plazas, especially in Mexico City, into inhabitable museums. And Aniceto Ortega, Ricardo Castro, and Gustavo Campa had composed a small number of operas on pre-Columbian topics: *Guatemotzin* (1871), *Atzimba* (1900), and *Le roi poète* (1901), respectively, provided cultural elites with relatable models of ancient Mexicans.[18]

Modernizing Mexico's economy and creating a homogenous, culturally mestizo nation out of a disparate population—to Indianize the mestizo and to mestizo-ize the indigenous—remained a priority after the Revolution. The war and the social and legal reforms embedded in the constitution of 1917 gave the project a new impulse and a political shift. Although indígena participation in the Revolution had been extensive and brought mestizos in contact with indígenas on an unprecedented scale, it had not been premised on any "Indianist" project made in the name of an indigenous identity and culture. Rather, indígena claims were agrarian, land ownership being vital to them and their immediate communities. Nevertheless, the presence and importance of the indigenous populations were fully acknowledged by the new political and intellectual elites: their assimilation into the Mexican nation would now be accomplished—optimistically and naively, or just as perversely, depending on one's point of view— through persuasion, education, and the respect for native culture. As the theory of *mestizaje* acquired full political weight *indigenismo*, a more enlightened way to assimilate indigenous communities, was developed. Crucial in this shift were the theories, writings, and concrete policies of philosopher José Vasconcelos and anthropologist Manuel Gamio (and later, Alfonso Caso and Moisés Saenz) from their positions in the new ministries of education, agriculture, and indigenous affairs.[19]

The implementation of indigenista policies was one of the main tasks of the government after the Revolution. With important exceptions, such as in the war against the Yaqui in 1926, federal rural schools and teachers substituted for the army, and it was in these schools that negotiations between the state project and traditional community life took place.[20] Thanks in great part to Gamio, modern archeology and anthropology developed exponentially and in tandem with indigenismo, producing new, actionable knowledge about both pre-Columbian and contemporary indigenous cultures.[21] Indigenismo was, again, not the result of a self-motivated indigenous agenda. The indígenas continued to be homogenized and constructed from outside, this time by mestizos for whom self-recognition in the indigenous/pre-Columbian culture, now turned into an idealized and valuable asset, was crucial. Empirical evidence points to a gulf between twentieth-century indigenous populations and their pre-Columbian ancestors.[22] The construction of ancient Mexican cultures as the Mexican past was an explicit agenda, and the result of literacy and education that most indígenas did not have. After the Revolution, educators and artists, like Diego Rivera in painting or Carlos Chávez in music, sought to create the link between present and past for the potential benefit of both indígenas and mestizos.

Chávez's "Indian Problem"

Born in 1899, Chávez came of age in the midst of the historical processes described above and actively threw himself into them. The decade of the Revolution—Chávez's teenage years—saw an increased interest in the traditional and popular musics of Mexico through composer Manuel M. Ponce's advocacy of the *canción mexicana*.[23] Ponce, a pioneer in the research on rural peasant music, used its melodies in his compositions as a means of creating a nationalist style. Notably, he considered this music not historically Mexican but acculturated European, and in his early writings he discarded the possibility of any indigenous (or African, for that matter) contribution to it. For him, pre-Columbian peoples had been barbarians, and as such, he speculated, their music must have been like that of present-day "primitive" peoples, such as some African tribes.[24] In the 1910s most well-established musicians, such as composer Gustavo Campa and music historian Alba Herrera y Ogazón, agreed with him on matters pre-Columbian.[25]

Among the many consequences of the displacement of large masses of people during the Revolution was the growing acquaintance across the population with each other's regional cultures and the discovery by urban artists and intellectuals of popular arts. In the 1920s and '30s a much-celebrated cultural efflorescence took place in high art, as painters and musicians combined celebratory representations of popular culture with avant-garde techniques. In music, the *canción mexicana* and other rural mestizo musics and dances were at the center of the creative and educational efforts of composers and teachers, beginning with the expansion of federal education and the musical education of urban workers, led by José Vasconcelos. However, in the early 1920s very little was yet known of indigenous dance and music, nor was it often presented to the general public. The month-long centennial celebration of the conclusion of the War of Independence in September 1921, for example, featured the performance of mostly mestizo music, the only exception being the presentation of a series of Yaqui dances.

It was while attending the centennial celebrations that Chávez, for whom indigenous music was not entirely foreign, conceived the idea of addressing not the mestizo but the pre-Columbian component of Mexican culture by writing *El fuego nuevo*, a ballet on an Aztec topic.[26] Chávez was easily able to find a topic in the existing scholarship on Aztec life, but finding the music for his ballet was a different proposition. In the fall of 1921, Chávez composed, or rather arranged, a *pascola* dance whose source is Chavero's *Historia antigua y de la conquista*, the first volume in the magnum opus of Porfirian historical scholarship, *México a través de los siglos* (Mexico Through the Centuries).[27] Chavero's merits as a historian had already been discussed at the time of publication, due mainly to his tendency to offer, often on the basis of half-accurate or incomplete information, a vivid and (and at times too imaginative) re-creation of pre-Columbian civilizations to his modern and Western-educated readers, for whom the pre-Hispanic world was foreign and remote. Chavero situated music within a context of song and dance, whose description is clearly aimed at extolling—or reimagining for the reader—the brilliance of pre-Columbian civilizations and the depth of character of their members. Music "was but a note within the harmonious concert formed by the poetry, with its brilliant metaphors, the bizarre circles of dancers with costumes of dazzling plumage and resplendent gold, the colorful temples, and the tropical turquoise sky." A little later, he added: "In their music was reflected the restless, bellicose, and turbulent nature of some of those peoples, and at times [the music] was like a rain of tears in their songs of death."[28]

In *Historia antigua*, Chávez would have encountered general descriptions of pre-Columbian percussion—the teponaztli, huéhuetl, tortoise shell, and rattles made of clay, gourds, or bone—and wind instruments—the conch or sea snail shell, and flutes and whistles made of reed or clay.[29] He would have pictured their sound with the help of Chavero's paraphrases of descriptions left by sixteenth-century Spanish missionaries and soldiers-chroniclers, for whom Aztec music was deafening, lugubrious, ear piercing, and strange. Finally, he would have also learned about the occasions in which the noblemen sang, and others in which those instruments were used in war and religious ceremonies. As for melodies,

Chavero indicated only that "we can formulate an idea of such music through certain songs that have been preserved, even though they must have been subject to modifications with the passage of time."[30] Indeed, the melodies he reproduced are tonal and modal, post-Conquest melodies. In short, Chávez would have come away from this reading with the idea of an awe-inspiring, magnificent pre-Columbian civilization that included extensive music making on intriguing non-Western instruments, and little else.

What was the state of knowledge on pre-Columbian music in those decades? What other scholars might Chávez have consulted? The accounts left by soldier-chroniclers like Bernal Jiménez del Castillo and missionaries and priest-scholars such as Juan de Torquemada provide a wealth of information on societal aspects of music making, but none of these authors transcribed any of the music they heard or left a description of their melodies, rhythms, or musical systems. Collating sixteenth-century codices, instruments, and dictionaries of indigenous languages, scholars had amassed by the late nineteenth century a reliable knowledge of the kinds of instruments available. As for the musical instruments found in archeological excavations, the most dedicated nineteenth-century scholars of pre-Colombian antiquities had paid little attention to them as musical instruments, concentrating instead on the symbols and characters depicted in their decoration.[31] The rattles and whistles, and the one-patch drums of the family of the huéhuetl provide no information on pitches, of course, but from the teponaztlis and the flutes scholars in the 1920s and '30s attempted to obtain information on scalar and intervallic systems.

Only a few surviving instruments were available in the 1920s. It is therefore necessary to consider the limits imposed on Mexican scholars by both the scarce sources and the nature of this inquiry. Equally important is to consider the historiographical premises and ideological constraints under which they labored. As late as 1925, Rubén M. Campos felt the need to draw the attention of scholars to pre-Columbian music as a field of inquiry, beginning with the question of whether pre-Columbian music had in fact existed.[32] Campos and an assistant were apparently also the first Mexican musicians to play on the instrument collection of the Museo Nacional, the main institution for the study of ancient cultures, in order to determine the instruments' tuning, range, and scales. The following year, José G. Montes de Oca reported his findings on the same instruments in a small book on indigenous dances. In 1931, in a monograph titled *Nociones de historia de la música mejicana*, Miguel Galindo discussed his study of teponaztlis and Aztec flutes.[33] The most thorough studies of pre-Columbian instruments, however, were conducted by the engineer Daniel Castañeda and musician-scholar Baqueiro, who in 1930 reported on the Aztec and Purépecha flutes of the Museo, and by Castañeda and composer Vicente T. Mendoza, whose *Instrumental precortesiano*, an ambitious study on percussion instruments, appeared in 1933.[34]

During his tenure as director, from 1929 to 1934, Chávez turned the Conservatorio Nacional de Música (CNM) into a powerhouse of music research by hiring new professors and founding several academies charged with bibliographic, field, and speculative (cabinet) research on Mexican music.[35] Castañeda, Baqueiro, and Mendoza were members of the academies, and their writings on the pre-Columbian flutes were published in the journal *Música: Revista mexicana*, founded and directed by Chávez. One of the academies' goals, as Castañeda explained in a lecture delivered on 7 March 1930, was to collect the ceremonial music of contemporary indígenas for the purpose of analyzing their melodies, rhythms, harmony, and scales. A second goal was to formulate a theory of pentatonicism, since "all the primitive melodies of the four continents, and even the Peruvians and those of the redskins of North America are pentatonic, and so must be ours." Such a theory, he claimed,

> is of vital importance to guide and direct . . . the analysis of our autochthonous melodies. And this is so, because the case would be exceptional and unique—impossible, as far as we know—if the musical production of our peoples were not to fall under the same gravitational pull as all the music of the primitives: pentatonicism.[36]

Castañeda subscribed to European theories of evolutionism that viewed the history of humankind as a linear march toward progress, in which some cultures—those of Europe—marched ahead of the others. Thus Europeans could learn about their own remote past by studying the "primitive" peoples of the present day who had remained in an earlier evolutionary stage.[37] For Castañeda, the pre-Columbians too had been primitive peoples, and he considered his study of their flutes as a logical extension of European research on primitive instruments. According to his understanding of history, cultures progress from using "defective" scales made of a few—three, four, or five—pitches to the superior European seven-pitch scales.[38]

Castañeda was not alone in this belief. European evolutionism in its many guises strongly impacted the Mexican intelligentsia in the late nineteenth and early twentieth centuries, including Chávez and his scholars, in ways that will not be addressed here. Needless to say, this Eurocentric premise directly contradicted these musicians' purpose of exalting their pre-Columbian past and led to a number of small and large-scale ambivalences and contradictions. For example, whereas most of these scholars agreed that the two tongues of the teponaztlis are tuned in major seconds, minor thirds, or perfect fifths, with major third and perfect fourth appearing less frequently, there were much wider discrepancies concerning the five Aztec flutes. Most scholars agreed that all flutes produced only five sounds, but only Castañeda claimed all five of them produced anhemitonic collections (without semitones). Galindo and Montes de Oca both reported semitones, with the former claiming that one flute produced only four pitches at minor third intervals.[39] These discrepancies, which can be due to the age of the instruments and differences in the different abilities of the scholar-performers, show the difficulty of trying to tease out of archeological evidence a uniform scalar or intervallic system for pre-Columbian, or even just Aztec music.

Further on, Castañeda found that the Aztec flutes were tuned at different pitches but all produced the pentatonic scale that can be obtained by the pitches C–D–E–G–A, or "at least, that was the ideal pursued by our original musicians of the Empire of Anáhuac [Aztec]."[40] This conclusion was the result of Castañeda's direct empirical research, although in the same article he tried to support this conclusion mathematically, with conflicting results. Castañeda also proposed that in their original state four hundred years earlier, the flutes had produced two other collections of pitches by overblowing, based on the second (the octave above the fundamental) and third (the twelfth) overtones in the series. In that case the third collection would have produced a sixth pitch, B in our hypothetical scale, a seventh above the fundamental. But Castañeda rejected the idea that the Aztecs would have altered their allegedly ideal scale. He instead explained away the sixth pitch by proposing that when overblowing the musicians must have played the entire melody using exclusively the pentatonic collection based on the third overtone (G–A–[the offending] B–D–E), without going back to the lower collection.[41] Castañeda also glossed over the fact that the fifth pitch of the scale is always lower with respect to Western tuning standards.

Unlike his colleagues, Castañeda studied the three flutes at the Museo Nacional that belonged to the ancient Purépecha, or Tarascan, culture. There he found five-pitch collections, two of them made of whole tones, and a third comprising a major pentachord. Considering the possibility of overblowing, Castañeda concluded that the flutes may have been able to produce Western major scales, with the addition in the whole-tone scales of "extraneous" pitches resulting in chromaticisms he explained away as a "Baroque ornament."[42]

How could these conflicting results be reconciled? Castañeda proposed that ancient Purépecha music must have reached a stage of evolution superior to that achieved by the Aztec. Following Oswald Spengler's theory of the development, splendor, and decadence of cultures, Castañeda suggested that the Purépecha culture, older than the Aztec, was already in decadence at the time of the Conquest—hence the Baroque chromatic intrusions—whereas the Aztec was still in a bellicose adolescence. But as its development was truncated by the Conquest, the Aztec civilization logically never attained a superior stage. Caught in a contradiction between his desire to extol Aztec music and the potentially negative conclusions to which his own premises had given rise, Castañeda was careful to praise the Aztecs for having "one of the purest musical primitivisms among human cultures."[43]

Castañeda—and Chávez—probably knew Raoul and Marguerite d'Harcourt's ambitious study of Andean music, whose conclusions were first published in *La musique indienne chez les anciens civilisés d'Amérique* and later more fully in *La musique des incas et ses survivances*.[44] The d'Harcourts claimed that Quechua music was based on anhemitonic pentatonic collections, and that it is possible to separate the pre-Columbian from the mestizo in contemporary indigenous Andean music. Earlier, in the late nineteenth and early twentieth centuries, Karl Lumholtz and Konrad Theodor Preuss had visited northwestern Mexico on ethnological trips in which they collected and transcribed melodies from the contemporary, semi-nomadic Tarahumara, Tepehuano, Cora, and Huichol groups.[45] The melodies reveal no uniform scalar or melodic system, and although a few are pentatonic and anhemitonic, most are not. More common are melodies made of fewer than five pitches. In a comparative chapter on Andean music and that of Spain and other American cultures, the d'Harcourts expressed their frustration with what they saw as shortcomings in the Preuss and Lumholtz melodies, collected among backward peoples—*retardataires*—who had little in common with the sedentary, urban, complex Aztec society.[46] But they were equally frustrated by the work of other foreign and Mexican scholars, such as Ponce, Elfego Adán, Gamio, Eleanor Hague, Frederick Starr, and Arthur Morelet, whose research in central and southern Mexico had produced nothing but melodies with clear European influence.

The d'Harcourts concluded that no Aztec music had survived, advancing two possible explanations: either Aztec music had never had the strength and personality needed to survive or the Spanish Conquest, which had been more brutal in Mexico than in Peru, had obliterated it.[47] Perhaps something could still be salvaged with very systematic research—to which scholars should rush—in Mexico's mountainous regions. Their own research, they concluded, had fully demonstrated the superiority of Andean music over any other American music.[48]

As a reputable, thorough scholarly work of its time, *La musique des incas* accomplished what Chávez, Castañeda, Mendoza, and Baqueiro had as their goal and exerted a powerful influence on them. There are no direct citations of this publication in Castañeda's or Chávez's writings. It is nevertheless safe to suppose they knew the work, as they do paraphrase it. Chávez was also familiar with Marguerite d'Harcourt's *Mélodies popularies indiennes*, from which he took melodies to use in concerts in Mexico City in 1924.[49] Furthermore, in a lecture on Aztec music in 1928, Chávez spoke about Aztec musical systems with great authority, probably derived from his reading of the d'Harcourts' work, whose conclusions on the existence of five pentatonic modes with structurally important quasi-cadential pitches also find echo in Chávez's words:

> The Aztecs showed a predilection for those intervals which we call the minor third and the perfect fifth; their use of other intervals was rare. . . . This type of interval preference, which must undoubtedly be taken to indicate a deep-seated and intuitive yearning for the minor, found appropriate expression in modal melodies which entirely lacked the semitone . . . . Aztec melodies might begin or end on any degree of the five-note series. In discussing their music one might therefore appropriately speak of five different melodic modes, each of them founded on a different tonic in the pentatonic series. Since the fourth and seventh degrees of the major diatonic scale (as we know it) were completely absent from this music, all the harmonic implications of our all-important leading tone were banished from Aztec melody.
>
> If it should seem that their particular pentatonic system excluded any possibility of "modulating"—which some feel to be a psychological necessity even in monody—we reply that these aborigines avoided modulation (in our sense of the word) primarily because modulation was alien to the simple and straightforward spirit of the Indian. . . . For those whose ears have become conditioned by long familiarity with the European diatonic system, the "polymodality" of indigenous music inevitably sounds as if it were "polytonality."

> (Polytonality in music we might say is analogous to the absence of perspective which we encounter in aboriginal painting. The paintings of the pre-Conquest codices show us what this absence of perspective means.) It seems evident that either the aborigines possessed an aural predisposition, or that an ingrained habit of listening was developed among them, which we today do not possess. They were thus enabled to integrate into meaningful wholes the disparate planes of sound that (in the European way of thinking) clashed in their music.[50]

Commenting on this lecture, Robert Stevenson observed "how completely Mexican musical opinion had reversed itself during the 1920s. Characteristics that previously had been looked upon as basic faults in the indigenous music of Mexico—its 'minor quality,' its 'monotony,' its 'simultaneous sounding of different pentatonic melodies' which are out of tune with each other in our way of thinking, its fondness for 'two or more rhythms the beats of which never coincide'—all these qualities previously thought of as crude distortions came now in the 1920s to be regarded not as defects but as virtues."[51] Moreover, by assimilating pentatonic polymodality to polytonality, and praising the indigenous ability to integrate disparate planes of sound into wholes, Chávez opened the door to primitivist modernism as the appropriate style for an Indianist, modern, Mexican music.

The Musical Construction of the Mexican Indigenous

The scenario for *El fuego nuevo* is very freely based on the Aztec ritual of the "New Fire," in which priests propitiated the cyclical rebirth of fire, and with it life, every fifty-two years. The extant manuscript of the ballet, which dates from 1927, includes Chávez's account of the myth in a paraphrasis borrowed from Juan de Torquemada and Chavero.[52] Although these sources do not describe a collective or grandiose ceremony, Chávez imagined a vast ritual celebration proceeding from a dance of terror (that the fire may not be reborn) to communal joy, as priestesses and warriors join the priests and occupy increasingly higher steps on a pyramid bathed in colorful changing light.

Chávez may have included teponaztlis and whistles in the original *Fuego nuevo* score, now lost. In any event, the 1927 full manuscript includes three kinds of whistles and three pairs of teponaztlis. Although the score

Example 1a. *El fuego nuevo*, "Danza del terror," rehearsal letter H1, mm. 4–10.

calls only for high, medium, and low whistles, they are expected to produce the minor third, believed to permeate Aztec music. The teponaztlis too are tuned in thirds, major and minor: F–A–C–E, G–B♭–D–F, and C–E–G♯–B. Each individual teponaztli thus complies with the tuning of a pre-Columbian one, although each pair of teponaztlis can also produce a major or minor seventh as well as a major, minor, or augmented chord. With the addition of D♯ in one of the two sets of timpani, the pitches

Example 1b. *El fuego nuevo*, "Danza del terror," rehearsal letter H3, mm. 3–8.

Example 1b. Continued

produced collectively are those of the C scale with both minor and major third, sixth, and seventh. This is the basic pitch collection of the ballet. The chromatically altered C-scale allows Chávez to produce copious dissonant harmonic intervals, such as we see in the two sets of timpani, and between these and the teponaztlis, in the excerpts from the "Danza del terror" shown in Examples 1a and 1b.

These examples show other features that would become staples of Chávez's Indianist style. The composer showed an early predilection in his music for a steady, almost mechanical rhythmic pulse. In his Indianist pieces, this pulse is maintained by consistent binary rhythmic figures, as opposed to the triple, and 3-against-2 figures employed in his abstract music or in his musical representations of machines. Despite this deliberate monotony, in "Danza del terror" the instruments never settle into a single rhythmic motive; instead, motives travel unexpectedly from

Example 2a. *El fuego nuevo*, "Danse des guerriers," rehearsal letter T, mm. 1–4.

Example 2b. *El fuego nuevo*, "Danse des guerriers," rehearsal letter Y, mm. 1–8.

one instrument to another, and the music gives the impression of being improvisatory and even wild. With these features and a gradual increase in dynamics, textural density, and tone color, Chávez here created an extended, primitivist dance of terror for (rudimentary) wind and percussion instruments.

The various dances of *El fuego nuevo* contain a profusion of short melodies that often dissolve into busy rhythmic figuration extending over many measures, particularly in the woodwinds, lending the ballet an impressionist tint. At other times Chávez develops the melodies by sequence (Example 2a). These procedures for working out melodic materials are similar to those he employed in his early chamber music. The melodies are consequently rather hyperactive and stand in contrast to the pleasant, pastoral, fully stated melodies of later Indianist works. The melodic motives are often pentatonic within themselves but violently juxtaposed to other motives that are based on a different pentatonic collection, whereby the overall collection of the melody is actually larger and often very chromatic (Example 2b).

Four years after *El fuego nuevo*, Chávez began to compose a second Aztec-based ballet, *Los cuatro soles*, which depicts the myth of the cyclical creation and destruction of the world by major natural catastrophes related to water, wind, fire, and earth. Each of these cycles is called a *sol* (sun).[53] The ballet's scenario thus lends itself to an exciting cyclical

Example 3. *Los cuatro soles*, "Sol de agua," rehearsal no. 15, mm. 1–8.

representation of birth, development, and destruction, each containing a central *danza*. Perhaps because of his reading of the d'Harcourts, the melodies in *Los cuatro soles* are much more consistently pentatonic. Yet some, such as the main theme in "Danza de agua," are disrupted by the shift to other potentially different (here whole-tone) collections (Example 3). This melody, however, remains diatonic much longer; its rhythm and general character have a childlike simplicity, and its first phrase exhibits a gentle arch form. The traditional Western association of the oboe and, in this case, the English horn with the pastoral contributes to its character, although, in a fortunate coincidence, Chávez may simultaneously be alluding to the indígena reed instrument, the *chirimía*.[54] The melody is accompanied by a percussive but quiet, simple, and steady rhythmic motive in the xylophone (or teponaztli) and lower strings.

Chávez's most extended use of a single pentatonic collection is in the beautiful initial "Preludio," which returns in abridged form between "Sol de agua" (Sun of Water) and "Sol de aire" (Sun of Wind). The music begins in a low register from which it slowly ascends (despite short wave-like descents). Out of this Chávez builds a mysterious and melancholy extended melody in the bass, propelled to a moving yet sober climax by the exceptional use of conjoint triplets and an upward leap by a fourth. The melody is accompanied by the most majestic of Aztec instruments,

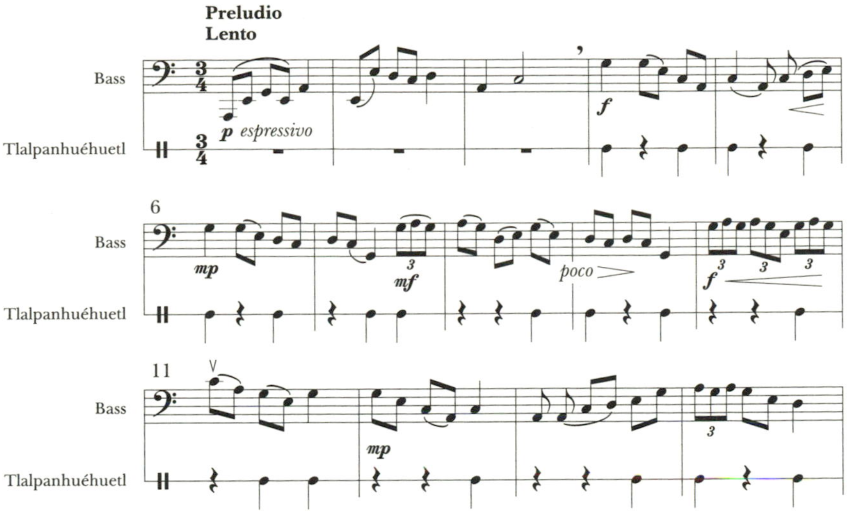

Example 4. *Los cuatro soles*, "Preludio," mm. 1–14.

the tlalpanhuéhuetl (Example 4). If "Danza de agua" constructs the indigenous as simple and innocent, the "Preludio" adds a deeper dimension of melancholy and sobriety, even stoicism.

Chávez represents, or constructs, yet another aspect of the pre-Columbian/indigenous in the open-ended, apparently improvised theme of "Danza de aire" (Example 5). Here, in a hectic *forte e preciso* melody, consistently based on a D-flat pentatonic collection, a choir of piccolo, flutes, and oboes seems to re-create the high-pitched clay and reed flutes described in sixteenth-century chronicles. The narrow ambitus of the melody, which changes "randomly" under Chávez's very tight control; the monotonous, simple percussion; and the drone-like open fifth in the harmony are all traditional indicators of primitive and/or archaic musics in Western culture. Yet they are equally recognizable as ingredients of modern primitivist music. Finally, the dissonant harmonic treatment of the D-flat melody, the open A–E fifth, and the countermelodies in violins and cellos denote equally well the primitive, the modernist, and—to us—the alien-sounding music of ancient Mexicans.

The final "Danza de tierra" (Dance of Earth) contains three melodies. This dance was included in the 1940 MoMA concert, and Herbert Weinstock, in his notes for the concert, explained that "this is the only section of the ballet in which use is made of musical themes Chávez had heard used by Indians in their religious dance of our own times. . . . Their

Example 5. *Los cuatro soles*, "Sol de aire," rehearsal no. 41, mm. 1–5.

distinction, their originality, leave no doubt that they are traditional and of very ancient origin."[55] The notes reproduce two of the dance's three themes. One is an asymmetrical, repetitive anhemitonic pentatonic melody; the other, shown in Example 6, a melody based on a descending major pentachord. A third melody, on a modal seven-pitch scale with a more Western, square-phrased structure, was not shown.[56] All are rhythmically simple, in the childlike fashion of "Danza de agua," as if to suggest the sincerity of the Aztecs' devotion to the goddess Centéotl, which is represented in this dance. The melody is accompanied in primitivist

Example 6. *Los cuatro soles*, "Sol de tierra," rehearsal no. 94, mm. 1–4.

homorhythm by parallel melodies that create pseudo-archaic, stacked open fifths, but also dissonant sevenths.

After failing to arrange the premieres of *El fuego nuevo* and *Los cuatro soles* in New York in 1927–28, Chávez finally conducted their first performances in Mexico City with his Orquesta Sinfónica de México on 4 November 1928 and 22 July 1930, respectively. Notably, neither the Aztec scenarios, nor the modernist style of the ballets went over well with audiences and critics. Audiences left, doors slammed, and critic Manuel Barajas, for example, wrote:

> The moment came to listen to "El Fuego Nuevo." . . . The composer and musicographer Aaron Coplan [*sic*] tells us about this work: "For the first time [Chávez] abandoned European influences and turned his eyes to his own country for inspiration. . . . Just as Debussy and Ravel reflect the French clarity, delicateness, ingenuity and spirit, so Chávez learnt to write music that reflects the spirit of Mexico." . . . I sincerely hope that Copelan [*sic*] is telling the truth and that his opinion is correct. As far as I am concerned . . . although there were moments in which listening to this ballet sent a shock down my back, in general, I sincerely confess that I did not understand. . . . [As for] the public: part of it applauded and acclaimed [the work], the other part remained perplexed, not knowing what to do.[57]

Such was the audience's reticence that Chávez did not insist.[58] Their puzzlement and coldness were in part caused by the music's lack of any audible referent in the Mexican soundscape. Moreover, composers and audiences had by then already validated a nationalist trend based on mestizo popular music of the nineteenth century. In 1926 and 1927 musicians in Mexico City gathered in a congress and called for submissions of newly composed nationalist music for a competition that was won by José Rolón and Candelario Huízar. In contrast to Chávez's epic re-presentation of the Aztec as the Mexican, Rolón's *El festín de los enanos* and Huízar's *Imágenes* are pieces of a rather intimate nature, based on children's stories and rural weddings and landscapes, and Mexican audiences received them enthusiastically.[59]

A second cause was the ballet's modernist style. Chávez, as a result of the style of his own works, the image of himself he presented to the public, and his programming of at least one twentieth-century composition in each concert of the OSM's first season was considered the most radical of Mexico's composers, and the task he undertook of "promoting, even imposing (that is the way it should be) new music" upon Mexican audiences was seen as a crusade against Mexico's traditional backwardness.[60] From the beginning the audience for the OSM was intensely polarized, and as late as 1934 critic Salomón Kahan noted that the public "seems to have developed a tradition of hissing the works of Carlos Chávez."[61]

Chávez let ten years pass between the composition of *Los cuatro soles* and his next Indianist piece, the far better known *Sinfonía india*, composed in New York in 1935 on an invitation from William Paley to write a work to be premiered over the CBS radio network.[62] Written in a single movement, *Sinfonía india* is a formally innovative, modern symphony based on sonata-form principles but also containing elements of a multi-movement cycle. First and second themes are exposed in the tonic and subdominant, respectively, and developed immediately. In turn, the development section (Poco lento) has its own new theme and acts like a slow middle movement inserted into an ongoing sonata structure. The themes are not developed motivically, but rather are restated several times in all their extension with increasingly complex contrapuntal textures and varying orchestrations that include the use of several indigenous musical instruments. The recapitulation presents first and second themes in the tonic and a coda containing elements of the introduction. Chávez adds a Finale in the subdominant, however, that subverts the teleological orientation of sonata forms.

The repetitiveness and rich and colorful counterpoint operate as signifiers of non-European musical practices—of heterophony in general

Example 7a. Preuss and Hornbostel, transcription of Cora song, "The Course of the Sun."

and at times of the indigenous "pipe and drum" performance practice. The first section of the second theme, for example, is exposed, *cantando*, by the E-flat clarinet over an arpeggiated countermelody in the B-flat clarinet, and a simple, binary rhythmic figure in the tenor drum that nevertheless introduces a 3-against-2 opposition with the triplets in the theme (rehearsal nos. 27–28, mm. 1–8 in the score). In the Poco lento, the flutes, oboes, and E-flat clarinets deliver the theme majestically, over a quasi-hypnotic steady rhythm in the strings, percussion, trumpets, and harp (rehearsal nos. 47–52). The *fortissimo* in the woodwinds, the dissonant, pseudo-archaic quartal harmony, and the presence of the harp create an intense yet contained climax, reminiscent of Chávez's Greek-tragedy inspired *Sinfonía de Antígona* (1933). The Finale is characterized by a driving rhythmic impulse, and crescendos at the end of each section led critic Olin Downes to speak of this piece's "savage reiteration" and "barbaric rhythmism."[63]

During the years that Chávez was the head of the Conservatorio and the Departamento de Bellas Artes, the Secretaría de Educación Pública commissioned several musicians close to him, including Sandi and Francisco Domínguez, to do research on indigenous communities.[64] Probably as a result of the increased ethnographic activity around him, in *Sinfonía india* Chávez used melodies from contemporary indigenous groups that have no relation to the Aztec civilization.[65] The symphony's first theme is one of the Cora melodies recorded by Preuss in 1905 (see Example 7a).[66] This melody is in B-flat major and has several phrases of irregular length. In the symphony, Chávez gives the time signature as 3/2, as opposed to the

Example 7b. *Sinfonía india*, rehearsal no. 9, mm. 1–5.

compound 6/4 also suggested by Preuss and Hornbostel, which would give the melody a dance-like character. Yet Chávez does suggest a 6/4 meter in the percussion's rhythmic figures, and then further complicates this polymeter by accentuating the initial trumpets' line on every third eighth note, as if in a 12/8 time signature (Example 7b).

For the second theme and that of the Finale Chávez used the Seri melodies "I Coos" and "Jime Eeke," respectively, transcribed by Domínguez on a 1933 field trip to the Yaqui, Mayo, and Seri regions.[67] The second theme is a six-pitch, G-mode melody in gently flowing triplets, which Chávez sets in transparent textures. The borrowed theme of the Finale is one of the few collected by Domínguez that is based on an anhemitonic pentatonic collection. I have not been able to identify the source for the theme of the slow middle section, which is based on a minor pentachord.

Finally (and ironically, as Gerard Béhague states), the two sections of the work that we can be sure are entirely original—the introduction and coda—create a contrast with these tunes, being composed on anhemitonic pentatonic collections based on B-flat and E-flat.[68]

Thus Chávez, here again, built part of his most famous Indianist music on the European conception of non-European cultures as primitive. But by juxtaposing the contemporary modal and tonal melodies with his own pentatonic representation of the indigenous, Chávez creates an ideological dissonance that underscores the contradictions underlying his own theoretical assumptions, and in so doing subverts his construction from within. Indeed, Chávez's earlier search for a representation of Aztec music through pentatonicism is still present. But this music stands on the margins while Chávez gives center stage to contemporary indígenas and their newer melodies. What is most ironic about the *Sinfonía india*—this central piece of the "Aztec Renaissance"—is that at its core lies a mestizo, post-Conquest music: the music of twentieth-century indígenas.

The first performance of the *Sinfonía india* in Mexico, on 31 July 1936, was very well received. The preseason publicity had been intended to bring about precisely this reaction, and evidently it worked. But Chávez's audience could not be so easily manipulated. More important reasons for the success of the symphony probably lay in the fact that, for the first time, Chávez had presented his audience with an audibly tonal composition, driven by rhythm, but built around either energetic or emotionally moving modal melodies, with beautiful orchestral colors and the kind of rhythmic complexity that despite its polyrhythms and constant cross-relations between binary and ternary rhythmic patterns remained anchored in a clear metric grid. Moreover, despite its innovative modified sonata form, the piece can be parsed aurally as a tone poem, with a fast-slow-fast ternary structure that Mexican audiences found reflected their own inner moods.[69]

The Aztec or the contemporary indigenous have never been the preferred representation of the Mexican for Mexican audiences and composers. And Chávez was not alone in his quest for signifiers of the indigenous in the 1920s; Antonio Gomezanda, Rolón, and Ponce imagined Aztec music as well.[70] But many of Chávez's signifiers, regardless of their historical and ethnological accuracy, or lack thereof, became standard musical symbols of the indigenous. Rhythmically simple, anhemitonic pentatonic melodies, set in clear textures over a steady binary rhythm, found their way into compositions by students and colleagues, either as the main material or as a passing allusion to the indigenous. For example, the moving but sober melodic style of the prelude to *Los cuatro soles* is central to Silvestre Revueltas's *Cuauhnáhuac*. And Candelario Huízar's two Indianist symphonies—"Oxpaniztli" and "Cora"—are inconceivable without Chávez's music, ideas, and activity at the helm of the OSM.

Chávez constructed the indigenous from outside, as having a homogeneous identity, and from a loving but nevertheless paternalistic perspective. Contradicting his avowed intention of revaluing Mexico's past, Chávez internalized a European conception of the pre-Columbian as the primitive other, and built some of his most famous music on this assumption. Thus his musical representation of the indigenous, and of the Aztec in particular, is loaded with contradictions and ambivalence. In my view, this makes his music all the more compelling. Nevertheless, as a historical agent, Chávez did what he set out to do. He gave Mexicans the means to imagine, should they so wish, both sober, modest, even stoic indigenous contemporaries—members of their own mestizo nation—and a glorious, striking pre-Columbian past.

NOTES

1. In the first chapter of *Music in Mexico* (New York: Thomas Y. Crowell, 1952), Robert Stevenson commented on the MoMA concert and on Chávez's role in Mexico's "changing attitudes towards ancient aboriginal music" in the 1920s (1–7). Stevenson called this period an "Aztec Renaissance," a name scholars have used thereafter.

2. Carlos Chávez, introduction to *Mexican Music: Notes by Herbert Weinstock for Concerts Arranged by Carlos Chávez as Part of the Exhibition Twenty Centuries of Mexican Art* (New York: Museum of Modern Art, May 1940), 5.

3. MoMA, press release for "Twenty Centuries of Mexican Art Being Assembled for the Museum of Modern Art," 21 February 1940, available at www.moma.org/momaorg/shared/pdfs/docs/press_archives/585/releases/MOMA_1940_0016_1940-02-20_40220-14.pdf.

4. The Spaniards called all native populations "indio(s)" for well-known reasons. Anthropologists use the more respectful noun "indígena(s)." In this essay I will use both "indígenas" and the more cumbersome "indigenous populations." Mexicans are of mixed race and stand in a racial continuum; depending on one's definition of indígena, and on how one slices the continuum, there are more or fewer indígenas in Mexico's population. For a concise and thought-provoking analysis of race relations in Mexico, see Alan Knight, "Racism, Revolution and Indigenismo," in *The Idea of Race in Latin America*, ed. with an Introduction by Richard Graham (Austin: University of Texas Press, 1990), 71–113.

5. Chávez, "Introduction," 9–10.

6. Ibid., 5.

7. Ibid., 8.

8. Carlos Chávez, *Xochipilli: An Imagined Aztec Music* (New York: Mills Music, 1964), 1, 2.

9. Aztecs are more properly known as Mexica. The most comprehensive catalog of Chávez's compositions and writings is Robert L. Parker, *Carlos Chávez: A Guide to Research* (New York: Garland, 1998).

10. Leonora Saavedra, "Carlos Chávez's Polysemic Style: Constructing the National, Seeking the Cosmopolitan," *Journal of the American Musicological Society* 68/1 (2015): 99–150.

11. In *Pirámide*, Chávez referred to pre-Columbian ideas about the origin of the world to represent the origins of humankind. Chávez also set to music two Nahuatl—the language of the Aztecs and their descendants—texts in *Lamentaciones* (in Spanish translation, 1962) and *Nonantzin* (1972).

12. Knight, "Racism, Revolution and Indigenismo," 72–75. See also R. Douglas Cope, *The Limits of Racial Domination: Plebeian Society in Colonial Mexico City, 1660–1720* (Madison: University of Wisconsin Press, 1994).

13. On liberalism in Mexico, see Richard Weiner, *Race, Nation, and Market: Economic Culture in Porfirian Mexico* (Tucson: University of Arizona Press, 2004); Charles A. Hale, *The Transformation of Liberalism in Late Nineteenth-Century Mexico* (Princeton: Princeton University Press, 1989).

14. See, for example, Dirk Raat, "Los intelectuales, el positivismo y la cuestion indígena," *Historia mexicana* 20 (1971): 412–27; and Moisés González Navarro, "Las ideas raciales de los científicos, 1890–1910," *Historia mexicana* 37 (1988): 565–83.

15. See Paul N. Edison, "Conquest Unrequited: French Expeditionary Science in Mexico, 1864–1867," *French Historical Studies* 26/3 (2003): 459–95; and Nancy N. Barker, "The Factor of 'Race' in the French Experience in Mexico, 1821–1861," *Hispanic American Historical Review* 59 (1979): 64–80.

16. Justo Sierra, "México social y político: Apuntes para un libro," *Revista nacional de ciencias y letras* 1 (1889): 13–19, 170–81, 213–20, 328–36, 371–80; and Andrés Molina Enríquez, *Los grandes problemas nacionales* (1909; repr., Mexico City: Era, 1981). Sierra responded, in particular, to Gustave LeBon, "L'influence de la race dans l'histoire," *Revue Scientifique*, third series, 15 (April 1888): 525–32; and Henry Summer Maine, *Popular Government* (London: John Murray, 1885).

17. Manuel Orozco y Berra, *Historia antigua y de la conquista de México* (Mexico City: Tipografía de Gonzalo Esteva, 1880); Alfredo Chavero, *Historia antigua y de la conquista*, vol. 1: *México a través de los siglos: Historia general y completa del desenvolvimiento social, político, religioso, militar, artístico, científico y literario de México. . .* , ed. Vicente Riva Palacio (Mexico City and Barcelona: Ballescá y compañía, 1887–89).

18. See, for example, Daniel Schávelzon, ed., *La Polémica del arte nacional en México, 1850–1910* (Mexico City: Fondo de Cultura Económica, 1988); Barbara Tenenbaum, "Streetwise History: The Paseo de la Reforma and the Porfirian State, 1878–1910," in *Rituals of Rule, Rituals of Resistance: Public Celebrations and Popular Culture in Mexico*, ed. William H. Beezley, Cheryl E. Martin, and William E. French (Wilmington, DE: Scholarly Resources, 1994), 127–50.

19. Manuel Gamio, *Forjando patria (pro nacionalismo)* (Mexico City: Librería de Porrúa Hermanos, 1916); José Vasconcelos, *La raza cósmica* (1925), in *Obras completas*, vol. 2 (Mexico City: Libreros Mexicanos Unidos, 1957–61), 903–1068; José Vasconcelos and Manuel Gamio, eds., *Aspects of Mexican Civilization* (Chicago: University of Chicago Press, 1926).

20. Mary Kay Vaughan, *State, Education, and Social Class in Mexico* (DeKalb: Northern Illinois University Press, 1982).

21. For a history of archeology and anthropology in Mexico, see José Lameiras, "La antropología en México: Panorama de su desarrollo en lo que va del siglo," in *Ciencias sociales en México: Desarrollo y perspectiva* (Mexico City: El Colegio de México, 1979), 107–80; Miguel Bernal, *Historia de la arqueología en México* (Mexico City: Porrúa, 1979).

22. For a critique of post-revolutionary anthropology and indigenismo, see Margarita Velasco, Arturo Warman et al., *De eso que llaman antropología mexicana* (Mexico City: Editorial Nuestro Tiempo, 1970); Guillermo Bonfil Batalla, *México profundo: Reclaiming a Civilization*, trans. Philip Adams Dennis (Austin: University of Texas Press, 1996); Judith Friedlander, "The National Indigenist Institute of Mexico Reinvents the Indian: The Pame Example," *American Ethnologist* 13 (1986): 363–67.

23. Ricardo Miranda, *Manuel M. Ponce: Ensayo sobre su vida y su obra* (Mexico City: CONACULTA, 1998); Leonora Saavedra, "Manuel M. Ponce y la canción mexicana," *Heterofonía* 42/142 (January–June 2010): 155–82.

24. Manuel M. Ponce, "El folklore musical mexicano: Lo que se ha hecho, lo que puede hacerse," *Revista musical de México* 1/5 (15 September 1919): 5–9.

25. See Alba Herrera y Ogazón, *El arte musical en México* (Mexico City: Dirección General de las Bellas Artes, 1917).

26. As a child Chávez had spent summers in the state of Tlaxcala, where he was exposed to indigenous musical performances. See Carlos Chávez, "Mexican Music" in *Renascent Mexico*, ed. Herbert Weinstock and Hubert Herring (New York: Covici Friede, 1935), 199–218, 209–10.

27. On Chávez's *Pazcola* and *El fuego nuevo,* see Leonora Saavedra, "Carlos Chávez's Polysemic Style," 109–113.

28. Chavero, *Historia antigua y de la conquista*, 795. All translations are mine.

29. The teponaztli or teponaxtle was a hollowed-out log into which two marimba-like tongues are made by incisions. The huéhuetl is a large, cylindrical one-patch drum.

30. Chavero, *Historia antigua y de la conquista*, 797.

31. See, for example, Eduard Seler, "Die holzgeschnitzte Pauke von Malinalco und das Zeichen Atl-Tlachinolli," in *Gesammelte Abhandlungen zur Amerikanischen Sprach- und Altertumskunde*, vol. 3 (Graz: Akademische Druck- u. Verlagsanstalt, 1960), 221–304.

32. Rubén M. Campos, "Los instrumentos musicales de los antiguos mexicanos," in *Anales del Museo Nacional de Arqueología, Historia y Etnografía*, 4th period, 3 (1925): 333–37. What Campos really meant to ask is whether the pre-Columbians had music as conceived in the Western world, as opposed to nonsensical noise. Campos's writings on the subject were later collected in his *El folklore y la música mexicana: Investigación acerca de la cultura musical en México (1525–1925)* (Mexico City: Secretaría de Educación Pública, 1928).

33. José G. Montes de Oca, *Danzas indígenas mejicanas* (Tlaxcala: Imprenta del Gobierno del Estado, 1926); Miguel Galindo, *Nociones de historia de la música mejicana* (Colima: El Dragón, 1931).

34. Daniel Castañeda, "Las flautas en las civilizaciones azteca y tarasca: 1. Civilización azteca," *Música: Revista mexicana* 8 (15 November 1930): 3–26; Castañeda, "Las flautas en las civilizaciones azteca y tarasca: 2. Civilización tarasca," *Música: Revista mexicana* 9–10 (December 1930–January 1931): 19–45; Castañeda and Vicente T. Mendoza, *Instrumental precortesiano: Investigaciones de la Academia de Música Mexicana del Conservatorio Nacional de Música* (Mexico City: Secretaría de Educación Pública, Publicaciones del Museo Nacional, 1933).

35. Between March 1933 and May 1934, Chávez took a leave from the CNM to become the head of the Departamento de Bellas Artes. Both were part of the Secretaría de Educación Pública (SEP).

36. Daniel Castañeda, "Las academias del Conservatorio N. de Música," *Música: Revista mexicana* 1 (April 1930): 6–13, 11.

37. See Alexander Rehding, "The Quest for the Origins of Music in Germany Circa 1900," *Journal of the American Musicological Society* 53/2 (2000): 345–85.

38. As archeological research has produced more sources it is now clear that pre-Columbian instruments could produce two- to seven-pitch diatonic scales, as well as chromatic and microtonal ones. See, for example, Samuel Martí and Gertrude Prokosch Kurath, *Dances of Anáhuac* (Chicago: Aldine Publishing, 1964). For a critique of Martí's historiographical premises, see Robert Stevenson, "Reflexiones sobre el concepto de música precortesiana en México," *Heterofonía* 114–15 (1996): 25– 37.

39. The possibilities of half-covering and double-stopping were not considered in any of these studies.

40. Castañeda, "Las flautas ... 1. Civilización azteca," 13.

41. Ibid., 14.

42. Castañeda, "Las flautas ... 2. Civilización tarasca," 29.

43. Ibid., 27.

44. Raoul and Marguerite d'Harcourt, *La musique indienne chez les anciens civilisés d'Amérique*, in *Encyclopédie de la musique et dictionnaire du Conservatoire*, part 1, 3337–71 (Paris: C. Delagrave, 1913–22); and *La musique des incas et ses survivances*, 2 vols. (Paris: P. Geuthner, 1925).

45. Carl Lumholtz, *Unknown Mexico: A Record of Five Years' Exploration Among the Tribes of the Western Sierra Madre, in the Tierra Caliente of Tepic and Jalisco, and Among the Tarascos of Michoacan*, 2 vols. (New York: Charles Scribner's Sons, 1902); Konrad Theodor Preuss, *Die Nayarit-Expedition: Textaufnahmen und Beobachtungen unter mexikanischen Indianern*, 2 vols. (Leipzig: B. G. Teubner, 1912).

46. Raoul and Marguerite d'Harcourt, *La musique des incas et ses survivances*, 217.

47. Ibid., 218–19. The authors had already advanced this argument in *La musique indienne*.

48. Ibid., 230.

49. Marguerite Béclard d'Harcourt, *Mélodies popularies indiennes (Équateur, Pérou, Bolivie): Recueil de 55 mélodies harmonisées* (Milan: Ricordi, 1923).

50. Stevenson, *Music in Mexico*, 6–7. I have not been able to locate the original lecture, which is quoted at length in Jesús C. Romero, "Música precortesiana," *Anales del Instituto Nacional de Antropología e Historia* 2 (1947): 229–57, 252–53. There are important differences between Stevenson's and Romero's versions of the lecture. For example, Stevenson's "a deep-seated and intuitive yearning for the minor" becomes in Romero "an intuitive knowledge of the minor chord."

51. Stevenson, *Music in Mexico*, 7.

52. The manuscripts for *El fuego nuevo* and *Los cuatro soles*, discussed below, are located at the New York Public Library for the Peforming Arts.

53. The ballet went through several revisions before arriving in its final form in 1930.

54. The *chirimía*, or Spanish shawm, was introduced by the Spaniards but has remained in use in post-Conquest indigenous cultures.

55. MoMA, *Mexican Music: Notes by Herbert Weinstock*, 31.

56. See Leonora Saavedra, "Of Selves and Others: Historiography, Ideology, and the Politics of Modern Mexican Music" (PhD diss., University of Pittsburgh, 2001), 294–300.

57. Manuel Barajas, "Crónicas musicales" (Mexico City), *El Universal*, 5 November 1928.

58. Chávez programmed his ballets only a few more times within a couple of years of their premiere. To my knowledge *El fuego nuevo* was never performed again. Chávez programmed an excerpt of *Los cuatro soles* in 1940, as seen, and recorded the full ballet in the mid-1960s. It was finally staged in Mexico City in 1951, with sets and costumes by Miguel Covarrubias and choreography by José Limón. The scores have not been published.

59. Ricardo Miranda, *José Rolón y su música* (Mexico City: CONACULTA, 2007); Saavedra, "Of Selves and Others," 187–95.

60. Manuel Casares, "Crónicas musicales: El cuarto concierto de la Sinfónica Mexicana," *Excélsior*, 14 December 1928.

61. Salomón Kahan, "Música," *El universal gráfico*, 22 June 1934.

62. On *Sinfonía india*, see Robert L. Parker, *Carlos Chávez: Mexico's Modern-Day Orpheus* (Boston: Twayne, 1983), 70–72; Roberto García Morillo, *Carlos Chávez: Vida y obra* (Mexico City: Fondo de Cultura Económica, 1960), 88–95.

63. Olin Downes, "Chávez Conducts Boston Orchestra," *New York Times*, 11 April 1936; and "Chávez Conducts 'La Mer,'" *New York Times*, 19 February 1937.

64. Domínguez and Sandi only collected music associated with ceremonies and communal feasts, and discarded all music making that did not agree with their notions of authenticity. Yet indigenous communities do have, then as now, rich expressive cultures into which they have rightly incorporated anything they have deemed suitable.

65. Chávez's program notes are unclear as to the provenance of the melodies he used.

66. Theodor K. Preuss and Erich M. von Hornbostel, "Zwei Gesänge der Cora Indianer," *Zeitschrift für Ethnologie* 6 (1906); repr. in Theodor K. Preuss, *Die Nayarit-Expedition: Textaufnahmen und Beobachtungen unter mexikanischen Indianern,* vol. 1: *Die Religion der Cora-Indianer in Texten nebst Wörterbuch Cora-Deutsch* (Leipzig: B. G. Teubner, 1912), 367–81.

67. Domínguez's report was published much later, in Baltasar Samper, Francisco Domínguez, Luis Sandi, and Roberto Téllez Girón, *Investigación foklórica en México: Materiales,* 2 vols. (Mexico City: Instituto Nacional de Bellas Artes, Departamento de Música, 1962). The melodies Chávez used can be found in vol. 1, 204 and 208.

68. Gerard Béhague, *Music in Latin America: An Introduction* (Englewood Cliffs, NJ: Prentice Hall, 1979), 136.

69. See Gerónimo Baqueiro Foster, "Por el mundo de la música: La Orquesta Sinfónica de México," *Excélsior*, 3 August 1936; Manuel Barajas, "Música y músicos: Soberbia inauguración de la temporada de la Orquesta Sinfónica de México," *El Nacional*, 6 August 1936; and Victor Reyes, "La música en México y en el extranjero," *El Universal Ilustrado*, 13 August 1936.

70. See, among other compositions, Ponce, *Canto y danza de los antiguos mexicanos*; Antonio Gomezanda, *Xiutzitzquilo*; and Rolón, *Cuauhtémoc*.

Non-Repetition and Personal Style in the *Inventions* and *Solis*

AMY BAUER

Recent scholarship shows how the indigenous, neoclassical, and avant-garde elements of Chávez's early music reflect a complex network of allegiances.[1] But little has been written about the later music, especially the challenging chamber works that demonstrate the composer's continuing interest in a high modernist style that challenges listener and performer alike. As Chávez entered the 1960s and continued to teach and conduct ever more widely, his compositional output followed two divergent tracks: traditional works intended for large ensembles and familiar venues, and experimental compositions that—with several exceptions—were written for solo instrument or small ensembles. This chapter looks at the later *Solis* for chamber ensembles (*Soli II*, 1961, and *Soli IV*, 1966) and the *Inventions* for piano (1958), string trio (1965), and harp (1967), works that occupy a singular position within Chávez's late output.[2]

The abstract language and forms of the *Solis* and *Inventions* attempt to forge a personal, progressive compositional legacy that resists imitation, capitulation to neoclassical formulas, or "repetition" in its broadest sense, distinct from the more fulsome language of the symphonies and dramatic works that preceded them. In these works Chávez explored a central idea first sketched in *Soli I* but now pursued within the context of an advanced harmonic language, one indebted to twelve-tone technique but only intermittently serial. *Soli I*, written for an unconventional ensemble of oboe, clarinet, bassoon, and trumpet, was commissioned in 1933 for the New York League of Composers and exhibited clear allegiances to jazz and native Mexican influences akin to other works of the 1930s. But it also represented one of the composer's first attempts at non-repetitive writing. *Soli I* reflected a desire to forgo traditional techniques such as sequence, development, and structural symmetry in favor of a kind of endlessly unfolding counterpoint. Chávez's linear progressions left behind the mnemonic signposts of Wagnerian endless melody for a constantly evolving musical discourse that favored "the element of renewal rather than repetition."[3]

In 1958–59 Chávez held the Charles Eliot Norton Chair of Poetics at Harvard University. The fourth of the Harvard lectures, which were collectively published in 1961, was devoted entirely to "Repetition in Music."[4] Here Chávez analyzed rhythm and symmetry in all of its musical forms with copious examples, from the two-note motive of Beethoven's Ninth Symphony, through the vagaries of meter and metric feet, to the principles that structure a symphonic movement. But Chávez chose to close the essay on a more philosophical note, one that considers the future of music and repetition in general. If Beethoven's Ninth Symphony pointed toward a new music, it is partly because the composer finally relinquished a mechanical play with motive to explore continuous melodic expression.[5] Hence Chávez valorizes non-repetition—the active expectation of newness—as a desirable, even ethical way forward, while "lazy memory," which relies on repetition, corresponds to a passive approach to life.[6] Against the common association of similarity and symmetry with the "good," and contrast and disorder with the "bad," Chávez advocates for the notion of "constant rebirth, of true derivation: a stream that never comes back to its source; a stream in eternal development, like a spiral, always linked to, and continuing, its original source, but always searching for new and unlimited spaces."[7]

All of the *Inventions* and the *Solis* partake of this spirit of "eternal development," which may explain some of their shared structural and harmonic traits. The former include the lack of breaks between sections, rapidly shifting rhythmic divisions, and a formal design determined more by tempo than texture or style. Chávez's harmonic language varies among the five featured works but relies in every work on the periodic use of major sevenths and minor ninths as harmonic intervals, as well as the contrast of whole-tone and chromatic harmonies—specifically the "Viennese" trichord (0, 1, 6)—to distinguish the shift from one phrase to another.[8]

The *Inventions*

As Robert Parker notes, a good 30 percent of Chávez's output was written for piano, reflecting the composer's long experience as a performer and improviser.[9] Hence the eighteen-minute, single-movement *Invención* suggests Chávez's comfort with exploring an early extended exercise in non-repetition for this instrument. *Invención,* written in 1958 and premiered in April of that year, fuses the rhythmic complexity of the Seven

Example 1. Hidden repetition in *Invención*, mm. 1–9.

Pieces (1923–30), the contrapuntal voice independence of the Ten Preludes 1937), and the extreme chromaticism of the 1949 Etudes, without any evident structural repetition.[10] *Invención* may appear to be based on a serial, ten-note subject, but it is written in a free atonal style, its only concession to its Baroque namesake being the primarily duple rhythmic divisions and the lack of clear section breaks. *Invención* is organized roughly by three expressive divisions (Con anima, mm. 1–183; Lento, mm. 184–238; Vivo, mm. 239–468), which are further demarcated by twenty-one finer tempo gradations. Each section shifts freely in texture, from the two voices that prevail in mm. 1–34 to three and four, and six-voice harmonies punctuate the close of each section (mm. 178, 210, and 461).

The *Invención* is thoroughly chromatic but not serial, adhering rigorously to the principle of non-repetition; duplication is restricted to extremely subtle recurring pitch and intervallic motives, as shown in an analysis of the opening "subject" in Example 1 (mm. 1–9).

At moments the work attains a certain modal clarity, as when tonal triads announce the first Pochissimo meno mosso, il tempo sempre giusto section in the bass (mm. 20–24), or float above that bass in the right hand (measure 28 and mm. 153–54). A clear diatonicism emerges at several points, before dissolving almost immediately into the prevailing chromatic.[11] Several grand Romantic gestures emerge during the Lento section (mm. 184–238), notably at mm. 204–5, measure 210, which rests for two beats on the hexatonic hexachord $HEX_{3,4}$, and mm. 213–15. The latter passage cadences on an implied D-seventh chord (asserted again within a six-voice D-eleventh harmony in measure 223), and the Lento closes with a stepwise descent in bass from G to C (mm. 236–38). Yet these moments are fleeting, mere glimpses of the type of homage to Chopin captured by the *Etudes* within an otherwise rigorous contrapuntal exercise. *Invención* approaches the coda through a rousing hocket-like passage that returns to the texture of the beginning, yet without the merest hint of a recapitulation (mm. 354–84).

Invention II for violin, viola, and cello, written seven years later, features the same type of kaleidoscopic melodic motion, but sets it within the context of a concertante texture that includes only occasional deviations in texture. Three movements and an extended coda are identified solely by tempo markings: Molto moderato (mm. 1–60), Molto lento (mm. 61–97), Vivo (mm. 98–181), and a closing Pochissimo meno mosso (mm. 182–217). As in the *Invención* for piano, slight figures recur in the background to shape the inexorable flow of the work: melodic chromatic and whole-tone trichords, the frequent appearance of the "Viennese" trichords (0, 1, 4) and (0, 1, 6), and the reappearance of the E/A fifth at the transition to a new section. For instance, the *Invention*'s "exposition" cadences with (0, 1, 6) in measure 25, followed by a transition that pits chromatic and whole-tone figures against one another to lead into a new section, as shown in Example 2 (mm. 25–31). Yet the second section commences in measure 30 with a twelve-tone canon launched in cello and composed of five successive rows.[12]

As the durations of each canonic voice are unique and never repeat, the lead voice is soon left behind; the end of the canon is signaled by the unison C_4–$D\flat_4$ in the upper strings (repeated as D_3–B_4 in cello), whereupon

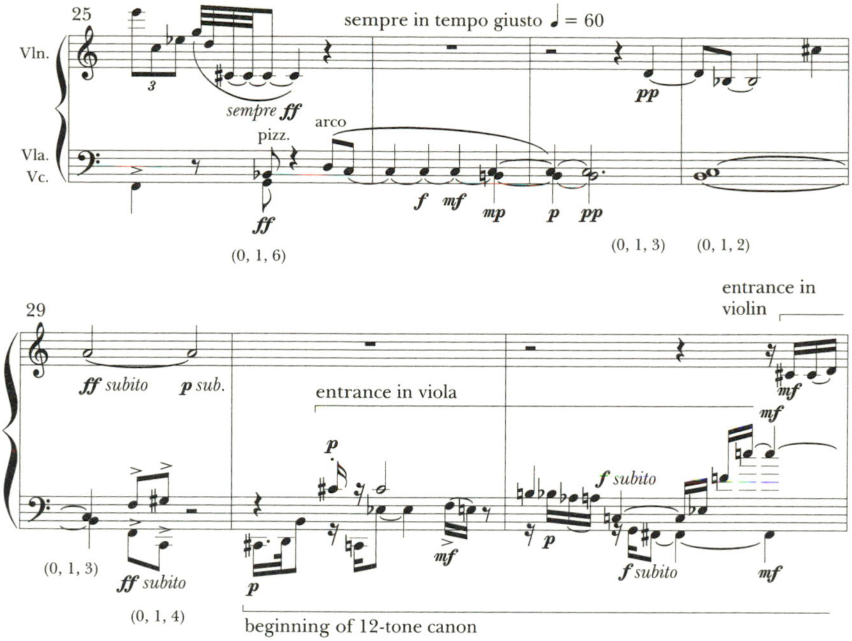

Example 2. First transition and beginning of canon in *Invention II*, mm. 25–31.

the *Invention* returns to the fantasia-like character of the opening. The first movement builds to a *furioso* climax in measure 60, pitting quintuplets against duple and sextuplet divisions of the beat, prior to the measure rest that signals the onset of the second movement. The Lento opens with series of four sustained chords, followed by a kind of faux imitation, involving all three strings in a continually evolving conversation, punctuated by diatonic and whole-tone vertical trichords that open up the harmonic texture.[13]

The Vivo begins with a twelve-tone solo in violin that dissipates into free atonality when joined by viola (measure 110); the viola soon abandons the violin for a duet with the cello in measure 123. A series of vertical harmonies slow the advance of the Vivo, beginning with a (0, 1, 3) trichord in the highest register in measure 134 (F_5–$G\flat_6$–E_7). The Vivo's central passage gives some idea of Chávez's approach to harmonic and rhythmic variation within the context of non-repetition. A delicate diatonic cadence in mm. 164–65 asserts a temporary focus on D. Yet this is followed by a series of rotating, non-repeating chromatic hexachords in an even half-note rhythm, which culminates in the single harmonic repetition of the series: pitch-class set (0, 1, 2, 4, 7, 8) (Forte's 6–z17, measure

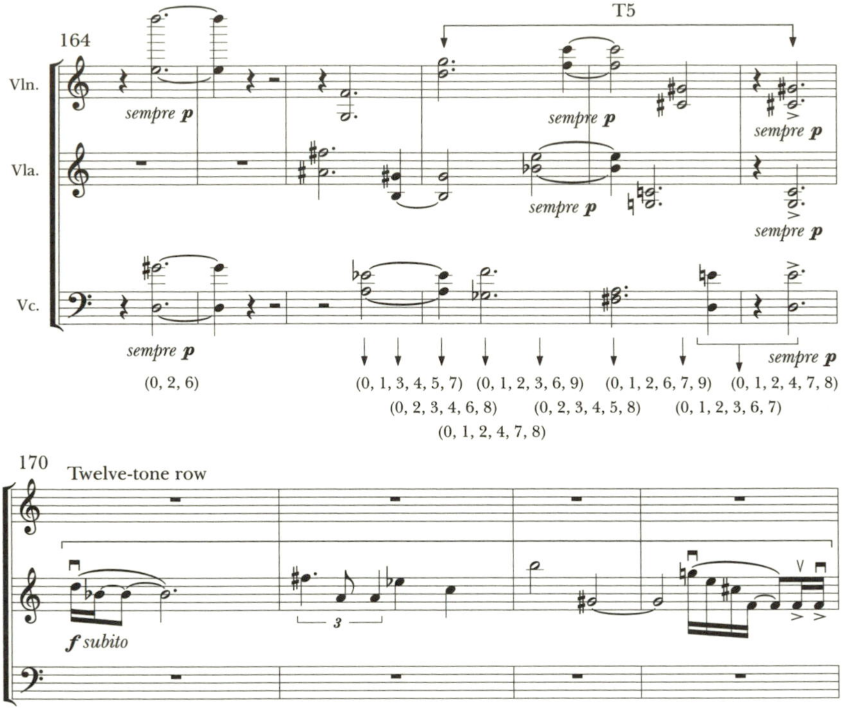

Example 3. Central passage in the Vivo, *Invention II*, mm. 164–73.

169). Here the viola launches a solo from D, once again articulating a twelve-tone row featuring nine different rhythmic values, as shown in Example 3.

The viola is joined by cello with an eleven-note row in cello (measure 175) en route to the Coda, which begins with an extended passage in harmonics on all three strings (mm. 182–94), after which the Pochissimo meno mosso continues with strummed quadruple stops in all voices punctuated by brief runs. The final harmonies shift from chromatic to hexatonic, accumulating pitches until reaching a ten-note chord at the close, voiced over the same low C that anchored the opening bass line in mm. 3–9.

Chávez completed the *Invention III* for solo harp, dedicated to Nadia Boulanger, in 1967. *Invention III* is a fascinating curio, as Chávez makes a virtue out of the limited chromatic possibilities available on the harp. The first nineteen bars run through every possible horizontal, vertical, and contrapuntal permutation of the [0, 1, 2, 3] tetrachord (spelled B♯, C♯, D, E♭), and the next twenty-three measures subject its transposition by semitone to the same endless variation (C♯, D, E♭, F♭). Various degrees

Example 4. Voice exchanges in *Invention III*, mm. 61–63.

of harmonic and melodic closure are distinguished by subtle variations in the registral placement and doubling of harmonic semitones and chromatic trichords. Tempo indications again mark out three unequal sections, the first of which closes on $C\sharp_2/D_3$ (measure 32), while the second, slower section ends on its inversion ($D_2/C\sharp_3$, measure 55). As the *Invention* progresses, larger sections are separated by a return to the opening tetrachord, or its transposition and abridgment to a dyad or trichord (as in mm. 72–112). The final section traces a web of voice exchanges between adjacent pitch classes, as shown in Example 4, and the central trichord gradually ascends in pitch from [2, 3, 5] to [6, 7, 9] (mm. 72–100). In formal terms the *Invention* traces an arc from B♯ to A, as the [6, 7, 9] trichord contracts and inches downward once again to close with the trichord that opened the work [1, 2, 3] in measure 128.

Soli II and *Soli IV*

Chávez gave the name *Soli* to a group of movements characterized by two features: each instrument of the movement receives a solo but without reducing its fellows to the role of mere accompaniment.[14] The second *Soli*, a quintet for winds, was commissioned in 1961 by the Inter-American Music Festival Executive Committee and premiered the same year by the Philadelphia Woodwind Quintet at the Second Inter-American Music Festival in Washington, D.C. The quintet would pick up the thread of *Soli I* almost three decades later, but discard its overt neoclassical and indigenous references in favor of a purist approach to the principle of non-repetition.[15]

Soli II relies much more heavily on twelve-tone techniques than either of the two chromatic *Inventions*. Although Chávez notes that a "minimal amount of repetition through symmetry is implied (almost ironically) by the designation of the movements as Sonatina, Rondo, Prelude, and

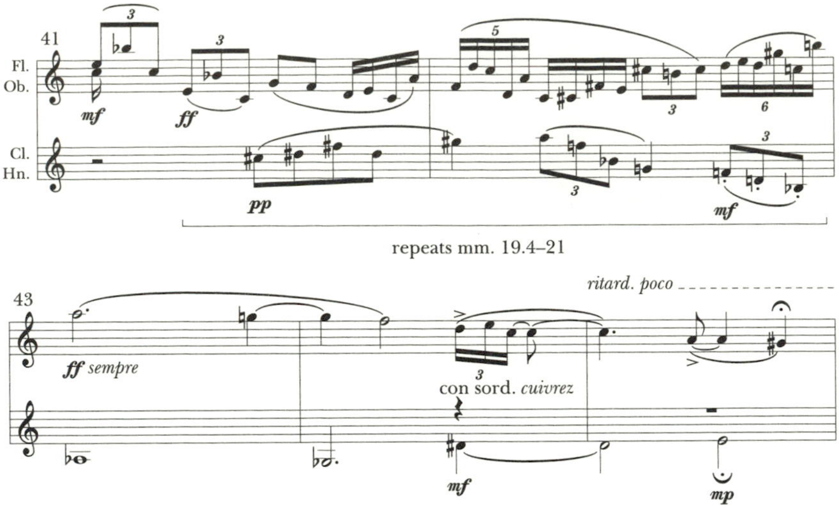

Example 5. Close of Preludio in *Soli II*, mm. 41–45 (reduction).

Aria," he does not mention that the Aria and Sonatina are based almost exclusively on all-combinatorial twelve-tone rows that carry their own inherent repetitive properties.[16] Much like the *Inventions*, *Soli II* contains no obvious section breaks, features concertante writing almost throughout, and establishes an arch form through shifts in tempo and rhythmic activity, relying—as in *Invention III*—on major sevenths and minor ninths to mark phrase closure. Unlike the *Inventions*, *Soli II* bears an obvious debt to Chávez's earlier neoclassical works, with contiguous movements identified with formal descriptors. And *Soli II* has a pronounced lyrical character, with a more relaxed approach to contrapuntal invention. Each movement features a different solo instrument, although there are few unaccompanied lines, and the poignant harmonies that shape its evolving form draw equally from diatonic and chromatic collections, although its harmonic language remains resolutely atonal.

The opening Preludio begins with an inverted wedge between flute and bassoon, but features flute throughout, traversing a range of styles punctuated by trichordal, diatonic cadences every four or five bars. The flute abandons a rhapsodic atonality for a climactic, fully twelve-tone melody in mm. 37–40, only to subside into a slightly altered repetition of three bars (mm. 19, beat 4–21) in mm. 41–42. This leads into a contrapuntal cadence with horn that introduces a major third over E as the closing harmony, as shown in a harmonic reduction as Example 5 (mm.

41–45). This third resolves into an E-seventh chord to begin the Rondo, which is cast in ABABCBAB form: A, mm. 46–53; B, mm. 54–91; A2, mm. 92–99; B2, mm. 100–15; C, mm. 116–37; B3, mm. 138–40; A3, mm. 141–45; B4, mm. 146–89.

The Rondo's refrain is characterized by staccato articulation, and—surprisingly—is repeated verbatim in A2 (A3 brings back only the final 5 measures of A). The B sections by contrast are denser, played legato, and feature terraced dynamics. These sections contain only minor, hidden repetitions, and are distinguished from C primarily by the latter's sparse texture, and the half-note three-chord punctuations played in hemiola prior to the return of A (at mm. 134–36 and 137). The final B section ends on two diatonic harmonies: a symmetrical (0, 1, 5, 6) tetrachord (measure 180), that shifts to a diatonic B–C♯–G♯ trichord (0, 2, 5) before fading to B–C♯ to introduce the Aria (mm. 182–89).

The bassoon picks up the C♯ that ends the Rondo, yet continues it with a twelve-tone solo that launches the Aria. The solo runs through each form of the row: R1, followed by P1, I1, and RI1, before dissolving as the flute joins the bassoon in canon.[17] Trichordal partitions of the row produce three (0, 1, 6) harmonies, and the whole-tone trichord, which suggests a dominant harmony (0, 2, 6); thus the Aria has a homogenous harmonic character defined by the tritone and its transposition or suspension. This may explain why Chávez places a rare emphasis on one pitch class—B♭, sustained by flute and clarinet in mm. 210–16—to anchor the Aria, although the movement's form is again defined primarily by tempo and texture, as it moves from largo (♩ = 46–48) to piu mosso (♩ = 60) and back.

The main theme of the Sonatina references the atonal lyricism of the Preludio and Rondo, and its subordinate theme is constructed with an all-combinatorial row beginning on the pitch-class B. As in the Rondo, the primary theme returns almost exactly in the recapitulation, and the subordinate theme returns in transposition. The Sonatina's featured instrument is clarinet, which opens the exposition with a sprightly main theme, one that includes a five-note chromatic scale motive that recurs throughout the exposition (mm. 242–67), as shown in a harmonic reduction of the opening three bars, Example 6.

By contrast, the subordinate theme (mm. 267–92) is more lyrical, relying—as in the Aria—on all four forms of its combinatorial row (P11, I11, R11, RI11), and—once again—including a brief canon, this time between clarinet and bassoon. The development (mm. 292–339) references both main and subordinate themes, bringing back P11, I11, and RI11 forms of the row, while the recapitulation reintroduces the subordinate theme

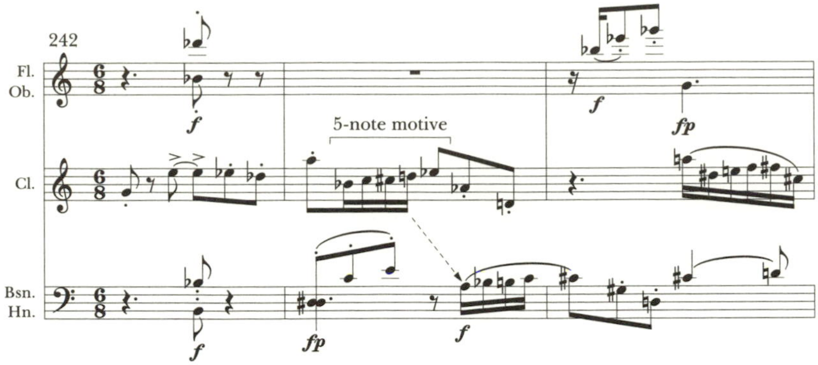

Example 6. Opening of Sonatina, *Soli II*, mm. 242–44.

with its inversion and retrograde inversion at the perfect fourth (I4 and RI4). The clarinet returns to the main theme in the coda (mm. 390–406).

The Finale traces a slow arch form as a showcase for horn, beginning with a high neighbor figure on B–C♯–B succeeded by an elegant descent. Plaintive harmonies mark regular cadences (mm. 411, 414, 417) before shifting to a concerted section with horn, which precedes the ensemble's slow march to the cadence in measure 440. The suite-like construction of *Soli II* suggests a reversion to neoclassical archetypes. Yet its five movements skillfully mask the repetition of slight motives and row forms within the constantly evolving dialogue based on the principle of non-repetition that characterizes all of Chávez's works.

The challenges of composing an extended work with this principle come into sharper focus in the later *Soli IV* for brass trio, as they did in the second *Invention*. *Soli IV* for French horn, trumpet, and trombone was commissioned in 1964 by Mario di Bonaventura for the Hopkins Center Congregation of the Arts Festival at Dartmouth College. Chávez's claim that "it has about it a rather special kind of 'atonality'" is a bit ingenuous, given *Soli IV*'s severe chromatic language.[18] The quasi-serial, seven-note "row" that begins the work in the trombone is composed of the chromatic segment E–E♭–D–C♯–G–G♯–F♯. Yet *Soli IV* soon reveals itself as a cousin of the *Invention* for harp. Although *Soli IV* employs a free circulation of the total chromatic, Chávez works primarily with four- or five-note chromatic segments within a given passage. As in the *Inventions* and *Soli II*, sections are determined primarily by tempo markings and slight shifts in texture and style. Occasional instrumental solos are overshadowed by the constant interplay among ensemble members. This evolving melodic interplay is punctuated frequently by sharp vertical harmonies, which

Example 7. A pointillistic texture gives way to chords in *Soli IV*, mm. 119–25.

consist almost universally of the chromatic trichord (0, 1, 2), with (0, 1, 3) preceding it on occasion to form a two-chord "cadence." Each section of *Soli IV* is introduced by trumpet or trombone, and the entire work boasts continual shifts in articulation (including muted passages and glissandi) and a quasi-serial use of terraced dynamics.

Whereas the lyrical first section is moderately paced, the following section strikes a lively tone (mm. 30–42). Announced by trumpet, the second section includes frequent repeated notes and hocket-like rhythmic interplay. Sections identified at mm. 43 and 85 continue in the same vein, until the pause in measure 92 that precedes the penultimate section. Here a *subito* attack in trombone leads to a long glissando cadenza (mm. 100–103) that introduces a slow final section (♩ = 50). A second long glissando in trombone leads into a pointillistic section (measure 112), succeeded by sedate, homorhythmic chords (measure 124). A harmonic reduction of this section shows how the pitch travels resolutely by chromatic step toward and away from dissonant cadence points (Example 7).

The passage launches an evenly paced cycle through varied dynamics and articulations that culminates in a third, measured trombone glissando that ends the work with a final (0, 1, 2) harmony: trombone on high E♭$_5$, joining the trumpet's F$_5$ over E$_4$ in horn. As in the *Invention* for harp, chromatic dyads, trichords, and melodic segments travel through every possible registral permutation, aided by a volley of distinct articulations; this confined harmonic language, in the context of a trio, serves to bring the individual character of each instrument and its expressive qualities more clearly to the fore.

Reflecting on his earlier career in the Harvard Norton Lectures, Chávez stated: "To try to be 'national' seemed a good way to try to be personal."[19] The chamber works of the late 1950s and 1960s represented a new notion of the personal for the composer, coming as they did at the height of his international influence and renown. If, as Chávez wrote at the close of "Repetition in Music," "The man, his character, what he has to say, his need for communication, all these are in the last analysis the ensemble of deep causes that determine unity and cohesion in a work of art," then progress and the pursuit of a personal style were synonymous.[20] The pursuit of unity and cohesion in art become the measure of an artist's character. Both meet in the composition of a music like that found in the *Inventions* and the *Solis*: a music that renounces the repetition of past styles, conventions, and iconic identities in favor of a unique approach, one dedicated to a singular, constantly evolving musical fabric that expresses the personal in the spirit of the universal.

NOTES

1. See especially Alejandro L. Madrid, *Sounds of the Modern Nation: Music, Culture, and Ideas in Post-Revolutionary Mexico* (Philadelphia: Temple University Press, 2008); and Carol A. Hess, *Representing the Good Neighbor: Music, Difference, and the Pan American Dream* (Oxford: Oxford University Press, 2013).

2. *Soli III*, as an orchestral work, will not be addressed here, although it does feature a concertante group consisting of bassoon, trumpet, viola, and timpani as continually interacting "soloists."

3. Carlos Chávez, liner notes to *Soli I/ Soli II/ Soli IV*, Odyssey LP, Y31534 (1972).

4. Carlos Chávez, *Musical Thought* (Cambridge: Harvard University Press, 1961).

5. Ibid., 80.

6. Ibid., 82.

7. Ibid., 84.

8. Pitch-class sets follow the conventions established in Allen Forte, *The Structure of Atonal Music* (New Haven: Yale University Press, 1974). Distinct octatonic and hexatonic collections are identified by a subscript denoting the first unique semitone in each collection when counting upward from C (0), e.g., $OCT_{0,1}$ denotes the collection that contains C and C♯/D♭ [0, 1, 3, 4, 6, 7, 9, 10]. Square brackets refer to pitch-class sets in normal form (the pitch classes as found in the score), and parentheses indicate pitch-class sets reduced to prime form.

9. Robert L. Parker, *Carlos Chávez: Mexico's Modern-Day Orpheus* (Boston: Twayne, 1983), 33.

10. William Masselos premiered the *Invención* on 14 April 1958 in Cambridge, Massachusetts. Parker lists an earlier unofficial premiere by Masselos at La Maison Française in New York. Ibid., 40.

11. A diatonic B-flat-major collection appears in measure 37, and in measure 40, a G-major collection resolves into D. Other diatonic moments occur at measure 61, mm. 67–78, and mm. 118–19.

12. The canon begins with a row built on a hexachord combinatorial at T_9I [11, 0, 1, 2, 3, 5], followed by a row built on the all-combinatorial chromatic hexachord. The canon then returns to the same hexachord as at the beginning, but in a different order; the fourth and fifth rows duplicate that same row with hexachords switched on each repetition. As in Webern's practice, the end of each row shares a pitch with the beginning of the next, and several rows feature occasional, Schoenbergian "swapped" dyads; that is, F–G becomes G–F.

13. The Lento opens with two symmetrical harmonies: the Dorian hexachord on C (mm. 62–63, [0, 2, 4, 5, 6, 8]) and the major-minor tetrachord (measure 67, [3, 6, 7, 9]), followed by the unrelated hexachords [4, 6, 7, 8, 9, 0] and [4, 6, 7, 9, E, 0].

14. Chávez, liner notes, *Soli I/ Soli II/ Soli IV*.

15. The relation of *Soli I* to *Soli II* is explored in Lyman Bruce Blanton, "Two Chamber Works of Carlos Chávez which Include Clarinet: Soli 1 and Soli 2" (DMA diss., University of South Carolina, 1998).

16. Chávez, liner notes, *Soli I/ Soli II/ Soli IV*.

17. Rows are identified by the pitch-class number that begins each referential P (prime) and I (inversion) form. R (retrograde) and RI (retrograde inversion) are identified by their final pitch class.

18. Chávez, liner notes, *Soli I/ Soli II/ Soli IV*.

19. Chávez, *Musical Thought*, 14.

20. Ibid., 84.

Music and the Marketplace: On the Backstory of Carlos Chávez's Violin Concerto

DAVID BRODBECK

> I am delighted to learn that your Concerto for Violin and Orchestra is at last to receive its New York premiere. Naturally, I am sorry that the team to present it is Leonard Bernstein and Henry Szyring [*sic*] instead of Carlos Chávez and Viviane Bertolami. I would like the music to get the reading it deserves.
>
> —Murray D. Kirkwood to Carlos Chávez, 30 August 1965

In January 1947 Carlos Chávez received a letter out of the blue from a man named Murray D. Kirkwood, a public relations writer for International Telephone and Telegraph in New York (IT&T). It brought the offer of a commission to write a violin concerto for the professional debut of Kirkwood's twenty-year-old wife, Viviane Bertolami, who was about to complete her study with Efrem Zimbalist at the Curtis Institute of Music.[1] Seeking to assure Chávez of his wife's credentials, Kirkwood made mention of her earlier appearances with the Boston Pops Orchestra (1943) and the Quebec Symphony (1946) and reported Zimbalist's conviction that she was a violinist to whom Chávez "could deliver his music with all confidence." Of himself he wrote:

> I am not a wealthy man, for I am only one of the editors of a magazine published by my employer. I enclose a copy . . . that was recently published on Mexico. Nevertheless, I have my savings and can borrow a little if necessary. . . . Should you be so kind as to write the concerto for my wife, I will pay you and be certain that she could not have a happier inspiration for her professional career than to begin it with the music of Carlos Chávez.

The magazine in question was the *International Review*, an IT&T house organ, and Kirkwood was no doubt counting on drawing Chávez's attention to his lead article "Mexico: Phoenix of the Americas," published in the issue of November 1946. This offered a bird's-eye view of the history of Mexico from the pre-Columbian era to the presidency of Manuel Ávila Camacho, then entering its final weeks. Although Kirkwood focused on the social, political, and economic realms, his opening sentence suggests it was Mexico's contemporary cultural life that had stimulated his use of the metaphor of a Phoenix reborn—and perhaps also the idea of whom to commission for the concerto: "Anyone who explores Mexico beyond the beaten path or, without leaving home, listens to music by Carlos Chávez or looks at paintings by Diego Rivera or José Clemente Orozco, finds himself drawn to the conclusion that in modern Mexico, the Americas have produced their first indigenous culture since the days of the Aztecs."[2]

If Kirkwood hoped the story of his relatively modest personal circumstances, combined with flattery, might lower Chávez's asking price, he was mistaken: when the composer tentatively accepted the commission in his reply of 1 February, he set his fee at $2,500. (This was $500 more than Benny Goodman paid Chávez's friend Aaron Copland for his Clarinet Concerto around the same time. Goodman later recalled that even $2,000 was considered "good money" in those days.)[3] Chávez promised to deliver the concerto by 1 November 1947, gave the violinist exclusive performing rights for the 1948–49 and 1949–50 concert seasons, and reserved the copyright in his own name and the right to publish the work with whomever he chose.

Meanwhile Kirkwood arranged to meet Arthur Judson, the powerful head of Columbia Concerts, Inc., and the manager of the New York Philharmonic.[4] We cannot know exactly what was said in this meeting, and it may be that neither man was entirely forthcoming. But the probable gist of their discussion can be pieced together from letters they exchanged later that year.[5] Kirkwood hoped Judson would agree to represent his wife and help launch her career with Chávez's concerto. Judson seems to have promised nothing, but he did offer some advice. Perhaps doubting the broad appeal of Chávez's music, he suggested considering someone else for the commission, mentioning Bohuslav Martinů, Erich Wolfgang Korngold, and Louis Gruenberg as composers who had recently written concertos that had done well in the United States. Kirkwood, in turn, asked whether having a concerto by Chávez would position his wife to begin her career with a tour of South America as a buildup to her debut in the United States. Judson responded by saying such a tour would be easier to bring off if Chávez gave the premiere of the work with his Orquesta Sinfónica de México (OSM) but apparently did not agree to arrange the tour or any subsequent appearances in the United States.

Kirkwood gave Chávez only a limited briefing on this conversation in a letter of 25 February 1947: "I have discussed with . . . Judson . . . the possibility of a South American tour for my wife, in order to introduce your concerto throughout the hemisphere. He points out the extreme importance, in that case, of giving the work its world-premiere performance in Mexico City, under your direction." To the conditions set out in Chávez's letter of 1 February, Kirkwood now added a new one of his own in line with Judson's advice regarding the premiere. Never imagining the composer would not agree to this, Kirkwood closed in expectation of an imminent coming to terms: "Neither my wife nor I has any wish to limit you in any way regarding the nature of your composition. However, it may interest you to know that, of your works which we have heard, our favorite is *Sinfonía India*."

Kirkwood must have been surprised to learn from the composer's reply of 18 March that Chávez would turn down the commission if it were tied to accepting Judson's suggestions. What Kirkwood could not have known was that Chávez was already looking for a way to dissolve the OSM and was therefore in no position to promise to perform with it any work he had not yet even begun to write. Moreover, although he said nothing to indicate this, it seems likely the composer would have bristled at the plan of using a South American tour to build interest in performances in the United States because it smacked of Pan-Americanism. Chávez wanted nothing to do with this ideology of postwar hemispheric solidarity under the leadership of the United States in its battle against Communism. He saw himself as a modern composer, and not a particularly Latin American one, and certainly not one looking for a friendly welcome by the "good neighbor" to the north on the basis of Pan-Americanism.[6]

Responding on 21 March, Kirkwood expressed his disappointment, especially since, as he now put it, Judson had declared a Mexican premiere under the composer's direction to be a necessary condition in order to arrange a South American tour and later appearances with major orchestras in the United States. (Here Kirkwood seems to have conflated what Judson said about the first performance with his own more encompassing plans for what might ensue from it.) Nevertheless, Kirkwood agreed to Chávez's terms, subject to his wife's approval of the finished concerto in both the violin-piano and orchestral scores. This new condition was made necessary, he implied, because he could find no manager who would guarantee a performance of the concerto in the United

States without first seeing the score, since Chávez was not known for his violin music. (Here Kirkwood was probably thinking of Judson's comments about Chávez vis-à-vis Martinů, Korngold, and Gruenberg.) For the composer this settled matters, since, as he wrote back on 31 March, he did not accept commissions subject to approval when submitted and thus considered the matter closed.

But then the story took an unexpected turn—and probably a fateful one, as we shall see. Judson's opinion was not something to be taken lightly. In a recent article, which Kirkwood could not have missed, the *New York Times* had with good reason called him "the most powerful figure in the music business."[7] Through Concert Management Arthur Judson, Inc. (one of seven divisions of Columbia Concerts), Judson managed the careers of nearly every leading conductor working in the United States as well as many of the soloists to whom they might offer engagements. Even knowing this, Kirkwood decided to take a gamble. "I am about to pit my judgment against that of Mr. Judson," he explained to Chávez in a letter of 4 April. "My wife and I are agreed that, if it should come to a choice between you and Judson, we would choose you." At least this way, he added, "we shall have a concerto which will be an inspiration to my wife and to everyone else who knows great music when he hears it—that is, if you are still willing to undertake the concerto upon your original terms." Hoping to seal the deal, he even made those terms more favorable to the composer by extending the deadline for submission to January 1948.

In his reply, dated 21 April, Chávez not only assented to the revised terms but also unexpectedly raised Kirkwood's hopes regarding the premiere: "I cannot promise to arrange that Viviane Bertolami play the concerto with the Orquesta Sinfónica de México, but if it appears possible to [do so], I would be happy to engage her." Delighted by this news, Kirkwood sent the agreed-upon down payment of $1,250 on the composer's fee. In the letter accompanying the check, dated 25 April, Kirkwood implicitly encouraged Chávez to hold nothing back: "I should tell you my wife's musical allegiances waver between Bach sonatas for the violin and boogie-woogie Harlem jazz for the piano. In other words, she takes her music straight, by preference. That is why we both like yours."

Writing three days later, Kirkwood updated Judson on all the recent developments:

> Your advice regarding the possible reaction of our musical public to violin concertos by Chávez, Martinů, Korngold, and Gruenberg forced my wife and me to face a vital fact: namely that we would rather gamble upon success with Chávez than

> to purchase a sure thing with any one of the other three. So, we definitely commissioned him last week. The man's integrity impresses us. He refused to accept the commission without the premiere attached, as you know. But, now that we have commissioned him without it, he takes pains to indicate its possibility.[8]

Details regarding rental fees and possession of the full score during the two-year period of Bertolami's exclusive rights to the work remained to be settled over the next several weeks, but matters were finally brought to a warm and gracious conclusion in Kirkwood's letter to Chávez of 10 June:

> Your patience has so often overcome the barriers of distance, language, and letters—to say nothing of prospective managers—that my wife and I like to think of you as a friend. . . . During these last weeks, when we more than half expected you to abandon the Concerto, we found comfort and hope by listening to your *Sinfonía India*, *Sinfonía de Antígona*, and your arrangement of the Buxtehude *Chaconne*. That hope has been justified, and we look upon the future with renewed confidence—thanks to you.[9]

Where Is Chávez?

As the months passed, Chávez missed deadline after deadline to complete the work. It is not difficult to imagine why. Administrative duties associated with the OSM had long absorbed much of his time and energy, and the strain placed on his compositional activity had only grown more acute since January 1947, when, in the very month in which Kirkwood offered the commission, Chávez accepted an appointment by Miguel Alemán, Mexico's newly elected president, to be the founding director of the Instituto Nacional de Bellas Artes (INBA). In light of this, it was wishful thinking on his part to accept a commission to provide Bertolami with a concerto that she could use for her debut during the 1948–49 season. In fact, Chávez failed to complete the work in time for performance during either of the two seasons thereafter.

The Kirkwoods were remarkably patient in the face of the long delay in delivery, especially in view of all that was riding on the commission. To make the best of a bad situation, Chávez sent Bertolami installments of the music as these were completed in violin-piano score, beginning with the first, on 4 March 1948.[10] Although the composer gave the Kirkwoods to believe the work would be completed by the end of the summer, this deadline too passed without further word or music. Finally, in a letter of 4 November 1948, Kirkwood made a polite yet clearly concerned inquiry. It may well have been a guilty conscience about his failure to deliver the concerto as promised that finally convinced Chávez the moment had come to be free of his administrative burdens once and for all and devote himself at last to his creative activity. In a letter of 17 November to his New York publicist, Herbert Barrett, the composer announced his intention to resign his position at INBA and to suspend the OSM.[11] Updating Kirkwood on the same day, Chávez promised to step down soon from his position at INBA and to turn his attention to the commission at hand. (He said nothing about his plan to suspend the OSM, however, perhaps not wanting to let on that no performance with that group would ever be possible.)[12]

In March 1949 Chávez resigned his position as director of the OSM after twenty-one years, and the orchestra ceased operations. In a subsequent burst of activity, the composer was able to dispatch the next section of the concerto at the end of that month. Chávez finally met the Kirkwoods for the first time in September 1949, during one of his frequent visits to New York, and used that opportunity to coach Viviane and her accompanist, Harry Kondaks, on the music they had received thus far. But thereafter work slowed once more, owing no doubt to Chávez's failure to follow through on his planned resignation from INBA, where he remained through the end of Alemán's presidency in 1952.[13] Bertolami thus went without any continuation of the concerto until April 1950, when Chávez sent the third installment. This included the cadenza, but, as the violinist would soon learn, there was still a good deal of music to come, albeit nothing that was entirely new. With the end finally in sight, the Kirkwoods joined Chávez in June for a week in his home in Acapulco to work out the details of Viviane's interpretation.

What Chávez finally produced was a long and structurally complex work, a far cry indeed from the colorful and compact *Sinfonía india* that had initially sparked the Kirkwoods' interest. Nicolas Slonimsky inimitably characterized the concerto as "eight linked movements of which the last four, separated from the first four by a florid violin cadenza, recapitulate in reverse the basic four movements, so that the entire work becomes an equilibrated specular octad possessing a perfect chirality" (Table 1).[14] The opening four movements at once function as a large-scale

Table 1. Chávez, Violin Concerto (Formal Overview)

Exposition				**Capstone**	**Recapitulation**			
Largo	*Allegro*	*Largo*	*Scherzo*	*Cadenza*	*Scherzo*	*Largo*	*Allegro*	*Largo*
Rehearsal No:	11	67	85	104	105	132	149	178
Introduction	Fast mov't	Slow mov't	Variations I–IV	Variation V	Variations VI–IX	Slow mov't	Fast mov't	Coda
	Tutti 1 beginning at 53			Begins Lentamente, later becomes much faster with many tempo changes	Tutti 2 through 138; Scherzo theme from 85 played simultaneously with its inversion at 124	Solo returns at 139; Largo theme from 73 inverted at 137		

exposition and together serve as a slow introduction, fast movement, slow movement, and scherzo-like theme and variations. The reverse recapitulation (with the slow introduction now serving as a coda) includes several passages in which material from the exposition is played in inversion, either alone or in combination with their original melodic shapes. (A few characteristic examples are noted in Table 1.) The fast and slow movements are linked by the first of the work's two tuttis. The second serves as the recapitulation of the scherzo and continues halfway through the returning slow movement. The soloist otherwise plays continuously and is given ample opportunities for virtuosic display. The capstone of the essentially melodic work is the long cadenza inserted between the two halves of the scherzo. This features substantial passagework but also develops certain rhythmic ideas from the fast movement and scherzo and includes, near its end, a modified inversion of the theme with which the concerto opens and closes, the only other appearance in the work of this critical thematic material (Examples 1a and 1b).[15]

Chávez had not yet written out the entire orchestral score by the time of the Kirkwoods' Mexican visit. But in a letter of 10 July 1950, he was able to send word he had finally completed his work.[16] Kirkwood's return letter, accompanied by payment of the balance of the composer's fee, is lost, but must have been full of enthusiasm, joy, and probably great

Example 1a. Chávez, Violin Concerto, introduction (beginning).

Example 1b. Chávez, Violin Concerto, cadenza (ending).

relief.[17] It was time now for him—without the assistance of Judson or any other manager—to go in search of a conductor to lead what he hoped would be his wife's belated debut in the 1951–52 season.

Not Ormandy

In early August 1950 Kirkwood met with Herbert Barrett to discuss the rollout of the concerto (and, of course, his wife's career).[18] The two agreed it would be best to turn first to Eugene Ormandy, music director of the Philadelphia Orchestra, perhaps because of his long-standing ties to the Curtis Institute and its director, Efrem Zimbalist.[19] This was a good bet, too, because Chávez and Ormandy had long been on good terms with one another. Responding to Barrett on 10 August, Chávez wrote:

> I am glad you met the Kirkwoods. She is a talented violinist but she still has to mature and, as I told them in Acapulco, she still has to practice for one year at the rate of five or six hours a day in order to master my concerto. I am interested in her success and I hope that she will play the Concerto well after such practice. Therefore, I shall be happy to introduce her to as many conductors as we think advisable.[20]

Writing on the same day to Murray Kirkwood, Chávez included a draft of a letter of introduction to Ormandy.

Things moved quickly over the next few months. On 17 September the *New York Times* released a brief notice of the work's completion (much shortened from the draft that Kirkwood had given Barrett in August). On 4 October Bertolami performed the work for Zimbalist, who declared it "strange music . . . but powerful and *very* impressive."[21] Shortly thereafter Chávez sent his letter to Ormandy, and Kirkwood himself followed up with the conductor a week later to request a date when his wife and her accompanist could play for him.[22] Scheduling proved somewhat difficult, but an audition was finally arranged to take place at Philadelphia's Academy of Music on 27 November.

The next day Kirkwood made a detailed report to Chávez on how it had gone. Although Ormandy was impressed by Viviane's playing, he held out no hope of programming the concerto in its current form. The problem, as he saw it, lay in the work's great length, which ran to nearly 45 minutes. "American orchestras are not content merely to accompany soloists," he explained, and "our audiences become restless with new works that demand their attention for more than 20 minutes." For the concerto to be successful, in Ormandy's view, it would need to be cut substantially to a length of around 18 to 20 minutes. Speaking off-the-cuff the conductor even suggested one possible way of achieving this concision, by omitting all the music following the first tutti through the end of the second.[23]

Ormandy was not entirely discouraging, however. Indeed, he promised to recommend the concerto to his board of directors if Chávez agreed to shorten it. He could make no guarantees about the board's decision, however, and indicated that, were he able to schedule the concerto, this would not be until the 1952–53 season, since he had already committed himself to several other new works for the next season.[24] With that in mind, he encouraged Kirkwood to approach Dimitri Mitropoulos, the newly named music director of the New York Philharmonic, as well as Arthur Judson, who, he thought, might be able to place it sooner with another orchestra. He even offered to speak to Judson about the matter on Kirkwood's behalf.

When Kirkwood expressed doubt about Chávez's willingness to cut his work as the conductor had suggested, Ormandy, as Kirkwood reported, laughed and said:

> I know what you mean. Chávez is a fighter. I have seen him fight for what he believes in, right out there [motioning toward auditorium]. Although he is my friend, although I have high regard for him as a truly great man, the fact

> remains that his music has not been popular in this country. It will be the same with this concerto, unless he compresses it.

Toward the end of his lengthy report, Kirkwood added: "You will be interested in a telephone call that I had from Viviane a little while ago. 'Murray,' she said, 'the more I think about changing this concerto the madder I get. I love every note of it.' That is my opinion, too."

A fighter (like Chávez) as well as gambler (as we have seen), Kirkwood wrote to Ormandy on the same day he reported to Chávez and brashly endeavored to explain the concerto's unusual arch-like structure.[25] The next day, still smarting from this initial defeat at the hands of Ormandy, he sent Chávez a clipping from the *New York Times* that included a review of the Philadelphia Orchestra's Carnegie Hall performance the previous night of Copland's Clarinet Concerto.[26] The accompanying note read: "The attached clipping carries its own moral. Evidently Ormandy, like Heifetz, is attracted by novelty rather than newness, and is equally blind to greatness." Whatever the merits of Kirkwood's assessment of Ormandy's tastes, Copland's concerto, at a length of about 17 minutes, responded to the exigencies of the marketplace in a way that Chávez's did not.

Chávez did not comment directly on Ormandy's decision to perform his friend's concerto, but his reply to Kirkwood on 6 December is otherwise telling:

> It has always been my belief that new works with a new content, expressed in new forms and manner of speech, are not easy to get at first acquaintance. It seems to me that is the case with this Concerto. . . . It is just too bad that good works are difficult to grasp at first. On the other hand, easygoing works, that have immediate success, prove in time not to keep their appeal and become cheap and trivial very soon. It just happens that there are two ways: the hard, and the easy. You have picked the hard way and you are naturally confronting all the difficulties involved, that is to say, all the hardship.
>
> The Concerto cannot be abridged. You understand very well that, and I was deeply satisfied reading what you quote from Viviane at the end of your letter of 28 November. So there is nothing but facing the situation as it is, to try other conductors, and to wait.

Although Chávez seemed receptive in this response to Ormandy's idea of turning next to Mitropoulos, he advised doing so "directly rather than through Judson" and offered to send a personal letter along the lines of what he had written to Ormandy a few months earlier. Yet he soon had second thoughts, suggesting in a quick follow-up letter of 14 December that Leonard Bernstein would be a better bet than Mitropoulos. (This made sense in that Bernstein, who was not tied to a permanent post, was frequently engaged to conduct orchestras in Boston, New York, Tel Aviv, and elsewhere.) By the time Kirkwood learned of the composer's change of heart, however, he had already written directly to Mitropoulos himself, describing the work as Chávez's "considered challenge to classic form and modern content."[27] In the event, this letter never reached its intended recipient, but since neither Kirkwood nor Chávez could have known that yet, the idea of approaching Bernstein was dropped for the time being, and a performance with Mitropoulos and the New York Philharmonic remained the immediate goal.

Particularly worthy of note is Chávez's advice not to approach Judson directly. The two had a long history, dating at least back to when Judson engaged him to lead two weeks of concerts with the New York Philharmonic in 1936–37. Although Chávez became one of Judson's conducting clients, he was not happy with his manager's work and for much of the 1940s had negotiated occasional guest conducting engagements in the United States on his own. But when he began looking for more frequent appearances in the United States after dissolving the OSM, he naturally thought it best to try to make things work with his manager, who was best positioned to help him.[28] Twice, in December 1949 and April 1950, the two met in New York for discussions. Chávez conveyed his desire not only for guest conducting appearances but also for a permanent position with a major orchestra in the United States.[29] When nothing materialized at first, he may well have taken this as a sign of retaliation for his earlier practice of accepting engagements on his own, which, of course, had freed him from paying any commission. It could not have helped that as director of INBA he had been drawn into a misunderstanding with Judson in 1948 over the latter's proposed use of Mexico City's Palacio de Bellas Artes for concerts he hoped to produce there as part of his Community Concerts series, or that in 1947, as we have seen, Kirkwood had disregarded Judson's advice to commission someone else to write his wife's debut concerto after Chávez's refusal to promise a Mexican premiere. In other words, the composer had good reason to be wary of Judson.[30]

Chávez shared none of these concerns with Kirkwood, however, and instead concluded his letter by turning away from the performance question and back to the music itself and those for whom it had been written:

> Now let me tell you the way I personally feel. I am very happy to have written this work and to see that it has had its first great success with Viviane and yourself. This success . . . is real because it is based on a thorough knowledge of and understanding of the work, whereas Mr. Ormandy's refusal is based on a hurried first and single impression and on other considerations, i.e. the making of programs for his concerts, which do not at all concern my work.

Not Mitropoulos

On 29 January 1951 Chávez finally dispatched a brief letter to Mitropoulos letting him know about the concerto and asking him to hear Bertolami perform it. Soon thereafter the composer was back in New York and once again met with the soloist and her accompanist for a coaching session. Shortly after that Kirkwood learned his own letter to Mitropoulos had gone astray, and so on 14 February he wrote once more to request an audition.[31] In his response, dated 19 February, Mitropoulos indicated he would be happy to hear Chávez's concerto but only out of personal curiosity, as he saw no possibility of performing it anytime soon. Not only were his Philharmonic programs fully booked for the next two years, he wrote, but there was also the question of balancing the public's demand for traditional repertoire and his personal commitment to contemporary music, a matter of some importance in a time of financial difficulties such that the orchestra was planning to make a public appeal for contributions.[32] He explained:

> From experience, we have learned that when a soloist whose box office is usually good plays a contemporary concerto, the box office is poor. On the other hand, if we put a contemporary work on the program and have at the same time a soloist playing something well-known, the box office does not suffer so much. In view of that fact, I decided not to accept for a while any contemporary concertos and [to] present only contemporary works written for orchestra alone.

Kirkwood responded on 21 February by demonstrating the same nerve he had shown in his last letter to Ormandy:

> Your Board Member and my good friend Chester Burden called on me last week for advice concerning your orchestra's

> forthcoming fund campaign. We agreed that the basic appeal . . . must rest on the orchestra's valid claim to be an educational institution of national importance. I hope that the campaign . . . will succeed in freeing you from the deadening influence of the box office, at least to the extent of permitting introduction of an occasional concerto on its merits. For if the box office is to determine your programming absolutely, there is no valid argument . . . for voluntary contributions. Until then, it is apparent that you are not free as conductor of the Philharmonic to help us realize our personal ambitions. But as Dimitri Mitropoulos, you can still help the Chávez Concerto gain the recognition it deserves.

Urging the conductor to hear the work even if he saw no chance of performing it, Kirkwood concluded by asking, "May we have the opportunity to win your support for a worthy cause?"

This somewhat heavy-handed tactic did the trick, and the audition with Mitropoulos finally took place, on only seven hours' notice, on 10 May. As he had done in the case of his wife's audition with Ormandy, Kirkwood reported to Chávez at length the following day. Although the conductor liked much of what he heard, he too was troubled by the concerto's lengthy form, which, in his view, "defied 'the classic Greek ideal of proportion.'" Particularly problematic, he felt, were the more "contemplative" passages, which were "too long, too personal, and too lacking in musical and rhythmic interest to hold the attention of audiences from north of the border," even supposing that they might appeal to those with "a more serene outlook on life." (The ethnic essentialism of this remark surely did not go unnoticed by the cosmopolitan composer, a self-proclaimed "Latin of Manhattan," whose home away from home had for years been the Barbizon Plaza Hotel on Central Park South.)[33] Mitropoulos went on to make a striking comparison: "Stravinsky writes mechanically and his Concerto does not approach the heights that this achieves. . . . But it is concise, which means that an audience does not have to like it already in order to listen to it. Therefore, it has a chance of being heard often enough to become popular."[34] Facing the same practical concerns as Ormandy, Mitropoulos too was convinced the work would have to be cut or else not be heard. Chávez showed little patience in his reply for the conductor's line: "I really don't know what is—'the classic Greek ideal of proportion,' as applied to music. And what music, Greek, Bach, or our present day music? I feel sorry for Directors of Music whose first consideration is box office."[35]

Although Chávez was himself no longer a director of music of his own orchestra, he found himself back on the podium in Mexico in the early months of 1951 as guest conductor of a short season of concerts with INBA's Orquesta Sinfónica Nacional (OSN). That spring, thinking he might return for a second season with the ensemble in the winter of 1952, he raised the possibility of giving the premiere of the concerto at that time.[36] On 2 September 1951, with his engagement for another season with the OSN now fixed, Chávez wrote directly to Bertolami for the first time to ask her to perform the work with him on 1 and 3 February 1952. (The dates were later pushed back four weeks to 29 February and 2 March.) In the formal offer sent by INBA under separate cover, the performer's fee was set at $1,250 (half of what Chávez received for composing the work). On 5 September Bertolami wrote back to INBA to accept.[37]

The premiere of a major new work by Chávez was much anticipated in Mexico and widely reviewed, mostly favorably, in the local newspapers.[38] The only proper review of the concerto to appear in the United States was by Charles Poore for the *Christian Science Monitor*, who described the work as "highly original . . . characteristically virile, and impelling; and at the same time dissonant, its motifs being based on extremely discordant intervals."[39] More remarkable was a feature article appearing in *Time* on Bertolami's belated debut. Entitled "45 Minutes in Mexico," this unsigned story was written by Chandler Thomas, the magazine's New York–based music critic, with the aid of background information provided by Murray Kirkwood during the weeks leading up to the premiere.[40] Among other things, Kirkwood shared with Thomas copies of his correspondence with Judson, Ormandy, and Mitropoulos. But even though he "like[d] a good fight," as he explained in a letter of 1 February 1952, he enjoined Thomas from airing his complaints about these powerful figures in public, since he knew that would only damage his wife's prospects. What Chandler produced, then, was a delightful human-interest story. Here Viviane is described as "a tall, dark-haired girl with a passing resemblance to Hedy Lamarr," and we read of how she and her husband were inspired by listening to the *Sinfonía india* to spend their savings to commission from its composer a concerto for her to play at her professional debut. Not surprisingly, no mention is made of the disappointment and bitterness experienced along the way to the first performance. At the same time the article uncritically invoked a whole set of preconceived and largely inapt notions in describing the music as "undiluted Chávez—bursting with repeated-note, marimba-like rhythms, themes sometimes curiously plaintive, sometimes broad with the flavor of mesquite and wide-open spaces, and orchestrated throughout with all the colors of a Mexican serape."[41]

From practically the moment Chávez invited Bertolami to perform the work with the OSN, Kirkwood began once more to woo Arthur Judson, who, after all, had suggested a premiere in Mexico City in the first place.[42] Nothing ever came of this, but Judson did at least do the violinist one favor, albeit indirectly, by way of his dealings with Chávez. In late February 1952, rather at the last moment, Judson arranged for Chávez to be invited to conduct the Los Angeles Philharmonic in its concerts of 27 and 28 March (in Los Angeles) and of 30 March (in neighboring Long Beach).[43] It is perhaps not surprising that Chávez included on his programs his own new concerto, with Bertolami as soloist. Thus within a single month, and more than five years after Murray Kirkwood first made contact with the composer, Viviane Bertolami gave both the world and U.S. premieres of Chávez's long-awaited Violin Concerto.[44]

The music heard in the two cities was not identical. With the experience of the Mexico City performances fresh in his mind, Chávez made the decision to do what he had once insisted he could not do, namely, shorten the long work. Notably, Bertolami learned of this only three days before the first concert in Los Angeles, when the composer arranged for her to come to his hotel room and, on the spot, worked through the changes with her. These excisions, evident from crossovers in the autograph score, were made in the first half of the scherzo, the cadenza, the second tutti, the restatement of the Allegro moderato, and the coda. And with that what had been "45 Minutes in Mexico" now became "35 Minutes in the United States," with no damage done to the concerto's symmetrical structural design.[45]

Why Not Bertolami?

In August 1953 Bertolami and Kondaks performed the revised version in an afternoon concert at Tanglewood, with Chávez, Aaron Copland, and Herbert Barrett in attendance. A few months later Copland wrote a warm testimonial letter for Bertolami's use in furthering her career.[46] But despite numerous efforts made by Kirkwood throughout these years with conductors such as Leonard Bernstein (Boston Symphony), Pierre Monteux (San Francisco Symphony), Thor Johnson (Cincinnati Symphony), Thomas Scherman (Little Orchestra Society), Malcolm Sargent (BBC Symphony Orchestra), Wilfred Pelletier (Orchestre Symphonique de Québec), Désiré

Defauw (Orchestre Symphonique de Montréal), and Howard Mitchell (National Symphony)—and notwithstanding Bertolami's personal request (written in French) to the Boston Symphony's Charles Munch—she never again played Chávez's work with a major orchestra.[47]

Judson might well have had something to do with this. Like Ormandy and Mitropoulos, nearly all the conductors the Kirkwoods contacted were under his management. That none agreed even to hear the work is certainly suggestive.[48] Then, too, there was a time not all that long ago when talented female soloists—even one who looked like a Hollywood movie star—were the victims of outright discrimination in the world of concert music. Sex appeal was not always used to sell classical music in the way it is today. But the defeating of the Kirkwoods' grand plan can be attributed in part, as we have seen, to Chávez's work itself. The concerto was in no way written with the demands of the marketplace in mind and perhaps partly for this reason failed to catch on with the conductors on whom Bertolami would have to rely. It was going to be difficult enough for a young, unknown female violinist who lacked Judson's support to establish herself with the public as a major virtuosa. To try to do so with a work as challenging and uncompromising as Chávez's concerto—one demanding to be taken straight, with no mixer or chaser—made that dream all the harder to achieve. For the work to find its way with the public, it would, in truth, require a more powerful advocate than the young artist for whom it was written.

A New (Male) Champion (and an Old Female One, Too)

In 1962 Chávez began a lengthy correspondence about the concerto with Henryk Szeryng, the Polish-born, naturalized-Mexican violinist who had recently been named Mexico's cultural ambassador. The composer sent Szeryng the music in July and in December reported his delight at the news the violinist had begun to learn it.[49] At the same time Mills Music, a New York firm headed by Arthur Cohn, accepted the work for publication. The two eventually turned their sights on a performance with the composer's longtime friend Leonard Bernstein and the New York Philharmonic. Fresh off a performance of Chávez's new Sixth Symphony, Bernstein looked with interest at the score in June 1964. Like Ormandy and Mitropoulos before him, he too had questions about the work's form—or, to be more precise, about one critical part of it. Still, the conductor promised to give serious consideration to performing the concerto upon his return from sabbatical in the 1965–66 season.

On 17 June 1964 Bernstein reported all this to Chávez:

> I have just read your violin concerto, and find it admirable—so different from the symphony! I think it could be a very successful concert piece, and I will think seriously about doing it when I return to harness.
>
> But Carlos, have you thought about redoing the Coda? It's a wonderful section, by far the most dramatic & interesting; and yet it leaves me with the inescapable feeling that it's more like an introduction than a coda. I guess one of the reasons is that according to the symmetrical arch of the total form, once the opening material returns we wait in vain for the decisive motive  from the introduction. Somehow the piece doesn't really seem finished, which is a *lástima*, since the work moves so successfully throughout. Do let me have your thoughts.

Chávez's reply to this friendly suggestion was written in a warm, yet characteristically stubborn and determined tone that the Kirkwoods would have recognized:

> I have your note of June 17. It is only natural you have hit [on] one of the hidden problems of the work.—A work that follows such an elaborate process of integration, being as you say a "symmetrical arch," an integral mirror. The nascent elements have to be also the ending elements but in a sort of matured way.—It is true, the sense of finishing is implicit, not explicit: it is not a final-final, a Finale-Finale. I would think of a simile (excuse me, *toute proportion gardée*): the endings of the early Chaplin films, with an impossible near Finale: the man slowing walking out, gradually disappearing, his back turned to the audience.—We come to a close after so many things have happened, so that it is not a Finale, just a necessary stop. The thing is: what has happened; to constantly "move throughout"; since nothing really finishes, life always recommences.
>
> Your reaction pleases me enormously because it shows tremendous insight to grasp the essence of the work. I am sure if, as I hope very much, you do the Concerto, you will find the way to work out the closing section as it is, a tutti of the orchestra in low trills, sinking into the distance, the Solo Violin reminiscing as an unbeatable idea.[50]

Bernstein was won over, and the concerto was eventually scheduled for the following season.

Szeryng immediately sought to make the most of the opportunity provided by this development for good advance publicity. After the dates on the Philharmonic's subscription calendar were fixed, he suggested a number of promotional schemes involving the Mexican ambassador in Washington and the Consul General in New York, as well as the orchestra and publisher.[51] He also engaged the services of Audrey Michaels, a New York classical-music publicist associated with his manager, Sol Hurok. Twice in the spring of 1965 Michaels contacted Chávez in this regard. Of particular interest is her second letter, dated 3 June, in which she sought to ascertain whether the violinist would be giving the world premiere, the American premiere, or merely the New York premiere.[52] Notably, although Chávez had described the hoped-for New York performance as the concerto's "*estreno*" (premiere) in a letter to Szeryng on 23 March 1964, he quickly thought the better of that obvious misrepresentation, using in his next letter instead the expression "*re-estreno*" (second premiere).[53]

To Szeryng the way the performance was publicized was no small matter. This is evident in his letter to Arthur Cohn of 4 July 1965, with a copy to Chávez:

> Now, may I ask you a favor. Miss Michaels [is] inquiring on how Maestro Chávez came to entrust me with this important premiere of his concerto. She needs this information urgently, and thinks it would make a magnificent story, and it would be connected with the fact of a hemispheric event, namely the premiere of Mexico's and Latin America's foremost composer's work, by Mexico's cultural ambassador in cooperation with the leading U.S. conductor. However and unfortunately, we both know that the concerto was originally commis[s]ioned by Mr. Kirkwood for Miss Bertolami. If you would write to the Maestro about obtaining a short note on the concerto, and my spiritual and artistic connection with the same, using your customary tact, and taking advantage of the Maestro's exquisite diplomacy, I feel that without indulging in any basic inaccuracies, the situation could be saved and solved in my favor. If either yourself or Maestro Chávez agree to write a short note about how the concerto came into my hands, (with out [*sic*] mentioning the names of the persons involved in the commission) would you please send it to Miss Michaels at your earliest convenience.

Chávez's reply to Szeryng, dated 12 July, was evasive: "I have received a copy of the letter you sent to Arthur Cohn, and he has also been in communication with me in this regard. Very soon you will receive my answer to your question." That the composer never followed up with the promised answer—evident from Szeryng's letter to Chávez of 6 September—suggests he wanted to have nothing to do with the violinist's deceptive plan.

But by then it didn't matter. Oddly enough, as it had done thirteen years earlier at Murray Kirkwood's instigation, *Time* again stepped in to play a role in telling the concerto's convoluted story. Now, however, the subject of promotion was not Viviane Bertolami but Henryk Szeryng. Appearing in the issue of 3 September was an admiring profile of the violinist, no doubt based on information provided by Michaels.[54] This concluded with the false report that in his forthcoming performances with the New York Philharmonic Szeryng would be "premiering a violin concerto by Carlos Chávez, Mexico's foremost contemporary composer." Edward Downes's program note put this lie to rest. Using information supplied by the composer, Downes reported the concerto had been commissioned by Kirkwood for Bertolami, who had given the first performances thirteen years before. There is a brief mention of some later changes in orchestration, but nothing suggesting Szeryng's performances constituted anything like a premiere (or even a *re-estreno*).[55]

What was now only the New York premiere took place in the concerts of 7–9 and 11 October 1965. Writing in the *Saturday Review*, Irving Kolodin found much to like in the concerto, which he described as "rewarding" and "provocative" music that "treats the instrument as a means of musical expression rather than as a prima donna or musical acrobat." After describing the work's unusual symphonic structure, he acknowledged it all might sound "formidably formal." And yet, he writes, "Chávez's ideas are varied, his manipulation of them absorbing. For the most part, the flow of ideas gave rise to the form in which they were expressed, one of among other reasons the concerto left an affirmative feeling about a rehearing."[56]

As it happens, Murray Kirkwood made a tape recording of the radio broadcast of the performance of 9 October.[57] This gives aural evidence of the two substantial elisions taken in these New York performances. The first occurs in the cadenza, which Szeryng cut by twenty-five bars (from rehearsal letter V to rehearsal letter b). The second, probably initiated by Bernstein, comes in the Largo section of the second tutti, whose extraordinarily long (and beautiful) oboe solo was cut by fourteen bars (from rehearsal number 134 to rehearsal number 137).[58] Writing to

Chávez on 14 June 1967, Viviane Bertolami reported she was at work again on the concerto and was using the recording her husband had made of Szeryng's performance as a point of reference. She said nothing about the abbreviated oboe solo, but the shortened cadenza was of course a matter of pressing interest. She inquired whether the composer had authorized the excision. Chávez's reply of five days later was clear: "No changes whatsoever have been authorized by me. Henryk made the cut in the cadenza because I could not force him not to do it."[59]

Early the next year, Chávez and Szeryng began making plans to record the concerto with the Orquesta Sinfónica Nacional. Particularly notable in this regard is Chávez's letter to Szeryng of 5 May 1966: "I am thinking that I will take to Mexico for the recording one of the best oboists there is, and I am not going to make the cut in the [second] tutti. It would please me very much if you were not to make the cut in the cadenza, for let us hope this shall be a *definitive* recording."[60] The concerto was recorded in Mexico City in August 1966 and released the following year by CBS Masterworks.[61] Chávez's liner notes—which delighted Copland because they were "very Chávez-y and charming"—present at somewhat greater length the description of the work's unusual form that he had provided for Edward Downes's program notes for the New York performances two years earlier.[62] Here again Chávez credits Murray Kirkwood with the commission, although this time, presumably out of deference to Szeryng's wishes, he made no mention of the violinist for whom the work had been written. Notably, while the CBS recording does restore the cut in the oboe solo, it appears Chávez was not able to convince Szeryng to perform the entire cadenza. What was produced, then, was not a definitive recording, although it is indeed a very fine performance, what Copland called "a *musical* pleasure."[63]

There was one performer, however, who did respect the composer's intentions. On 26 February 1968, Viviane Bertolami, accompanied by Connecticut's Norwalk Symphony Orchestra, performed the concerto in public for the first time since 1952. The tape recording made by Murray Kirkwood on this occasion reveals his wife played every note of the work he had commissioned Chávez to write for her some twenty years earlier. The orchestral playing in this recording may be less than ideal, but the performance turned in by the soloist is its own musical pleasure and must have been meaningful to her and her husband in ways we can only imagine.

NOTES

1. Murray D. Kirkwood to Carlos Chávez, 10 January 1947. This letter was written in Spanish. Chávez replied in English, the language in which the extensive correspondence between Chávez and the Kirkwoods continued thereafter, running to well over a hundred letters written over at least twenty-seven years. Since both men kept copies of their outgoing letters, a more or less complete record is preserved in both the Fondo Carlos Chávez, Archivo General de la Nación (henceforth AGN) and in a large private collection of correspondence and audio recordings in New York I will call the Kirkwood Family Papers (hereafter KFP). Although Chávez wrote fluently in English, he occasionally misspelled a word or used an unidiomatic locution; I invariably retain the original text here. When Spanish proper nouns and other words are given by Kirkwood and other native English speakers without the proper diacritics, however, I correct the orthography without comment. I am grateful to several members of the Kirkwood family for their willingness to support this research. I am especially grateful to Anne C. Kirkwood for several thoughtful conversations pertaining to her mother's career and for otherwise assisting me in this project.

2. "Mexico: Phoenix of the Americas," *International Review of the International Telephone and Telegraph Corporation* 2/5 (November 1946): 1–11, quoted at 1.

3. Goodman is quoted in Aaron Copland and Vivian Perlis, *Copland Since 1943* (New York: St. Martin's Press, 1999), 94.

4. On Judson, see James M. Doering, *The Great Orchestrator: Arthur Judson and American Arts Management* (Urbana: University of Illinois Press, 2013).

5. Letters of 6 October (Kirkwood to Judson), 7 October (Judson to Kirkwood), and 8 October 1947 (Kirkwood to Judson), KFP.

6. Three years later Kirkwood may have caught an inkling of the composer's attitude when he demurred at the idea raised by his longtime friend and supporter Frances F. Paine of performing the concerto under the sponsorship of the Pan-American Society, since that might put "emphasis on extra-musical considerations such as Pan-Americanisms." Chávez to Kirkwood, 10 October 1950, in reply to Kirkwood's letter to him of 25 August 1950.

7. "Portrait of a Concert Manager," *New York Times*, 9 February 1947.

8. Letter of 28 April 1947, KFP. Still hoping that Judson might consent to represent his wife, Kirkwood enclosed two tickets for her forthcoming graduation recital in Philadelphia. Judson returned the tickets with his regrets in his reply of 30 April. From Kirkwood's letter to Chávez of 15 May 1947, we can assume that at this point he began looking elsewhere for management of his wife's career, including the National Concert and Artist Corporation, Judson's main rival.

9. The reference here is to a four-disc 78-rpm recording of the three works made by Chávez in the 1930s in the Victor Musical Masterpiece Series, Victor Red Seal M 503 (manual sequence) and DM 503 (automatic sequence).

10. Unfortunately, the present whereabouts of this and all other such manuscripts is unknown.

11. A copy of Chávez's letter to Barrett is preserved in AGN.

12. On the following day, Chávez wrote more expansively and personally about these decisions to Copland, explicitly describing how the press of his duties had left him "unable to finish my Violin Concerto, of which only one third is done." Chávez to Copland, 18 November 1948, Aaron Copland Collection, ca. 1900–1990, Library of Congress. It thus appears that by the middle of November Chávez had made little or no progress on the concerto since 4 March, when he described the first installment sent to the Kirkwoods as "a little less than one-third of the Concerto."

13. Chávez's continued work at INBA was probably related to feelings described in his letter to Copland of 18 November 1948: "México is a country in which almost every thing is to be done. If one is requested to do a work of social, cultural character for the benefit of the community, one cannot refuse; or rather, one refuses but is forced to accept."

14. Nicolas Slonimsky, *Music Since 1900*, 6th ed., ed. Laura Kuhn (New York: Schirmer, 2001), 456.

15. See also Roberto García Morillo, *Carlos Chávez: Vida y Obra* (Mexico City and Buenos Aires: Fondo de Cultura Económica, 1960), 135–40; David Hamilton, "Current Chronicle," *Musical Quarterly* 52 (1966): 90–93; and Robert L. Parker, *Carlos Chávez: Mexico's Modern-Day Orpheus* (Boston: Twayne, 1983), 87–88.

16. The autograph full score, preserved in the Performing Arts Division, New York Public Library (NYPL) JOB 84–11, no. 121, is end-dated "México, Acapulco / Marzo-Julio 1950 / Carlos Chávez." The autograph violin-piano score (JOB 84–11, no. 32) is end-dated "Carlos Chávez / Julio 1950."

17. Chávez acknowledged receipt of the $1,250 balance of his fee in a reply dated 25 July 1950.

18. Kirkwood to Herbert Barrett, 5 August 1950, KFP.

19. Kirkwood to Chávez, 3 August 1950; Barrett to Chávez, 4 August 1950, both AGN.

20. Chávez to Barrett, 19 August 1950, AGN.

21. Zimbalist is quoted in Kirkwood's letter to Chávez of 5 October 1950.

22. Copies of Chávez's letter to Ormandy are preserved in AGN and KFP. A copy of Kirkwood's letter to Ormandy of 17 October is preserved in the latter.

23. This would have resulted in a large-scale ternary structure with one interior tutti and no cadenza, destroying what for Chávez was the concerto's raison d'être as a complex structure combining elements of sonata form and sonata cycle in an entirely new way.

24. One of these very likely was a new violin concerto by the violinist-composer Boris Koutzen, who had enjoyed a long working association with Ormandy and the orchestra. Unlike Chávez's concerto, this work was written in a conservative, romantic style and was considerably shorter in length. This concerto was given its premiere by the Philadelphia Orchestra on 22 February 1952, with the composer's twenty-one-year-old daughter, Nadia, as soloist.

25. Kirkwood to Eugene Ormandy, 28 November 1950, KFP. No reply from Ormandy is extant.

26. Olin Downes, "Ormandy Offers 2 Novelties Here," *New York Times*, 29 November 1950.

27. Kirkwood to Dimitri Mitropoulos, 11 December 1950, KFP.

28. All this is made clear in Chávez's letter to Herbert Barrett of 18 June 1949: "In spite of the fact that as we know very well Arthur did not work for me during the last eight or nine years, but I rather succeeded in receiving invitations in spite of him, I think at this present moment we should contact him first." Chávez goes on to authorize Barrett to negotiate with Judson on his behalf and discusses the possibility of severing ties with the manager if he showed no definite interest. Chávez's other correspondence with Barrett from this period shows how distressed he was by the mishandling in the United States of the announcement of the OSM's dissolution, which he feared might have a detrimental effect on his conducting prospects in the United States (Fondo Carlos Chávez, AGN). The *New York Times* erroneously attributed Chávez's resignation to recent labor disputes and poor critical notices. Those issues were related instead to the Orquesta Sinfónica Nacional del Conservatorio, a part of INBA but not Chávez's orchestra. See "Chávez Resignation, Disbands Orchestra," *New York Times*, 12 March 1949. A follow-up notice corrected some of this misinformation ("Mexico," *New York Times*, 20 March 1949), but the report of difficulties with the musicians' union and the press was repeated in a story headed "Chávez

Quits Post as Leader of Mexico Symphony," in *Musical America,* March 1949, 1, the last paragraph of which repeats verbatim that of the first *New York Times* report.

29. The gist of the discussions can be drawn from Chávez's letter to Judson of 21 April 1950, AGN.

30. Community Concerts was another division of Columbia Artists Management, Inc. (formerly Columbia Concerts, Inc.). Chávez described the misunderstanding with Judson in this connection in a letter to Barrett of 7 July 1948, AGN.

31. All correspondence cited in the next several paragraphs is preserved in KFP.

32. On the orchestra's budgetary difficulties, see "Philharmonic Aim Is to Cut Deficit," *New York Times,* 3 April 1951, which discusses the proposal to create a "Friends of the Philharmonic" among public-spirited individuals. On Mitropoulos's commitment to contemporary music, see "Mitropoulos Radiant: Conductor Finds Century Rich in Music Accomplishment," *New York Times,* 21 December 1951.

33. Anthony Mancini, "Still Composing," *New York Post,* 31 January 1965.

34. Kirkwood to Chávez, 11 May 1951, KFP. In an earlier letter to Chávez of 12 March 1951, Kirkwood had reported some "interesting contrasts" Viviane had drawn between the same two concertos, those in which Chávez's work comes out ahead of Stravinsky's for its "grandeur," originality, and rewarding technical challenges.

35. Chávez to Kirkwood, 31 May 1951, KFP. As music director of OSM, Chávez had taken a much less conservative approach. He gave his audiences a steady diet of challenging new works and eventually made some progress in getting them to respect, if not love, the modern repertoire he favored. See Leonora Saavedra, "Of Selves and Others: Historiography, Ideology, and the Politics of Modern Mexican Music" (PhD diss., University of Pittsburgh, 2001), 273.

36. Chávez to Kirkwood, 26 April and 14 May 1951, KFP. In both letters Chávez encouraged Kirkwood to continue seeking performances in the United States.

37. The formal offer is lost, but we can infer its contents from Bertolami's reply of 5 September 1951, KFP. That Viviane Bertolami's voice has not been heard up to now speaks volumes about the place held by women during this period in both the conjugal and professional spheres. Indeed, after Viviane accepted the offer, Murray immediately stepped in to handle matters once more.

38. These reviews are preserved in AGN.

39. Charles Poore, "Chávez Concerto in Première," *Christian Science Monitor,* 8 March 1952.

40. "45 Minutes in Mexico," *Time,* 10 March 1952, 76. Kirkwood's correspondence with Thomas is preserved in KFP. Thomas may not have traveled to Mexico City to hear the premiere, but he at least heard the work in a private performance given by Bertolami and Kondaks in the Kirkwoods' New York apartment.

41. For a critique of discourse of this kind, see Leonora Saavedra, "Carlos Chávez's Polysemic Style: Constructing the National, Seeking the Cosmopolitan," *Journal of the American Musicological Society* 68/1 (2015): 99–150.

42. In addition to the correspondence between Kirkwood and Judson from 1947 cited above, KFP includes several letters exchanged between the two from the years 1951 to 1955.

43. Barrett evidently learned that Judson, who, as noted, had done little to further Chávez's conducting career, had secured this engagement and for this reason advised the composer to pay him a commission. Barrett to Chávez, 25 February 1952; Chávez to Barrett, 20 March 1952; and Barrett to Chavez, 24 March 1952, AGN. It is not hard to read between the lines of Judson's acknowledgment of Chávez's payment: "Thank you very much for the check for commission on the Los Angeles engagement. Very often people who engage conductors wish to communicate with them personally and I, of course, can have no objection to this but as a general rule they ask us about it." Judson to Chávez, 12 April 1952, AGN.

44. For reviews of the performances in California, see Albert Goldberg, "Chávez Work Features International Night," *Los Angeles Times*, 28 March 1952; Patterson Greene, "Concert Heard New Chávez," *Los Angeles Examiner*, 28 March 1952; and Mary Lou Zehms, "Composer Directs Own 'Concerto,'" *Long Beach Press-Telegram*, 31 March 1952.

45. Six years later, as he readied the score for publication, Chávez made a few additional unspecified revisions. These appear to have involved only minor details of articulation and the like, and the version performed by Bertolami and Chávez in Los Angeles could not have been substantially different from what eventually appeared in print. Requesting the revised score in a letter of 23 July 1958, Kirkwood explained that his wife hoped to "rebuild" her performance based on "the final, definitive version." Kirkwood to Chávez, in AGN.

46. A copy of the letter, dated 30 December 1953, is preserved in KFP.

47. Relevant correspondence is preserved in KFP.

48. On Judson's ability to hinder the careers of even the most established artists who dared to cross him, see Joseph Horowitz, *Classical Music in America: A History of Its Rise and Fall* (New York and London: W. W. Norton, 2005), 416–21.

49. Relevant correspondence between the composer and violinist is preserved in AGN. They corresponded mostly in English but occasionally in Spanish; translations from the Spanish are my own. These letters correct somewhat the information provided in Parker, *Carlos Chávez*, 141n, which is based on information shared in a letter to Parker of 26 December 1980 from Szeryng's London representative, Mary-Clare Adam. I am grateful to Christina Taylor for providing me with a copy of Adam's letter, which is preserved in the Latin American Music Center, Catholic University of America, Washington, DC.

50. Letter of 21 June 1964. Both letters quoted here, along with several others related to these performances, can be viewed on pp. 2–3 and 79–80, respectively, of the Leonard Bernstein Papers, Nov. 15, 1963–Jun 22, 1966, New York Philharmonic Digital Archives (http://archives.nyphil.org/index.php/artifact/5485d881-7f09-4303-be1c-272b4b1f44c9/fullview#). The original of Bernstein's letter to Chávez is preserved in the Performing Arts Division, NYPL, (JOB 93–4), f. 2 (MAI–17883).

51. Szeryng to Chávez, 23 November 1964 and 21 April 1965, in ibid. Chávez agreed with these ideas in general, although he thought the Ministry of Foreign Affairs should handle any matters involving the diplomatic corps; see his letters to Szeryng of 8 December 1964 and 27 April 1965, AGN.

52. Michaels to Chávez, 24 May and 3 June 1965, AGN. The file also includes other letters cited in this discussion.

53. Chávez to Szeryng, 23 March and 28 May 1964, AGN.

54. "Violinists: Cultural Ambassador," *Time*, 2 September 1965, 52.

55. See New York Philharmonic Digital Archives, Programs, 1965–66 Season, Subscription Season (http://archives.nyphil.org/index.php/artifact/240a917a-c652-4b99-a980-ca173d935c8a/fullview#page/1/mode/2up). A copy of the information Chávez sent Downes is preserved in AGN. Also available in the New York Philharmonic Digital Archives are notes and questions related to Downes's intermission broadcast interview with Chávez on 9 October 1965 (http://archives.nyphil.org/index.php/artifact/8441bfaa-fa9b-4bf6-90d2-29c14154bf50/fullview#page/17/mode/1up).

56. Irving Kolodin, "*Don Carlo* with Schippers and Bumbry," *Saturday Review*, 23 October 1965, 54. Because these concerts came toward the end of a twenty-three-day newspaper strike, the concerto received no other reviews.

57. Available on YouTube (https://www.youtube.com/watch?v=CwXrIALqNYQ) is what purports to be a live recording of one of the Szeryng-Bernstein performances from October 1965 but is instead a copy reproduced at nearly a half-step sharp from a commercial recording released two years later.

58. Both cuts are marked in Bernstein's conductor's score, which can be viewed in the New York Philharmonic Digital Archives (http://archives.nyphil.org/index.php/artifact/a4aaea54-4ee2-4536-aa2d-94c4b5058fa2/fullview#page/1/mode/2up).

59. Bertolami to Chávez, 14 June 1967; and Chávez to Bertolami, 19 June 1967, AGN. Bertolami replied to Chávez on 24 June: "Your letter was very welcome. I prefer your concerto as you wrote it" (ibid). These letters also touch on two smaller changes that Szeryng introduced in the cadenza (replacing the lower note E with D at two bars before rehearsal letter M, and substituting the note E♭ for E in the trill at two bars before rehearsal letter u), both of which Chávez disavowed.

60. Chávez to Szeryng, 6 May 1966, AGN. This file contains several other letters related to this project.

61. Carlos Chávez, *Chavez: Violin Concerto; Chávez-Buxtehude: Chaconne*, Henryk Szeryng, soloist, cond. Carlos Chávez, Orquesta Sinfónica de México, CBS Records, 32 11 0064. The recording went out of print by the early 1970s, and Chávez was unable to induce CBS to reissue it. See the correspondence preserved in AGN. The only other commercial recording of which I am aware is of an unauthorized abridged version of the score by Enrique Arturo Diemecke, issued in 2002 as *Carlos Chávez, Dos Conciertos*, Pablo Roberto Diemecke, soloist, cond. Enrique Arturo Diemecke, State of Mexico Symphony Orchestra, Prodisc, 27299.

62. Copland to Chávez, 15 October 1968, Performing Arts Division, NYPL, (JOB 93–4), f. 6 (MAI–17886).

63. Ibid.

PART III

Chávez's Greater World

Carlos Chávez and the Mexican "Vogue," 1925–1940

HELEN DELPAR

On page 60 of the June 1929 issue of *Vanity Fair* magazine are photographs of five individuals under the heading "Men of Mexico."[1] Four are visual artists: Luis Hidalgo, José Clemente Orozco, Miguel Covarrubias, and Rufino Tamayo. The fifth photograph is of Carlos Chávez. The inclusion of these photographs in a stylish periodical testified to the then current and growing appreciation in the United States for the cultural production of Mexico. The earliest manifestation of this appreciation was the enthusiasm shown for the work of Mexico's contemporary painters, especially muralists such as José Clemente Orozco. Interest in Mexican music came later and was concentrated on the person of Chávez.

The "enormous vogue for things Mexican," to quote a phrase that appeared in a *New York Times* article in 1933, had numerous origins and dimensions.[2] It was partly linked to the Mexican Revolution, which had ravaged the country from 1910 to 1920 and had ended in a fitful stabilization in the 1920s.[3] The United States dispatched troops into Mexico twice during the Revolution (1914, 1916), and the two countries came close to war during 1916. As the violent phase of the Revolution came to a close, many in the United States were alarmed by provisions of the new constitution of 1917, which seemed to threaten American investments in the country, especially in agriculture and the petroleum industry, to the chagrin of investors such as William Randolph Hearst, Edward Doheny, and William F. Buckley. President Venustiano Carranza (1915–20) did little to enforce the objectionable constitutional articles, but his successors Álvaro Obregón (1920–24) and Plutarco Elías Calles (1924–28) undertook limited agrarian reform and seemed bent on limiting private-property rights in petroleum as prescribed by the constitution. Although the latter issue was temporarily settled by a compromise, relations between the two countries remained tense through the mid-1920s. Moreover, when Mexico recognized the Soviet Union in 1924, it seemed as if the government was embracing Bolshevism and was perhaps the center of a radical conspiracy to spread Bolshevism throughout Central America. Devout Catholics in the United States also objected to anticlerical features of the constitution and the Calles administration's determination to enforce the offending articles, which led to a bitter and violent conflict in the late 1920s.

Underlying these sources of tension was the long-standing disdain of Americans for the Mexican people. Many deemed them unfit for self-government because of their racial heritage, believed that dictatorship was the only means by which they could be ruled, and lamented the demise of the regime of Porfirio Díaz, who had been ousted by the Revolution in 1911. Disdain was also exhibited in popular culture, especially in motion pictures, in which the Mexican "greaser" was the favorite villain—cowardly, treacherous, and no match for the American hero.[4]

There were, of course, American leftists and liberals of various stripes who were sympathetic toward the Revolution and believed that it was necessary to correct evils that for centuries had afflicted the Mexican masses, especially peasants of indigenous extraction.[5] These individuals—among them Carleton Beals, Frank Tannenbaum, and Ernest Gruening—spent extended periods in Mexico after 1920 and wrote articles and books articulating their views. Though they agreed that all was not perfect in Mexico, they hoped for greater sympathy for the country from the United States and were opposed to any plan to intervene in it, as some conservatives demanded.

By the later 1920s revolutionary momentum seemed to have stalled as agrarian reform was virtually halted under Calles, who emerged as Jefe Máximo (Maximum Chief) after the assassination of Obregón in 1928. Dwight W. Morrow, the U.S. ambassador from 1927 to 1930, though tied to American banking interests, also sought to ease tensions. These revived, however, under Lázaro Cárdenas (1934–40), who undertook an ambitious program of agrarian reform and in 1938 suddenly ordered the expropriation of the petroleum industry.

These political and economic controversies were, however, hardly likely to produce an "enormous vogue of things Mexican" in the United States, though they did keep Mexico at the center of national attention. Many other forces were at work, both within Mexico and in the States. Among the most prominent was the cultural and artistic ferment associated with the Revolution that emerged in the 1920s. Mexican intellectuals, artists, and political leaders now repudiated the elitist, Europeanizing culture that they claimed was a hallmark of the fallen regime and instead embraced indigenous and mestizo culture as the basis of national identity.

Accordingly, folk and popular art became highly valued as expressions of the Mexican's innate aesthetic abilities, with a major exhibition mounted in Mexico City in 1921.[6] Even more significant was the explosion of muralist painting beginning with the appointment of José Vasconcelos as Minister of Education in 1921. He and his successor, José Manuel Puig Casauranc, gave the walls of public buildings under their jurisdiction to Orozco, Diego Rivera, and other artists who created epic scenes of the Revolution as well as of popular culture. The murals were objectionable to some Mexicans, but to the artists and their supporters they furthered nationalist revival through their themes and advanced democratic aims by being accessible to all.[7]

In literature, popular themes were also evident. The era saw the emergence of a genre known as the novel of the Mexican Revolution, signaled by the rediscovery in the mid-1920s of *Los de abajo* (translated as *The Underdogs*), a work originally published in an El Paso Spanish-language newspaper in 1915. Its author, Mariano Azuela, a physician who had served with the forces of Francisco Villa, had a jaundiced view of the Revolution but captured much of the disorder and confusion that characterized the fighting. Other works in the genre include *Los caciques* (*The Bosses*, 1917) and *Las moscas* (*The Flies*, 1918) by Azuela and the novelized memoir *El águila y la serpiente* (*The Eagle and the Serpent*, 1928) by Martín Luis Guzmán. In the 1930s novels were often centered around Indians, the presumed beneficiaries of the Revolution, but who had actually gained little.

A renaissance in art music also occurred, much of it as a result of the creative and organizational efforts of Carlos Chávez. He incorporated indigenous themes and instruments into some of his compositions, but his work also reflected the influence of Stravinsky and other modern composers. As director of the Orquesta Sinfónica de México (OSM), created in 1928, he introduced Mexican concert-goers to new music and made special arrangements to allow workers and children to attend concerts. The example of Chávez shows that despite the nationalist and indigenous orientation of Mexico's post-revolutionary creative leaders, they by no means shunned international modernist trends. Many Mexican painters, including Rivera and David Alfaro Siqueiros, spent years studying art trends in Europe, and Rivera was first exhibited in New York in 1916 as an artist of the Cubist school.

International modernist influences were less evident in the novels of the Mexican Revolution, but the individuals associated with the Contemporáneos literary movement, such as Salvador Novo and Xavier Villaurrutia, praised American poets such as Ezra Pound, Carl Sandburg, and T. S. Eliot in their journal, which carried the same name as their movement (1928–31). The Contemporáneos group also arranged for the performance of plays by Eugene O'Neill and other modern dramatists. In 1932 Chávez wrote the incidental music for Sophocles's *Antigone,* in Jean Cocteau's version, presented by the avant-garde group Teatro Orientación.

It would also be incorrect to conclude from contemporary discourse linking the artistic renaissance to the Revolution that national themes had been absent from Mexican art, literature, and music before 1910. A Mexican school of painting had been identified by 1700, and the eighteenth and nineteenth centuries saw the emergence of painters such as Miguel Cabrera (1695–1768), Agustín Arrieta (1802–1874), and José María Velasco (1840–1912), who incorporated Mexican scenes and landscapes into their work.

Mexico's nineteenth-century literary figures also incorporated national themes into their writings, starting with what is considered the first Mexican novel, *El periquillo sarniento* (*The Mangy Parrot,* 1816) by José Fernández de Lizardi. Mexican settings and characters are also prominent in the writings of Ignacio M. Altamirano, who in 1871 called on his countrymen to declare their intellectual independence from Spain and create a literature reflecting the local environment. His principal works include *La Navidad en las montañas* (Christmas on the Mountains, 1871) and *El Zarco: Episodios de la vida mexicana en 1861–63* (El Zarco the Bandit, 1901).

In music, national elements were less fully developed than in art or literature. During the colonial period, Spanish forms prevailed even in works composed in Mexico, though some religious hymns and devotional songs, known as *villancicos,* might contain indigenous words or phrases. In the nineteenth century, European forms and subjects remained dominant, but Aniceto Ortega, composer of patriotic marches, wrote the opera *Guatimotzin* (1871) on an Aztec theme, with the Mexican soprano Ángela Peralta in a leading role. The continuing dominance of European values is shown in the 1901 opera *Le roi poète* by Gustavo E. Campa, about the poet-king Nezahualcóyotl, which had a French libretto. But in 1904, Melesio Morales's *Anita* had a Mexican theme and a libretto in Spanish.

During the 1920s and 1930s, Mexico's cultural trends resonated in the United States, not only among liberals and leftists, who were likely to hail all the products of the Revolution, but also among conservatives and the apolitical who hoped for a similar renewal in American cultural production. In part these sentiments reflected a surge in cultural nationalism in the United States, which emerged from the First World War as a global economic hegemon while Europe lay prostrate. As Carleton Beals, a journalist who spent long periods in Mexico, explained in 1923 after a visit to Spain and Italy: Europe "was weary, weary to death, rigor mortis already in its veins."[8]

Cultural nationalism could be seen in the new interest in American folk art, which received its first formal exhibition in 1924. The same year saw the inauguration of the American Wing of New York City's Metropolitan Museum of Art, which displayed antiques in sixteen period rooms that proclaimed the value of American arts by displaying them alongside the treasures of the Old World. The value of America's past was also asserted in such constructions and collections as Colonial Williamsburg and Delaware's Winterthur Museum, both begun in the 1920s.[9]

Although members of the American artistic community had been well aware of European modernism at least since the Armory Show of 1913, no single school prevailed. Many looked for native sources for American art and viewed the Mexican movement as worthy of emulation. As Thomas Hart Benton recalled: "I saw in the Mexican effort a profound and much-needed redirection of art towards its ancient humanistic functions. The Mexican concern with publicly significant meanings and with the pageant of Mexican national life corresponded perfectly with what I had in mind for art in the United States. I also looked with envy on the opportunities given Mexican painters for public mural work."[10] The search for an authentically American music also gripped many composers in the United States, among them Aaron Copland, who became a close friend of Chávez.

Still another aspect of Mexican life attracted those Americans who were repelled by the standardization and regimentation of their machine-dominated, industrialized society. Despite Mexico's poverty, conditions there, especially in rural areas, seemed to afford a life that was more authentic and coherent than that of the United States. These sentiments became even more pronounced during the Great Depression, which showed that modern industrial society could not even be counted on to provide continuing economic well-being. Exemplifying this attitude was Stuart Chase's best-selling *Mexico: A Study of Two Americas* (1931), which compared the so-called Middletown (Muncie, Indiana), which recently had been the subject of sociological analysis by Robert and Helen Lynd, and Tepoztlán, a village that was the subject of a pioneering community study by Robert Redfield.[11] Chase concluded that though Tepoztlán would benefit from electricity and other modern conveniences, on balance its people were better off than those of Middletown, for they had economic security.

Americans could obtain information about cultural trends and general conditions in Mexico from a variety of sources. Travel to Mexico from the United States by rail and ship was relatively easy for the numerous journalists, artists, writers, and academics who wished to visit the country as conditions improved in the 1920s. A summer school (*cursos de verano*) at the Universidad Nacional attracted dozens of Spanish teachers from the United States each year as well as prominent figures such as John Dewey, recruited as a lecturer in 1926. Starting in the mid-1920s Hubert C. Herring, a Congregationalist minister, conducted an annual seminar in Mexico during which participants had access to government officials and were exposed to the new Mexican art.[12] In 1935, Herring's *Renascent Mexico* included an essay on Mexican music by Chávez.[13]

Soon these cohorts of dedicated visitors were joined by a rising tide of American tourists. Starting in the late 1920s, the Mexican government made systematic efforts to expand tourism from the United States by encouraging the building of new hotels and other facilities and by the construction of a highway from Laredo, Texas, to Mexico City, which was completed in 1936. Americans, lured by the promise of martinis, pre-Columbian pyramids, and relatively low costs, traveled to Mexico in increasing numbers, especially during the Depression years. Accordingly, while Mexico accounted for only 4.6 percent of American spending on foreign travel in 1923, the figure had increased to 16.7 percent ten years later.[14]

Meanwhile, those unwilling or unable to travel to Mexico had many opportunities to acquaint themselves with its cultural developments, thanks in part to the efforts of various individuals who devoted themselves to the promotion of Mexican culture in the United States. Among Mexicans the most prominent, if at times controversial figure was José Juan Tablada, a poet and man of letters living in New York, who was employed as a cultural ambassador by the Mexican government during the 1920s and early 1930s. Launching what he called a "holy crusade" on behalf of Mexican culture, he published several articles on contemporary art, notably "Mexican Painting of Today," which appeared in *International Studio* in January 1923 and contained an assessment of current trends as constituting a renaissance. Tablada also introduced Chávez to the French composer Edgard Varèse, who had lived in New York since 1915 and premiered Chávez's *Otros tres exágonos* on 8 February 1925 with the International Composers' Guild.[15] Walter Pach, an artist and critic who lectured at the summer school in 1922, published several articles on Mexican art and arranged for Rivera and other painters to be included in the annual exhibition of New York's Society of Independent Artists in 1923.[16]

Three American women—Alma Reed, Anita Brenner, and Frances Flynn Paine—also promoted Mexican art and culture. Reed, already noted for her articles on Maya archeology, became Orozco's chief backer in the United States and in 1929 opened a gallery, the Delphic Studios, to showcase his work and that of other artists.[17] Brenner published numerous articles in the United States on Mexican art and other subjects and wrote a major study, *Idols Behind Altars* (1929), in which she stressed the close relationship between Mexico's art and its national identity. Although Brenner's primary focus was art, she knew Chávez in Mexico City and saw a great deal of him when they were both in New York in 1926–28, concluding that he was "a very great artist indeed."[18] Paine was also enthusiastic about Chávez. After his return to Mexico from the United States in 1928, she urged Elizabeth Cutter Morrow, wife of the ambassador, to act as his "*patroncita*." "There is absolutely no doubt as to his genius," she wrote, "and that he can hold his own with the greatest of modern composers. . . . He deserves whatever recognition and encouragement we can extend to him."[19] While in Mexico, Mrs. Morrow sat on the board of directors of the OSM.

Given these conditions, it is not surprising that many Mexican artists and musical figures traveled to the United States after 1920. In 1927 Howard S. Phillips, editor of *Mexican Life*, observed that these émigrés probably constituted "the greatest cultural mission that has ever gone forth out of a country as small in population as Mexico. This group is an aesthetic vanguard that is building up respect and admiration for Mexico in the outside world."[20] Indeed, the composer Ignacio Fernández Esperón, better known as Tata Nacho, who had spent six years in New York, asserted in 1925 that Mexican artists were welcome there. "There is a sincere and noble sympathy that we should take advantage of to strengthen the bonds of friendship between the two peoples and make our art known. . . . Mexicans who are worthy always find a favorable reception."[21] He added that he always won applause when he presented Mexican music in New York. This was certainly different from the reception accorded the Mexican tenor José Mojica during his first visit to the United States in 1916, when he was advised not to sing Mexican songs or wear Mexican costume because of anti-Mexican sentiment.[22] Tata Nacho's optimism may have been encouraged by the Theatre Guild's inclusion of a segment called "Rancho Mexicano" in its musical revue *Garrick Gaieties*, which ran for 231 performances on Broadway in 1925. Tata Nacho provided the music for the segment and staged the dances, which included the folk dance *jarabe tapatío*, and Miguel Covarrubias designed the set for the segment.[23]

Mexico's cultural émigrés left their country for the United States for a variety of reasons. Some were unhappy with the Mexican government or with their chances for artistic or economic fulfillment there. This was the case with Orozco, who spent most of the period 1927–34 in the United States. There artists might find validation from critics, a larger audience for their work, and greater financial returns. In addition, musical figures might have been influenced by articles in the Mexican press that described New York as the musical capital of the world, offering a seemingly infinite variety of concerts, operas, and popular music.[24] According to Chávez's biographer Roberto García Morillo, the composer was especially impressed during his first visit to New York in 1923 by the high quality of American orchestras, the advanced technology for the diffusion of music, and the dynamism of jazz.[25]

Some émigrés received a temporary stipend from the Mexican government, but in general they faced financial hardship, as did Chávez and Rufino Tamayo, with whom he roomed during his 1926–28 stay in New York. In addition, they might have to alter their work to make it acceptable to U.S. audiences. Anna Indych-López has shown how Orozco was unable to generate interest in his series of drawings *Horrores de la Revolución* until he changed the name to *Mexico in Revolution* and began making lithographs of the series that "cleansed [it] of the horrific details of civil strife and struggle in order to make its commercial debut in the United States a commercial success."[26]

It should be noted that the exodus of Mexico's cultural emigrés during the 1920s coincided with a substantial outflow of ordinary Mexican migrants, who traveled mainly to California and the Southwest as agricultural laborers and to Chicago and other cities in the Midwest. During the decade, the population of Mexican origin in the United States rose from approximately 725,000 in 1920 to nearly 1.5 million in 1930. With the start of the Great Depression, however, there were cries that Mexicans were depriving U.S. citizens of employment and were a drain on welfare services. The result was the deportation and repatriation of large numbers of Mexicans, by some estimates perhaps as many as one million.[27]

When relations between Mexico and the United States were strained, individuals in both countries took advantage of the "vogue" and used culture to try to defuse tensions. This was especially true of the Mexican government, which in 1922 dispatched folk art recently exhibited in Mexico City to the United States, a time when there were no formal diplomatic relations between the two countries. The exhibit traveled only to Los Angeles, where it was formally inaugurated by the mayor, George E. Cryer, and officials of the city's chamber of commerce, and reportedly attracted an average daily attendance of 3,000–4,000 during its two-week run. At a luncheon held in conjunction with the exhibit, the Mexican consul, Leandro Garza Leal, emphasized the values shared by the two peoples: "The ideals of the Pilgrims were the same in basis as those of the Mexican Revolutionists, first against the Spanish in 1810, against the French in 1863, against Díaz in 1910, and against [Victoriano] Huerta in 1913. Like your ancestors the Mexicans were fighting for life, liberty, and the pursuit of happiness as they understood it."[28]

Diplomatic relations between the countries were resumed after the Revolution, in 1923, but tensions were by no means dispelled. In 1928 a two-part exhibit was presented at the Art Center in New York that was clearly intended to improve relations between the two countries, as the director of the center, Alon Bement, believed that "cultural relations" formed "the basis of true understanding between nations." The Mexican government offered to finance the show, which featured folk art and work by contemporary painters, but Bement rejected the offer for the folk art segment, asserting that the Art Center wanted "the native craftsmen [to] understand this movement to be an American recognition of Mexican crafts." The folk art exhibit was financed by a $5,000 grant from a Rockefeller philanthropy, the General Education Board, but the Mexican government provided the funding for the modern art section.[29]

Official support also helped to expose American audiences to popular Mexican music, song, and dance by "*típica*" orchestras that toured the country starting in the late 1920s. Such orchestras were first formed in the late nineteenth century, often to represent the government at world's fairs. In 1928 Miguel Lerdo de Tejada, a veteran composer and performer, led one such orchestra on a ten-month tour of the United States, supposedly to thank Americans for Charles Lindbergh's recent flight to Mexico. A highlight of the tour for the performers, who were dressed as *charros*,[30] was an engagement in New York's Palace Theater. A critic in the *Herald Tribune* commented: "It is doubtful if more charming melody from stringed instruments than that of the Tipica group can be heard anywhere else in the world."[31] Between the matinee and evening performances at the premiere dignitaries in attendance were treated backstage to a Mexican dinner prepared by the orchestra's own chef, which included "an appetizing if fiery mixture of turkey and red peppers known as 'mole.'"[32] While still in New York, the orchestra was presented with a gold medal on behalf of the Mexican Chamber of Commerce of the United States by Acting Mayor Joseph V. McKee, who donned Mexican costume for the occasion.[33]

An exhibition of art in 1930, even larger than that of 1928, was also intended to promote better relations between the two countries, which had become more harmonious after the arrival of Ambassador Morrow in 1927. Morrow, despite his banking background, eschewed the anti-Mexican animus of his predecessor, James Rockwell Sheffield, and President Calles had apparently halted revolutionary initiatives. Morrow is credited with conceiving what became known as the "Mexican Arts Exhibit," which was on display at New York's Metropolitan Museum of Art in the fall of 1930 and traveled to thirteen other cities.[34]

Organized by René D'Harnoncourt, future director of New York's Museum of Modern Art (MoMA), with the support of the Mexican government, the show included fine art, especially works by Rivera and other contemporary painters. However, these were somewhat overshadowed by the profusion of folk and decorative art, which, according to the catalogue, represented "the truest form of self-expression of the Mexican people." The show garnered generally favorable reviews and attracted large crowds, perhaps as many as 450,000 nationally, and may have altered U.S. perceptions of Mexico. An editorial in the *New York Times* noted that although Mexico seemed "so alien, so remote . . . when we are privileged, as now, to seek her national point of view, in terms of art that has been so wisely and comprehensively chosen, barriers tend to go down and there grows a neighborly impulse toward reciprocity."[35]

Cultural diplomacy was even more evident in the origins of another major exhibit, *Twenty Centuries of Mexican Art*, which opened at MoMA in May 1940 and ran for four months.[36] The show took place at a time when relations were severely strained, mainly because of the expropriation of Mexico's foreign-owned petroleum industry in 1938 by the Cárdenas administration. Mexico promised compensation for the seized properties and gained the sympathy of some U.S. officials, who were trying to encourage hemispheric solidarity in view of the deteriorating international climate. Oil company executives were adamantly opposed to the move, however, and mounted a powerful anti-Mexico campaign in the U.S. media.

Ironically, a key figure in organizing the exhibition was Nelson A. Rockefeller, who was president of MoMA as well as a shareholder in Standard Oil of New Jersey, which had a subsidiary in Mexico. Rockefeller, who had traveled extensively in Latin America and was knowledgeable about Mexican art, visited Cárdenas in October 1939 when negotiations were at an impasse.[37] He suggested mounting a major show at MoMA to coincide with the World's Fair. Cárdenas agreed, and the Mexican government eventually financed half the cost of the exhibition, with the museum covering the rest.

The exhibition, in 1940, was larger than the 1930 show, and differed from it in several respects. It included pre-Columbian pieces, for the first time, and an expanded section on colonial art, and folk art was assigned a less prominent role. One similarity to its 1930 predecessor was its linkage of Mexico's modern art to the Revolution. According to Miguel Covarrubias, who was in charge of assembling the modern art collection: "The artistic liberation of Mexican art runs closely parallel to the social and political liberation of the nation itself."[38]

The show generated largely favorable reviews that emphasized the artistic gifts of the Mexican people. Critic Emily Genauer, for example, wrote that everybody "who saw the exhibition left it with a most profound respect for Mexico, for her rich artistic tradition, for the brilliance of her civilization, when our own land was a wilderness, for the versatility, inventiveness and gaiety of her peasant art. . . . It's the feeling American art lovers have long held for France and Italy."[39]

Twenty Centuries of Mexican Art differed from its predecessors in still another respect. The museum organized a two-week series of concerts of Mexican music in conjunction with the exhibition. In 1927 Frances Flynn Paine had contracted with the new Roxy Theater to present Chávez's ballet *El fuego nuevo* in anticipation of the Art Center show the following year, but the project had fallen through.[40] In the 1940 announcement of the concerts, however, Rockefeller stated that they were intended to present music as an integral part of Mexico's artistic culture.[41] Chávez organized the series of concerts and conducted three of them; the others were conducted by Eduardo Hernández Moncada. The programs offered an overview of Mexican music, which Chávez defined as "the Indian music of the ancient Mexicans; the music of Spanish or other origin implanted in Mexico, and, finally, the production in Mexico of a mixture of these elements."[42] Only three of the pieces performed were intended for concert presentation: an eighteenth-century mass by José Aldana and two works by Chávez, *Xochipilli: An Imagined Aztec Music*, which featured modern replicas of ancient Aztec instruments, and dances from the ballet *Los cuatro soles* (*The Four Suns*). The other offerings consisted of traditional songs and marches arranged for orchestra and contemporary music of the Yaqui Indians.

Rockefeller's remark and MoMA's sponsorship of the concerts indicate the growing acceptance in the United States of Mexican music as part of the artistic renaissance stemming from the Revolution of 1910. Chávez, recognized as Mexico's most important composer and musical entrepreneur, played a leading role in promoting this narrative, which emphasized the indigenous or mestizo roots of the renaissance. A 1935 article in the *New York Times* noted, "What Diego Rivera has been doing in the field of art, what the revolutionary regime has been doing in politics and social emphasis, is likewise being accomplished in the field of music," and cited Chávez as the presiding genius of this transition.[43]

Chávez elaborated on this theme in a 1939 *New York Times* article in which he reviewed ten years of concerts by the OSM for workers and peasants. The concerts "were a step in Mexico's cultural renascence," which had begun in 1921 and was still under way. Initially, painting was in the forefront, and "music limped along for a time." Now music reflected two "fundamental principles" that the painters had adopted, that "art must be national in character but universal in its foundations and that it must reach the vast majority of the people."[44]

Chávez was ideally suited to become the personification of Mexico's musical renaissance at the peak of the "vogue." No other émigré, except possibly Miguel Covarrubias, developed as many friendships with members of the American cultural elite, as shown by Chávez's relations with Copland, Henry Cowell, Paul Rosenfeld, Claire R. Reis, Minna Lederman, and others. His compositions not only reflected the commitment to modernism that these espoused but also the Americanist notes they endorsed. Chávez's positions as musical director of the OSM (1928–49) and director of Mexico's National Conservatory of Music (1928–34) gave him a visibility and authority none of his contemporaries could match. These qualities were further strengthened by his numerous writings, both in Mexican and American publications, and by extensive and generally positive commentary about his work in the U.S. press from an early date.[45]

Chávez's New York connections led to the performance of his compositions on several occasions during the 1920s. Varèse's premiere of *Otros tres exágonos* has been called "the first significant performance of his music in the United States."[46] "The Dance of Men and Machines," the fourth movement of his ballet-symphony *H.P.* (*Horsepower*), was included in another International Composers' Guild concert on 28 November 1926. According to Olin Downes in the *New York Times*, who called Chávez "the Mexican composer of radical bent," the audience laughed at the "shrill and discordant sounds" of the music, but a critic in *Musical America* found "humor in the combination" of Mexican folk tunes and sounds associated with industry, "and eerie fancy as well."[47] Chávez played some of his own music at the first Copland-Sessions concert on 22 April 1928, which included a Sonata for Piano and Three Sonatinas for piano and other instruments. Once again Downes was unenthusiastic, but the critic of *Musical America* declared, "The heavy rhythm with the Mexican Indian themes employed by Mr. Chavez, made his works the most interesting of the evening."[48]

A much more glittering occasion was the U.S. premiere of the complete ballet version of *H.P.* by the Philadelphia Grand Opera Company on 31 March 1932. The music was performed by members of the Philadelphia Orchestra under the baton of its director, Leopold Stokowski. Diego Rivera, fresh from his highly successful one-man show at New York's MoMA, designed the decor and costumes. Catherine Littlefield was the choreographer. The ballet purported to show the presumably beneficial relationship between the South, with its bounty of tropical products, and the machine-driven North. Frances Flynn Paine served as a kind of midwife in the birth of this event, having interested Stokowski in the ballet and hoping to take advantage of the "enormous amount of . . . interest in Mexican things in the United States."[49]

The well-publicized premiere attracted a distinguished crowd: "all musical and social Philadelphia as well as pilgrims from New York."[50] The critics' verdict, however, was mixed, particularly with respect to Chávez's music; and a recent study proclaimed the event "a Pan-American communication failure."[51] Modern commentators may interpret the theme of the ballet as representing U.S. imperialism in Latin America, but the contrast between these two regions was a commonplace during the early twentieth century, informing as it did such works as Chase's *Mexico*. It is also worth noting that Marc Blitzstein found that "since Chávez's music is hard, not soft, literal, brutal and unperfumed, we were offered the paradox of a 'Southern' composer dealing most successfully with the 'Northern' aspects of his theme."[52] At the time of *H.P.*'s premiere, Stokowski was recently returned from his second trip to Mexico, where he had traveled to rural areas and listened to indigenous music.[53]

For Chávez, the years after 1932 brought new accolades and opportunities in the United States. In 1935 William Paley, president of the Columbia Broadcasting System, invited Chávez to compose a work that might be performed on the CBS radio network. The result was *Sinfonía india*, which he premiered with the Columbia Symphony Orchestra on 23 January 1936. The following year Chávez made his debut as a guest conductor with the New York Philharmonic, launching his conducting career in the United States. In the late 1930s, he often included some of his own compositions in the concerts he conducted, among them an orchestral suite derived from *H.P.*, his *Sinfonía de Antígona*, and *Sinfonía india*. In February 1937, *Time* magazine placed Chávez firmly within the vogue for things Mexican:

> Poets and painters have swarmed over Mexico, inordinately praised its crude-colored landscapes, its dark slow-moving

> Indians, its Aztec remains. . . . In painting, no one has done more to work out a native style than Diego Rivera. In music, no one has done so much as his good friend Carlos Chávez, the swart young mestizo who can make a full orchestra suggest swishing gourds and shrill clay pipes.[54]

Thanks in part to the efforts of Chávez, music, along with art, won recognition as part of Mexico's post-revolutionary cultural renaissance. To members of the American musical community, Chávez's strong commitment to modernism, along with his use of indigenous instruments and themes, exemplified what they sought to do with American music. Meanwhile, despite periods of strained U.S.-Mexican relations during the 1920s and 1930s, both governments used music, as well as art, to smooth the rough edges of diplomatic differences.

NOTES

1. "Men of Mexico," *Vanity Fair*, June 1929, 62.

2. "Noted Woman Archeologist," *New York Times*, 15 April 1933. The occasion for the article was the recent death of archaeologist Zelia Nuttall, a longtime resident of Mexico City.

3. The literature on the Mexican Revolution is enormous. For a recent survey, see chapters 14–16 in William H. Beezley and Michael C. Meyer, eds., *The Oxford History of Mexico*, rev. ed. (New York: Oxford University Press, 2010).

4. See Helen Delpar, "Goodbye to the 'Greaser': Mexico, the MPDDA, and Derogatory Films, 1922–1926," *Journal of Popular Film and Television* 12 (Spring 1984): 34–41.

5. For an analysis of the range of U.S. views from left to right toward the Revolution, see John A. Britton, *Revolution and Ideology: Images of the Revolution in the United States* (Lexington: University of Kentucky Press, 1995).

6. See Rick A. Lopez, "The Noche Mexicana and the Exhibition of Popular Arts," in *The Eagle and the Virgin: Nation and Cultural Revolution, 1920–1940*, ed. Mary Kay Vaughan and Stephen E. Lewis (Durham, NC: Duke University Press, 2006), 23–42.

7. For an overview of post-revolutionary trends in painting and the other arts, see Helen Delpar, "Mexican Culture, 1920–1945," in Beezley and Meyer, eds., *Oxford History of Mexico*, 508–34.

8. Carleton Beals, *Glass Houses: Ten Years of Free-Lancing* (Philadelphia: J. B. Lippincott, 1938), 175.

9. Helen Delpar, *The Enormous Vogue of Things Mexican: Cultural Relations between the United States and Mexico, 1920–1935* (Tuscaloosa: University of Alabama Press, 1992), 133; Marshall B. Davidson and Elizabeth Stillinger, *The American Wing at the Metropolitan Museum of Art* (New York: Alfred A. Knopf, 1985), 6.

10. Thomas Hart Benton, *An American in Art: A Personal and Technical Autobiography* (Lawrence: University Press of Kansas, 1969), 61–62.

11. Delpar, *The Enormous Vogue of Things Mexican*, 69–72; Britton, *Revolution and Ideology*, 105–10.

12. Delpar, *The Enormous Vogue of Things Mexican*, 18–20, 47–49, 72–74.

13. Hubert Herring and Herbert Weinstock, eds., *Renascent Mexico* (New York: Covici Friede, 1935).

14. Delpar, *The Enormous Vogue of Things Mexican*, 16, 57–58; Dina Berger, *The Development of Mexico's Tourist Industry: Pyramids by Day, Martinis by Night* (New York: Palgrave Macmillan, 2006).

15. Alejandro Ugalde, "The Presence of Mexican Art in New York between the World Wars: Cultural Exchange and Art Diplomacy" (PhD diss., Columbia University, 2003), 108–17; Christina Taylor Gibson, "The Music of Manuel M. Ponce, Julián Carrillo, and Carlos Chávez in New York, 1925–1932" (PhD diss., University of Maryland, 2008), 133; José Juan Tablada, "Nueva York de día y noche," *El Universal*, 12 October 1930, sec. 4, 3, 11.

16. Ugalde, "Mexican Art in New York," 117–21.

17. Delpar, *The Enormous Vogue of Things Mexican*, 34–36, 83–84, 147–48.

18. *Avant-Garde Art and Artists in Mexico: Anita Brenner's Journals of the Roaring Twenties*, ed. Susannah Joel Glusker, 2 vols. (Austin: University of Texas Press, 2010), 2:603.

19. Frances Flynn Paine to Elizabeth Cutter Morrow, 14 September 1928, Box 61, Elizabeth Cutter Morrow Papers, Smith College, Northampton, MA.

20. "Exodus or Reconquest," *Mexican Life* 3 (November–December 1927): 34.

21. Roque Armando, "'Tata Nacho' y la música popular mexicana," *Revista de revistas* 15 (31 May 1925): 20.

22. José Mojica, *I a Sinner: The Autobiography of Fray José Francisco de Guadalupe Mojica, O.F.M.* (Chicago: Franciscan Herald Press, 1963), 181. Mojica later had a successful career with the Chicago Opera Company and in early talking motion pictures filmed in both Spanish and English. In 1941 he entered a Franciscan monastery in Lima.

23. "'Rancho mexicano' in Gaities," (New York) *Sun*, 12 June 1925.

24. See, for example, Luis Lara Pardo, "La música mexicana en Nueva York," *Revista de revistas* 10 (2 November 1919): 24–25, and Salvador Ordóñez Ochoa, "La vida musical en Nueva York," *Excelsior: Nuestra revista de los jueves*, 13 February 1930 and 20 February 1930.

25. Roberto García Morillo, *Carlos Chávez: Vida y Obra* (Mexico City: Fondo de Cultura Económica, 1960), 26.

26. Anna Indych-López, *Muralism Without Walls: Rivera, Orozco, and Siqueiros in the United States, 1927–1940* (Pittsburgh: University of Pittsburgh Press, 2009), 64.

27. Jaime R. Aguila, "Mexican/U.S. Immigration Policy Prior to the Great Depression," *Diplomatic History* 31 (April 2007): 207–25; Francisco E. Balderrama and Raymond Rodríguez, *Decade of Betrayal: Mexican Repatriation in the 1930s* (Albuquerque: University of New Mexico Press, 1995). See also Delpar, *The Enormous Vogue of Things Mexican*, 16–17, 81–82.

28. Delpar, *The Enormous Vogue of Things Mexican*, 135–36.

29. Ugalde, "Mexican Art in New York," 176–82; Alon Bement to Charles R. Richards, 21 September 1927; and W. W. Brierley to Charles R. Richards, 20 October 1927, Box 321, folder 3342, General Education Board Collection, Rockefeller Archive Center, Pocantico Hills, NY.

30. A charro is a traditional horseman from Western Mexico. The charro became iconic of Mexican culture during the Golden Age of Mexican cinema, in the 1930s and 40s, when it became synonymous with honor, dignity, skill, and bravery in the rural world. They differ from the American cowboy in etiquette, tradition and social status (*Ed.*).

31. Percy Hammond, "Mexican Tipica Players Please Palace Audience," *New York Herald Tribune*, 13 March 1928. See also John Koegel, "Compositores mexicanos y cubanos en Nueva York, c. 1880–1920," *Historia Mexicana* 66 (October–December

2006): 559–75, and Mario Talavera, *Miguel Lerdo de Tejada: Su vida pintoresca y anecdótica* (Mexico City: Editorial "Compás," n.d.).

32. "Mexican Official Band at Palace: Enthusiastic Applause Greets Native and Spanish Airs on Opening Program: Chili con Carne Served: Latin-American Consuls and Other Notables Present," *The World*, 13 March 1928.

33. "McKee honors Mexicans." *New York Times*, 21 March 1928.

34. Detailed accounts of the 1930 exhibit appear in Ugalde, "Mexican Art in New York," 189–211, and in Indych-López, *Muralism Without Walls*, 75–128.

35. Ugalde, "Mexican Art in New York," 206; "The Mexican Exhibit," *New York Times*, 15 October 1930.

36. On the 1940 exhibition, see Ugalde, "Mexican Art in New York," 396–459.

37. Ibid., 407. Rockefeller was also notorious for his role in the destruction of a Rivera mural in Rockefeller Center in 1934. See ibid., 260–97.

38. Jean Charlot, *Four Centuries of Mexican Art* (New York and Mexico City: Museum of Modern Art and Instituto de Antropología e Historia de México, 1940), 141.

39. Quoted in Ugalde, "Mexican Art in New York," 443.

40. Gibson, "The Music of Manuel M. Ponce, Julián Carrillo, and Carlos Chávez in New York," 165–66.

41. "Series arranged of Mexican Music" *New York Times*, 1 May 1940.

42. Carlos Chávez, "Introduction," in *Mexican Music: Notes by Herbert Weinstock for Concerts Arranged by Carlos Chávez as Part of the Exhibition: Twenty Centuries of Mexican Art* (New York: Museum of Modern Art, 1940), 9–10. See also Robert L. Stevenson, *Music in Mexico: A Historical Survey* (New York: Thomas Y. Crowell, 1952), 1–3; and Leonora Saavedra, "Of Selves and Others: Historiography, Ideology, and the Politics of Modern Mexican Music" (PhD. diss., University of Pittsburgh, 2001), 317–29.

43. Elgin Groseclose, "New Music in Mexico," *New York Times*, 28 July 1935.

44. Carlos Chávez, "Music in a Mexican Test Tube," *New York Times*, 2 July 1939.

45. Robert M. Stevenson, "Carlos Chavez's United States Press Coverage," *Inter-American Music Review* 3 (Spring–Summer 1981): 124–27.

46. Gibson, "The Music of Manuel M. Ponce, Julián Carrillo, and Carlos Chávez in New York," 133–36.

47. Olin Downes, "Music: More of the Ultra-Modern," *New York Times*, 29 November 1926, 16; R. C. B. B., "Modernists evoke laughter and applause," *Musical America* 45 (4 December 1926): 7.

48. Olin Downes, "Music: Presenting American Composers," *New York Times*, 23 April 1928, 20; I. L., "First Copland-Sessions Concert," *Musical America* 48 (12 May 1928): 20.

49. Frances Flynn Paine to Chávez, 17 September 1930, Fondo Carlos Chávez, Archivo General de la Nación, Mexico City.

50. John Martin, "Mexican Ballet in World Premiere," *New York Times*, 1 April 1932, 9.

51. See Christina Taylor Gibson, "The Reception of Carlos Chávez's *Horsepower*: A Pan-American Communication Failure," *American Music* 30 (Summer 2012): 57–93.

52. Quoted in Robert L. Parker, *Carlos Chávez: Mexico's Modern Day Orpheus* (Boston: Twayne, 1983), 110.

53. Gibson, "The Music of Manuel M. Ponce, Julián Carrillo, and Carlos Chávez in New York," 120–24; "Stokowski Returns," *New York Times*, 7 February 1931 and "Friends of Music Decade," *New York Times*, 5 April 1931; "Chokopul's Travels," *Time*, 11 April 1932.

54. "Music: Mexican in Manhattan," *Time*, 22 February 1937.

Carlos Chávez and Paul Strand

JAMES KRIPPNER

> Too often musicians spend their lives among musicians, and painters or sculptors or photographers like to be with the practitioners of their own art. I like to think that my long and close friendship with Paul Strand is an exception perhaps for both of us. My predominant interest in music, and his lifetime devotion to photography have enabled us to be friends.
>
> —Carlos Chávez, unpublished 1975 foreword to *Paul Strand: Sixty Years of Photographs*

Historical biography is a tenuous enterprise, one that permits only a partial reconstruction of complex lives and past experiences.[1] The task is made even more difficult when two individuals and the fraught concept of "friendship" are involved.[2] The quotation above demonstrates that Carlos Chávez considered Paul Strand a friend, a sentiment that Strand undoubtedly shared.[3] Though the two men enjoyed a sustained and cordial relationship, its meaning varied over time. Chavez's reference to his "long and close friendship" with Strand summarizes a relationship that waxed and waned over almost fifty years, crossing national as well as artistic borders.

Fortunately for historians, Chávez kept meticulous documentation. In the Archivo General de la Nación, his correspondence with Strand is divided into three separate sections: Paul Strand 1930–39, Paul Strand 1940–77, and Paul Strand 1975–77. Interestingly, the letters contained within these categories challenge the archive's categories and chronological divisions. At times they are composed by or addressed to people other than Paul Strand, are dated prior to or after the designated years, and discuss events that happened out of sequence or before the years referenced.

The letters' greatest density comes in the years 1932–40; they decline precipitously after this date though they conclude with a flurry of correspondence from 1975 to 1977. These sources, supplemented by texts and images scattered in archives and collections across the United States and Mexico, provide glimpses into the shared experiences and personal relationships of two twentieth-century modernist giants (though it should be noted that neither artist defined himself or his work in these terms).[4] They also reveal intriguing details about the surprisingly transnational artistic communities of Mexico City and New York City in the 1920s and 1930s; the cultural history of Mexico following the Mexican Revolution, especially during the years 1932–34 when Strand lived and worked in Mexico in response to Chávez's invitation; the cosmopolitan lives of two legendary artists sympathetic to Marxism from the mid-1930s through the Cold War decades following the Second World War; and the distance granted by the passage of time and the failing of memory as two long lives drew to a close in the mid-1970s. It is to the consideration of these four eras and their related themes that we now turn.

Artists and Borders, 1928–32

At Strand's memorial service on 16 October 1976, Chávez recalled that he first met the photographer in Taos, New Mexico, during the early 1930s. However, the passage of time was playing tricks with the composer's memory. The paper trail connecting these two artists clearly indicates that they met earlier in New York, where the young composer visited from December 1923 to March 1924 and again from September 1926 to July 1928.[5] During this latter trip Chávez apparently extended his limited finances by sharing an apartment with the painter Rufino Tamayo. He also began lasting collaborations with fellow musicians Aaron Copland, Edgard Varèse, and Leopold Stokowski.[6] These types of interactions were common in New York City in the 1920s, where the vibrant cultural scene brought together visual and performance artists, creating dense networks of artistic and personal exchange and of course frequent conflicts. The International Composers' Guild and the League of Composers, two contending organizations to which Chávez belonged, provide an example of these types of networks.[7] At times, the overlap between innovative currents in music and the visual arts became explicit, as when the League of Composers staged performances in the Anderson Galleries. This was the same building in which the photographer and gallery owner Alfred Stieglitz maintained his Intimate Gallery, devoted to his work and that of Arthur Dove, Marsden Hartley, John Marin, Charles Demuth, Paul Strand, and Georgia O'Keefe.[8] Though we lack precise details, it is clear that the friendship between Chávez and Strand originated in this milieu and would continue to develop when both artists visited New Mexico, prior to Strand's two-year sojourn in Mexico, where their most intensive collaboration took place.

Strand lived a long and legendary life as an art and social-documentary photographer. His career started when he joined an after-school photography club directed by Lewis Hine in 1908 and continued with his first major exhibition at Stieglitz's legendary gallery 291 in 1916. The publication of his photographs in the final issue of Stieglitz's *Camera Work* in 1917 signaled his emergence as arguably the world's foremost practitioner of what would later be called "straight photography," or photography prohibiting any manipulation of the negative, a stature he maintained until his death in 1976.[9] In the early 1920s Strand purchased an Akeley motion-picture camera and began experimenting with moving images. He would work with both photography and film through the 1930s before returning exclusively to photography in the 1940s.[10] Strand's friendship with Chávez and their interactions in New York, Taos, and Mexico undoubtedly influenced his artistic and political development. Strand specifically credited Chávez as a major influence in his embrace of socially committed art in the 1930s.[11] But their personal ties went beyond art and politics. On a more intimate and perhaps more interesting level, Chávez and his family provided companionship and emotional support for Strand in a number of ways. These included hosting him as their guest while he struggled with depression as his first marriage crumbled, ultimately ending with a divorce while in Mexico, in 1933.[12]

Unlike Chávez, Strand was a primarily visual person who wrote relatively infrequently, presenting unique challenges for those seeking to construct his historical biography. Written evidence demonstrating Strand's early relationship with Chávez comes primarily from letters written to Chávez by Strand's first wife, the artist Rebecca Salsbury. The correspondence captures something of the ambience of the time and place, and demonstrates a degree of familiarity allowing informal banter. For example, in an extensive letter dated 3 January 1929, Rebecca writes:

> We have been hoping to hear from you—but I know your concerts, babies, wife and Mexico are legitimately conspiring to keep you away from letters—while I, having more time, and the wish to have you know we have not abandoned you, am writing.

The letter discusses the thriving artistic and social scene in New York and notes that several sources report his concerts are going well. A connection to Strand is established when Rebecca writes, "If Stieglitz stays well Paul will have an exhibition this year—probably in March. I hope you will be here for it."[13] She also notes:

> I am glad the orchestra is a success—it was almost bound to be under your precise and eager leadership—I would like to hear something refreshing in music—You cannot imagine how thoroughly sterile and impotent all the music has been this winter. I imagine the writing is competent enough musically—but, as Clurman said, "There is no seed in the loins"—while I go further even than that and say there are no loins.[14]

Rebecca concludes with an accurate self-assessment of the content of her letter and an invitation for future visits:

> This is all the gossip I can give you. You must come soon and hear it all in person—You have been missed by us all this year—your name is often said—"any word from Carlos?" Paul sends love—and if you even have a moment, do write.

This series of letters continues with another dated 18 March 1930. In addition to frequent references to the musical and artistic scene in New York and Chávez's success in Mexico they discuss Rebecca's well-known 1929 trip to Taos with the artist Georgia O'Keefe (at that time Alfred Stieglitz's wife), as well as Rebecca and Paul's desire to travel to Mexico. The series concludes with a final letter in 1937, in which Rebecca notes her second marriage, to Bill James, and invites Carlos to visit them in Taos.[15]

Although Chávez may have been confused about the time and place of his initial meeting with Paul Strand, his 1976 eulogy contained an element of truth. Chávez and Strand met again in Taos in the early 1930s, an experience that cemented their friendship and led directly to Chávez's invitation to Strand to visit Mexico. We know that Strand made visits to New Mexico in 1930, '31, and '32, and that Chávez came to Taos on a commission from Mexico's Secretaría de Educación Pública (Ministry of Public Education, known by the Spanish acronym SEP) to study "the music of the Indian reservations in the United States" in 1931.[16] Both were certainly acquainted with the doyenne of Taos artistic society, Mabel Dodge Luhan, although Strand is known to have been disdainful of the gossipy demimonde that frequented Luhan's ranch, Los Gallos.[17] A diverse array of artists, writers, and intellectuals passed through Taos in the 1920s and 1930s and were frequently hosted by Luhan. Among them were D. H. Lawrence, Leopold Stokowski, Martha Graham, Mary Austin, Aldous Huxley, Robinson Jeffers, Willa Cather, Carl Jung, Ansel Adams, and Dorothea Lange.[18]

Though he wrote little about his time in New Mexico, Strand produced several photographs, including several biographical portraits of family and friends. These include portraits of his then-wife, Rebecca, and several friends in New Mexico, including Ward Lockwood, Gina Knee, Barbara "Bobby" Hawk, Cornelia Thompson and her daughter Nancy, and the Irish writer and revolutionary Ernie O'Malley. Strand also became friends with the radical author, playwright, and screenwriter Philip "Ted" Stevenson and the Irish poet and folklorist Ella Young, who lectured in the United States after serving prison time for running guns to the Irish Republican Army.[19] Among the biographical portraits that Strand produced in New Mexico was a lovely photograph of a relatively young Carlos Chávez (see Figure 1). In this image, Chávez appears to have an intense gaze focused somewhere beyond the camera, the texture of his sweater offset by the smooth surface of a dress shirt, his human form framed by a rectangular adobe wall, dense clouds, and a barely visible elevated landscape in the distance. Strand had an uncanny ability to convey a sense of intimacy in his photographic portraits. This photograph certainly indicates that Strand counted Chávez among the circle of friendly acquaintances he made images of while in Taos, and perhaps provides evidence of his familiarity with key aspects of Chávez's personality.

The first written source establishing a direct link between Strand and Chávez is a telegram Strand sent from Santa Fe on 16 November 1932:

> Plan driving in Car to Mexico City and Want [to] Bring Along Examples My Work could you Get and Send Me Laredo General Delivery Some Official Letter Identification Perhaps From Saenz Facilitating Entry Photographs Into Mexico and Photographing While There Will Reach Laredo About Ten Days Thanks and Affectionate Greetings Paul Strand.

Chávez responded to this telegram with an official letter of invitation from the National Conservatory on official SEP stationery, in Spanish, dated 19 November 1932. Chávez continues by asking the authorities to extend every possible courtesy to Mr. Strand.

Figure 1. Paul Strand, *Carlos Chávez, Taos, New Mexico, 1932.*
©Aperture Foundation, Paul Strand Archives.

Chávez simultaneously sent an informal personal letter, devoid of legalese, written in colloquial English and also dated 19 November 1932, to Strand in Laredo, Texas, where he was waiting to cross over into Mexico, noting how glad he was that Strand was coming and urging him to contact him if there were any problems during his journey. Thus began Strand's Mexican chapter, which depended entirely upon the invitation and subsequent support Strand received from Chávez. In addition to demonstrating the origins of the Chávez-Strand relationship, the early years in New York and the American Southwest reveal a youthful creativity and intellectual openness that is perhaps surprising given both artists' reputations for autocratic tendencies during the later years of their lives.

The Mexican Chapter, 1932–34

Chávez and Strand's most intense period of collaboration came after Strand traveled to Mexico armed with Chávez's letter of introduction.

During this era, from 1932 to 1934, they worked together to promote Strand's photographic work and filmmaking in Mexico. Chávez most likely supported Strand due to his cosmopolitan belief that high-quality art transcended national borders. He also sought to promote a positive image of Mexico abroad after the turmoil of the Mexican Revolution.[20] In Mexico, Strand enjoyed a successful exhibition of his photographs; obtained work, originally at the level of elementary school art instructor and later as the director of the Oficina de Fotografía y Cinematografía, the photography and filmmaking sector of SEP's Departamento de Bellas Artes; and finally, played a central role in the creation of the film *Redes* (1936; released as *The Wave* in the United States in 1937). Chávez was director of the Departamento de Bellas Artes from March 1933 to May 1934 and almost certainly created the department of photography that Strand was to direct.[21] In the end, Strand's collaboration with Chávez and his years in Mexico resulted in a visual archive consisting of 234 photographic negatives and 114 prints, as well as *Redes* (1936).[22] Despite Strand's intense productivity, he would depart Mexico abruptly in January 1935 in the midst of much controversy. He would not return until 1966, when he made a brief but important visit.[23]

Strand's exchange of letters with Chávez continued in Saltillo and Querétaro, as Strand journeyed south from Laredo, Texas, to Mexico City. We know that Strand arrived in Mexico City in early 1933, though the precise day remains a mystery. An exhibition of Strand's photographs was presented at the Sala de Arte of the SEP, from 3 to 15 February 1933. Strand's letter of introduction from Chávez stated that the SEP planned an exhibition of Strand's photographs, yet decades later Strand incorrectly recalled that the exhibition was unplanned: "When I came to Mexico I brought fifty-four prints along including last summer's work, with no idea of a public exhibition—anything but."[24] Chávez's influence was decisive in arranging for a public viewing of the photographer's work. According to Strand, "Chávez saw the things he felt Mexico should have the opportunity to see (photography)— All they knew was Tina Modotti and Edward Weston—not much to know in my humble opinion."[25]

According to Strand, the exhibit occurred because Chávez provided access to those in a position to make decisions in Mexico, especially Narciso Bassols, SEP's Minister of Education from 1931 to 1934. Chávez was a protegé of Bassols, and both were united in their belief in socialist education, which perhaps ironically did not erase older patterns of patron-client relationships in terms of implementation.[26] As Strand succinctly stated, "We showed the pictures to Bassols and he said yes."[27] Chávez had worked intermittently with the SEP throughout the 1920s, first as an inspector of music schools for workers and after 1928 as the director of the Conservatorio Nacional before becoming head of the DBA (Departamento de Bellas Artes or Department of Fine Arts). Strand's artistic work in Mexico was inextricably linked to his friendship with Chávez and the institutional access that Chávez provided. When Bassols and then Chávez lost their positions at the end of 1934 due to bureaucratic infighting at the SEP, Strand lost his most important patron and sponsor in Mexico, as well as control over the unfinished film tentatively titled *Pescados*, and ultimately released as *Redes*. Despite these and an array of personal problems, Strand managed to create an extraordinary though inevitably partial visual archive of Mexico during these years. The entire experience, including all the images that Strand produced, would not have occurred without the friendship of Chávez and Strand.

Following the photography exhibition at SEP's Sala de Arte, Strand spent April to September 1933 traveling through Mexico, accompanied by Agustín Velázquez Chávez, Carlos Chávez's nephew. Strand's visit to Mexico happened just after the avant-garde artistic experimentation of the so-called Mexican Renaissance of the 1920s and before the consolidation of the post-revolutionary Mexican state under the reformist administration of Lázaro Cárdenas. As such, his experience was somewhat idiosyncratic compared to that of the steady stream of foreign artists and intellectuals traveling in Mexico in the 1920s and 1930s, who were drawn by the cultural and political effervescence in the aftermath of the Mexican Revolution.[28] Velázquez Chávez played an important role as Strand's translator and guide, though the relationship ultimately ended in acrimony due to disputes over proper credits for the film *Redes*.[29]

In addition to providing Strand with his nephew's help, Chávez played a decisive role in finding Strand employment. In a letter to Chávez from Oaxaca dated 4 April 1933 Strand noted that in May he would decide whether to stay in Mexico or leave.[30] To allow him to extend his Mexican visit, Chávez found work for him first as an elementary school art teacher and then as the director of SEP's Oficina de Cine, a position Strand held while working on *Redes*. Although it seems unlikely he did much teaching of elementary school art, Strand did assist Velázquez Chávez in curating an exhibition of children's art in Mexico City and reviewed at least one public art program in the state of Michoacán.[31] It seems more likely that Chávez assigned Strand to this position so that he could pursue his photography with a salary and sanction from the SEP. In 1933, Strand, accompanied by Velázquez Chávez, photographed in the states of Michoacán, Hidalgo, Puebla, México, Oaxaca, Veracruz, and possibly Tlaxcala.[32]

Strand's efforts in photography would be complemented by his work in film, which occupied him from September 1933 through November 1934. Chávez's support of Strand's filmmaking was even more decisive than his assistance in terms of Strand's photography. On 26 November 1933, Strand wrote from Mexico City to his old friend Kurt Baasch in New York:

> As I think you know, Carlos was made Jefe of the Departamento de Belles [*sic*] Artes some months ago. One of the things he greatly wants to start is a program of movies to be made—according to ideas we both agree upon—movies which would have a social significance and meaning somewhat from the same point of view that the group works from—he induced me to stay and start the whole thing.[33]

Redes, which tells the story of fishermen in Alvarado, Veracruz, and their struggle to unionize, is widely considered a classic in the history of Mexican cinema.[34] The full story of the making of *Redes* has been told elsewhere.[35] The bureaucratic infighting involved throughout the making of this film offers a fascinating narrative to consider alongside the overwhelmingly masculine tale of working-class emancipation that is vividly though somewhat simplistically portrayed in the film.[36]

It is important, especially for readers unfamiliar with Mexican history, to frame Strand's work in the Oficina de Cine within a larger educational and political context. Chávez was in charge of the Oficina as director of the DBA, and he may very well have written the "Plan para la filmación de películas educativas," the overarching document that authorized the filming of *Redes*. Chávez proposed several of these broadly conceived projects when he was at the DBA, including, for example, plans for the socialist education of music students. All of this took place within the Mexican government's attempts to implement both socialist education and the third article of the Mexican Constitution, which stated, among other things, that education should be mandatory, free, and secular (that is, not controlled by the Catholic Church). The SEP, under the administration of Bassols, played a decisive role in realizing these goals. Correspondence pertaining to the filming of *Redes* also demonstrates the artistic and personal links between Chávez and Strand. Strand, besides asking for filming materials and larger budgets, writes in detail about the progress of the filming, indicating that Chávez is conversant with the project. In addition to sharing the writing and revising of the script, they discuss scenes, the content, the actors, etc., as well as hopes and frustrations, all expressed in personal and even intimate ways.[37]

In essence, the personal/institutional network supporting Strand's artistic work in Mexico fell victim to a bureaucratic coup. On 9 May 1934 Narciso Bassols resigned as Minister of SEP amid significant controversy. He was replaced by Ignacio García Téllez, who then replaced Chávez with Antonio Castro Leal as the new director of the Departamento de Bellas Artes. Rather than fire Strand outright, Castro Leal created a new Sección de Cine and placed Agustín Velázquez Chávez in charge. Initially, all of this maneuvering in Mexico City caused some confusion for the film crew working in Alvarado. One long-term consequence of the transition was that Strand ultimately lost control over the addition of the soundtrack and the distribution of the finished film. Another major consequence was that the commission for the film's musical score ultimately ended up with Silvestre Revueltas.[38] Strand maintained amicable relationships with both composers, but the historical record indisputably establishes that he had always believed that Chávez would compose the music for the film, and would later characterize as a "dirty trick" offering the film score to Silvestre Revueltas instead.[39]

On 25 August 1934, Strand wrote a letter to Antonio Castro Leal explaining his understanding of the situation:

> Yesterday I received copies of some correspondence from Carlos Chávez. It came as a complete and rather distressing surprise. Obviously it is not for me to judge the possibilities of his being able to write the music for "Pescados."—But in all fairness I think I should say that I had always counted on him for the music, never considered anyone else, and the reason I did not mention his name when you were here was only because it was so settled both in his mind and mine from the very beginning of this project that he would be the composer. He was eager to write the music and I was eager to have his music in "Pescados." I still am. However, if this was impossible, I want to say that the choice of Revueltas mitigates my disappointment, for I like his music and feel him to be, though less mature than Carlos, also a fine artist.[40]

Later that fall, Chávez sent an angry letter to Strand complaining about his removal from the writing of the musical score. Strand responded with a telegram on 4 November 1934: "There is plenty of Trickiness and Dishonesty Around as I now see but please Believe I have never Been Deliberately or Consciously Disloyal to you."[41] Though Strand and Chávez's friendship endured, the wound from this incident took a long time to heal for the composer. According to Chávez scholar and biographer Gloria Carmona, Chávez never saw *Redes* until she arranged a private viewing in her home in 1976—perhaps not incidentally the year of Strand's death.[42]

It would take several years to sort out the disputes surrounding the making of *Redes*. Strand left Mexico in January 1935, somewhat embittered though still proud of what had been achieved with *Redes* and on good terms with Chávez.[43] In a letter dated 15 January 1935, Jacob Strand, Paul Strand's father, acknowledged his son's earlier letter informing him that Chávez would be visiting New York City soon. In reference to Chávez, the elder Strand wrote: "We will do everything we can to make it pleasant for him, realizing how nice he has been to you. If Chávez will let me know, by wire, when he arrives (about the time of his arrival) I will be glad to meet him with the auto—and take him to the house."[44]

After the Mexican Chapter, 1935–74

Following Strand's exit from Mexico in 1935, the friendship between Carlos Chávez and Paul Strand moved into a new phase. The paper trail of correspondence linking the two maintains a density through 1940. The letters dwindle in the 1940s and appear to end in the mid-1950s before starting again in the late 1960s. This correspondence includes several letters between Chávez and Virginia Stevens, Strand's second wife, concerning the marketing in Mexico of Strand's *Photographs of Mexico* (1940). Strand's combination of art and social documentary, expressed with new maturity in *Photographs of Mexico*, would be refined in subsequent photographic studies created in the United States, France, Italy, the Outer Hebrides of Scotland, Egypt, Romania, Morocco, and Ghana.[45] For this reason, *Photographs of Mexico* can be considered a work of decisive importance in terms of Strand's artistic development and thus the history of modern photography. It also provides an important visual record of aspects of Mexican rural culture in the 1930s.

The selection and ordering of the twenty images in Strand's portfolio are distinctive. In total, they include one landscape; three primarily architectural photographs with an emphasis on gateways, doors, and windows; five examples of religious sculpture (one Virgin and four Christs in various stages of torment and crucifixion); and eleven portraits depicting men, women, and children, individually and together. The trajectory of the sequence—from physical landscape to built environment to the popular artistic practice of religious sculpture to portraits—reveals a historical sensibility and a finely attuned attention to detail. Strand's photographs construct a fragmentary visual archive of rural Mexico during this era, though the equation of these images with *México profundo*—deep, unchanging, timeless Mexico—may tell us more about the observer than about the content of the photographs or the context of their making.[46]

Virginia Stevens had a special interest in the success of this venture, to be sold only through advance subscriptions, since she had financed the initial printing of this selection of Paul Strand's photography of Mexico. Chávez assisted her by compiling first and second lists of prospective buyers drawn from the Mexican cultural and political elite, more than half of whom he personally contacted. Among the fifty names included in these lists were Jesús Silva Herzog, Luis Barragán, Daniel and Ismael Cosío Villegas, Dolores del Río, Alfonso Reyes, Moisés and Aarón Saenz, Emilio Portes Gil, Narciso Bassols, and Salvador Novo.[47]

Strand and Chávez also continued to communicate about the fate of *Redes*. On 25 October 1936, Chávez wrote to Strand that though he had not seen the film, he would have protested if he had known of any important changes. Chávez apparently continued to act as a champion of the film and Strand's contribution to it even after he left the DBA. One of Strand's most prized possessions appears to have been a framed copy of a letter from President Lázaro Cárdenas, dated 3 January 1938, congratulating him for his work on *Redes*.[48] Though it is impossible to know for sure why President Cárdenas wrote this letter to Strand, it seems likely that Chávez, despite his personal disappointment at losing the commission for the musical score, intervened to ensure that Strand received proper acknowledgment in Mexico for his work on the film. More than a year later, on 2 April 1939, Strand wrote to Chávez saying that he profoundly appreciated the letter from Cárdenas. He also noted that a friend had suggested making a film about the great Mexican revolutionary Emiliano Zapata. Strand wrote: "Some day I will like to make this film in Mexico, but *well*, by means of people like you and Miguel [Covarrubias] and a group capable of making a great heroic documentary. What do you say?"[49] Alas, a Strand-Chávez-Covarrubias film on Zapata never materialized, and all three artists moved on to other projects.

After this point, the letters between Strand and Chávez become markedly less frequent. On 5 September 1940, Chávez wrote to Strand noting that his book was a great success and agreeing to write a letter in support of Strand's (ultimately unsuccessful) application for a Guggenheim fellowship. On 10 May 1945 Chávez thanked Strand for a recent letter and informed him of the death of his sister Estefanía. Strand wrote to Chávez on 25 May 1951, hoping to locate the negative of *Redes*; Chávez responded a few days later saying he did not know anything about the negative though he would look into it and thanked the photographer for the copy of his book *Time in New England*.[50] A gap in the archival record appears from this time until the mid-1960s, as Strand prepared for a return visit to Mexico in 1966 and the subsequent 1967 re-release of *Photographs of Mexico*, with the new title *The Mexican Portfolio*. David and Brynna Prensky, acquaintances of Strand and owners of a leading Mexico City art gallery, in a letter dated 5 December 1965 noted: "Carlos Chávez is alive and quite active. He runs the composers workshop here and conducts with a fair degree of frequency as a guest conductor or on special occasions such as when his young hopefuls present their new works."[51] It seems likely that Chávez and Strand renewed their friendship as a result of Strand's 1966 trip and the 1967 publication of *The Mexican Portfolio*, though there is no written record of their meeting during this later visit to Mexico.

On 27 July 1966, Strand wrote to Chávez from Orgeval, France, saying: "I hope to be able to send you a new book about Egypt in the not too distant future." On 26 May 1969, Chávez wrote expressing his admiration for Strand's *Living Egypt*. On 22 April 1972, Chávez thanked Strand for sending him a copy of *Paul Strand: A Retrospective Monograph, The Years 1915–1968*. In January 1974, Chávez sent a note to Paul and Hazel (Strand's third wife) saying he would be in New York soon; they responded promptly, saying they hoped they would be able to meet and catch up during his visit.

Memory and the Tricks of Time, 1975–77

On 1 April 1976 Hazel Strand sent Chávez a telegram informing him of Paul's death; Chávez himself would die on 2 August 1978, a little more than two years later. As their long lives drew to a close, communication between Chávez and Strand increased, largely over a foreword that Chávez was to write for a book on Strand's work. Carlos Chávez wrote the words cited at the outset of this essay in the summer of 1975. The document from which they come is located in the Archivo General de la Nación within a sequence of letters from 1975 to 1977 between Chávez and Hazel Kingsbury Strand, and between Chávez and Michael Hoffman, at the time the editor and publisher of the Aperture Foundation. The letters reveal that Strand wanted Chávez to write the introductory notes to a published collection of his work, most likely the retrospective volume *Paul Strand: Sixty Years of Photographs*, published in 1976.[52] In the end, the

Chávez text was never published. What type of historical evidence does an unpublished rough draft provide?

On 16 July 1975, Michael E. Hoffman of the Aperture Foundation wrote to Chávez, stating: "My initial feeling about the two pages you kindly sent is that the text is too general and the laudatory remarks do not seem to carry the power of fact." Though Hoffman urged Chávez to revise the text and offered to provide translation from Spanish, Chávez was not able to do so, perhaps because of his own advancing age and declining health.

Though the text remained unrevised and unpublished, excerpts from it provide a fascinating way to begin and end this essay. After praising Strand's sense for creative experimentation, Chávez compared his work in photography to Beethoven's Ninth Symphony and Stravinsky's *Rite of Spring*. He concludes:

> Out of that accidental encounter in Taos my great admiration for Paul developed and turned into an enduring friendship. I convinced him to go to Mexico thinking that he would find material there of value for his experiments. After long, patient, enterprising and solitary traveling through much out-of-the-way Mexican country he found a great deal. In those days I was able to invite him to take a leading part in a cultural film project which I had originated. As head of the Department of Fine Arts of the Secretariat of Public Education I was working on a film program.
>
> The film Paul produced under this program, The Wave, is a magnificent piece. I wrote the music for it, and know the vitality of his contribution to our understanding of Mexican fisherman. I hope he is as proud of it as I am.

Apparently, the passage of time and the fading of memory allowed Chávez to recall some things while forgetting others.

NOTES

I am grateful to Leonora Saavedra for inviting me to contribute this essay and for sharing her research on Carlos Chávez. Portions of this article appeared previously in James Krippner, *Paul Strand in Mexico* (New York: Aperture Foundation, 2010).

1. On the limits of biography, see William St. Clair, "The Biographer as Archaeologist," in *Mapping Lives: The Uses of Biography*, ed. Peter France and William St. Clair (Oxford: Oxford University Press, 2002), 219–34.

2. On the complications of friendship, see Jacques Derrida, *The Politics of Friendship*, trans. George Collins (London and New York: Verso, 2005), esp. 49–74.

3. The introductory notes quoted in the epigraph can be found at the Archivo General de la Nación, Fondo Carlos Chávez (AGN). Unless cited otherwise, all archival documents cited in these notes are from this same archive. For a comprehensive study of Paul Strand's years in Mexico, see Krippner, *Strand in Mexico*. On his relationship with Chávez, see esp. 16–33.

4. These visual and many of the written sources are reproduced throughout Krippner, *Strand in Mexico*.

5. Helen Delpar, *The Enormous Vogue of Things Mexican: Cultural Relations between the United States and Mexico, 1920–1935* (Tuscaloosa: University of Alabama Press, 1992), 44; Krippner, *Strand in Mexico*, 16.

6. Delpar, *The Enormous Vogue of Things Mexican*, 86–90. In a fascinating 1971 radio interview with Charles Amirkhanian and George Cleve, Chávez discussed his first meetings with Varèse (ca. 1923–24) and Copland (in 1927) in New York. The interview, originally recorded for San Francisco's KPFA, is accessible at https://radiom.org/archivesphp?et=InterviewMusic&pageID=2radiom.org/detail.php?et+interviewMusic&omid+AM.1971.09.1.

7. Carol J. Oja, *Making Music Modern: New York in the 1920s* (Oxford and New York: Oxford University Press, 2000), 177–90.

8. Ibid., 190.

9. Krippner, *Strand in Mexico*, 22–25.

10. Ibid., 24–26.

11. Ibid., 75–79. For an understanding of Chávez's political thought in this era, see Leonora Saavedra, "The American Composer in the 1930s: The Social Thought of Seeger and Chávez," in *Understanding Charles Seeger, Pioneer in American Musicology*, ed. Bell Yung and Helen Rees (Urbana and Chicago: University of Illinois Press, 1999), 29–63. Overall context is provided in Mary K. Coffey, "The 'Mexican Problem': Nation and 'Native' in Mexican Muralism and Cultural Discourse," in *The Social and the Real: Political Art of the 1930s in the Western Hemisphere*, ed. Alejandro Anreus, Diana L. Linden, and Jonathan Weinburg (University Park: Pennsylvania State University Press, 2006), 43–70.

12. Krippner, *Strand in Mexico*, 29, 63–64.

13. The pioneering photographer, gallery owner, and publisher Alfred Stieglitz served as an important mentor to Strand until the relationship deteriorated amid personal and professional conflicts in the 1920s. Krippner, *Strand in Mexico*, 27.

14. Rebecca is referring here to Chávez's Orquesta Sinfónica de México. Harold Clurman was a theater director and founder of the Group Theater in New York. Krippner, *Strand in Mexico*, 27. See also Michael Denning, *The Cultural Front: The Laboring of American Culture in the Twentieth Century* (London and New York: Verso, 1996), 164.

15. On Rebecca Strand and O'Keefe's trip to Taos, see Geoff Dyer, *The Ongoing Moment* (New York: Vintage Books, 2005), 69–70.

16. SEP, Departamento de Archivo Histórico y Reprografia, Colección Personal Sobresaliente, Expediente Personal, Chávez Ramírez, Carlos. As cited in Krippner, *Strand in Mexico,* 21.

17. Krippner, *Strand in Mexico,* 21. See also Robert L. Parker, "Leopold Stokowski y Carlos Chávez: Contacto en Taos," *Heterofonía* 20/98–99 (January–December 1988): 4–11; repr. in Robert L. Parker, *Trece panoramas en torno a Carlos Chávez* (Mexico: CONACULTA/ Teoría y Práctica del Arte, 2010).

18. Rebecca Busselle and Trudy Wilner Stack, *Paul Strand Southwest* (New York: Aperture, 2004), 82–85.

19. Ibid., 83. Strand also produced several biographical portraits of Young.

20. On the Mexican context of the Chávez-Strand relationship, see Alfonso Morales Carillo, "Spanish for Your Mexican Visit: Paul Strand South of All Borders," in Krippner, *Strand in Mexico*, 239–64; and Helen Delpar, "Mexican Culture, 1920–45," in *The Oxford History of Mexico*, ed. Michael C. Meyer and William H. Beezley (Oxford and New York: Oxford University Press, 2000), 543–72.

21. Delpar, *The Enormous Vogue of Things Mexican*, 89.

22. Krippner, *Strand in Mexico*, 9–10. All of the images and a digitally remastered copy of the film are included in this work.

23. Ibid.

24. Strand, cited in Steve Yates, *The Transition Years: Paul Strand in New Mexico* (Santa Fe: Museum of New Mexico, 1989), 42.

25. Strand to Stieglitz, 5 February 1933, as cited in John B. Rohrbach, "Art for Society's Sake: Paul Strand's Photographic Visions" (PhD diss., University of Delaware, 1993), 113. Edward Weston and Tina Modotti are now considered to be among the giants of twentieth-century art photography. They arrived together in Mexico in 1923, with Weston leaving in 1926 and Modotti in 1929. The latter would return to Mexico in 1939, where she died in 1942. See John Mraz, *Looking for Mexico: Modern Visual Culture and National Identity* (Durham, NC, and London: Duke University Press, 2009), 82–87; and Sarah Lowe, *Tina Modotti and Edward Weston: The Mexico Years* (London and New York: Merrell, 2004).

26. On the promise and problems of socialist education during the Bassols era, see John Britton, *Educación y radicalismo en México*, vol. 1: *Los años de Bassols (1931–34)* (Mexico City: Secretaría de Educación Pública, 1976).

27. Strand, cited in *Paul Strand: Sixty Years of Photographs* (Millerton, NY: Aperture, 1976), 155.

28. The cultural ambience of Mexico City as well as the impact of Strand's exhibition at the Sala de Arte is brilliantly evoked in Carillo, "Spanish for Your Mexican Visit," 243–48, 251–53.

29. For Strand's version of events see Krippner, *Strand in Mexico*, 339–50, and chap. 4, 69–95.

30. Strand to Chávez, 4 April 1933, in *Epistolario selecto de Carlos Chávez,* ed. and introduced Gloria Carmona (Mexico City: Fondo de Cultura Económica, 1989), 160.

31. "Report of Paul Strand on Trip to Michoacán, June1933," Center for Creative Photography (CCP), Tucson, AZ, AG 17:31/Scrapbook.

32. Krippner, *Strand in Mexico*, 41; a map of Strand's travels in Mexico, 13.

33. Strand to Kurt and Isabel Baasch, 26 November 1933, CCP, AG 137, Kurt Baasch Collection.

34. Emilio García Riera, *México visto por el cine extranjero,* vol. 1: *1894–1940* (Guadalajara: Ediciones Era/Universidad de Guadalajara, 1987), 195; Krippner, *Strand in Mexico*, 280n2.

35. Krippner, *Strand in Mexico*, 69–95. See also Eduardo Contreras, *Silvestre Revueltas en escena y en pantalla* (Mexico: CONACULTA, 2010); and Robert L. Parker, "Carlos

Chávez y la música para el cine," *Heterofonía* 17/1 (January–March 1984): 13–27: repr. in Parker, *Trece panoramas*, 69–86.

36. Krippner, *Strand in Mexico*, 86.

37. For a detailed discussion of these issues, see ibid., 69–95. A glimpse of their personal relationship can be taken from Chávez's remark on missing conversations with Strand while sitting in the sun on his Mexico City terrace. Chávez to Strand, 16 March 1934, AGN.

38. Krippner, *Strand in Mexico*, 69–95.

39. Ibid., 86.

40. Strand to Antonio Castro Leal, 25 August 1934, AGN.

41. Krippner, *Strand in Mexico*, 86.

42. Carmona, *Epistolario selecto,* 209.

43. Strand's letter to Chávez, 27 August 1936, AGN, speaks about *Redes*'s honesty and beauty, and its usefulness to the working class, for whom it was made.

44. Jacob Strand to Paul Strand, 15 January 1935, CCP, AG 17:39:10.

45. Krippner, *Strand in Mexico*, 100.

46. Ibid., 45.

47. The complete lists compiled by Chávez are provided in Krippner, *Strand in Mexico*, 263–64.

48. The letter is reproduced in Krippner, *Strand in Mexico*, 91. It can be found in CCP, AG 17:29, Paul Strand Activities and Awards and Oversize Materials.

49. Strand to Chávez, 2 April 1939, in Carmona, *Epistolario selecto*, 284.

50. Krippner, *Strand in Mexico*, 64; Carmona, *Epistolario selecto*, 575, 955.

51. Paul Strand Archive, CCP, AG 17:26. See also Krippner, *Strand in Mexico,* 64.

52. A complete list of Strand publications can be found in Krippner, *Strand in Mexico*, 328–29.

Masters Carlos Chávez and Miguel Covarrubias: A Puppet Show

BY ANTONIO SABORIT
TRANSLATED BY REBECCA LEVI

In her diary for Tuesday, 25 May 1926, the young aspiring anthropologist Anita Brenner recorded the arrival from New York of "El Chamaco" (The Kid) Miguel Covarrubias and the Friday party celebrating his return to Mexico City after a three-year absence.

A few details survive from this celebration, memorable among the festivities of Mexico City's writers and artists. Ambassador-to-be Genaro Estrada performed an unexpected parody of *Carmen*, with a carnation in his mouth. Diego Rivera showed he was only human by breaking the rocking chair in which he was seated and falling to the ground, after which he improvised a lyre out of its remains. Painter Roberto Montenegro spent his time eating *pozole*[1] and empanadas with the women. Rose Roland, Covarrubias's girlfriend, sat on a glass of punch, then immediately left to change her dress. The printmaker Francisco Díaz de León and the poet Salvador Ugarte sang a *corrido* for Brenner.[2] Socialite and model Nahui Olín wandered around, grave and melancholic, while Senator Manuel Hernández Galván vacillated between happiness and sentimentality. Rivera's wife, Lupe Marín, went a little crazy and started going in and out of the bedrooms. The architect Carlos Obregón Santacilia sang in his baritone voice. The *estridentista* poet Arqueles Vela spent the time watching from a door.[3] The storyteller Mariano Silva y Aceves dedicated himself to taking care of the guests. And at the end of the night, songwriter Ignacio Fernández Esperón appeared, the same noisy "Tata Nacho" who, in the spring of 1925, had premiered his second ballet, *Garrick Gaieties*, supported by New York City's Theatre Guild, with sets, proscenium curtains, backdrops, and frivolous architectural pieces by Covarrubias.[4]

In the following days Brenner, a frequent Museo Nacional visitor, as well as the English translator of a series of lectures by anthropologist and archaeologist Manuel Gamio, recorded her encounters with

Covarrubias at the Museo, 13 Moneda Street. The meeting on Tuesday, the first of June, for example, may interest those who know that eventually Covarrubias would redesign the rooms of this very museum. On Wednesday the ninth, after passing by the Museo Nacional and perhaps even visiting the Fray Bernardino de Sahagún exhibition at the Biblioteca Nacional, Covarrubias invited Brenner to his house to listen to mariachi music. Later on El Chamaco, Rose, the caricaturist Matías Santoyo, and Brenner went to eat *tamales oaxaqueños* at the Café Colón and then went home so that Covarrubias could show them some of the films he had made about his meetings and trips. On Monday, 14 June, Brenner again met Rose and El Chamaco, and on Thursday, 17 June, when they got together for tea at Sanborns,[5] she found out that the couple was leaving for Tehuantepec.

In the diaries, all kinds of people come in and out of Brenner's circle: the composer Carlos Chávez; the painters David Alfaro Siqueiros, George Rufus Boynton, Jean Charlot, Francisco Goitia, Xavier Guerrero, Carlos Mérida, Máximo Pacheco, Fermín Revueltas, José Clemente Orozco, Rivera, and Rufino Tamayo; the architects Alfonso Pallares and Obregón Santacilia; the social activists Mary Doherty and Frances Toor; the archeologist George Vaillant; the historians Luis Castillo Ledón and Federico Gómez de Orozco; the poets Jaime Torres Bodet and José Dolores Frías; the journalists Carleton Beals, Ernest Gruening, and José Pérez Moreno; the editors Agustín Loera y Chávez and Vanegas Arroyo; the photographers Tina Modotti, José María Lupercio, and Edward Weston; the artists William Spratling and Jorge Enciso; the independent women of the time such as Concha Michel, Antonieta Rivas Mercado, and Elena Torres; the *rebozo*[6] maker León Venado; and the sculptor Ralph Stackpole.[7]

Brenner saw Rose and El Chamaco again upon their return from Tehuantepec. They dined together at the Café Colón on Wednesday, 7 July, and Rose showed Brenner the dresses she had brought back with her and told her about the beauty and the flowers of the isthmus. Two days later, on Friday afternoon, Brenner went to Chávez's studio to work on some ideas for the ballets for the next winter season, in which she was involved in some indeterminate way. Later on, she recorded the following in her diary:

> Carlos has an Indian sweetness and precision, a mask of an Indian. He is a man whose eyes have no center, a la D. H. Lawrence. Yet he is doing creative work. Four ballets:
> New Fire (Diego & Lazo)
> The White Prince (Genaro Estrada & Diego)

> The Miracle (Barreda & Covarrubias)
> H.P. (Diego)
> The little things I am supposed to work on. The idea is for simplicity, & dynamism.
> Thereby missed Barreda who came in this P.M.— Carlos gave me back the idea of work out of aimless confusion Diego brings on. Anything—anything, you don't have to be a genius. Only self-defense. And the revolution is a law, why be a Socialist *que son puras mentiras*[8]— He says—*"El que tiene más saliva traga más pinole. Y siempre será así."*[9] John Dewey here lecturing philosophy and education. But God knows I'm confused enough.[10]

Brenner was at work on various books, among them *Idols Behind Altars,* as well as other projects in her free time, such as contributions to the magazines *Forma*, *La Renaissance,* and *L'Art Vivant*, a ballet of her own invention called *The Return of Quetzalcóatl*, and even helped out with Jean Charlot's book, *The Mexican Mural Renaissance, 1920–1925*. On Tuesday, 27 July, Torres Bodet told her that his boss, José Puig Casauranc, Secretary of Public Education, wished to invite her and Rose for a meal at his house on Friday, 6 August.

On Thursday, 23 September, already in the final stretch of their stay in Mexico City, Rose and Covarrubias appeared briefly at Weston's studio to take a look at test prints of the portraits he had shot of them during their stay.[11] "Of Rose," noted Weston in one of his own diaries, "I have one at last for myself. Miguel I should like to do again, but they leave for New York tomorrow. They are both very agreeable, jolly persons—I like them."[12]

A cyclone in Veracruz—one that Rivera attributed to the enormous atmospheric shift caused by his own bodily mass from the city of Xalapa, where he was visiting at the time—hindered the progress of the *México*, the steamboat on which Rose and her "Kid" set sail.[13]

Anita Brenner was a year younger than Miguel Covarrubias and Carlos Chávez's junior by nine years. Nevertheless, the only "Kid" was Covarrubias the caricaturist, whose work appeared on 21 February 1925 in a brand-new weekly: *The New Yorker*. Only a few people in Mexico found out that Covarrubias's first submission was a portrait of the director of the Metropolitan Opera, Giulio Gatti-Casazza,[14] or that shortly thereafter his interest in music would show in his portrait of the critic Ernest Newman.[15]

Fewer still knew that El Chamaco's prestige led him him to design backdrops, hangings, and silhouettes for the Paris debut performance of singer Josephine Baker. "Precisely at the moment when black is being worn again, Josephine Baker's *Revue nègre* has arrived at Champs Elysées Theatre and the result has been unanimous," wrote Genet in *The New Yorker*. "Paris has never drawn a color line. It likes blondes, brunettes, or Bakers, more now than ever. The *première* looked like one of the Count de Baummont's exclusive parties, and began the smart theatrical season. Covarrubias did the sets, pink drops with cornucopias of hams and watermelons, and the Civil War did the rest, aided by Miss Baker."[16] Perhaps it would not be entirely incorrect to note that Covarrubias won the approval of the American theatrical community in the blink of an eye by way of *The New Yorker* and his cartoons. In 1925, his manner of depicting celebrities opened the doors of the gallery Valentine Dudensing and piqued the interest of the publishing house Knopf, which published his book, *The Prince of Wales and Other Famous Americans*.[17] Carl Van Vechten, the enthusiastic author of the book's preface, immediately sent a copy to the legendary Parisian home of Gertrude Stein on the Rue de Fleurus.[18] Before Covarrubias traveled to Mexico in May 1926, the *New Yorker* obtained a double portrait from him of Ernest Lawford and Vera Ross in the operetta *Iolanthe*.[19] As soon as the artist came back to Manhattan, he resumed his contributions with another theatrically themed cartoon dedicated to the star of the Ziegfeld Follies, Fanny Brice, and enjoyed the publication of a collection of songs edited by W. C. Handy that he illustrated, *Blues: An Anthology*.[20]

About the same time Covarrubias and Rose returned to New York, Chávez settled into the city for a two-year stay—even if, in 1925, Agustín Lazo had told him that he found Paris far from disappointing and a much better city.[21] In New York, Chávez, in addition to joining a small, active community of Mexican writers and artists, became involved in the work of his colleagues and contemporaries, who were led by the initiatives of Aaron Copland and Roger Sessions. "Now, the Mecca of music is no longer Paris, Milan, or Berlin," the poet José Juan Tablada wrote from New York at the end of 1926. "The center is here, with four splendid concert halls and two or three opera houses, without counting the many second-rate halls and hotels in which one can also hear select music." He continued:

> What everyone in Mexico should be aware of in all this is the complete, resounding triumph of a Mexican composer who is as well-known in the great musical circles of Europe and the United States as he is misunderstood and discouraged in our own country, where only a very reduced, select

group of people nurture, admire, and stimulate him: Carlos Chávez. This guy, at twenty-six, has already been a member of the International Composers' Guild for four years, during which his music has been well received on two occasions. He traveled to Europe, and first-class German publishing houses competed to publish his creations. He works tirelessly and only thinks about his art. He loves his homeland very much and is neither daunted nor upset by the indifference that surrounds him there. Now, he has just arrived with three new works: his suite *H.P.*, his ballet *The White Prince*, which Adolf Bolm will stage, and a Mexican dance, to which he is giving the final touches. Varèse chose Carlos Chávez's *H.P.* for the first concert of this season, and upon my faith, what I heard said about this work in Carnegie Hall filled me with pride as a Mexican and urged me to awaken my compatriots, so that they might immediately pay attention and encourage this great artist who arrived here a few days ago, disheartened from earning a hard living of eight pesos a day at the Olimpia movie theatre. So, after the *Pastoral* and *Rondino* of Colin McPhee, the Canadian; the three pagan hymns of the Londoner Goossens; the *Darker America* by the American William Still; and a *Lieder* [*sic*] by the Viennese Anton Webern, the audience, full of good wishes, prepared itself to hear the very modern *H.P.* by the Mexican Carlos Chávez, truly the best Mexican music that New York had heard up to then. The architecture, the volumes of sound, the beautiful coloring. The kid from Aguascalientes,[22] accompanied by Goossens himself, had to go out on stage four times to acknowledge the tempest of applause and approving comments that sounded so celestial to my ears after having suffered the roughness of other notes, notes the *Washington Post* finds so agreeable. A complete triumph! The Aeolian Hall, full to bursting with the most refined New York audience, its opinion makers: the artists and critics of the latest fashion."[23]

On Sunday, 26 December 1926, Chávez spoke to Tablada and thanked him for his words.[24] Later, Tablada would come to refer to a "Latin explosion in New York," writing in his newspaper columns about the presence of Mexican creators in the city.[25] The artists Emilio Amero and Pal-o-mar were already there. The choreographer Pedro Rubín and the artist Matías

Santoyo joined forces for the show *Río Rita*. Also wandering around were Adolfo Best Maugard—the author of *Método de dibujo* (Drawing Method), which Covarrubias had illustrated in 1923[26]—the engraver Carlos Tejeda, the painters F. Segura and Rufino Tamayo, and the caricaturists Ben-Hur Baz, Luis Hidalgo, and Jorge Palomino y Armando. As well as Covarrubias and Chávez, of course.[27] Nevertheless, Tablada did not fail to touch upon a topic familiar to all of them: his private concerns about the marked difference between the projects and the actual productions of the writers and artists.

In this sense Chávez was not an exception. In 1921, encouraged by the Russian choreographer Adolf Bolm and the Dominican writer Pedro Henríquez Ureña, he composed the libretto and score for *El fuego nuevo* (*The New Fire*), influenced by the diversity of the indigenous music he listened to as a child. Later on, in the mid-1920s, Chávez thought of writing a ballet with the help of writer and playwright Salvador Novo, but the project "remained in development because there were no possibilities of producing it."[28] Something similar happened to him with Octavio G. Barreda, who drafted the storylines for various ballets that Chávez would develop later on, two of which should be mentioned among his unfinished works. The first, *Suave patria* (Gentle Fatherland), would have included "September 15, fireworks, a parade, patriotic speeches, etc."[29] The other, which did not even reach the title stage, was "in a factory, with great screeches of machinery, anvils, saws, a workers' uprising and a final lynching of the owner, who is sent through a press and converted into useful things such as cuff links, *chorizos* or condoms—all sorts of things that everyone shares with great jubilation, ringing and hammering."[30] Barreda represented one side of Chávez's experience of New York. "Remember that we are disillusioned," Barreda told him on one occasion, "and that, in reality, we do not care much about that sophisticated thing currently called art."[31]

In September 1927, a year after El Chamaco's return to his Harlem escapades and while he was in Paris trying his luck, Anita Brenner settled in New York, where she continued to spend time with Carlos Chávez. One night at the beginning of October, he appeared at her apartment: "He is horribly intelligent and bad-tempered and therefore very diverting to listen to. He is as a rule silent, reserved, formal, because he says he is '*muy platicador*,'[32] and when he begins he won't stop. We liked it. Themes, music, the way the modern Mexican music would occur, New York, ballets, art, etc etc etc. He walked up and down the room with an Apizaco cane on each foot and drank cold tea and talked.[33] We like each other."

In New York, Chávez became interested in jazz, cinema, and a new kind of vaudeville. These were the true arts of the moment for both the composer and Covarrubias, with whom in 1927 Chávez tried to stage *El milagro de Nuestra Señora de Guadalupe* (The Miracle of Our Lady of Guadalupe). For this production, El Chamaco designed puppets that were to be made by Remo Bufano. Chávez asked Covarrubias, then in Paris, to see about the possibility of putting on his second "Aztec ballet," *Los cuatro soles* (The Four Suns) in the French capital, with the artist's sets and costumes. Over time, the composer would say that his idea for this piece's score, with its great scope and choreographic character, came to him from four images of the destruction of the world in the *Codex Vaticanus*, which Chávez and Covarrubias had consulted at the New York Public Library.

Bufano's high-quality marionettes had entered the limelight on 29 December 1925, when the then new League of Composers premiered *El retablo de maese Pedro* (Master Peter's Puppet Show), by Manuel de Falla, at Town Hall in New York.[34] As a poor immigrant in a city of poor immigrants and one of fourteen children, Bufano had never had enough. He preferred the life of the theater, the lyrical left, and the agenda of a modernist, radical company, the New Playwrights Theatre. It was there that he fortuitously discovered marionettes, perhaps without knowing about either Meyer Levin's work in his Marionette Studio Theatre in Chicago or the art of Lou Bunin. "Chamaco," Chávez wrote to Paris,

> I have spoken with Dos Passos, and he is very interested in the *4 Soles*. He has enough money for his theatre next season; Otto Kahn[35] kept his promise. In order for them to make a definitive decision about the *4 Soles*, they need you to send *immediately*, if not all, at least some of the drawings and sketches you have. I think there is no reason to waste an opportunity like this; tell me what you think and if you plan on being here next winter. I have heard that you are going to Russia; if that is true, you could take care of putting it on there, and I would take care of putting it on here. In that case, I would see what I could do about making copies of the score.
>
> Miss Lewisohn went to California and, before she left, told me that she would probably go to Mexico at the end of July or in August.[36] I asked her when she would open her theatre, and she told me that she herself did not yet know, but she thought it would be late in the season. So we do not

> have any obligation to wait for her, if they make us a good offer at the New Playwrights. This theatre is good; they are going to have a better space than the 52nd Street one they had last winter and will only produce new, modern works.

The ballet-pantomime *El milagro* exists halfway between puppet plays like the aforementioned *Maese Pedro* and the pantomimes of the beginning of the twentieth century, such as the ill-fated *A quelle heure partira-t-il un train pour Paris?* That production celebrated the ten-year anniversary of the Little Galleries of the Photo-Secession in January 1915 and, during the summer of 1914, involved Guillaume Apollinaire, Albert Savinio, Francis Picabia, and Marius de Zayas. However, it is more than likely that Chávez's interest in combining his music with dance and visual art is founded on the example of Sergei Diaghilev's celebrated Ballets Russes, which since 1909 had done as much "for modern art as for classic legs."[37] In any case, the projects *Los cuatro soles* and *El milagro* are testimony to the creativity that Chávez developed among his contemporaries at this time and proof of a very particular way of facing the challenges of modern musical expression. His letter to Covarrubias continues:

> Make sure you tell me what you think about the puppet ballet. I will devote myself to it completely as soon as you send the sketches to Bufano and he starts making the puppets. I already have part of the music and lots of notes, but I do not want to start working all out only to get stood up by you and Bufano. Bufano is extremely interested; the night before he left (at the end of last month), I had dinner with him, and he told me that he thought you were crazy, but despite his interest, he cannot work if you do not send him the designs.
>
> You need to send me a decision about the *4 Soles* and your drawings, otherwise we will miss this opportunity. This is the time in which they plan and program, and if we do not figure it out *right now*, we will be left out again.[38]

"It seems to me absolutely useless to try something here," Covarrubias replied to Chávez from France in mid-1927; the letter was without his usual humorous twist, but rather in the more serious tone he had adopted when he met Gertrude Stein.[39] In the same letter El Chamaco said that, given his meager success in Paris, he would leave for the African continent. Nevertheless, he honored his commitment and sent the sketches for Bufano.

Before continuing and highlighting the privilege that Chávez and his friends felt upon experiencing directly the messy, enthusiastic, creative, and unpredictable nature of the spaces that gave life to the performances of Jelly Roll Morton, George Gershwin & Co. (admired only at a distance, alas, by many of Chávez's contemporaries, such as Paul Hindemith, Ernst Krenek, Kurt Weill, and Bertold Brecht),[40] it is appropriate to point out that the ballet *Los cuatro soles* was never produced in New York. The Orquesta Sinfónica de México premiered the symphonic version at the Teatro Iris in Mexico City on 22 July 1930, and much later, on 31 March 1951, the Academia de la Danza and the Orquesta Sinfónica Nacional finally presented it as a ballet in the Palacio de Bellas Artes, with choreography by José Limón and sets and costumes by Covarrubias.[41] Because *El milagro de Nuestra Señora de Guadalupe* was never premiered, the location of the sketches that Covarrubias sent to Bufano is unknown.[42]

Brenner was a witness to and participant in all this, and she even found out that Frances Paine, a promoter of Mexican arts, was interested in staging Chávez's other ballet, *El fuego nuevo*, at the Roxy. In any case, Chávez did not lose sight of *Los cuatro soles*, believing it to be a much more feasible production. "Dear Chamaco," Chávez wrote that autumn,

> You must have already received my letter responding to yours from July. I have already given Bufano the sketches, and he says that he could finish the project by next January; he has a lot of work, and it could not be before then. During the summer he was out of the city and now is going to direct a show in Provincetown. He and Florence send their greetings.
>
> I haven't heard anything from Miss Lewisohn about *Cuatro soles*. The other day, she wrote me a letter and sent it to the consulate for immediate delivery, and our colleague Barreda had the kindness to bring it to me a week later. She wanted us to see each other during the few days that she was in the city, but when I received the letter she had already left. I have heard that the Neighborhood [Playhouse] will definitely reopen, but it is only hearsay.
>
> You may have been startled to hear that I am going to do the other Aztec ballet at the Roxy, but it is on the basis that they will give me carte blanche; the idea is to take advantage of all the theatrical elements they have to do the most new, original production possible. If they try to impose their methods on me, I will withdraw my work immediately, if all other options have been exhausted. If things go to my liking,

as they say they will, and we manage a good production, I think it will be something quite significant.

Considering that you have shown no signs of life and have not said when you are coming back, I am almost at the point of sending you an ultimatum. I have already written a lot of the music for *Milagro*, but as you know, I do not want to write it to set it aside. What are the ideas you have for the production? If you do not come back and if we do not work hard on the project together, time will slip by again. Besides, if the Roxy project goes as well as we hope, I think we will have to take advantage of the interest it might stir up right away.

So I thought that *Los cuatro soles*, *El milagro*, and *H.P.* would make a complete, varied program. It would be interesting to combine your work and Diego's; he told me before I left Mexico that if I did the ballet he would come. Remo was very interested in the idea and says that he would like very much to supervise the making of the costumes and sets for *Cuatro soles* and *H.P.* This would ensure faithfulness to the sketches. I spoke to Mrs. Paine about the matter, and we agreed to speak with Mr. Biment and Mr. Crowninshield. It could be in an already established theatre, or it could be our own, independent thing, if we get enough money. As you already know, I also have other small and medium-sized things with which we could maybe fill another performance, which we would do in agreement with you and Diego.

I do not think that another ultimatum is necessary for you to respond soon and say if you are coming back or not, that is, if you are going to stay in Tunis to live.

I do not think there is any point in communicating by letter. In order to make theatre some day, we need to be together. When you were here, I was in Mexico, and now that I am here, you are in Tunis. Let me know if there are possibilities of doing something in Tunis, but if not, what would you say if we all go to hell and see what we can do there?

What you sent me for *Cuatro soles* gives an idea of the work but nevertheless is incomplete and does not give a clear idea of the work. Without a doubt, Remo is very interested in doing *El milagro*, but I do not think that he would dedicate his time, now that he is so busy, if he does not see clearly. The two ballets that you have and *H.P.* are the only big ones

> (except *Fuego nuevo*, which Lazo did a long time ago). But what of it, if you are in Paris and Diego in Mexico?
>
> I already gave Harry part of my book on music, and in the next few days he is supposed to tell me what he thinks.[43]

The Harry in question was none other than Harry Block, editor at Knopf, "a very young chap, pleasant, Jewish, blond, and *requete águila*" ("really sharp"), in Brenner's description.[44] Chávez dedicated himself fully to composition. Brenner, meanwhile, followed Manuel Gamio's instructions and recommendations, tried to use her merit and previous studies to get into the anthropology classes and seminars at Columbia University. There she met the celebrated Franz Boas, who was more than familiar with Mexican life and culture, and joined the anthropology students' weekly meal at the Livingston Club. Brenner came and went as she pleased in the city neighborhoods that she knew like the back of her hand—the Village and Harlem.

Anita Brenner's appointment book is a mirror that reflects much of Carlos Chávez's activity in New York City during the second half of the 1920s: she sees the painter Rufino Tamayo, she converses with the critic and painter Walter Pach, she meets Freda Kirchwey at *The Nation*, Frances Paine offers her work on some Mexican topic, she briefly sees Diego Rivera on his way to France and one or two more possible stops like Russia, and at the end of the year she lends José Clemente Orozco a hand in settling into New York and introduces him to Chávez.[45]

Also in this *mexicanada* are the names of Carmen Marín[46] and former minister of education José Vasconcelos, witnesses of the *succès d'estime* that Covarrubias had managed in 1927 with the pieces he collected in *Negro Drawings*, his sketches of the neighborhood of Harlem and its inhabitants: the bejeweled black financier, the blues singer, the Sheik, the preacher, the Jazz Baby.[47] "In Harlem he found a society perfectly suited for his pencil," wrote the art critic Henry McBride in his daily column in *The Sun*.

> He at once proceeded to make a marvelous series of drawings. He has missed nothing, apparently, in the well-known list of types. . . . All these extraordinary people and their equally extraordinary activities have been recorded very exactly in the art of Covarrubias, and the book of these drawings . . . proves convincingly enough that in the young Mexican we have a caricaturist comparable in talent to the Frenchman

> Caran d'Ache. In the course of time he may go beyond Caran d'Ache, but to reach that degree of skill is in itself already astonishing. He is in the first, youthful, rapturous stage of recognizing lovely and too unbelievably amusing things in life. When he gets a little deeper into the puzzling maze of human existence and gets constructive impulses he may become a Daumier. He certainly has skill enough to be anything.[48]

In January 1928, after a party thrown by Ruth and Egmont Arens for Orozco, Chávez played "some of the music for the ballet" (which was perhaps *El milagro de Nuestra Señora*) "and a sonatina" in his apartment for Brenner and Orozco, as she noted in her diary. "Very fine. Clear, concise, beautifully built, pure—with the Indian feel to it."[49] This sonatina was one of the three sonatinas that Chávez would present, along with his Third Sonata for piano, in April at the Edyth Totten Theatre, on West 48th Street just off Eighth Avenue, as part of a concert series organized by Aaron Copland and Roger Sessions. The program also included Virgil Thomson with *Five Phrases from the Song of Solomon,* Theodore Chanler, and Walter Piston. Chávez wanted Brenner to establish a relationship with him and his musician friends as similar as possible to the one she already had with painters and writers. Indeed, this is what led her to visit Covarrubias at the beginning of February, just back from a year's stay in Europe and North Africa.Waiting for him at home was a copy of José Juan Tablada's book of poems, *La feria* (The Fair), illustrated by Matías Santoyo, George Hart, and El Chamaco himself.[50]

Brenner's intense memory of Jean Charlot led her to look for his equivalent in the friendly presence of Chávez. "His technique is very similar," she wrote on 22 February 1928. "Also, he has the same *saveur* of *appassionné*[51] and cold calculation when he approaches his work. He had the same look—utter, thorough, complete submission and absorption while listening to some music—that I saw in Jean once when he was kneeling in front of the confessional."[52] Chávez tried to teach Brenner to understand rhythm; he invited her to his musical analysis sessions in the company of Aaron Copland, they listened to and talked about Igor Stravinsky's *Oedipus Rex* until dawn, he sought her out at night, he informed her about his projects and explained them to her, and meanwhile she insisted on making a drawing of him: "He is making a good headway . . . they are beginning to play his stuff quite frequently. He is so very Indian in the way his mind works, and so clear and logical and simple. I believe him to be a very great artist indeed." A few lines later, she noted:

> I like the feeling of health and simplicity and utter absence of Bohemianism that obtains with the few I have met of the musicians. Of course, they are much more established than the artists (so-called), but anyway they are beginning to get an interest and an emphasis on American stuff based on American values (I think the identification of the values is somewhat due to Carlos), and that makes me feel so much more encouraged about them. No pose, no blinkers. (Or at least, less.)[53]

On Sunday, 22 April, Brenner occupied one of the 313 seats in the Edyth Totten Theatre and confided to her diary: "They played some of Carlos's things. Impressed again by the unity in them, and by the peculiar quality of insistence . . . they grow logically out of themselves and also grip you at the beginning and won't let you go—bulldog way. One was particularly lovely to me, and it is one I had not heard before . . . a cello-piano sonatina. There was a movement in it that went along like a small wild thing singing alone to itself, over and over again. A violin-piano sonatina had the *tristura*[54] of the Indian."[55] Copland, for his part, was more surprised by the large turnout of critics than by the quality of the music. "They all damned Chávez which I think is a sign of the real excellence of his music," Copland confided to Sessions.[56]

In June, Brenner was at a party that started at the Covarrubias apartment, "with the playing of their mariachi (Tamayo, Chamaco, Harry Block and brother) and then dinner at Tovar's with Chamaco, Rose, Tamayo, and then went walking and rowing in Central Park, eating cherries, and then we ended up at El Charro of Salomón de la Selva's brother, drinking *tepache*,[57] and then I came home about midnight." Then, Chávez appeared, having finished composing a foxtrot, "and bringing with him an *antología* of modern Mex. poetry with some dishwater in it of our friends the *putos*, but some excellent things and a beautiful one of Ramón López Velarde, which is called 'Suave patria.'"[58] A few weeks later, Chávez returned to Mexico and immediately formed the Orquesta Sinfónica de México.

For Brenner, New York was an opportunity to take her abilities and enthusiasm to the limit. She was invited to contribute to magazines like *The Arts* and *The Nation*, to translate Hernán Cortés and Bernal Díaz del Castillo for a book on the conquistadors, and to restructure the Peruvian room at the Museum of Natural History. She met Alfred Tozzer, Edward Sapir, Herbert Joseph Spinden, Alma Reed,[59] and Margaret Mead and wrote something for the *Encyclopedia Britannica*. She broke into a publishing world seemingly as limitless as the one El Chamaco experienced when Frank Crowninshield accepted him for *Vanity Fair*, a magazine that rather resembled an extremely exclusive club, with offices in the Graybar Building on West 44th Street.

The poet José Gorostiza, a kind of perverse shadow à la Pushkin, a Salieri to Chávez's Mozart—more literary than literal or real, of course—represented the other side of Carlos Chávez's New York experience and would remind the Mexican composer of his inescapable artistic pact with figures like Arnold Schoenberg, Alban Berg, and Anton von Webern. "You have forgotten *our* program," Gorostiza wrote him, months before Chávez proposed his three sonatinas to Aaron Copland,

> —ours, belonging to all of us who are obliged by artistic honesty to make unpopular art. You must abandon the idea of others liking your work for the reason you like it. There is a reason why you understand what you are doing and they do not. The issue is a different one: survival. Can you not do the pieces we have talked so much about—the *danzón*, the foxtrot, mainstream music—everything that makes money, anyway? Then, using our own resources, we could *pay ourselves* for the luxury of putting on more beloved projects.[60]

We can only imagine what this advice felt like to Chávez, especially in view of Covarrubias's accomplishments and discoveries, and his increasing popularity. Gorostiza tried to convince the composer to prolong his stay in New York: "I tell you, it is not yet time to do anything in Mexico," he said. "Someday it will be, and I think that then our immediate obligation will be to stay indefinitely in Mexico."[61] Agustín Lazo thought similarly and, around the same time, confided in Chávez his hope of realizing another project:

> Just a few days ago, I wrote to Xavier [Villaurrutia] about my desire that all those who are dear to me—who are precisely the people whom I admire spiritually and who are now scattered around the world—would stay in contact so that after these years of experiences and studies abroad, we could go home, in the universal spirit of making Mexico into something artistically interesting—beyond all politics, social or otherwise—so as to occupy a place in the world that belongs to us.[62]

In this whole story, the atmosphere of New York City and the experience of living there were notable influences. Sometimes with muddy boots, blinded by gusts of powdery snow, restricted in movement by a coat, gloves, a scarf. Other times in shirtsleeves. But always like a kind of pariah (as Tablada put it), or like prospectors, or even like ghosts in that "inferno of ridiculous, useless, abominable civilization."[63] Manhattan and its surroundings transformed them into captive fans of its endless mysteries and surprises. The very inhabitants of New York City were not only imprisoned "within rigid categorical imperatives, unconnected to our free will," as Tablada once wrote, "but rather were obliged to suffer what Dostoevsky considered the worst torment of the Siberian prison camp, the constant presence of other beings that strip us of the greatest and most precious of liberties, our inner life." But there was more. "In that case, freest New York paradoxically resembles the brilliant Slav's House of the Dead. Perhaps, while Dostoevsky endured such prolonged torment in the middle of the desolate steppes, in these populous streets Edgar Poe, his antipode and brother, suffered an incipient phobia of crowds."[64] In this "swift and spiritually somber city," the poet constructed an exceptional space. Slowly and progressively, he populated it with his favorite characters: Edgard Varèse, who was an admirer of Carlos Pellicer; Tamara Karsavina, "Léon Bakst's model . . . the star of the open-minded Diaghilev ballet"; Anna Ivanova Kustodiev, "one of the best interpreters of Wilde's *Salomé*"; and Jack Johnson, black boxer and world champion, who in Mexico had been the guest of playboys and Carrancista soldiers.[65] There was no other way to experience the city.

Long after the adventure died, Tablada made a diagnosis:

> New York, like the Persia of *One Thousand and One Nights*, like the Byzantium of the Greeks, like the Moscow of the tsars, the Venice of the doges and the Lutetia of *The Mysteries of Paris*, is a nucleus of lyrical romances and an emporium of adventures, only that its motives are not love or bravery, religion or courtly pomp, aristocracy, and power. A unique motive, a singular purpose, a unanimous objective moves the spirits, intensifies the virtues, launching beings into intrigues, conquests, battles and adventures: gold.[66]

In this nucleus, Mexican writers and artists, who arranged things to make this city their refuge and alibi, imagined more projects than they were able to accomplish in the magical flash of their first youth, before crossing the line of shadow that awaited them. But throughout the rest of their lives, though some grew apart from others because of work and love, they seem to have always been united by this largely unfinished task, now the inheritance of the following generations: the creation of audiences that would appreciate artistic expressions of the modern temperament. José Limón described part of Covarrubias's strategy: "Delight people. Give them beauty. Bring them to it. Let them see it, feel it, eat it, drink it. Instruct. Enchant. Then, see what happens."[67]

NOTES

1. Traditional Mexican dish. (*Trans.*)

2. Mexican narrative musical genre. (*Trans.*)

3. Estridentismo was a subversive, multi-disciplinary avant-garde movement in Mexico in the 1920s, similar to Dada, but with a leftist political agenda.

4. Susannah Joel Glusker, ed., *Avant-Garde Art and Artists in Mexico: Anita Brenner's Journals of the Roaring Twenties* (Austin: University of Texas Press, 2010), 1:162–63, 165.

5. Historic Mexico City drugstore and soda fountain, founded in 1903. (*Trans.*)

6. A *rebozo* is a traditional, finely made shawl. (*Trans.*)

7. Those referenced here were members of post-revolutionary artistic and intellectual circles, as well as foreign artists who visited Mexico, sometimes for long periods, and integrated into Mexican circles. See Helen Delpar's essay in this volume.

8. "which are pure lies." (*Trans.*)

9. "He who has more saliva swallows more *pinole*. And it will always be this way." *Pinole* is a corn-based powder, used to make a beverage, from Tabasco, Mexico. (*Trans.*)

10. Brenner's text is in English in original, as are all quotations from Brenner in this essay. *(Trans.)* Glusker, *Avant-Garde Art and Artists in Mexico,* 1:194 and 196. Agustín Lazo was a painter; Octavio Barreda, a writer and diplomat. They were both close friends of Chávez.

11. Some of these photographic test prints are preserved today in the Fondo Miguel Covarrubias, Archives and Special Collections, Biblioteca de la Universidad de las Américas, Cholula, Puebla. (Henceforth Fondo Miguel Covarrubias.)

12. Nancy Newhall, ed., *The Daybooks of Edward Weston,* vol. 1: *Mexico* (New York: Aperture, 1973), 192.

13. Glusker, *Avant-Garde Art and Artists in Mexico,* 1:263.

14. Gilbert W. Gabriel, "Maestrissimo!," *The New Yorker*, 21 February 1925, 9.

15. "Music," *The New Yorker*, 2 May 1925, 15.

16. Genet (Janet Flanner), "Paris Letter, November 6," *The New Yorker*, 21 November 1925, 32.

17. Miguel Covarrubias, *The Prince of Wales and Other Famous Americans*, preface by Carl Van Vechten (New York: Alfred A. Knopf, 1925).

18. Carl Van Vechten to Gertrude Stein, 9 September 1925, New York, in *The Letters of Gertrude Stein and Carl Van Vechten,* vol. 1: *1913–1935*, ed. Edward Burns (New York: Columbia University Press, 1986).

19. Miguel Covarrubias, "Unerring Ames at 'Iolanthe,'" *The New Yorker*, 15 May 1926, 25.

20. Miguel Covarrubias, "Fennie Brice in Erizona," *The New Yorker*, 30 October 1926, 30; W. C. Handy, ed., *Blues: An Anthology*, introduction by Abbe Niles, illustrations by Miguel Covarrubias (New York: A. & C. Boni, 1926).

21. Agustín Lazo to Carlos Chávez, 1925, Paris, in Gloria Carmona, ed., *Epistolario selecto de Carlos Chávez* (Mexico City: Fondo de Cultura Económica, 1989), 62.

22. Tablada is mistaken here. Chávez was born in Popotla, a suburb of Mexico City, and not in the state of Aguascalientes.

23. José Juan Tablada, "Nueva York de día y de noche," *El Universal* (Mexico City), 19 December 1926.

24. José Juan Tablada, *Diario (1900–1944),* vol. 4 of *Obras*, ed. Guillermo Sheridan (Mexico City: Universidad Nacional Autónoma de México, 1992), 291.

25. Tablada recorded in his diary that Covarrubias and Rose left New York for France on 15 January 1927, on board the *Paris*. See Tablada, *Diario (1900–1944),* 295.

26. Adolfo Best Maugard, *Método de dibujo: Tradición, resurgimiento y evolución del arte mexicano* (Mexico City: Publicaciones de la Secretaría de Educación Pública, 1923), 133.

27. José Juan Tablada, "Nueva York de día y de noche," *El Universal*, 27 March 1927.

28. Carlos Chávez, *Mis amigos poetas* (Mexico City: El Colegio Nacional, 1977), 37. Novo, in the plan for his unfinished work *par excellence*, wrote the name of Carlos Chávez and the year 1924. See Salvador Novo, *La estatua de sal*, Preface by Carlos Monsiváis (Mexico City: Colección Memorias Mexicanas, CNCA, 1998).

29. "September 15" refers to the traditional yearly celebrations that commemorate the beginning of Mexico's War of Independence in 1810.

30. Octavio G. Barreda to Carlos Chávez, 8 February 1925, in Carmona, *Epistolario selecto de Carlos Chávez*, 54.

31. Octavio G. Barreda to Carlos Chávez, August 1924, New York, in ibid., 48.

32. "very chatty." *(Trans.)*

33. Apizaco is a town in the state of Tlaxcala. *(Ed.)*

34. See Edgar Istel and Thedore Baker, "Manuel de Falla: A Study," *The Musical Quarterly* 12/4 (October 1926): 499. With its first program on 11 November 1923, the League of Composers proposed to encourage and support the production of new significant works. See Marion Bauer and Claire R. Reis, "Twenty-five Years with the League of Composers," *Musical Quarterly* 34/1 (January 1948): 1–14.

35. Otto Hermann Kahn was an investment banker and protector of the arts.

36. Irene Lewisohn had been co-owner of the off-Broadway Neighborhood Playhouse, and in 1928 opened the Neighborhood Playhouse School of the Theatre on the Lower East Side.

37. Genet, "Letter from Paris, April 9," *The New Yorker*, 15 April 1939, 86.

38. Carlos Chávez to Miguel Covarrubias, 9 July 1927, New York, Fondo Miguel Covarrubias.

39. Miguel Covarrubias to Carlos Chávez, 20 July 1927, Paris, in Carmona, *Epistolario selecto de Carlos Chávez*, 79. The meeting of Covarrubias with Stein is not mentioned here, but it is clearly implied in her correspondence with Van Vechten.

40. See Donald Spoto, *Lenya: A Life* (New York: Ballantine Books, 1989), 73–74.

41. Roberto García Morillo, *Carlos Chávez: Vida y obra* (Mexico City: Fondo de Cultura Económica, 1978), 41–42.

42. At the moment of this writing, the 30 cubic feet of the papers of Remo Bufano (1894–1948), stored in the De Grummond Children's Literature Collection at the University of Southern Mississippi, have not been processed. Since the material dates from 1919 to 1929, there is the possibility that Covarrubias's sketches for *El milagro* are included. The Detroit Institute of Arts holds in its archives marionettes from both the *Retablo del Maese Pedro* and the opera-oratorio *Oedipus Rex* by Stravinsky with libretto by Jean Cocteau—marionettes that are three meters tall. See A. S. Cavallo, "Heroic Puppets from Oedipus Rex," *Bulletin of the Detroit Institute of Arts* 35 (1955–56): 24–27; and Gil Oden, "Remo Bufano, Puppet Showman," *Bulletin of the Detroit Institute of Arts* 39 (1959–60): 17–19.

43. Carlos Chávez to Miguel Covarrubias, n.d., New York, Fondo Miguel Covarrubias. "What of it" is in English in the original.

44. Glusker, *Avant-Garde Art and Artists in Mexico,* 2:525.

45. "The other day, I met a young Mexican musician and composer who, it seems, is starting to have success here. He is called Carlos Chávez," Orozco wrote to his wife

Margarita in a letter from New York dated 25 December 1927. "They are already starting to play his compositions in serious concerts and are going to put on a dance of his in a theatre." In José Clemente Orozco, *Cartas a Margarita (1921–1949)*, compiled and annotated by Tatiana Herrero Orozco (Mexico City: ERA, 1987), 23.

46. Carmen Marin was the first director of the Museo de Arte Moderno in Mexico City, Lupe Marín's sister and Octavio G. Barreda's wife.

47. Miguel Covarrubias, *Negro Drawings*, preface by Ralph Barnton, introduction by Frank Crowninshield (New York and London: Alfred A. Knopf, 1927).

48. Henry McBride, "Covarrubias in Harlem," *The Sun* (New York), 24 December 1927, collected in Henry McBride, *The Flow of Art: Essays and Criticisms*, ed. Daniel Catton Rich, prefaces by Lincoln Kirstein and Hilton Kramer (New Haven and London: Yale University Press, 1997), 231.

49. Glusker, *Avant-Garde Art and Artists in Mexico,* 2:567.

50. Ibid., 2:583.

51. Translated as "flavor of enthusiasm" in ibid., 2:585.

52. Ibid.

53. Ibid., 2:602.

54. "sadness." *(Trans.)*

55. Glusker, *Avant-Garde Art and Artists in Mexico*, 2:606.

56. Aaron Copland to Roger Sessions, 23 April 1928, New York, in *The Correspondence of Roger Sessions*, ed. Andrea Olmstead (Boston: Northeastern University Press, 1992), 107.

57. Mexican beverage made with fermented pineapples. (*Trans.*)

58. Glusker, *Avant-Garde Art and Artists in Mexico,* 2:620. *Puto* is a pejorative colloquial term for homosexual. Brenner is probably referring to the poets known as Los Contemporáneos, close friends of Chávez's, who were often accused of being effeminate. *(Ed.)*

59. Alfred Tozzer and Herbert Joseph Spinden, anthropologists and linguists, were specialists in Maya culture. Edward Sapir, anthropologist and linguist, specialized in Native American languages. Alma Reed was a journalist with a lifelong interest in Mexican art and politics.

60. José Gorostiza to Carlos Chávez, 4 July 1927, in Carmona, *Epistolario selecto de Carlos Chávez*, 77.

61. José Gorostiza to Carlos Chávez, 20 September 1927, London, in Carmona, *Epistolario selecto de Carlos Chávez*, 81.

62. Agustín Lazo to Carlos Chávez, 11 August 1927, Paris, in Carmona, *Epistolario selecto de Carlos Chávez*, 80.

63. José Juan Tablada, "Nueva York de día y de noche," *El Universal*, 28 February 1926.

64. Ibid., 9 December 1928.

65. Venustiano Carranza was president of Mexico from 1915 to 1920, after having led the Mexican Revolution and the overthrow of dictator Victoriano Huerta. *(Trans.)*

66. José Juan Tablada, "Nueva York de día y de noche," *El Universal*, 10 and 21 September; 5 and 19 October 1924; 14 March, 6 June, and 25 July 1926.

67. *José Limón: An Unfinished Memoir*, ed. Lynn Garafola, introduction by Deborah Jowitt, foreword by Carla Maxwell, afterword by Norton Owen (Hanover, NH: University Press of New England, 1998), 131.

The Literary Affinities and Poetic Friendships of Carlos Chávez

SUSANA GONZÁLEZ AKTORIES
TRANSLATED BY REBECCA LEVI

Carlos Chávez's relationship with different cultural circles in Mexico and abroad is well-known. Few studies, however, elucidate fully the musician's various ties to other artistic disciplines, particularly painting, ballet, and literature. Chávez was not only an avid, consistent reader, but also had direct exchanges with his writer friends from which some of his literary interests emerged. In fact, he built a universe of shared values and tastes, guided by his affinity with texts and authors, who frequently passed on creative inspiration or posed attractive challenges for his compositions. At times, however, he was led by practical motives such as obligation, artistic trends, and opportunity.

Within Chávez's catalogue of compositions lies a wide, versatile range of literary references that he integrated, explicitly or discreetly, into his music. Furthermore, these relationships to literature are clearly neither temporary nor passing, since they reappear in different ways throughout the composer's nearly sixty-year musical career. Without pretending to exhaust this facet of Chávez's work, this essay offers a general perspective and maps these relationships by looking in particular to the close ties that bound the composer, in more than one sense, to a specific sector of the Mexican literary world: the group Los Contemporáneos. We will also examine the types of musical appropriation that Chávez explored, looking specifically at his settings of poems by Carlos Pellicer and Xavier Villaurrutia.

We can confirm the decisive role that literature played in Chávez's oeuvre by considering his vocal and choral pieces together with his poetically infused instrumental works.[1] Even the titles of his compositions show numerous literary influences, often alluding to specific texts; these references also appear in thematic musical allusions, as well as in his writings. Yet in the same way it is difficult to divide Chávez's work into compositional periods with clearly defined musical styles, it is equally difficult to separate his literary preferences by era.[2] The texts that influence his compositional poetics span the most distant moments and literary traditions; the references range far afield, from classical Greece to pre-Hispanic cultures. Alongside Sophocles's *Antigone* (the Jean Cocteau version of 1932)[3] and the Aeschylus tragedy *Prometeo encadenado* (*Prometheus Bound*), a cantata libretto adapted from the Trevelyan translation (1956), or Euripides's *Hippolytus* for a Salvador Novo adaptation, with the title *Upingos: Melodía para oboe solo* (1957), we also find Náhuatl texts translated into Spanish, as in *Lamentaciones* (1962). As for poetry, Chávez's repertoire includes samples that date from the Middle Ages through the twentieth century. Among the English poets, he favored Lord Byron, John Keats, and Percy Bysshe Shelley, whose respective poems "So We'll Go No More A-Roving," "Sonnet to Sleep," and "To the Moon" he set to music in Three Nocturnes (1942).[4] From French literature, he chose Victor Hugo for an early work, "Extase" (1918), and from the German, he set Heinrich Heine's "Du bist wie eine Blume" (1919).

As for Hispanic literature, Chávez evokes the adventures of Miguel de Cervantes' *Don Quixote* in Toccata for Orchestra (1947), composed for a theatrical production, which like *Hippolytus* was also adapted by Salvador Novo. From the modern era, there is Federico García Lorca's *Romancero gitano* (Gypsy Ballads), set as "La casada infiel" (The Unfaithful Wife; 1941). From Latin American literature, Chávez uses the poetry of Colombian José Asunción Silva in "Estrellas fijas" (Fixed Stars; 1919) and that of Brazilian Ronald de Carvalho in "Inútil epigrama" (Useless Epigram; 1923). Within Mexican literature of the time a highly venerated key figure for Chávez is Ramón López Velarde, from whose work he drew the words for *Tierra mojada* (Wet Earth) and "Todo" (Everything; 1932).[5] He is also interested in other Mexican poets, such as Carlos Gutiérrez Cruz, with *El sol, corrido mexicano* (The Sun, a Mexican Ballad; 1934), and Enrique González Martínez, with "Canto a la tierra" (Song to the Earth; 1946), as well as the members of Los Contemporáneos, as we will see.

Chávez and Los Contemporáneos

Although many international masters of the literary arts left a mark on Chávez's life and work, his most intense, lifelong intellectual exchange was with his own contemporaries. He borrowed freely from them for his compositions. Early on, Chávez, prompted by his shared interests with childhood friends like Carlos Pellicer, joined a circuit of young intellectuals and writers. The publication that helped consolidate these relationships was the magazine *Contemporáneos* (1928–32), a forum characterized by its a critical attitude toward the many reactionary, antiquated cultural ideas and visions—echoes of romantic, fin-de-siècle paradigms—that still dominated post-revolutionary Mexico. The journal's intention was to open the cultural panorama to a new, more inclusive cosmopolitan discourse.[6] The Contemporáneos group of poets included the three founding editors of the magazine—Jaime Torres Bodet, Bernardo Ortiz de Montellano, and Enrique González Rojo, Sr.—as well as Carlos Pellicer, José Gorostiza, Jorge Cuesta, Agustín Lazo, and Gilberto Owen.[7] Two other associates of this circle, poets Salvador Novo and Xavier Villaurrutia, had earlier founded the magazine *Ulises* (1927–28) as a vehicle for their cultural activities at Teatro Ulises. As artists of different origins, each cultivating his own style, these poets resisted being identified as a self-contained nucleus or labeled as a specific generation. However, even Villaurrutia's ironic witticism about a "group without a group" could not stop them from being associated with one another.[8]

Chávez did not directly participate in either of these magazines, except for a score he contributed to *Ulises* and the appearance of his name in the early issues of *Contemporáneos*.[9] Although his presence in these publications was limited, he remained close to the majority of their contributors, in particular to Novo, Pellicer, and Villaurrutia. It is thus not a surprise that in his 1973 lectures at the Colegio Nacional he called them "my poet friends."[10] Unlike the profiles on Pellicer and Novo that Chávez prepared for the occasion, only a few archival notes survive from his text on Villaurrutia. In them, Chávez references his years-long relationship with Los Contemporáneos:[11]

> We were not a group; friendship and shared views bound us together. We wanted a change, an injection of new ideas. Villaurrutia and Novo wanted to do theater, what is called experimental theater, and in the end, in 1927, they started the Teatro Ulises on Mesones Street. I had left Mexico in September of 1926, fleeing from the inaction and mediocrity of the Mexican musical scene. Xavier would write to me from time to time and would send me the *Ulises* magazine, which was published as part of the Teatro Ulises movement.

Chávez mentions in these notes that, despite Villaurrutia's requests for material, he never sent him a literary contribution for the magazine but only a "little piece of mine for piano that I had just finished composing in New York."

To trace the path along which these friendships emerged and developed, one must go back to the early literary gatherings of 1915. Chávez recalls these artistic meetings, known as *tertulias*, in his biographical sketch of Pellicer:

> I used to travel constantly from Jalapa to Veracruz, and in Jalapa, a small group of us would have literary parties at which Carlos Pellicer, who lived there at the time, would introduce us to Lugones, Chocano, Nervo, and Darío, and would read us his latest and already astonishing poems.[12]

He also mentions that upon his return to Mexico City, he became involved with the magazine *Gladios* (1916), founded by Pellicer and writer-diplomat Octavio G. Barreda, among others, which lasted only for two issues.

This circle of friends also used their contacts for an ongoing book exchange, especially for titles that were hard to find in Mexico. For example, in a letter of 18 June 1973 Chávez wrote to the poet's sister Teresa Villaurrutia with a special request:

> As you'll surely remember, Xavier Villaurrutia and I kept a close friendship and visited each other frequently.
>
> On one occasion, now quite some time ago, it must have been in the 1920s, I lent two books to Xavier that I would very much like to get back. I imagine that the books must be in his library, and what's more, they are easy to identify because they have my name in them. The first is a small book by Jean Cocteau, titled *Le coq et l'arlequin*, and it has an inscription for me from José D. Frías.[13] The other is a monograph on Picasso written in German.

Apart from books, as Chávez recalls, his "poet friends" shared some of their creations, which he integrated into his music. Later in this essay, I will refer in greater detail to Pellicer's poems in *Tres exágonos* (Three Hexagons; 1923) and *Otros tres exágonos* (Other Three Hexagons; 1924). There are others as well: "El segador" (The Reaper), by the same author, which appears in Three Poems for Voice and Piano (1938); the same composition features "Hoy no lució la estrella de tus ojos" (Today the Star of Your Eyes Did Not Shine) by Novo and "Nocturna rosa" (Nocturne: The Rose) by Villaurrutia.[14] Other poems by Villaurrutia were set by Chávez in *Cuatro nocturnos* for voice and orchestra (1939) and "North Carolina Blues" (1942).

The friendships with poets grew through intense epistolary exchanges, the documentation of which, though incomplete, gives us an idea of the content and quality of the correspondence. The Contemporáneos would elaborate on their first impressions of travel abroad, often to the United States, the United Kingdom, Spain, France, and Italy.[15] They also used the correspondence to discuss their aesthetic and ideological affiliations and to plan joint projects.[16] These included the vocal compositions already mentioned as well as the mise-en-scènes designed by theater director Celestino Gorostiza for *Antigone* at Teatro de Orientación in Mexico City at the end of July 1932, staged when his brother, poet José Gorostiza, was the administrative head of the Department of Fine Arts at the Ministry of Public Education. As for Novo, he created the mise-en-scène for *Don Quixote* in 1947, when Chávez was already director of the Instituto Nacional de Bellas Artes and Novo the head of the theater department. Next they collaborated on *Hippolytus* (1957). In addition to their written exchanges regarding joint projects—including those that for different reasons never saw the light of day, such as the "Aztec ballet" of 1925–26 with José Gorostiza's scenario[17]—their collaborations included writing journal reviews or program notes for performances of Chávez's work and even for the concerts he programmed for the Orquesta Sinfónica de México.

At the beginning, united by a youthful spirit, Chavez and his literary associates sought to nourish themselves intellectually and define themselves within Mexican culture. They showed passion, hunger for the quest, and enthusiasm for embarking on experimental, idealistic projects. With the passing of the years, as they took on public positions, whether in education, culture, politics, or diplomacy, their exchange of letters took on a different tone, which often had to do with professional collaboration. Here other interests would come into play, which in some cases caused friction, disagreements, or even irreparable fractures.[18] For example, José Gorostiza and Chávez became estranged after Chávez replaced him as head of the Department of Fine Arts. A series of reciprocal accusations followed that spread to the Mexican press between January and May of 1932.[19] Ferocious complaints about Chávez can also be found in letters, such as the one that Villaurrutia sent to Torres Bodet in 1933 (no exact date), in which he warns that "even Celestino [Gorostiza] has become a victim of the most German of German musicians, meaning Carlos Chávez."[20] Indeed, Chávez's positions of responsibility as director and mover of many institutions and cultural authorities—such as the

Orquesta Sinfónica de México, the Instituto Nacional de Bellas Artes, and the Colegio Nacional, along with various magazines and record companies—transformed him into one of the most powerful, influential artists to mold Mexican culture in the twentieth century. If his authoritarian nature and heavy hand distanced various people, deep-rooted loyalties and trust in one another after so many years of friendship allowed him to maintain his proximity to his closest circle—Novo, Pellicer, and Villaurrutia—in spite of occasional differences or complaints.

Chávez and Pellicer: Lines of Communication Drawn Between *Hexagons*

In Chávez's lectures at the Colegio Nacional on 24 September and 10 October 1973, titled "My Poet Friends" and subsequently published by the Colegio press, he paints a series of spoken portraits. Nourished by his personal memories, as well as by historical and biographical information, comments on literary criticism, and his own attraction to the poetic work, these essays sketch the poets' personalities and the value that, in the composer's opinion, each had as key figures within the Mexican cultural panorama.[21]

Chávez introduces Pellicer as a "friend from my early youth"[22] and describes him as a talented and precocious poet who revealed his personal style in his first book, *Devoted Blood, Colors in the Sea*: "Before he was twenty, the voice of our poet had stopped being a reflection, so as to emit its own light."[23] Unlike the more historical tone he adopts in his biographical sketch of López Velarde, Chávez puts a literary critical spin on Pellicer's portrait, relying on the observations of poet Alí Chumacero and writer and diplomat Antonio Castro Leal.[24] He uses their commentaries to help him argue that Pellicer inaugurated a new trend within the Mexican literary tradition, in contrast with López Velarde's work, which he considers

> parallel, but completely distinct and apart, because the lines of feeling and expression of the two poets, like the rails of a train track, never meet. . . . Both artists came from origins rooted in the same earth and watered by the same springs; they breathed the same moment, but there was never unison in their voices. Each one said his part, with his timbre, with his accent, and with his own language.[25]

In addition, Chávez acknowledges the social commitment of both, which did not, however, lead them to seek high governmental positions.[26] Chávez recognizes in Pellicer's work, beyond a profound connection with Mexico, an interest in the social reality that his country shares with the rest of Latin America.

Most inspiring to the composer is the intensity his poet friend achieves with the written word, creating images of landscapes with "elusive textures" that remind him of Lorca but also dazzle him with their singularity:

> But his extraordinary capacity to see color and light and make them vibrate is matched by his capacity to tell us about everything he sees, transformed into poetic images. . . . The poetry of the author makes objective values subjective. In describing the outside, the poet describes himself: the artist makes everything his, turns everything into his self.[27]

Regarding their more personal exchange, he remembers that Pellicer dedicated the poem "I Listen" to him in 1925 and shared unpublished manuscripts such as "Exágonos" with him.[28] These were later printed in the same issue of *Ulises* in which Chávez published his piece for piano.[29]

It is not surprising that Chávez mentions these poems in his biographical sketch of Pellicer, since they inspired his composition series *Tres exágonos* and *Otros tres exágonos*.[30] Six lines each, with an irregular meter (7 to 14 syllables), Pellicer's hexagons sketch a variety of situations and impressions. The resulting images seem dictated by impulse, rather than by rational coherence, and are often extraordinary. For this reason, these poems have been considered as works with a strong Surrealist influence. The themes range from the cliché of hopeless, unrequited love, as in "To Love. All of Life in Flames," to fantastical voyages in boats and nocturnal scenes, accompanied by dreamlike images and seasoned with a touch of irony, as in "The Ship Has Crashed into the Moon" or "When the Transatlantic Passed." Regarding these poems, Chávez comments:

> Without a doubt, Carlos knew what was happening in the world. Although the First World War, 14–18, coinciding with the second stage of our revolution, 14–17, left us relatively isolated, Pellicer could not have ignored the existence of the Futurists, of Giorgio de Chirico, of Marcel Duchamp, or of Dada, the movement baptized as such in 1916. In any case, his unbelievable artworks, such as "The Ship Has Crashed

> into the Moon" and many of his new forms of expression, were clearly a natural development of his own fantasy and delirious imagination, loaded intuitively with irrational poetic symbolism. . . . ["The ship has crashed into the moon"] has an enormous dynamic charge. It is about lived rather than dreamed moments, lived in an electrified, alert imagination.[31]

The reference to "The Ship Has Crashed into the Moon" hexagon explains Chávez's decision to include it as the first in his series *Otros tres exágonos*.[32] In both series Chávez generally preserves not only the brevity but the scintillating, witty, and at moments caustic spirit that Pellicer, the poet from Tabasco, gave to his verse. It is also clear that in these pieces, as in others from the early 1920s, the young Chávez found himself exploring musical resources of a more experimental nature. Scholars such as Robert Parker also find ties between these pieces and Schoenberg's *Pierrot lunaire* or Stravinsky's settings of Japanese poetry.[33] Leonora Saavedra, for her part, hears echoes of the *Catalogue de fleurs* by Milhaud and influences of Varèse, to whom the works were dedicated.[34]

By examining a few hexagons, we may appreciate how the text is linked to the music. In the poem that opens the first series with the lines "To love. All of life in flames," Chávez relies on the syllabic structure for the vocal line. At the beginning, the voice is required to perform a phrase that is more recited than sung—a kind of *Sprechgesang*—in keeping with the sharp, monotonous tone with which Pellicer begins the poem. Moved by destructive, scorching images, this voice seems to cry out desperately. As the poem develops, however, the vocal line becomes nuanced and muted, melting into and dialoguing with the dark, dense instrumental textures from which it was initially distinct.

The structure of the poem seems disjointed toward the end of the song, which begins with the enjambment of the fourth and fifth line—"silent love / in the sea"—merging into a single musical idea. Then, in the middle of the fifth line, the melody takes on new colors and shades that illustrate the sky-blue tone: "together with the sky." Here, the syntactic structure seems to take on more importance than that of the verse line, which until now had been respected. This provides a framework for the musical interpretation of the last part of the fifth line, when the beginning of a new sentence, "Only the soul," causes a caesura to appear behind the healing, tranquil image of the sky. This leads to another change in the character of the piece, not only rhythmically and melodically but also instrumentally, generating a tension that lasts until the dramatic denouement of the final line. These continual contrasts in the music allow the various faces of love to be thematized in sound; even if they are not symmetrically equivalent, as in an equilateral hexagon, they function as a metaphor for the geometric figure implicit in the poems. Love as a theme takes on different motives (impressions or images), which are juxtaposed against one another and illuminate the emotion's volatile, multiple essence.

The second hexagon of the series, "Arrive, Oh Sweet Hours," has a more narrative tone and begins like a calm awakening. At first the poetic subject's sweet, subtle sensation of being before the world rather than in a state of full consciousness predominates. Faithful to the intention of a poem that is full of sensuality and synesthetic impressions, the musical composition makes the "sweet hours" vibrate, as they awaken the world with "flowers / collected at night" and offer "better / profiles to things," transforming the soul, as announced at the end of the fifth line, into a "melody modulated over ancient colors." Even though the composition respects the poem's structural elements, such as enjambments, and has fewer changes or breaks than the preceding piece, the fifth line is once again interrupted—this time by an instrumental melody, one used until then as an illustrative tool for the poetic images.

In the settings of *Otros tres exágonos*, Chávez continues to follow the syllabic structure of the poems and insists on creating unexpected environments. One clear example of this is "The ship has crashed into the moon," perhaps the most abstract of the six poems because of the use of superimposed images, as in a cubist painting. Although Pellicer turns to a romantic theme, the night, he deconstructs it entirely as he recounts a series of unbelievable incidents: the crashing of the ship into the moon, the moon that is shipwrecked, and the presumable presence of travelers with luggage who assume the poetic voice and speak hidden truths in verse. These images appear independent from one another, without clear narrative or thematic development, which also explains why the poem is considered Surrealist.

Chávez's music aspires to support this interpretation by means of short, differentiated musical motives that generally reinforce the relaxed, playful, and ironic tone of the poem. The first line unleashes a series of images of a constative nature, followed by a long musical silence. The texture changes in the second line and moves toward a melody that lasts through lines three and four, where it imitates the stiff, clumsy but easy rhyming phrase of someone "speaking in verse." In the manner of some sonic hypotyposis, the moon goes under at the end of the fifth line, and then the music drags "our romantic efforts" with it in a parodical key, with a melody that gradually loses strength until it disintegrates.

The case of "Where is my heart going?" is similar to that of "To love. All of life in flames," not just for the particular spin placed on the theme of falling out of love, but also in the treatment of the voice. Musically, Chávez interprets the poem as having three different moments. At the beginning, the soprano's voice extends in a monotone across the first two lines, except for the questioning tone created by modulating only the final syllable. The vocal monotone contrasts with the text—"along this luminous avenue"—but is balanced by the agility of the instrumental melody. The contrast Chávez generates between the lyrical line and the instrumental arrangement underscores, with an expressionistic touch, the estrangement suggested by this deliberate disarticulation. The third line changes the dynamic by letting the voice adopt a spoken, almost colloquial tone that stresses the absurdity of the circumstances: "Good evening, Lady Disappointment." This greeting is followed by an exclamation that traverses three lines, in which Pellicer plows humorously over the ridiculousness of love: "But I was in the country / mortgaging sunsets / to edify my life!"

The last of the six *Exágonos*, "When the Transatlantic Passed," is the longest, due to the instrumental prelude that provides the atmosphere in which the ship travels "under the green-gold arc of dawn" while the "crowned mermaids" rise from the waters. The text becomes predominant only in the most Surrealist passage, when the mermaids ask the passengers for "sandwiches and champagne."

The public gave a warm welcome to both series of *Exágonos*, but particularly to the second, whose success was reported after its 1925 New York performance at Edgard Varèse's International Composers' Guild. By contrast, it is worth recalling an anecdote from the reception in Mexico, one with which Chávez, very much in the sharp, ironic tone of Pellicer, concludes the portrait of his friend:

> In 1924, when the *Seis exágonos* of Pellicer set by me premiered in Mexico, a musical maestro of the previous century said to me, horrified: "But by God! What does it mean to go through the countryside mortgaging sunsets?" I told him: "Look, Maestro, we mustn't forget that poetic language is poetic language. You or I would have said that we got away from it all (!) or something like that; Pellicer simply said that he went to the countryside. Now, as for the mortgage, well, look, one intuits poetry, one doesn't explain it. Who knows what the poet meant, but if we were to speak prosaically, we might understand, maybe, that from the beauty of the

sunsets the poet wanted to extract the riches with which he could establish his life's purpose."[35]

Chávez and Villaurrutia: Moving Through the Nocturnes

Chávez's portrait of Villaurrutia, sketched in the unpublished, unfinished notes for *Mis amigos poetas*, reveals that their relationship revolved around shared friendships and projects, which helps Chávez remember facets of Villaurrutia's personality:

> Xavier always appeared vivacious and sharp. I seem to remember him with a cheerful air and a touch of irony—his natural, everyday attitude. During some periods, we saw each other frequently, in the company of other friends. 1924, '25, '26. Novo, Tamayo, José Gorostiza, Abraham Ángel, and Rodríguez Lozano. Shortly thereafter, I introduced Agustín Lazo to the group.[36]

The notes are too brief, however, to reveal Chávez's opinion of his friend's poetry or the aesthetic or even ideological directions that Villaurrutia pursued.[37]

To complement these impressions, we turn to the concise portrait of Villaurrutia presented by Octavio Paz around that time in his introduction to a selection of his poems published by the Universidad Nacional Autónoma de México (UNAM):

> Villaurrutia was always concerned with the opposition between Classicism and Romanticism. These terms were not only historically and stylistically significant for him, but rather vitally and personally so. The opposition between them was his conflict, his drama. . . . Villaurrutia's poetry is defined neither by unity nor plurality, but rather by duality. His poetry begins with the consciousness of duality and attempts to resolve it into unity. But unity that does not destroy duality, but on the contrary, preserves it and is preserved in it.[38]

According to Paz, this duality is thematized in the constant motion of recurring opposites, such as "solitude/company, silence/noise, sleeping/

waking, time/eternity, fire/ice, full/empty, nothing/everything, etc. . . . The intermediary state, in the poetry of Villaurrutia, describes a moment of extreme attention at the core of the most extreme abandon: to sleep with one's eyes open, to see with one's eyes closed."[39] These issues, as well as the idea of permanent doubt, also appear in the nocturnes that so attracted Chávez's attention and, like Pellicer's hexagons, gave him ideas for his songs.[40]

The experience of including Villaurrutia's first nocturne, "Nocturne: The Rose," in Three Poems for Voice and Piano (1938), encouraged Chávez to set another four nocturnes a year later for soprano, contralto, and orchestra. "Nocturne I," "Nocturne: Dream," "Nocturne: The Statue," and "Nocturne: Nothing Is Heard" make up the movements of this piece, one of Chávez's longest vocal compositions.[41] Written between 1933 and 1938, Villaurrutia's nocturnes form a broad corpus, ultimately integrated into the book *Nostalgia de la muerte* (*Nostalgia for Death*; 1946).[42]

These poems share certain characteristics with Pellicer's earlier hexagons, such as the intensity of the poetic images and the reappropriation of the romantic night using a new aesthetic, connected to the free association of ideas. However, the works of the two poets differ in various ways, starting with their length: Villaurrutia's poems, thematically more ambitious, are less concise than the *Exágonos*.[43] As for tone, Pellicer's is more playful and ironic, whereas nostalgia dominates Villaurrutia's work, along with existential doubt, the result of questioning and searching for the meaning of man's existence. In these conditions, the night and its derivatives (darkness and shadow) offer a propitious environment for contemplation, shown as a sharp state of consciousness from which images emerge, depicting an inner experience translated through the senses. The dream, as slippery but as palpable as water, strengthens these images, which allow the lyrical "I" to transcend the very night and open itself to revelation, even when it cannot show any absolute truths.

Robert Parker provides a good summary of Chávez's methods of translating these poetic experiences to the musical level:

> Soloists appear individually in the first three movements . . . . The two singers join forces in the fourth movement. . . . Lyrical vocal melodies embody the essence of the dreamlike poetry, and the large but restrained orchestra accompanies sensitively without overshadowing the singers. The vocal lines, though challenging in respect to intonation and difficult intervals, are nonetheless "vocal" in character and idiomatic for the trained singer. Light orchestration, in a seemingly

> endless variety of colors, complex chromatic harmonies, polytonality, and nonpulsatile rhythm are the salient resources Chávez has assembled in surrealistic sound ambience befitting Villaurrutia's poems.[44]

"Nocturne I," which Chávez chose as the first piece in his composition, launches the principal motives: the night, the shadows, and the dream. The poetic subject, entirely exposed to the nocturnal experience, receives these elements through a multi-sensory, synesthetic awareness that is often ambiguous and is associated with Surrealist methods such as automatic writing: "the shadows [that] make you hear," "the bloody scream," "the haze of desire," "the sweat of earth," "smudges across my lips: / the sweet dream / of contact," etc.

The music re-creates the dark atmosphere, full of tension and suspense, as well as the constant contrasts. Divided into six stanzas of different lengths, unrhymed and mostly in heptasyllabic meter, the poem uses anaphora—"Everything that"—at the beginning of the first four stanzas, while in the fifth the recurring phrase suffers a small change by including a conjunction: "And everything that." This reinforces the accumulation of sensations encapsulated in an emphatic, all-embracing "Everything" in the sixth stanza. The poem as a whole gives an impression of simultaneity; this can be sensed in the saturation of verbs declined in the present tense: *sketches, reveals, undresses, makes hear, flare, makes emit, smudges, makes touch, dares, circulates, caresses, pushes under, lives, dies*.[45] This saturation contrasts with the subject's experience of solitude. Chávez translates this disparity into music not only through the contrasting use of high and low pitches, but by evoking romance on the stylistic level only to immediately deconstruct it by bringing out an instrumental line of musical economy, defined by slow rhythm, sustained notes, and the strategic use of rests. Thus the anaphora does not become a musical refrain but is transformed as the night progresses.

At moments, the instrumental solos communicate the mood rather than the environment, echoing the voice, like the flute that appears in the second stanza, when the "hard thudding silence" is announced. In other moments, the music anticipates the text, like the muted trumpet with the "bloody scream" in the same stanza. The melancholic tone toward the end seems to foreshadow the unresolved drama of a confirmed paradox: the knowledge that everything "lives in my deadening eyes, / and dies on my hardening lips."

"Nocturne: Dream," unfolding its wings, contrasts musically with the tension and suspense experienced in the first movement and poem. Without abandoning the dark tone, Chávez begins with a more fluid melody and a syllabic setting. It should be noted that Villaurrutia dedicated this poem to the Franco-Uruguayan poet Jules Supervielle, who instead of following the Surrealist trend of automatic writing, proposed a lyrical vigilance toward the links between one's inner world and the outside one. Divided into nine stanzas (each four or five lines long, with the last two at two lines each), the poem presents a largely hexasyllabic structure, and Chávez takes advantage of this consistency by playing with melodic symmetry and its inversions. The poem evokes the theme of the dream as a voyage through different dimensions that intersect, while menacing Death is sung about in a dark, monotonous way. The body that carries itself to its own deathbed remains divided until it catches up with sleep, which finally folds its wings.

"Nocturne: The Statue," which Villaurrutia dedicated to painter Agustín Lazo, who initiated him into Surrealism,[46] has been interpreted as a Surrealist poem because of the way in which images are presented.[47] It also contains clear references to Supervielle's poem "Saisir," in both the theme and the syntactic structure with which it begins. The first of two stanzas, barely two lines long, sets the scene of the dream: "Dream, dream of night, the street, the stairway / and the scream of the statue unrounding the corner"—as if taken from a Giorgio di Chirico painting. Rhythmically the most nimble of the four songs and melodically the most playful, this piece re-creates the exploratory, experimental tone of the poem and introduces it with a staccato articulation, as if to imitate the depersonalized, almost automatized vision of the lyrical "I" who speaks in infinitives: "Dream, dream of night"; "Run to the statue, and find only the scream, / long to touch the scream, and find only its echo, / long to grasp the echo, and find only the wall / run to the wall and touch a mirror"; etc.[48]

This last line marks a musical interruption in this movement, as Chávez uses cymbals to depict the collision with the mirror. This collision leads to the encounter with the assassinated statue, which happens in a state of consciousness that the song presents as pensive and slightly distressed. But the suspense is once again interrupted by the obstinate, mechanical melody that represents the dream and its succession of erratic events while the subject interacts with the statue. The poem does not culminate in a dramatic moment, but rather in a scene that borders on the absurd: "shuffle the chips of its fingers / and repeat in its ear a hundred times a hundred hundred times / until you hear it say: 'I'm dying of sleep.'" In this musical passage, the staccato melody in the background contrasts with the gradual draining of the dream, interpreted with a deceleration of tempo.

Finally, "Nocturne: Nothing Is Heard," structurally the most complex poem—decidedly polymetric, with use of anaphora to open semantic and syntactic games—seems an ideal way to close the song cycle and with it the thematization of sleep and death. At the beginning, Chávez evokes the deserted, silent, and desolate environment of the lyrical "I" who sings her death suspended in a minor key. Again, free association predominates in this architecturally abstract setting; one tries to imagine, but all turns out to be slippery and undefined. The contralto sings: "in this loneliness with no walls / at this hour when angles are escaping / I leave my bloodless statue in the tomb of my bed." Chávez captures "the slow-moving moment / in the interminable descent" musically, until it falls into silence—as the "invisible piano" also falls beyond the reach of fingers.

The confirmation that only "a glance and a voice" remain marks the turning of the song toward an ambiguous state of existence. When the question becomes explicit ("what are lips? what are glances that are lips?"), a change in vocal register happens: the soprano appears. But soon it is the contralto's turn to speak again, and she keeps affirming the ambiguity of her existential situation: "and my voice is no longer my voice / within this unwetting water / within this plate glass air / within this purple fire that slashes like a scream / In the miserable game of mirror to mirror / my voice is falling." The composer sees this doubt and alienation of the body and its senses as an opportunity for a performative display, which results in a musical and semantic game of mirrors, captured in a passage that reveals the homophony of the words: "my voice is falling / and my voice incinerates / and my voice in sin narrates / and my voice in sin elates / and my poison scintillates." Chávez creates the musical effect of this sea of reflections by alternating the contralto and soprano voices. The final lines, which talk about "the pulse in my temples" as "a dead telegraph no one is answering," return to the aridity and monotony of the beginning of the piece and culminate with the line, "for sleep and death have nothing more to say," sung by both voices in unison for the first time.

This brief tour through the different connections that Chávez established with the world of letters—as a reader, critic, friend, powerful public figure on the Mexican cultural scene, but above all as a composer—confirms the existence of an open field of scholarship so rich and astonishing that it calls out for more detailed, comprehensive studies. May this essay serve simply as a small taste, the sketch of a spoken portrait or a floating image, as in a dream of Villaurrutia's, eager to be completed.

NOTES

1. By Robert Parker's estimate, poetry-based compositions were some 20 percent of Chávez's musical output. Robert L. Parker, *Carlos Chávez: Mexico's Modern-Day Orpheus* (Boston: Twayne, 1983), 57.

2. In Chávez's music, works that have nationalist elements and use traditional techniques coexist alongside more abstract, experimental pieces. Robert L. Parker, "Carlos Chávez: A Panoply of Styles," and Leonora Saavedra, "Carlos Chávez y la construcción de una alteridad estratégica," in *Diálogo de resplandores: Carlos Chávez y Silvestre Revueltas*, ed. Yael Bitrán and Ricardo Miranda (Mexico City: CONACULTA, 2002), 118–24 and 125–36, respectively.

3. Chávez's decision to base his piece on Cocteau's version of *Antigone* is not surprising, given the latter's influence among young Mexican intellectuals and artists who in those years were open to new aesthetic paradigms.

4. For a complete list of influential poetry, see Parker, *Carlos Chávez*, 57.

5. Chávez devotes some time to the memory of López Velarde, eleven years his senior, in an important lecture titled "Mis amigos poetas" (My Poet Friends), given at the Colegio Nacional in 1973.

6. Los Contemporáneos were faulted as Europeanizers who lacked commitment to Mexican issues. Several, however, such as Xavier Villaurrutia and Salvador Novo, involved themselves directly in the struggle for Mexican cultural definition by participating in such movements as the Frente Único de Lucha Contra la Reacción Estética (FULCRE, Unified Front Against Esthetic Reaction) of 1932.

7. The group belonged to a generation of young, urban, educated writers—poets, playwrights, and essayists—who shortly after the Revolution gained access to positions of political and literary prominence. For some of them this was partly through their association with José Vasconcelos, Minister of Education, 1921–24.

8. Xavier Villaurrutia, "La poesía de los jóvenes de México," in *Obras: Poesía, teatro, prosas varias, crítica*, ed. Miguel Capistrán, Alí Chumacero, and Luis Mario Schneider (Mexico City: Fondo de Cultura Económica, 1953), 819–35.

9. The brief "Solo" for piano, written in an abstract, modernist style, appeared in *Ulises* 1/2 (1927): 80–81. Chávez is also mentioned in the seventh issue of *Contemporáneos* (1928) as one of the first figures linked to a new type of Mexican nationalism in the arts. The article, written by Aaron Copland and translated into Spanish, was originally published in *The New Republic* as "Carlos Chávez: Mexican Composer," 2 May 1928. See also Guillermo Sheridan, *México en 1932: La polémica nacionalista* (Mexico City: Fondo de Cultura Económica, 1999), 46.

10. Carlos Chávez, *Mis amigos poetas* (Mexico City: Colegio Nacional, 1977).

11. Unpublished materials used in this essay are from Fondo Carlos Chávez, Archivo General de la Nación (AGN), Mexico City. Although Chávez elaborated no definitive text on Villaurrutia, he did give a lecture at the Colegio Nacional in 1944 in which he referred to the discursive devices in Villaurrutia's Surrealist style that spawned some of his own musical ideas. See Parker, *Carlos Chávez*, 60.

12. Chávez, *Mis amigos poetas*, 24. The writers Leopoldo Lugones (Argentina, 1874–1938), José Santos Chocano (Peru, 1875–1934), Amado Nervo (Mexico, 1870–1919), and Rubén Darío (Nicaragua, 1867–1916) were members of the Modernista movement in Latin America. They wrote poetry and essays, were journalists and editors of literary magazines, and during a certain period of their lives held diplomatic positions in their own countries. Darío is considered the foremost Modernista poet.

13. José Dolores Frías (1891–1936) was a poet and journalist from Querétaro, Mexico, and the first Mexican foreign correspondent during the First World War. In his many

visits to Paris, he became acquainted with writers and artists living in that city, including Jean Cocteau.

14. All translations of Villaurrutia's poetry are from *Nostalgia for Death: Poetry by Xavier Villaurrutia*, trans. Eliot Weinberger (Port Townsend, WA: Copper Canyon Press, 1993).

15. These trips allowed them to discover the work of authors such as Jean Cocteau, T. S. Eliot, and Luigi Pirandello, for whom they would become the first Spanish-language translators and editors.

16. On the many references to music in Los Contemporáneos' correspondence, see Luis Ignacio Helguera, "Los contemporáneos y la música," *Pauta* 18/79 (2001): 5–17.

17. The correspondence mentions an unnamed "Aztec ballet" which may have been *Los cuatro soles* or yet another project.

18. Sometimes the friendships helped establish strategic connections, such as when Pellicer put Chávez in contact with José Vasconcelos. With others, the relationship was limited to cordial contact and mutual interests, as documented in the written exchange that Chávez maintained with Jaime Torres Bodet from 1954 to 1955.

19. Regarding this debate, see Sheridan, *México en 1932*, 462; and Evodio Escalante, "Contemporáneos y estridentistas en el estadio del espejo" in *Los contemporáneos en el laberinto de la crítica,* ed. Rafael Olea Franco and Anthony Stanton (Mexico: El Colegio de México, 1994), 397.

20. Sheridan, *México en 1932*, 462.

21. The biographical sketch of López Velarde, for example, is loaded with historical and personal or family anecdotes. In *Mis amigos poetas*, Chávez attributes his understanding of the value of literary discourse to López Velarde and Pellicer (13).

22. Ibid.

23. Ibid., 19.

24. Alí Chumacero (1918–2010), apart from being a prominent poet and winner of several awards, became a key literary figure as editor of literary journals such as *El hijo pródigo* and *México en la cultura*, and as chief editor of the publisher Fondo de Cultura Económica. Antonio Castro Leal (1896–1981), well-known as an essayist, occupied several important positions in cultural administration, and was the president of the Universidad Nacional Autónoma de México and Mexican ambassador to UNESCO.

25. Chávez, *Mis amigos poetas*, 29.

26. Ibid.

27. Ibid., 29, 31.

28. Ibid., 23.

29. Carlos Pellicer, "Exágonos," *Ulises* 1/2 (1927): 55.

30. Both were composed for tenor or soprano, flute/piccolo, oboe/English horn, bassoon, viola, and piano, although Chávez initially wrote *Tres exágonos* as a piece for soprano or tenor and piano.

31. Chávez, *Mis amigos poetas*, 31–32.

32. Further on in his biographical sketch of Pellicer, Chávez cites the complete "Where Is My Heart Going?" which would become the second in the *Otros tres exágonos* series.

33. Parker, *Carlos Chávez*, 58.

34. See Leonora Saavedra, "Carlos Chávez's Polysemic Style: Constructing the National, Seeking the Cosmopolitan," *Journal of the American Musicological Society* 68/1 (2015): 99–150, 118.

35. Chávez, *Mis amigos poetas*, 32–33.

36. Artists Rufino Tamayo (1899–1991), Abraham Ángel Card Valdés (1905–1924), and Agustín Lazo (1896–1971) often collectively exhibited their work. Although they all incorporated nationalist elements in their paintings, they departed from the mainstream nationalism of the Mexican muralists, developing independent styles through their choice of color and topics and the incorporation of naïf (Ángel) or surrealist (Lazo) elements.

37. In the earlier mentioned Colegio Nacional lecture of November 1944 Chávez addressed Villaurrutia's quasi-Surrealist stream of consciousness and "explained that any archetypical forms or procedures in music would be incompatible with the basic tenets of surrealism. He argued that 'psychic automatism,' for example, unforeseeable impulses, guided by the subconscious with all its complexity and mystery, enters into the process of musical creation and is thereby suitable for a surrealistic text." Parker, *Carlos Chávez,* 60.

38. Octavio Paz, "El pliegue y sus dobles," introduction to *Xavier Villaurrutia: 15 poemas* (Mexico City: Universidad Nacional Autónoma de México, 1977), 3–6.

39. Ibid., 4–5.

40. The other Villaurrutia poem that Chávez set is "North Carolina Blues" (1937), also from *Nostalgia de la muerte*. This more ideological, socially conscious work is dedicated to Langston Hughes, for whom Villaurrutia was the Spanish translator. The composition, for mezzo-soprano or baritone and piano, premiered in 1942, although Chávez started working on it in 1939, as stated in a letter of 23 December of that year, in which he asks Villaurrutia to meet with him and the English translator to discuss his adaptation. For more detail about "North Carolina Blues," see Stephanie Stalling's essay in this volume.

41. Parker, *Carlos Chávez*, 60.

42. On the different published editions of the Nocturnes, see Pilar Gil Soler, *Xavier Villaurrutia, entre el clasicismo y el simbolismo: Estudio comparativo y análisis prosódico-retórico de su poesía* (Valencia: Ediesser, 2008), 40 and 299–300.

43. Luis Ignacio Helguera correctly defines these differences in general terms: "If Villaurrutia is the nocturnal poet, Pellicer is the poet of light, of a hundred-degree Tabasco sun." Luis Ignacio Helguera, "Los contemporáneos y la música," *Pauta* 28/79 (July–September 2001): 5–17.

44. Parker, *Carlos Chávez*, 60.

45. Pilar Gil Soler recognizes the influence of the French Decadent Movement and Symbolism in this approach. See her *Xavier Villaurrutia,* 305.

46. Olivier Debroise, "La inmóvil permanencia de lo mutable," *Revista de Bellas Artes: Homenaje nacional a los Contemporáneos* 8 (November 1982): 55, cited in Gil Soler, *Xavier Villaurrutia*, 43.

47. Villaurrutia "confesses, in addition to his personal participation in the Surrealist movement of his time, that 'Surrealism'—he affirms—'lives among us as a possibility for expression. . . . I, too, in some parts of my poetry, have been a Surrealist without even meaning to be.'" José Luis Martinez, interview in (Mexico City) *Novedades*, 14 January 1951, quoted in Eugene L. Moretta, *La poesía de Xavier Villaurrutia* (Mexico: Fondo de Cultura Económica, 1976), 50.

48. In the original Spanish, all of these verbs are in the infinitive form: "Soñar, soñar la noche"; "Correr hacia la estatua y encontrar sólo el grito / querer tocar el grito y sólo hallar el eco, / querer asir el eco y encontrar sólo el muro / y correr hacia el muro y tocar un espejo." *(Trans.)*

The Composer as Intellectual: Carlos Chávez and El Colegio Nacional

ANA R. ALONSO-MINUTTI

Responding to an ideological and political impulse to modernize the country after the Revolution, the Mexican State supported the creation of institutions, periodicals, and award systems that provided the financial structure for an intellectual elite to thrive. The most prestigious of these is El Colegio Nacional (National College), founded in 1943 under the presidency of Manual Ávila Camacho. At the core of its constitution lies the belief that the knowledge produced by its members will strengthen "the national consciousness."[1]

Among El Colegio Nacional's fifteen founding members, Carlos Chávez stood out as one of the most influential figures in the development and orientation of the musical and cultural practices of the country. During his long tenure at El Colegio, Chávez successfully fulfilled the mission he set for himself as a member: to give a number of educational lectures to the general public each year at the building where El Colegio is located, in downtown Mexico City. Interested in securing a place for music within this circle, Chávez established the role of the composer *as* intellectual. In Chávez's model, the composer-intellectual follows a modernist ideology of musical progress, which in turn serves as a support system for avant-garde practices.[2] Over seventy years later, the model he created still stands. Chávez's successors at El Colegio, Eduardo Mata (1942–1995) and Mario Lavista (1943–), have performed this role while guaranteeing state support for the creation and performance of Mexican contemporary concert music.

In what follows I aim to investigate the ways in which Chávez, as founding member and first musician in the country to be granted official recognition as an intellectual, used El Colegio Nacional as a platform to cultivate a didactic modernity. He did so by institutionalizing the format of *concierto-conferencias* (lecture-concerts) as a central pedagogical tool to enlighten the general public and by incorporating a model of musical modernity aligned with a cutting-edge intellectuality. Archival research, as well as interviews and personal correspondence with some of El Colegio Nacional's members, workers, and performers provided the groundwork for the present study.[3]

Institutionalizing Culture

The creation of El Colegio Nacional, as Ignacio Sánchez Prado and others have suggested, was the result of a long process of institutionalization of Mexican culture that began during the 1920s and 1930s, and provided a "definite step toward the professionalization of the intellectual class of the country."[4] As Sánchez Prado states, the creation of this type of institutional system allowed intellectuals to enjoy a certain degree of autonomy and at the same time granted them platforms of unprecedented stability.[5] The primary objective of El Colegio Nacional has been to "disseminate and to spread the philosophical, literary, and scientific culture of the Republic"[6]—mostly through a series of free lectures given by its members to the general public during a ten-month period. The federal government, through the Ministry of Public Education, provides each member an equal monthly allowance from January to November.[7] By decree, the members of El Colegio are prohibited from publicly adhering to an overtly political agenda, primarily because of the belief that any political interest could potentially "cloud" the conscience of the member (teacher) and the audience (student).[8]

Although the different disciplines among El Colegio's members are meant to represent "all branches of knowledge and culture," the fields of the founding members showed a significant inclination toward the arts. Eight out of fifteen individuals—chosen by Octavio Véjar Vázquez, head of the Ministry of Public Education—were professionals within artistic disciplines: novelist Mariano Azuela, composer Carlos Chávez, poets Enrique González Martínez and Alfonso Reyes, and painters José Clemente Orozco and Diego Rivera (see Figure 1). Nevertheless, in El Colegio's membership since 1943 there has been a lack of representation of the performing arts, music being the exception.[9] Music may not have been regarded an obvious choice as an intellectual discipline at first, and Chávez might have faced the need to justify its inclusion.

New affiliations with El Colegio are made possible only when a post becomes vacant either by death or resignation, and after an internal process of nomination and evaluation. The original membership grew from fifteen to twenty within a year and, in 1971, that number was doubled

Figure 1. Founding members of El Colegio Nacional (1943). Top, l. to r.: José Clemente Orozco, Diego Rivera, Isaac Ochoterena, Ignacio Chávez, Antonio Caso, Alfonso Reyes, Carlos Chávez; bottom, l. to r.: Manuel Uribe Troncoso, Mariano Azuela, Ezequiel A. Chávez, Enrique González Martínez, Manuel Sandoval Vallarta, José Vasconcelos.

to forty. From 1943 to 2014 El Colegio has had a total of 94 members. It was not until 1985 that it accepted its first female member, art historian Beatriz de la Fuente, who remained the only woman until the inclusion of psychologist María Elena Medina Mora in 2006 and, a year later, anthropologist Linda Rosa Manzanilla Naim.[10]

Chávez's inclusion within El Colegio's founding members was not surprising. He had gained national and international reputation not only as an avant-garde composer since the mid-1920s, but also through his leadership (since 1928) of the Orquesta Sinfónica de México and the Conservatorio Nacional. Moreover, he had served as head of the Fine Arts Department of the Ministry of Public Education (1933–34). Through these posts, as Robert Parker, Leonora Saavedra, and Alejandro Madrid have demonstrated, Chávez became one of the most influential figures in the development and orientation of the musical and cultural practices of the country.[11]

El Colegio's main mission resonated with Chávez's ongoing commitment to educating the people as a means to achieve social progress. If

Chávez was to achieve this mission, the central question became: What kind of music would adequately contribute to the education of the general public? As we will see, the musical repertories he chose to present and the topics he addressed, both at the *concierto-conferencias* and in the writings he published for El Colegio, assisted in the establishment of a particular type of musical intellectuality.

Performing Modernity: The *Concierto-Conferencias* at El Colegio Nacional

Chávez covered a great variety of subjects in his lectures at El Colegio, but art music remained his main focus.[12] Delineating the parameters of greatness in art was imperative for him, and the *concierto-conferencias* became a useful platform from which to shape the musical practices that would be regarded as intellectual. Chávez's commitment to this goal was closely connected to his devotion to a process of social transformation.

Starting with the basic teaching of the parameters of art music, Chávez centered his inaugural series of nine lectures at El Colegio in 1943 on general topics of music appreciation, and for the next two years (1944–45) mainly covered the elements of music.[13] The first major composer Chávez addressed extensively was Beethoven (1944), whom he presented as a hardworking composer embracing an organicist compositional method, thus setting him up as a model for other composers.[14] To Chávez, Beethoven symbolized the artist that endures, the solitary genius that creates, and whose music enlightens.[15]

Once Chávez had established a model for the composer-intellectual within the mainstream lineage of Western art music composers, he proceeded to lay out the place of Mexican music within an international frame. Starting in 1946, Chávez began to offer a significant number of lectures focused on introducing Mexican concert music to the broader public. Of the seventy lectures Chávez gave during his first decade at El Colegio (1943–53), almost half (thirty-three) focused on Mexican music; twenty-one on general aspects of music appreciation; and fourteen on Beethoven.

Chávez's emphasis on national music went hand in hand with his internationalist agenda to promote a universal repertory in order to generate an educated general public. He stated: "As we continue [to ensure] equilibrium between native music and universal classical [music], we believe we are building a well-rounded and well-educated public in our country, a public of all social classes, which is truly democratic."[16] This statement resonates with El Colegio's main objective of providing free education for the masses (given by specialists), and at the same time emphasizes the importance of placing Mexican music along with the European in a universal repertory.

In his 1949 series Chávez devoted twenty lectures (twice the required number) to the study of Mexican music. He began by addressing the legacy of the nineteenth century, and subsequently covered the first four decades of the twentieth century. Although it is impossible to determine exactly the content of his lectures due to the lack of recordings or transcriptions, we can infer the historical progression he followed by looking at the lectures' titles as printed in the annual El Colegio *Memorias* (yearbooks). During the following year (1950) Chávez devoted nine more lectures to the study of Mexican music from 1900 to 1950, in which, after tracing the ancestry of Mexican music to Western music—particularly French and German—he outlined what he perceived as the deficiencies of national music with regard to its European counterpart.

Although concerts might not have been originally regarded as legitimate intellectual activities by members of El Colegio, Chávez managed to justify them as such and persuaded the members to consider them as pedagogical tools. In a letter to Silvio Zavala, president of the Colegio's Council, the composer requested that three concerts programmed for 1953 substitute for lectures he had not imparted the previous year, for "a good concert teaches in the sense that it *instructs* the audience in the art of music and exposes the art in a way that it can be known and appreciated. . . . A verbal dissertation about music could, at most, awaken the curiosity of receiving the authentic musical *teaching*, which is *listening* to the music."[17] Thanks to the composer's persuasive skills and tenacity, traits that characterized him throughout his life, performances of concert music were established at El Colegio for decades to come. As with numerous other external initiatives, Chávez found in this institution a platform that granted financial support for the production and consumption of new music.

The format of the *concierto-conferencia* became the perfect vehicle for Chávez to couple his own music with that of his international counterparts. Each *concierto-conferencia* would begin with a piece or set of pieces preceded or followed by a short lecture in which Chávez would provide a brief historical contextualization and easy-to-follow analytical observations. The second half of the program would often consist of a second hearing of the first half. This arrangement proved not only to be a useful pedagogical tool, but also allowed for first (and second) hearings of works in progress.

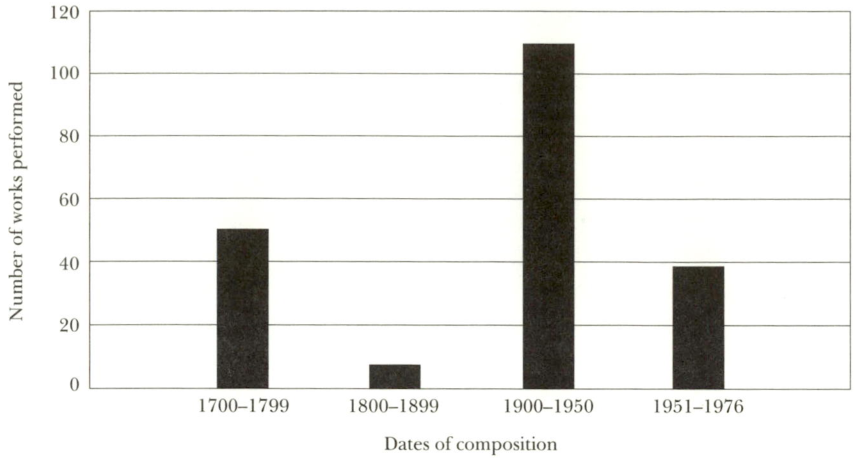

Figure 2. Chávez's *concierto-conferencias*, El Colegio Nacional, 1953 to 1976.

From 1953 onward the composer programmed mostly post-1900 music (see Figure 2), and included regular performances of his own music —particularly works *not* associated with his nationalist or indigenist output.[18] Chávez, fully conscious of the general public's reluctance to assimilate new music, believed in the power of instruction to remedy the separation between composer and listener.[19] Being the only musician at El Colegio granted him complete power of decision in terms of repertory and choosing guest performers. In addition, the lack of a concert admission charge allowed Chávez not to feel pressured about pleasing an audience.

The pieces Chávez selected in his programs, especially those from his European and U.S.-American counterparts, exerted significant influence on other Mexican composers. According to Aurelio Tello, Chávez's 1954 lecture on dodecaphony, which was followed by a program of works by Schoenberg, Berg, and Webern, caused a wider embrace of the twelve-tone method by "practically all young composers in Mexico."[20] Chávez's programming of twelve-tone music reflected his interest in exposing a well-appraised and revered compositional trend, rather than an attempt to impose a personal predilection for the system. Even though he rarely embraced serial techniques in his own music, he believed in the importance of introducing young composers and the general public to compositions that were deemed relevant at an international level. In his essay "El dodecafonismo en México," published in the *Memorias*, Chávez regarded the twelve-tone system as "the next step" in music composition.[21] Following this impetus, a year later he organized a concert at El Colegio that included the *Sinfonia per orchestra d'archi* by Franco Donatoni, as well as *Tres piezas para orquesta de cuerda,* Op. 23, by Spanish-born Rodolfo Halffter, who is credited with introducing the twelve-tone method to Mexico in the 1940s.

The events that Chávez organized during the 1950s at El Colegio were eventually regarded by the local media as one of the summits of musical activity in Mexico City. As critic Salomón Kahan expressed, "Each one of Chávez's *concierto-conferencias* has constituted one of the highest points of their respective musical year in this city."[22] Kahan went on to report that Chávez's concerts attracted such a large audience that many remained standing. From the first season in 1953 to the last, in 1976, Chávez organized a total of sixty-nine *concierto-conferencias* of which twenty-five were solely devoted to his music (a little over a third), with ten others including at least one of his works. This makes Chávez the composer most performed at El Colegio (see complete list of those works in Table 1 at the end of the essay).[23]

Establishing the *concierto-conferencias* as events focused on new music was also possible thanks to the significant honoraria Chávez could grant to high-profile performers and chamber ensembles. Among them, pianist María Teresa Rodríguez (1923–2013) was not only the most frequently featured performer at El Colegio, but also the only female musician who had ever been considered as a pre-candidate for membership.[24] From the very first time Chávez invited a guest performer—pianist Miguel García Mora in 1950—up to the very last event, he never ceased to include guest solo performers and chamber groups. Hence, through El Colegio, Chávez provided a valuable financial support system for Mexican performers—a responsibility he fully believed belonged to the state.

During the 1960s Chávez continued premiering European and U.S.-American high modernist music, such as Pierre Boulez's *Structures* for two pianos in 1960, Edgard Varèse's *Déserts,* and Karlheinz Stockhausen's *Zeitmasse,* both in 1964. For the performance of *Zeitmasse* Chávez invited—for the first and only time—a guest conductor: Eduardo Mata, who at the time was a stellar student of Chávez at the Conservatorio Nacional.

Although works by Latin American and U.S. contemporaries were often performed in Chávez's *conciertos-conferencias*, he rarely programmed works by younger Mexican composers. During a 1969 lecture titled "Composición de vanguardia en México," Chávez raised his concern for the younger composers' fascination with "novelty" and their lack of "the solid foundation that only classical techniques grant."[25] He ultimately concluded that among the younger generation of Mexican composers, only two had demonstrated having a solid foundation and being worthy of national attention: Héctor Quintanar (1936–2013) and Eduardo Mata, who had been his students at the *taller de composición (*composition workshop).[26] At the end of the lecture, María Teresa Rodríguez performed Mata's *Sonata para piano* from 1960.[27] Chávez introduced the work by highlighting "the excellent approach to modern technique . . . in a well-conceived, original and singular work."[28] This represented the only occasion Chávez programmed a piece by a younger Mexican composer at El Colegio Nacional, hence strengthening the mentor-disciple relationship that characterized the configuration of this intellectual elite.[29] Moreover, the fact that Chávez chose to program this piece at a time when Mata had largely abandoned composition to pursue his conducting career might also have strengthened the view of Mata not only as a conductor, but also as composer-intellectual.[30]

Performing Modernity: Chávez's Essays in the *Memorias* of El Colegio Nacional

The centralized channel for the communication of the activities of El Colegio's members are the *Memorias* published annually by the institution. Apart from containing a detailed report of all activities, each of these yearbooks includes a number of texts written by the members, ranging from full-fledged specialized research articles to short opinion pieces on diverse matters. There is no restriction as to the length, scope, and nature of the texts, and all members are invited to submit as many articles as they wish.[31]

Throughout his tenure at El Colegio, Chávez submitted only a handful of essays to the *Memorias*.[32] Since Chávez was such a prolific writer, this leaves one to speculate about this self-imposed limitation. Perhaps he regarded his *concierto-conferencias* as a kind of publication in themselves.[33] Given that the *Memorias* were the most important publication of this institution, Chávez might have chosen what to publish strategically, in order to consolidate music as an intellectual discipline and shape the role of the composer as an intellectual.

Chávez established the figure of the composer as an individual with extraordinary abilities, an intellectual whose output *should* be regarded as masterwork. He begins his 1952 essay "Vivaldi-Bach" with a categorical definition of Vivaldi as "a star; a great inventor; a great enlightened man."[34] He describes Vivaldi's compositional process as formalist—one focused primarily on a balance of form—but asserts that his individuality as a composer is the result of his genius, which in turn makes him not a craftsman but an artist.[35] This focus on form is also present in his essay "Arte americano," in which Chávez affirms that individuals on the American continent should be regarded as heirs of Western culture as much as Europeans. Hence, the search for originality in American art should not be looked for in the ways of a "nationalism inspired in localism and limitation," but in the universal search for the equilibrium of form.[36]

Chávez's emphasis on the importance of compositional individuality was further exposed in his essay "Pierre Boulez" (1960). He contextualized Boulez's *Structures* as a direct result of Webern's serialism. Chávez's modernist belief in musical progress lay behind his commitment to promoting certain kinds of new music. To that end, he quoted what Stravinsky said to the Argentinean press while in Buenos Aires: "We cannot speak a lyrical language or a pathetic language anymore. We must use a scientific language, a language of precision." Chávez followed the implications of this quotation by stating that whether the listener liked this music was of no importance, for ultimately the historical value of this new scientific musical language was something no one could deny.[37] The modernist flair of this statement reminds us of the posture adopted by Milton Babbitt in his famous "Who Cares if You Listen," published just two years prior to Chávez's essay. However, Chávez's attitude toward his audience was much more inclusive than Babbitt's, at least in principle. Finally, Chávez concluded that music has no intrinsic value.[38] By closing his essay with this statement, the composer was conforming to El Colegio's main ideological standard: *Libertad por el saber*, or freedom through knowledge, a goal that, at least in principle, is not meant just for the educated, but turns knowledge into something that should be accessible to *all*.[39]

Chávez's Legacy

During the ceremony in honor of Chávez on 11 May 1981 Jaime García Terrés, then president of the Colegio Council, centered his homage on the composer's extraordinary efforts as a cultural promoter. Chávez's devotion to the history of Western art music, as well as his focus on Mexican music in the context of El Colegio's *conciertos-conferencias*, responded to an ulterior motive: "Both fields of study converge in a single goal: the consolidation of a Mexican music; the coming together of seeds able to fructify for the benefit of our country and our future."[40] García Terrés's speech testifies to Chávez's success in incorporating music as an intellectual discipline.

After Chávez's death, no musician was inducted until 1984, when Eduardo Mata became a member of El Colegio. By the 1980s, Mata's superb credentials as an orchestra conductor of international fame—he was conductor of the Dallas Symphony Orchestra in the late 1970s, and guest-conducted many other orchestras—would have been strong enough reason to nominate him for membership. But Chávez had introduced Mata as both a composer and a conductor to this intellectual circle decades earlier, and his reputation as Chávez's heir played an important role. García Terrés made this clear in a speech given at Mata's induction, in which he recalled Chávez's words in the early 1960s: "'If Mata wanted, he could be the best prepared of my successors.'"[41]

Not only had Mata achieved a reputation of creator/promoter, but he was also regarded as a composer with an intellectual foundation.[42] His activities within El Colegio during his ten-year tenure were limited, in part due to his active conducting schedule abroad. In his inaugural speech he, like Chávez before him, felt compelled to diagnose the state of Mexican contemporary art music, and proposed that in order to counteract its shortages it was necessary to promote the "great masters" so that the public could assume them as theirs. He reintroduced Chávez's format of *concierto-conferencias,* although he gave only four series of these events during his time at El Colegio.[43] In the first of these, titled "El intérprete musical en la segunda mitad del siglo XX," (The performer in the second half of the twentieth century), he addressed the issue of the historically informed performance practices of eighteenth-century music, followed by a performance of Pergolesi's *Stabat Mater* and Bach's *Brandenburg* Concerto No. 6. Like Chávez, Mata gathered some of the best performers in the country for his series at El Colegio.

Mata paid homage to Chávez as a mentor and composer by dedicating *concierto-conferencias* to his memory. Besides programming Chávez's music on two occasions, he also organized a concert of contemporary Mexican music in which he included Mario Lavista's *Reflejos de la noche* for string quartet. Mata's introduction of Lavista's music to El Colegio may have foreshadowed Lavista's later inclusion in this intellectual circle.[44] Apart from his inaugural speech, Mata published only one of his lectures in the Colegio's 1994 *Memorias,* where he reinforced the vision of Chávez as "the greatest musician Mexico has produced." The label "musician" in his text is meant to include Chávez's efforts as a conductor and composer—both of which resonated with Mata's own trajectory.[45] At this point in his career, Mata had already left his post as artistic director of the Dallas Symphony Orchestra and had expressed a desire to return to Mexico and devote more time to composition.[46] Unfortunately, those plans did not come to pass, for he was killed in a plane crash in January of the following year (1995). Even with such a limited presence at El Colegio Nacional, Mata's musical practices served to continue the legacy already outlined by Chávez.

Only three years after Mata's death, Mario Lavista was appointed a member of El Colegio. By the time he was admitted, in 1998, Lavista had already been granted acceptance to the Academia de Artes and obtained the Premio Nacional de Artes y Ciencias. Lavista's appointment to El Colegio could have been in part the result of being regarded a disciple of Chávez by other members, but his nomination was also indebted to the mentorship he received early in his career from members of the literary circle associated with La Casa del Lago in the late 1960s, especially from its director, writer Juan Vicente Melo.[47] Through Melo Lavista became acquainted with other poets who were to become members of El Colegio, among them José Emilio Pacheco, García Terrés, Octavio Paz, and Salvador Elizondo—all remaining close to Lavista's career from an early stage.[48] In contrast to Mata's conducting career, Lavista had attained national and international reputation not only as a musician but also as a prolific writer and chief editor of the music journal *Pauta*.[49]

In his inaugural speech, Lavista offered an examination of both technical and aesthetic aspects that had shaped the musical panorama of the twentieth century, contextualizing his own path as a composer.[50] He saw his place within this circle more as a creator and less as a promoter, as Mata had. Throughout his tenure at El Colegio, Lavista has organized more than seventy lecture-recitals, published more than fifty texts in the annual *Memorias*, and released half a dozen recordings with El Colegio's support. Though he has not programmed much of his own music in his *concierto-conferencias*, he has reprinted some of his scores for chamber and solo music in the *Memorias*. For Lavista, El Colegio has been an extraordinary platform that has allowed him to introduce to the general public contemporary music little known in Mexico, performed by the best performers and chamber ensembles of the country.[51]

Throughout El Colegio's existence, the model of the composer as intellectual established by Chávez, one that promotes the performance and study of avant-garde contemporary music through *conciertos-conferencias*, has prevailed. Thanks to Chávez's leadership and strong initiatives within this elite, El Colegio remains a space for new music, both national and international, to be performed by thriving, extraordinary performers. Chávez's didactic modernity, in which music is understood as an intellectual discipline, has allowed for the critical exploration of musical affairs in our time. The figure of the composer-intellectual within this national elite seems destined to live for years to come.

Table 1. Chávez Works Performed in *Concierto-conferencias* at El Colegio Nacional, 1953–1976

Date	Title of Lecture	Title of Composition	Performers	Other Works Performed
29 April 1953	AMERICAN MUSIC	Ten Preludes for piano	Carlos Chávez	Villa-Lobos, *Bachiana Brasileira* No. 6 for flute and bassoon Copland, Sextet for piano, clarinet and string quartet
7 October 1954	VOCAL MUSIC BY MAESTRO CARLOS CHÁVEZ	"Extase" (Victor Hugo), "Du bist wie eine Blume…" (Heine), "Inutil epigrama" (R. de Carvalho), "Estrellas fijas" (J. A. Silva) *Seis Exágonos* (Pellicer) "Amar, toda la vida en llamas," "Llegad, oh dulces horas," "Amada, déjame ver la luna," "El buque ha chocado con la luna," "A dónde va mi corazón?", "Cuando el trasatlántico pasaba¿" "El segador" (Pellicer) "La casada infiel" (García Lorca), "Todo" (López Velarde) "Hoy no lució la estrella de tus ojos" (Novo), "Nocturna rosa" (Villaurrutia), "North Carolina Blues" (Villaurrutia) *Cuatro nocturnos* (Villaurrutia) "Nocturno," "Nocturno sueño," "Nocturno de la estatua," "Nocturno en que nada se oye"	Carlos Puig, Agustín Oropeza, Alberto Caroldi, Alfredo Bonilla, Marcelino Ponce, Eduardo Hernández Moncada, Irma González, Concha de los Santos, Carlos Chávez	None

Table 1. Continued

Date	Title of Lecture	Title of composition	Performers	Other works performed
29 October 1954	STRING ORCHESTRA, EARLY AND MODERN MUSIC	Symphony No. 5	Members of the Orquesta Sinfónica Nacional; Franco Ferrari, concertino	Bach, *Brandenburg* Concerto No. 4 Schoenberg, Suite for string orchestra, Op. 35
18 November 1955	DIVERSE FORMS OF "ATONALITY"	*Energía*	Rubén Islas, Agustín Oropeza, Sally van den Berg, Anastasio Flores, Guillermo Robles, Louis Salomon, Leo Kreuz, Felipe Léon, Ignacio Cahue, Ivo Valenti, José Luis Hernández	Varèse, *Octandre* Schoenberg, Wind Quintet, Op. 26
2 December 1955	SELECTIONS FROM THE OPERA *PÁNFILO Y LAURETTA* BY CARLOS CHÁVEZ	*Pánfilo y Lauretta* [*Los visitantes*] From Act 1: Aria: tenor (Pánfilo); Recitativo: soprano and tenor; Aria: soprano (Lauretta); Recitativo: soprano, contralto, and tenor; Aria: contralto (Elisa); Terzetto: soprano, contralto, and tenor; Recitativo: baritone (Dioneo); Duetto: soprano and tenor (Psiqué y Cupido) From Act 2: Duetto: baritone and bass; Madrigale: soprano, contralto, tenor, and baritone; Aria: bass (Lázaro); Duetto: soprano and tenor (Magdalena and Centurión)	Maritza Alemán, Concha de los Santos, Carlos Puig, Miguel Botello, Salvador García Larios, Carlos Chávez, Eduardo Hernández Moncada	None

Table 1. Continued

Date	Title of Lecture	Title of composition	Performers	Other works performed
20 August 1957	LATIN AMERICAN MUSIC	Symphony No. 5	Members of the Orquesta Sinfónica Nacional; Franco Ferrari, concertino	Bartók, Divertimento
1 August 1958	CHORAL MUSIC	Three Nocturnes "Sonnet to Sleep" (Keats), "To the Moon" (Shelley), "So We'll Go No More A-Roving" (Byron) "A Woman Is a Worthy Thing" (16th century), *A! Freedome* (John Barbour) "Arbolucu, te sequeste" (Spanish popular song) *Tierra mojada* (López Velarde)	Coro de Madrigalistas	de Falla, *Balada de Mallorca,* text adapted by Mosén Jacinto Verdaguer
6 August 1958	CHAMBER MUSIC	*Soli I* for oboe, clarinet, bassoon, and trumpet	Members of the Orquesta Sinfónica Nacional	Revueltas, *Ocho por radio* Villa-Lobos, *Choros* No. 7
22 November 1960	TWO QUARTETS BY CARLOS CHÁVEZ	String Quartet No. 1 String Quartet No. 3	Lener Quartet: Higinio Ruvalcaba, José Smilovitz, Heberto Frölich, Imre Hartman	None
8 June 1961	PIANO MUSIC BY CARLOS CHÁVEZ	Seven Pieces for Piano *Invención**	William Masselos	None

Table 1. Continued

Date	Title of Lecture	Title of composition	Performers	Other works performed
15 July 1963	REPETITION IN MUSICAL FORM	*Tierra mojada* *Soli II*	Cristina Ortega, Graciela Saavedra, Gilda Cruz, Hortensia Cervantes, Dora de la Peña, Osvelia Hernández, Eduardo Angulo, Francisco Amador, Rogelio Vargas, Angel Ramírez Rubén Islas, Sally van der Berg, Anastasio Flores, Louis Salomon, Vicente Zarzo	None
27 July 1965	THE SECOND POST-WAR	*Invention II**	Hermilo Novelo, Gilberto García, Sally van der Berg	Stockhausen, *Klavierstück XI*
19 August 1966	MUSIC FOR PERCUSSION	*Tambuco**	Carlos Luyando, Zeferino Nandayapa, Xavier Sánchez Cárdenas, Homero Valle, Félix Montero, Abel Jiménez, Fidel Pérez, Carlos Chávez	None
27 September 1967	THE KINETIC FACTOR IN ATONAL MUSIC	*Soli IV**	Louis Salomons, Vicente Zarzo, Felipe León, Clemente Sanabria	None
4 October 1967	CHOPIN: MELODY AND HARMONY	Three Etudes to Chopin (*Tres estudios a Chopin*) *Estudio IV: Homenaje a Chopin*	María Teresa Rodríguez	None
20 June 1968	MUSICAL DRAMA	Selections from Act 1 of *Los visitantes*	Victora Zúñiga, Dora de la Peña, Eduardo Angulo, Roberto Bañuelas, Carlos Chávez	None
24 June 1968	MUSICAL DRAMA	Selections from Act 2 of *Los visitantes*	Victora Zúñiga, Dora de la Peña, Eduardo Angulo, Roberto Bañuelas, Carlos Chávez	None

Table 1. Continued

Date	Title of Lecture	Title of composition	Performers	Other works performed
27 June 1968	MUSICAL DRAMA	Selections from Act 3 of *Los visitantes*	Victora Zúñiga, Dora de la Peña, Eduardo Angulo, Roberto Bañuelas, Carlos Chávez	None
5 August 1969	MUSICAL COMPOSITION	*Invención**	María Teresa Rodríguez	None
7 August 1969	MOTIVIC COMPOSITION	Double Quartet*	Gildardo Mojica, Gys de Graaf, Anastasio Flores, Louis Salomon, Hermilo Novelo, Daniel Burgos, Gilberto García, Sally van der Berg	None
13 October 1971	MY EARLY WORKS	*Four Nocturnes* "Vals elegía," "Vals íntimo I," "Vals íntimo II," "Vals íntimo III" Etude I, Etude II, Etude III	María Teresa Rodríguez	None
18 October 1971	MUSIC IN MEXICO IN THE LAST 25 YEARS	Sonatina for cello and piano*	Sally van der Berg, María Teresa Rodríguez	Beethoven, Trio for piano, clarinet, and cello, Op. 11
20 October 1971	CREATION, RENOVATION	*Cuarteto de Arcos III* *Invention II* *Variaciones* for violin and piano	Luz Vernova, Vladimir Wulfman, Gilberto García, Sally van der Berg, María Teresa Rodríguez	None
18 September 1973	THE LIED	"Extase" (Víctor Hugo), "Inutil epigrama" (Ronald de Carvalho), "Du bist wie eine Blume" (Heine), "Estrellas fijas" (J. A. Silva)	Irma González, María Teresa Rodríguez	Schubert, "Die böse Farbe," "Auf dem Wasser zu singen" Schumann, "Widmung" Debussy, "Récit et air de Lia"
20 September 1973	FORM AND STEREOTYPICAL FORMS	*Invención** Preludes II, IV, and VIII*	María Teresa Rodríguez	None

Table 1. Continued

Date	**Title of Lecture**	**Title of composition**	**Performers**	**Other works performed**
24 September 1973	MY FRIENDS THE POETS: NOVO AND LÓPEZ VELARDE	"Nocturna rosa (Villaurrutia),* "North Carolina Blues" (Villaurrutia),* "Hoy no lució la estrella de tus ojos" (Novo),* "Todo" (López Velarde),* "La casada infiel" (García Lorca)*	Rufino Montero, María Teresa Rodríguez	None
27 September 1973	THE ART OF THE PIANO	Sonata III* Six Etudes*	María Teresa Rodríguez	None
1 October 1973	MY FRIENDS THE POETS: PELLICER AND VILLAURRUTIA	*Seis exágonos* (Pellicer)* *Cuatro nocturnos* (Villaurrutia)*	Carlos Puig, instrumental ensemble Guillermina Higareda, Rufino Montero, María Teresa Rodríguez	None
4 October 1973	*LOS VISITANTES* (THE VISITORS)	*Los visitantes*:* Aria, Pánfilo: "Psyche, be welcome…"; Aria, Lauretta: "I am too young to fear…"; Duetto, Cupid and Psyche; Aria, Lauretta: "Then it was all true!"; Duetto, Centurion and Magdalen; Aria, Cupid: "Once more, my bride"; Diálogo, Pánfilo: "What do you want of me?" Lauretta: "Your love…"; Aria, Cupid: "Let her abuse me…"	María Luisa Salinas, John Aler, María Teresa Rodríguez	None
20 June 1974	COMPOSERS OF TODAY	Seven Pieces for Piano	Alan Marks	Davidovsky, *Synchronisms* No. 6 for piano and electronic sounds Boulez, Piano Sonata No. 1

Table 1. Continued

Date	Title of Lecture	Title of composition	Performers	Other works performed
24 June 1974	THE PIANO ETUDE	Two Early Etudes Three Etudes to Chopin *(Tres estudios a Chopin)* *Estudio IV: Homenaje a Chopin* Four New Etudes (*Cuatro nuevos estudios*)	María Teresa Rodríguez	None
1 July 1974	CREATION, INVENTION	*Nonantzin* Fragmento Two arias for soprano from *Los visitantes* Two duets from *Los visitantes*	Choir Cristina Higareda, María Teresa Rodríguez Cristina Higareda, Carlos Puig, María Teresa Rodríguez	None
11 November 1976	RETROSPECTIVE OF PIANO MUSIC, IN THREE SESSIONS	Sonata III Three Etudes to Chopin (*Tres estudios a Chopin*) *Estudio IV: Homenaje a Chopin* *Estudio a Rubinstein* *Five Caprichos*	Alan Marks	None
18 November 1976	RETROSPECTIVE OF PIANO MUSIC, IN THREE SESSIONS	Seven Pieces for Piano *Invención*	William Masselos	None
25 November 1976	RETROSPECTIVE OF PIANO MUSIC, IN THREE SESSIONS	Sonatina Ten Preludes Four New Etudes (*Cuatro nuevos estudios*)	María Teresa Rodríguez	None

* Repeated in second half of the program.

NOTES

1. The original decree was published on 13 May 1943 as *Artículo 2º*. See *El Colegio Nacional 60 Años 1943–2003*, ed. Rosa Campos de la Rosa (Mexico City: El Colegio Nacional, 2006), 13–14. All translations in this article are mine.

2. Chávez was responding to a need to guarantee state support for new music in Mexico, given the lack of Mexican and modern music in the programming of concerts organized by prominent private organizations in public spaces. See Leonora Saavedra, "Los escritos periodísticos de Carlos Chávez: Una fuente para la historia de la música en México," *Inter-American Music Review* 10/2 (1989): 89.

3. El Centro de Información of El Colegio Nacional was created in 2004 to function as an on-site archive. Currently it does not have complete documentation of all events prior to 2004. Most of the programs of Chávez's concerts are kept at the Centro, but only a handful of recordings of his lectures have been preserved.

4. Ignacio Sánchez Prado, *Naciones intelectuales: Las fundaciones de la modernidad literaria mexicana* (Lafayette, IN: Purdue University Press, 2009), 144.

5. Ibid., 144–45.

6. Antonio Caso, "Libertad por el Saber," in *El Colegio Nacional 60 Años*, 71.

7. Although not publicly disclosed, the approximate amount of the monthly stipend each member receives from January to November is Mex$100,000 (pesos), which is equivalent to US$6,883 (as of January 2015). In order to receive this substantial stipend for the month of December as well the member needs to have fulfilled at least 75 percent of the projected annual lectures.

8. Caso, "Libertad por el Saber," 62.

9. See *El Colegio Nacional 60 Años*, 7.

10. This imbalance in gender representation has yet to be fully addressed, although recently there have been several isolated initiatives to counteract it.

11. See Robert L. Parker, *Carlos Chávez: Mexico's Modern-Day Orpheus* (Boston: Twayne, 1983); Leonora Saavedra, "Carlos Chavez, I. Biografía," in *Diccionario de Música Española e Hispanoamericana,* vol. 3, ed. Emilio Casares Rodicio (Madrid: Sociedad General de Autores y Editores, 1999); Alejandro L. Madrid, *Sounds of the Modern Nation* (Philadelphia: Temple University Press, 2008).

12. In the context of his activities at El Colegio Nacional Chávez showed no interest in promoting popular or indigenous music, which had absorbed him for years. Chávez might have regarded art music as the most appropriate to fulfill El Colegio's aims. However, his position regarding popular and folk musics, a topic covered extensively in his writing, cannot be easily described. Leonora Saavedra points out that Chávez's differentiation between the popular and cultivated arts was based on the degree of technical development produced in societies where differences in social classes exist ("Los escritos periodísticos de Carlos Chávez," 85). For Chávez, once a society reached higher cultural, social, and economic levels, the popular arts would "inevitably evolve in the direction of so-called great art." See Carlos Chávez, "Gran arte y folklore," in *Carlos Chávez Obras II: Escritos periodísticos (1940–1949),* ed. Gloria Carmona (Mexico City: El Colegio Nacional, 2000), 288.

13. Some of the titles of Chávez's lectures from these years are "Introducción al estudio de la armonía musical" (1943), "Estudios sobre la forma musical" (1944), and "Estudios y ejercicios necesarios a la creación musical: Sonido, melodía, armonía y ritmo" (1945).

14. Beethoven was a recurrent subject in Chávez's writings of the period, and he programmed Beethoven's music extensively. His lecture of 11 November 1944 was titled "Beethoven." Most likely, its content and scope might have derived from his previous essay "Beethoven: Algunos apuntes," published in *El Universal,* 23 June 1944.

15. Chávez stated: "Although there are millions of persons who play and have played Beethoven's music, there was only one person, Beethoven, who was able to write such music. The more scarcity, the more value; the more value, the greater the need to preserve." See Carlos Chávez, "La notación musical," in *Carlos Chávez Obras II: Escritos periodísticos (1940–1949),* 106.

16. Carlos Chávez, "Música en México," in ibid., 282–83.

17. Carlos Chávez to Silvio Zavala, 16 April 1953, Fondo Carlos Chávez, Archivo General de la Nación.

18. Special thanks to Wojciech Milewski for his work on this graph. Chávez programmed eleven works by Igor Stravinsky at his *concierto-conferencias*—in 1953, 1957, 1960, 1962, and 1971—making Stravinsky the composer most performed at El Colegio after Chávez himself. Other twentieth-century composers programmed on more than one occasion were Arnold Schoenberg (1954 and 1955), Anton Webern (1954 and 1965), Erik Satie (1958 and 1965), Aaron Copland (1953 and 1961), Edgard Varèse (1955 and 1964), Rodolfo Halffter (1955 and 1969), Manuel de Falla (1958 and 1970), Karlheinz Stockhausen (1964 and 1965), and Pierre Boulez (1960 and 1974).

19. See Leonora Saavedra, "Música y vida musical en los escritos periodísticos de Carlos Chávez," in *Signos: El arte de investigación,* ed. Esther de la Herrán (Mexico City: INBA, 1988), 207.

20. Aurelio Tello, "La creación musical en México durante el siglo XX," in *La música en México: Panorama del siglo XX,* ed. Aurelio Tello (Mexico City: Fondo de Cultura Económica, 2010), 514.

21. Carlos Chávez, "El Dodecafonismo en México," in *Memorias del Colegio Nacional 1954* (Mexico City: El Colegio Nacional, 1954), 69–70.

22. Salomón Kahan, "Conciertos-conferencias de Carlos Chávez," *El Universal,* 15 June 1961.

23. Some Chávez works included in his *concierto-conferencias* are the String Quartets No. 1 and No. 3; Symphony No. 5; *Soli(s)* 1, 2, and 4; *Tambuco*; *Energía*; selections of his opera *Pánfilo y Lauretta* (later *Los visitantes*); and multiple vocal works, such as *Seis exágonos* and *Cuatro nocturnos*. For a complete list, see Table 1.

24. Ruy Pérez Tamayo, interview with author, Mexico City, 26 July 2012.

25. Although addressing Chávez's criticism is beyond the scope of the present study, I can suggest that he might have been responding to the growing popularity of graphic notation and aleatoricism during the 1960s, of which Manuel Enríquez was a main proponent. Chávez firmly believed in the composer's total control over the musical work.

26. Carlos Chávez, audio transcription of lecture titled "Composición de vanguardia en México," Centro de Información, cat. no. 1359, 14 August 1969. Chávez held a composition workshop at the Conservatorio Nacional de Música in the early 1960s.

27. The *Sonata para piano* is Mata's first and last work within total serialism. Mata later considered the piece to be "a meager contribution to post-Schoenbergian 'neo-academicism' . . . written when I was 19, when twelve-tone technique (by then already *passé*) really interested me as a discipline. I was beginning my studies with Carlos Chávez. The technique's meticulousness was my obsession during those years." See Juan Arturo Brennan's liner notes for *Apuntes para piano: Música mexicana para piano de los siglos XX y XXI,* Mauricio Náder, piano, Quindecim Records, QP200 (2009).

28. Chávez, "Composición de vanguardia en México."

29. Roderic Ai Camp, who spent more than three decades researching the processes behind the configuration of intellectual elites in Mexico, reported that nearly half of El Colegio's members active in the early 1980s were disciples of other members. See Camp, *Intellectuals and the State in Twentieth-Century Mexico* (Austin: University of Texas Press, 1985), 156.

30. Throughout Mata's life, he continued to be regarded by many as both a composer and conductor. Much research needs to be done to substantiate the relevance of Mata's

output in the history of Mexican music. See Gloria Carmona, *Eduardo Mata (1942–1995): Fuentes documentales* (Mexico City: CONACULTA, 2001).

31. The *Memorias* are available in some bookstores in Mexico City and are currently sold inexpensively at El Colegio's library, though their distribution is otherwise quite limited. Seen in this light, the direct audience for the *Memorias* is first and foremost the members of El Colegio.

32. The essays are "Vivaldi-Bach" (1952), "Arte americano" (1952), "Canto y melodía" (1954), "Dodecafonismo en México" (1954), "Pierre Boulez" (1960), and "Mis amigos poetas: Ramón López Velarde" (1973).

33. Besides the handful of essays Chávez wrote for the annual *Memorias*, he published some of his lectures with El Colegio. Unfortunately, the institution lacks a complete list or record of such individually published lectures. Some held at El Colegio's library are "El arte eleva," from 1968 (inauguration speech for the Arts Academy); "Debussy y la Guerra del 14" and "Falla en México," both from 1970 (lectures given at El Colegio); and a pair of short essays, "Oro . . . no vale" and "Lira de Orfeo," published together in 1972.

34. Carlos Chávez, "Vivaldi-Bach," in *Memoria de El Colegio Nacional 1952* (Mexico City: El Colegio Nacional, 1952), 183.

35. Ibid.

36. Carlos Chávez, "Arte americano," in ibid., 187–90.

37. Carlos Chávez, "Pierre Boulez," in *Memoria de El Colegio Nacional 1960* (Mexico City: El Colegio Nacional, 1960), 66.

38. Ibid.

39. Chávez believed the composer should never compromise his artistic integrity even when audiences disapproved—an example being his Violin Concerto, as David Brodbeck's essay in the present volume shows—though he was in turn committed to educate the public in what he deemed great music.

40. Jaime García Terrés, "Discurso de homenaje en memoria del Maestro Carlos Chávez," in *Memoria de El Colegio Nacional 1981* (Mexico City: El Colegio Nacional, 1981), 109.

41. Jaime García Terrés, "Respuesta al discurso de Eduardo Mata en el acto de su ingreso al Colegio Nacional, el jueves 9 de agosto de 1984," in *Memoria de El Colegio Nacional 1984* (Mexico City: El Colegio Nacional, 1984), 150.

42. Many individuals, both inside and outside El Colegio, regarded Mata not only as a composer and conductor but also as an intellectual. For instance, Sergio Vela states: "Eduardo was a man who had a great intellectual foundation. He was not the type of musician who concentrates all his energy in the music." See Verónica Flores, *Eduardo Mata a varias voces* (Mexico City: CONACULTA, 2005), 171–72.

43. See Eduardo Mata, "Discurso de ingreso al Colegio Nacional el jueves 9 de agosto de 1984," in *Memorias del Colegio Nacional 1984* (Mexico City: El Colegio Nacional, 1984), 143–44. The four *concierto-conferencias* mentioned represent only the events that took place at El Colegio's building. This account does not include concerts and lectures given elsewhere. Mata's series of *concierto-conferencias* at El Colegio are "El intérprete musical en la segunda mitad del siglo XX" (1987), "Tres conciertos en homenaje a Carlos Chávez" (1988), "Tres gigantes de la música americana" (1991, works by Aaron Copland, Silvestre Revueltas, and Julián Orbón), and "Concierto-conferencia: Homenaje a Carlos Chávez" (1994).

44. The program of this concert also included compositions for string quartet by Federico Ibarra, Julio Estrada, Arturo Márquez, and Manuel Enríquez, performed by Cuarteto Latinoamericano.

45. Eduardo Mata, "Concierto-conferencia en homenaje a Carlos Chávez," in *Memorias del Colegio Nacional 1994* (Mexico City: El Colegio Nacional, 1994), 60. The *concierto-conferencia* took place on 25 October 1994. The works Mata programmed for that night were *Energía* (1925), which Mata claimed anticipated Chávez's theory of no repetitition;

the *Suite para doble cuarteto* (1947), written for Martha Graham's ballet *Dark Meadow*; and *Xochipilli* (1940), written for the exhibition *Twenty Centuries of Mexican Art* at New York's Museum of Modern Art.

46. Mario Lavista, interview with author, Mexico City, 4 May 2012.

47. Lavista began teaching at La Casa del Lago as a substitute for Mata, who had recently left to conduct the Orquesta Sinfónica de Guadalajara (1966).

48. Lavista's adherence to this literary group in the late 1960s brought him attention in the public arena as a promising young composer. See Ana R. Alonso-Minutti, "Forging a Cosmopolitan Ideal: Mario Lavista's Early Music," *Latin American Music Review* 35/2 (Fall–Winter 2014): 169–96.

49. Lavista's active involvement with literary circles and his constant writing endeavors in multiple venues are reasons why, according to Ruy Pérez Tamayo, a current member of El Colegio, he is "much more a member of El Colegio than Mata himself, for Mata was primarily a conductor." Ruy Pérez Tamayo, interview with author, Mexico City, 26 July 2012.

50. Mario Lavista, "El lenguaje del músico: Discurso de ingreso," in *Memorias del Colegio Nacional 1998* (Mexico City: El Colegio Nacional, 1998), 13.

51. Among the numerous events Lavista has organized at El Colegio (up to 2012) were concerts devoted to single composers, such as George Crumb, Carlos Chávez and Silvestre Revueltas, Boguslaw Schaeffer, John Cage, Dmitri Shostakovich, Conlon Nancarrow, Arnold Schoenberg, Frédéric Chopin, György Kurtág, and Elliott Carter. Lavista also has chosen to center his concerts around solo performers or chamber groups, such as Sinfonietta Ventus, Stefano Scodanibbio, Alberto Cruzprieto, Federico Bañuelos, Quinteto de Alientos de la Ciudad de México, Cuarteto Latinoamericano, Aki Takahashi, Carlos Prieto, Edison Quintana, BBC Singers, Ensamble 3, Onix, Horacio Franco, Tambuco, and Duplum Dúo, among many others.

Portraits of Carlos Chávez: Testimonies of Collaboration

ANNA INDYCH-LÓPEZ

Throughout his long and influential career as a composer and cultural promoter, Carlos Chávez had a significant impact on the development of modern Mexican art and was one of the critical figures of the period known as the Mexican Renaissance. In addition to his strong personal relationships with visual artists such as Rufino Tamayo, he collaborated directly with Agustín Lazo, Miguel Covarrubias, and Diego Rivera on sets, costumes, and scenography for his various musical projects, making him a central figure of the Mexican cultural vanguards. In both his artistic collaborations and in his role as a cultural *animateur*, Chávez played an important role in advancing the post-Revolution project of national consolidation based in part on the recuperation of indigenous cultures. While some of the visual artists of the period looked to the compositional, stylistic, or iconographic elements of pre-Columbian art, Chávez broadened those efforts by salvaging and furthering knowledge about pre-Hispanic musical instruments and by inventing an imaginary Aztec music.[1] Like his counterparts in painting, he combined references from colonial, folk, indigenous, academic, and modern music to create a new form of modernism. This new cultural production—one could call it a form of mestizo modernism[2]—emerged as Mexico's unique take on the primitivism that was prevalent throughout Europe and the Americas.

Beginning in the 1920s Chávez, in partnership with various artists, helped to forge this significant cultural shift and became one of its unwavering supporters well into the twentieth century. As a cultural ambassador with strong and direct ties to the United States, especially New York, where he was based at various times, Chávez also played an important role in promoting a vision of Mexican culture abroad. It is no surprise, then, that he should be the subject of numerous portraits, varying from large-scale painted canvases to quick, quirky, yet revealing sketches by artists who sought to capture the personality and physical idiosyncrasies of this cultural authority and diplomatic powerhouse.

Chávez's best-known partnership with a visual artist remains his collaboration with Diego Rivera on the symphonic ballet *H.P. (Horsepower)*. The premiere took place in Philadelphia on 31 March 1932, shortly after Rivera's high-profile retrospective organized by New York's Museum of Modern Art had traveled to the Pennsylvania Museum of Art (now the Philadelphia Museum of Art).[3] Musicologist Christina Taylor Gibson has illuminated this celebrated alliance, which generated much pre-performance publicity, even as we lack much knowledge of the degree to which the two artists directly interacted.[4]

As was common in the period, critics and reporters focused not only on the production itself and the artists' accomplishments, but also sought out exotic physical attributes that they believed authenticated the supposedly "native" perspectives of the creators. According to Taylor Gibson, "The biographical articles about Chávez invariably embellished his connection to native Mexicans. For example, although most of Chávez's ancestors were criollos, or Spanish in descent, articles proclaimed him 'half-Indian and half-Spanish.' Physical descriptions matched the exaggerated characterizations of his mestizo heritage."[5] Indeed, a reporter from the *Public Ledger* focused on Chávez's "picturesque shock of smokey black hair as fluffy as a baby's" and declared that "his hair is a fine sublimation of the typical Indian locks."[6] That same shock of puffy hair is the emphasis of many of the early portraits of Chávez by his artist friends. Unlike the reviewers who mistakenly attributed an Indian heritage to the composer (and infantilized natives by characterizing their fine hair as similar to a baby's), artists such as Rivera turned Chávez's coiffure into a marker of his vanguard style, persona, and work.

Rivera's ink portrait of Chávez published in the May–June 1932 issue of *Modern Music* (Figure 1) accompanied an article by Paul Rosenfeld that celebrated Chávez's unique American modernity.[7] The bust-length portrait, which concentrates on the composer's face, conveys an aura of intellectual seriousness—enhanced by the round-rimmed glasses, formal attire, and stern expression manifested by his downturned lips and slight furrow of his brow—with a sense of playfulness. For example, Chávez's tie bows slightly upward in the middle, echoing the unruly curlicues of his tousled locks above; similarly, his dark and heavy eyebrows reiterate the curved rims of his glasses. With a simple economy of means, a formal play of contrasting gradations and widths of curvilinear and whimsical lines, Rivera is able to achieve Chávez's likeness and also to

Figure 1. Diego Rivera, *Carlos Chávez*, 1932, ink on paper. Published as *Carlos Chávez: A New Portrait* in *Modern Music* (May–June 1932).

capture a sense of introspection and whimsy, as if one of those curly locks might disappear off the page and turn into one of his musical notations. Providing the viewer with enough anecdotal details, Rivera balances realism with restraint, making for a sparse, clean, and modern portrayal that bears his signature style while still bringing out his sitter's personality and their mutual interest in modernism. The portrait is also in keeping with Rivera's many illustrations published in a host of journals, books, and periodicals of the time, suggesting that though the artist apparently made this portrait for the sitter (it is dedicated to Chávez), he might well

Figure 2. Miguel Covarrubias, *Carlos Chávez*, 1940. Sketched in May 1940 for *Modern Music* during rehearsals of the Mexican program in conjunction with the exhibition *Twenty Centuries of Mexican Art* at New York's Museum of Modern Art.

have known it would be reproduced in *Modern Music* on the occasion of the premiere of *H.P.*

In May of 1940, *Modern Music* featured another portrait of Chávez, a caricature by artist Miguel Covarrubias (Figure 2). He sketched the composer during rehearsals of concerts that accompanied the large-scale *Twenty Centuries of Mexican Art* exhibition at the Museum of Modern Art in New York, the modern art section of which was curated by Covarrubias.[8]

Figure 3. Miguel Covarrubias, *Lightning Conductors*, 1937, National Portrait Gallery, Washington D.C. Published in *Vogue*, 15 November 1937.

Besides their collaboration on this show, the two artists maintained a strong personal relationship in Mexico and New York and worked closely together on numerous projects throughout the years, most significantly when Covarrubias designed the costumes for the 1951 staging of Chávez's ballet *Los cuatros soles*. Covarrubias's portrait, like Rivera's, features Chávez's tuft of black hair as a central element. By reducing his portrait to a few spare lines, Covarrubias amplifies the whimsy in his caricature. The shock of hair becomes one of the primary identifying elements, along with such abstracted details as the exaggerated heavyset arch that stands in for an eyebrow, the plus sign that substitutes for an eye, and several horizontal and scraggly lines that mark the sideburn as if they were the bars of a musical score come to life. The quirkiness of Covarrubias's portrayal is emphasized by the abundant jacket lapels that frame Chávez's wide and squared jaw. Three years earlier, the artist had included a similar representation of Chávez in his illustration *Lightning Conductors*, published in *Vogue* magazine, in which the facial features are also reduced to an arch and a simple plus mark (Figure 3).[9] Apart from its imaginative nature, Covarrubias's substitution of a plus sign for the eye is open to several interpretations. It could, for example, be taken for a squint or a sparkle. Indeed, photographs and portraits of Chávez from the 1930s consistently show him wearing glasses, though these were abandoned in later years and do not appear in Covarrubias's caricatures; conceivably, the plus sign represents the composer squinting. In the *Vogue* image, Chávez is the only modernist among the composers and conductors depicted and is nearest to the electrical tower hovering in the background. Perhaps Covarrubias portrayed him as looking toward the future? Or the plus sign may suggest that his eye is a positive electric charge, given that Chávez had published a book on music and electricity the same year as the *Vogue* caricature.[10] In 1928, Mexican writer Anita Brenner compared Chávez's "utter, thorough, complete submission and absorption, while listening to . . . music" to the look she saw in the face of artist Jean Charlot once "when he was kneeling in front of the confessional."[11] Covarrubias's portrait captures this sense of complete aural absorption by modulating the depiction of the eye.

Six years later in 1946, one year before Chávez became the founding director of the Instituto Nacional de Bellas Artes (INBA), Rivera created another portrait of the composer, one that contrasts significantly with that of 1932. The whimsicality of the early portrayal is now replaced with a more serious visual approach (Figure 4). To begin with, Rivera uses pencil and a masterfully academic drawing technique to create a neoclassicizing likeness of Chávez. With Ingres-like precision Rivera creates an exquisitely realistic portrayal, almost tender in its attention to detail and smooth tonal gradations. As with earlier portraits, however, Chávez's expression is stern; in this profile view his eyes wander off into the distance, as if he is contemplating the future. More heavy-set, hair receding, and generally more volumetric, Chávez's massive figure fills the pictorial space. The curly locks and thick brows are still there, but what takes precedence is

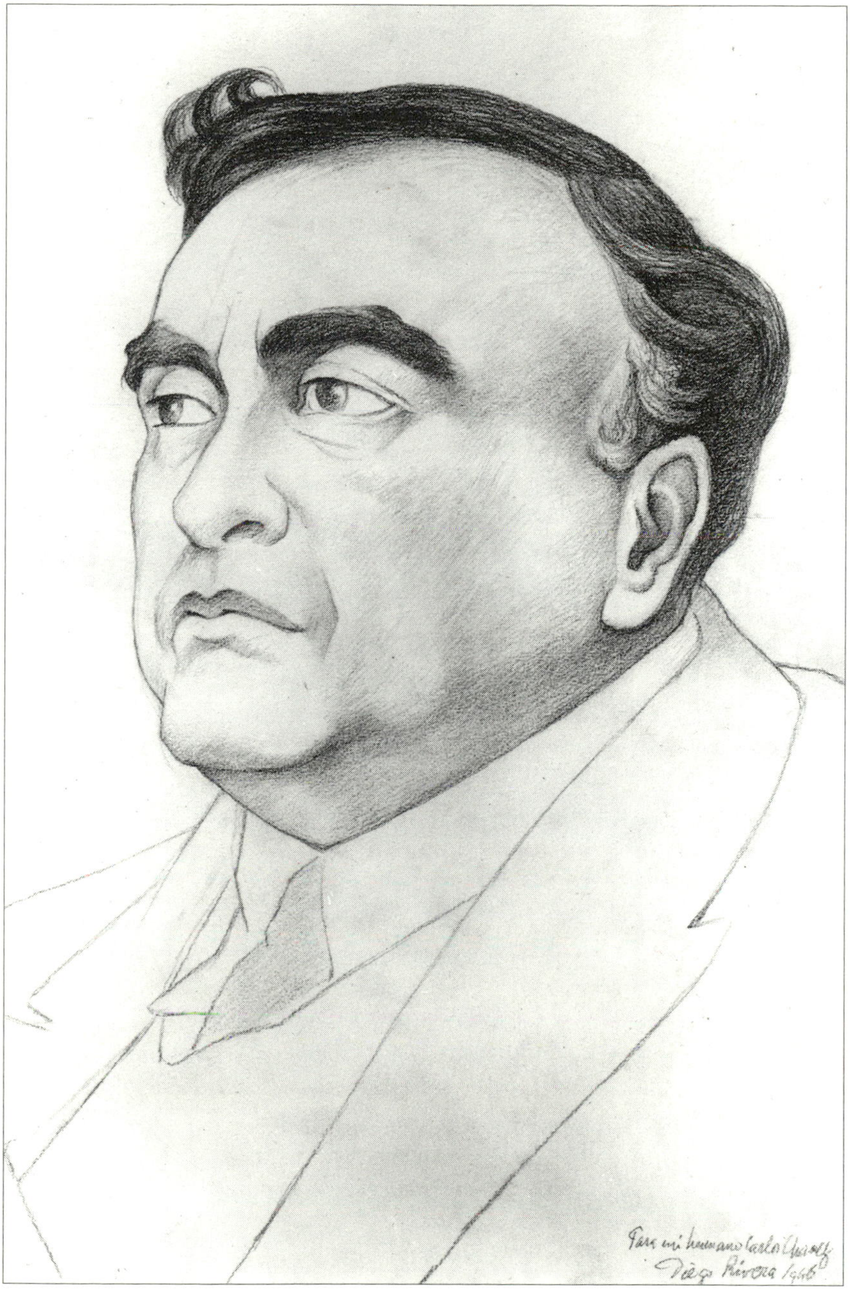

Figure 4. Diego Rivera, *Carlos Chávez*, 1946, graphite on paper.

Figure 5. David Alfaro Siqueiros, *Carlos Chávez*, 1948, pyroxylin on wood, Museo de Arte Moderno, Mexico City.

the general straightforward presence of the composer, making this more the portrait of a figure whose cultural authority is about to be recognized officially.

Although they never formally collaborated on a project together, the artist David Alfaro Siqueiros commemorated Chávez in painted form in 1948 (Figure 5). Siqueiros's portrait conveys a similar sense of officialdom as the Rivera drawing from 1946. The composer sits in a chair and turns

Figure 6. Rufino Tamayo, *Carlos Chávez*, ca. 1971.

away from the viewer in a comparable profile view. Chávez's expression here is stern; indeed, the facial expressions of the two portraits are almost identical. Yet Rivera's portrait privileges Chávez's massive head, whereas Siqueiros focuses instead on Chávez's body, specifically his exaggerated left arm, injecting the portrait with his signature modern Baroque style, animating the composition. Loose, expressive brushstrokes on the arm suggest dynamism and movement; the composer seems enveloped in a whirlwind of abstract shapes and strokes. It is a fitting representation of Chávez at midcentury, shortly after taking on the role of the director of INBA, a position in which he would make some controversial decisions that led to his falling out with several artists, including Diego Rivera.[12]

The last portrait considered here, by Rufino Tamayo (Figure 6) depicts Chávez in his later years, although it was executed by an artist who had known him from the early days of 1926, when they traveled to New York City and became roommates. Although both had great success in New York, Tamayo and Chávez never officially teamed up on a musical production. Nevertheless, Tamayo benefited greatly from Chávez's stewardship of the INBA, enjoying unprecedented attention from the Mexican state during this period.[13] Chávez and Tamayo also shared a love of music and guitars, and in the early days hosted a slew of parties and home concerts; some have suggested that Tamayo's many paintings of guitars refer to these soirées and could therefore be considered veiled portraits of Chávez. This late depiction of the composer was published as the cover of Rodolfo Halffter's *Carlos Chávez, catálogo completo de sus obras* in 1971 and is based on a photograph of the artist. Although the implacable eyebrows remain, the famous tuft of hair is gone, and all sense of whimsy has dissipated. In these later years Chávez, as a result of various disputes and controversies, had become alienated from the Mexican music world. Nonetheless, Tamayo's line drawing, which suggests an engraving, etches the composer's familiar visage forever in our memory.

NOTES

1. I would like to thank Ted Freed, a student in my Fall 2014 Modern Mexican art class, who informed me of Chávez's collection of pre-Columbian musical instruments.

2. Tace Hedrick, *Mestizo Modernism: Race, Nation, and Identity in Latin American Culture, 1900–1940* (New Brunswick, NJ: Rutgers University Press, 2003). Hedrick does not discuss Chávez.

3. *Diego Rivera*, exhibition at Museum of Modern Art, New York, 22 December 1931 to 27 January 1932. The exhibit traveled to Philadelphia's Pennsylvania Museum of Art, 2–10 February, and then to that museum's 69th Street Community Center Branch, 11–29 February 1932.

4. Taylor Gibson shows in detail the extent to which the collaboration between Chávez and Rivera remains unclear, given that there is no written evidence to provide clues about their mutual conception of the ballet or its design. Yet by comparing the composer's scores, especially last-minute changes made in 1931–32, with Rivera's set designs, Taylor Gibson reveals the ways in which the two Mexican artists, unlike the others involved with the collaboration who emphasized pan-American harmony, may have shared an ambivalence about North-South relations and offered an implicit critique of modern industrial life. Taylor Gibson argues that the lack of direct collaboration between Rivera and Chávez, as well as the divergent agendas of the team members, led to the mixed post-performance reception. Christina Taylor Gibson, "The Reception of Carlos Chávez's *Horsepower*: A Pan-American Communication Failure," *American Music* (Summer 2012): 157–93.

5. Ibid., 168.

6. "Stokowski Opens 'Parley' on Ballet," *Public Ledger* (Philadelphia), 5 March 1932, quoted in ibid.

7. Paul Rosenfeld, "American Composers: VIII: Carlos Chávez," *Modern Music* (May-June 1932): 153–59.

8. *Modern Music* (May–June 1940): 202.

9. The illustration *Lightning Conductors*, published in *Vogue*, 15 November 1937, and now in the collection of the National Portrait Gallery in Washington, includes caricatures of Toscanini, Stokowski, Rodzinski, Koussevitsky, Barbirolli, Ormandy, Damrosch, and Chávez (the smallest figure at the bottom). Reproduced in *Miguel Covarrubias: Cuatro Miradas/Four Visions* (Mexico: Editorial RM, 2005), 112.

10. Carlos Chávez, *Toward a New Music: Music and Electricity*, trans. Herbert Weinstock, with eight illustrations by Antonio Ruíz (New York: W. W. Norton, 1937; repr., New York: Da Capo Press, 1975). Acknowledgment is due to Leonora Saavedra who made me aware of this book and brainstormed with me about the possible meanings of Covarrubias's *Vogue* illustration.

11. Anita Brenner, diary entry, 22 February 1928, in Susannah Joel Glusker, *Avant-Garde Art and Artists in Mexico: Anita Brenner's Journals of the Roaring Twenties* (Austin: University of Texas Press, 2010), 2:585.

12. Rivera broke ties with Chávez in 1952 when the composer refused to send one of the artist's Communist-themed works to a large-scale exhibition of Mexican art in Paris.

13. When Chávez was head of the INBA (1947–52), the Palacio de Bellas Artes hosted a Tamayo retrospective (1948); Tamayo was given a one-man show at the Venice Biennale (1950); his *Homenaje a la raza india* was featured in the 1952 Paris exhibition of Mexican art (for which Chávez refused to send Rivera's work); and later in 1952 Tamayo received a commission to execute two murals for permanent installation at the Palacio de Bellas Artes.

The Modernist Invention of Mexico: Carlos Chávez, the Mexican Revolution, and the Cultural Politics of Music

LEON BOTSTEIN

Octavio Paz harbored few doubts about his ability to write "with dignified authority" about painting. But he could not do so for music, which he loved. As Paz observed, "A Panofsky of music, capable of deciphering the origin and significance of each sonorous figure is unimaginable."[1] The visual could be read and translated into language, but, for Paz, "the code of music—the scale—is abstract: units of sound empty of meaning."[2] In his *Essays on Mexican Art*, Paz reproduces a Maya marine shell, a "ritual trumpet," to highlight its intricate asymmetrical formal beauty, as if to underscore that in Mesoamerica "art was not an end in itself" or "beauty a separate value," but an art whose "speech is always expressive": "a logic of forms, lines, and volumes that is at the same time a cosmology."[3] Music suggested for Paz an art form immune to such claims, a realm of pure beauty, autonomous and individual.

Paz's confession reveals more than the eloquently phrased but familiar observation, deeply rooted in Western aesthetics, that music possesses an inherent insularity. Rather, Paz's sidestepping of a discussion of music, particularly Mexican music in the twentieth century, mirrors an ambivalence and unease with the history of high-art musical culture in modern Mexico, a culture that emerged from the Mexican Revolution parallel to the stunning and internationally recognized accomplishments of Mexican painters.

By writing on Mexican painting, Paz understood that he was inserting a particular Mexican achievement into a cosmopolitan account of art history.[4] Art history traditionally concerns itself with a self-referential or autopoietic history of objects and images that are valued on the basis of aesthetic judgment. But despite the prominence of artist biographies in the construction of art history, the materials of this history consistently offer themselves up to be "deciphered" in terms of their origins and historical significance. The illusion of realism and representation is central to the making of art. The social function of art invites elucidation; the subject is a sensory object that invites contemplation linked to meaning. All these factors come together powerfully when considering the group of great modern Mexican painters.

Writing about Mexican art meant writing about Mexican history. Each of the painters that most concerned Paz—the three great Mexican muralists José Clemente Orozco, Diego Rivera, and David Alfaro Siqueiros, and the Mexican painter with whom Paz felt the greatest affinity, Rufino Tamayo—could be understood from two distinct but intertwined perspectives. First was the formal character of their art, notably the way an individual painter appropriated and adapted modernist strategies prevalent in Europe and the United States. In each case, the use of form and color and transformation of imagery—the subjective vision of the artist—could be understood in terms of sources and a history independent of Mexico. All these artists had spent time in Europe and North America. The grand tradition of Western, and in particular European art had left its mark. In Orozco's work, Paz found traces of Goya, Ensor, Toulouse-Lautrec, and above all, the influence of German Expressionism. Rivera's painting revealed a debt to El Greco, Poussin, Picasso, and Cézanne. In Siqueiros, the evocation of movement and the dynamic sense of form were reminiscent of Italian Futurism.[5]

The second and most indispensable source of understanding was the relationship between each of these artists and Mexico, specifically the prolonged ten-year Mexican Revolution that began in 1910.[6] The Revolution provided the inspiration and the patronage that brought, for the first time, four Mexican painters into the pantheon of art history as innovators and masters whose work was itself worthy of imitation and emulation beyond the borders of Mexico.

The centrality of the Revolution inspired the invention of a Mexican nationalism through art—particularly high art. That national sentiment was expressed through the appropriation and adaptation of European modernism in a manner that could represent the Mexican past and its destiny. For Paz, the Mexican experience accounted for the aesthetics—the "deformations" of the human figure in Orozco and Siqueiros, for example—and gave the works a moral content beyond their merely formal character. They were expressions of individualistic subjectivity—the Mexican—vis-à-vis the world and an ideological criticism directed "against society and the state."[7]

Each of the muralists adapted modernist techniques from European contemporaries in the service of signaling, through art, a new beginning for Mexico. Such a beginning included a "resurrection" of the Mexican pre-Columbian past together with the sense of a victorious new age. The three muralists incorporated elements of popular culture, Indian civilization, a buried "spiritual" past, and the collective sensibilities of the Mexican people. Aesthetic modernism was more than an assertion of revolution. It helped define the Revolution and its conception of the nation. The distinctive character of Mexican painting—its synthesis of modernism and the material and spirit of Mexico, past and present—also shifted Mexico onto center stage in the debate about the modern age and its culture. Mexico became a theater appropriate for scrutinizing the interplay between aesthetics and politics, beauty and justice in contemporary life.

Might the same significance be accorded the vibrant post-revolutionary music that evolved in Mexico after 1920? Consider two aspects of the Mexican muralists' art. First, its public character: the murals' accessibility, scale, and integration into the urban landscape gave the works a capacity to redefine the politics of public space. The murals heightened the significance of architecture. Second, the muralists appropriated modernist strategies in order to construct a historical narrative for the Mexican nation. Rivera in particular emerged as the official iconic representative of a "new," coherent, unified Mexico—even if the political agenda of the Revolution was fractured, ranging from the elite's call for mere electoral reform to radical schemes for land reform or a return to the traditional land system of the *ejido*, a mix of communal and private property.

Holding the Revolution together was the desire for a shared vision of modern Mexico transcending class, status (Indian, *criollo*, and *mestizo*), and a deeply rooted regionalism; that vision was plausible and successful on account of the framing of a shared distinctive Mexican heritage and history, a common past, and therefore a potentially vibrant shared nationality. As the Revolution became institutionalized into a state apparatus with one dominant party, Mexican painting became a defining symbol internationally of the legitimacy of this post-revolutionary nationalism. Could that also be said of modern Mexican music?[8]

Before contemplating this question, it may be helpful to pay attention to Paz's reading of Rufino Tamayo. Although close in age to Siqueiros, Tamayo distanced himself from the overtly political posture of Orozco, Rivera, and Siqueiros. Yet more than the other three painters, Tamayo drew on the formal qualities of pre-Columbian and Mexican popular art in his work and transformed them through "modern aesthetics," as Paz put it. In so doing he distanced himself from a recognizable modern "Mexican" school. However, the Mexican reality was consistently present. Tamayo's commitment, for Paz, transcended the political in the name of national

Figure 1. Rufino Tamayo, *Cosmic Terror*, 1954, oil on canvas. Museo Nacional de Arte, Mexico City.

identity. He cultivated an asceticism of vision, a "primordial gaze" through which he expressed a critique of reality (Figures 1 and 2). Through modern painterly means, the objects undergo an instinctual poetic transformation that reveals an essential reality beyond any stylized, identifiable Mexican school. Tamayo embodies for Paz the enigmatic but most noble aesthetic consequence of the new beginning sparked by the Mexican Revolution: a synthesis between the internationalist claims of artistic individuality—and therefore the deeply personal—and an allegiance to Mexican place

Figure 2. Rufino Tamayo, *Girl Attacked by a Strange Bird*, 1947, oil on canvas. Museum of Modern Art, New York.

and history, all without concession to an ideology, whether the anarchism of Orozco or the Marxism of Siqueiros and Rivera.[9]

Tamayo gave the most eloquent evidence of Mexico's revolutionary achievement. In the space of less than half a century, Mexico succeeded in creating an artist worthy of a place in a cosmopolitan account of culture regardless of his nationality. The "Mexican" needed no longer to be defined reductively in terms of folklore and history. It is ironic that although Paz privileged Tamayo above the Mexican muralists, he remained silent on the matter of Mexican music, even though the closest analogue to Tamayo in twentieth-century Mexican musical history was Carlos Chávez.[10] If the significance of the Revolution for Mexican concert and classical music has been largely obscured by the fame and success of the three great muralists who came to represent modern Mexico in the 1920s, when the state became the patron of Mexican culture, a partial exception must be made in the case of Chávez. He alone achieved in his own time a reputation and prominence at home and abroad, particularly in North America, comparable to that of Rivera and colleagues. Chávez collaborated with Rivera but personally, and ultimately ideologically, he was closest to Tamayo. They were even roommates in New York.[11]

More to the point, Tamayo and Chávez shared an approach to the integration of the national agenda with the formal challenges of aesthetic modernism. When asked which composer was dearest to him and most influential on his art, Tamayo answered: J. S. Bach.[12] Just as Chávez, when called upon to reform music education and performance standards in Mexico during the presidencies of Miguel Alemán in the 1940s and Luis Echeverría in the early 1970s, insisted that the Mexican composers and performers needed to steep themselves in the European classical models and modern masters, and not content themselves with the other indispensable task—the study of Mexican folklore, popular culture, and history.[13] Both Tamayo and Chávez shared the conviction that the Mexican (both the pre-Conquest heritage and the Hispanic legacy) must be transformed through a self-conscious modernism if it was not to degenerate into decoration and a reductive symbol of exoticism.

Paz's suggestion that locating a link between formal, aesthetic content and revolutionary politics would not be possible for music reflects more than his personal conception of music. It mirrors a public perception that has ceded a virtual monopoly to the Mexican painters in defining a modern twentieth-century Mexican sensibility. Although Chávez's music reflects modernist Mexican aesthetics and the complex underlying politics, notably between 1920 and 1940 (if not thereafter), his music, once widely performed, has largely disappeared from the international music scene. Silvestre Revueltas, the other Mexican composer of the same era to make a mark beyond Mexico—and a protégé of Chávez—also has at best a marginal place in the repertory and history of music (in part owing to his short life), sustained largely by a sense of exoticism.[14]

Nonetheless, Paz's refuge behind a quite standard epistemological notion of music as abstract and seemingly without meaning masks the rich history of the classical music tradition in Mexico before and after the Revolution. Music, as a social and cultural practice, experienced extensive patronage under the dictator, modernizer, and art patron

Porfirio Díaz. Emerging from the era of Benito Juárez, Díaz ruled for thirty-four years, legitimized by seven orchestrated elections. He was lionized in Europe and North America. His ambitions are perhaps best symbolized by the Palacio de Bellas Artes in Mexico City. Much like the Paris Opéra, it was planned as a tribute to autocracy, only to be finished after the Revolution—with murals by Rivera, Siqueiros, and Orozco inserted into an architecture initially designed to celebrate the Europeanization of Mexican culture under the Porfirian regime.[15]

Indeed, Porfirian patronage resulted in the domination of French, Italian, and German models in music. Salon and concert music had established themselves among the elite. The Porfirian legacy in music—best represented by the nation's leading composer Manuel M. Ponce—can be compared with its parallel in painting, for example through the work of Hermenegildo Bustos (1832–1907), José María Velasco (1840–1912), and even the more prescient José Guadalupe Posada (1852–1912), whose influence on Mexican modernism can be compared to that of Ponce in music.[16] The canvases of Velasco and Bustos are of the same refinement and quality as those of their counterparts in Europe—the so-called academic genre of landscape and portrait painters. In Posada the riveting power of his caricature is matched with an astonishing sense of movement and form. Much as Ponce did in classical music, Posada's originality left its permanent mark on Mexican modernist art.[17]

Music, like painting, was given a powerful impetus by the Mexican Revolution, particularly in the popular forms that celebrated and chronicled the era and the victory over autocracy. In 1911, during the Revolution's first phase under Francisco I. Madero (when Chávez was twelve years old), Ponce argued for the integration of the folkloric into the realm of concert and art music. His ambition mirrored European models: the appropriation of folk materials (in Mexico dance and song forms dating from after the Conquest) into Classical and Romantic art forms. Ponce sought to create a new "national" style along a European model.

By 1921, when Chávez came into public view, Ponce's approach probably seemed to him outdated and tame.[18] Something more radical appeared necessary. Indeed, the very essence of the Revolution was the creation of a decisive break with the past—a self-conscious severing of the illusion of historical continuity with the Porfirian era.

Chávez took a decisive step beyond Ponce and seized on the opportunities provided by the Revolution. Writing in 1916, the seventeen-year-old Chávez understood that the folkloric riches of Mexico could easily permit Mexican music to "achieve a place on par with the Russians."[19] He believed that what Mexico had to learn was akin to what Bartók had done with his research into rural folk music. The task was to use "strange" but popular sources in terms of form, pitch, sonority, and rhythm to fashion an "original" Mexican, modern school of composition.

Not surprisingly, Chávez harbored a lifelong admiration not for Rimsky-Korsakov but for Stravinsky.[20] Recognition of the debt owed by Stravinsky's brand of modernism to archaic folkloric materials—audible in *Le sacre du printemps* and later in *Les noces*—informed Chávez's early identification of the Russian example as relevant to the Mexican. "I am talking of modernism," the young Chávez wrote, "and well, modernism arises in response to a need of evolution . . . from a need for something new."[21]

Music is, to a large extent a public art form; for Chávez in particular the public function lent music its importance as an instrument capable of realizing the national revolutionary goal and gave it an affinity to the work of the Mexican muralists. For Chávez, the ambitions of the Revolution included using music education and the distribution of folk and popular music as part of the project of breaking the boundaries of regionalism and of fostering "mutual knowledge" among Mexicans (replacing ignorance about the diversity in the nation), not only in the countryside but also in the cities. Similarly, the public representations of a shared Mexican history became the central justification of the genre of the mural in public buildings.[22]

At the start of Lázaro Cárdenas's presidency in 1934, Chávez drew a distinction between the support of education and culture under the Porfirian regime and the goals of the Revolution. Before, high art and culture had been used as a means of exploitation of the poor and the proletariat—a way to exert domination. Now the task was to generate art that would be a "weapon of social justice." The project of turning Mexicans into weak copies of Europeans had failed; therefore it was incumbent on the Revolution to "increase the productive and creative power" of the ordinary Mexican who is surrounded by the vitality of "peasant art." As Chávez observed in 1930, "Revolutionary political organization—established and maintained with courage and action—brings closer all the factors of Mexican culture and synthesizes a tradition that will give us, no doubt, a sense of nationality. Then we will have a national culture and art." Chávez concluded, "The Mexican painters of today found the Mexican tradition of painting that the academicians prior to the Revolution denied without knowing it."[23]

Chávez was intent on founding a tradition in Mexican music parallel to that of the visual artists. His career, like that of Rivera, was closely bound up with the Mexican government, but more so. Chávez turned out to be a master politician. He fought competing interests, held vital positions, shrewdly outmaneuvered competitors, and wrote extensively on the future of Mexican music, articulating an official national and populist ideology. This included rhetorical attacks on the primacy of the European, and on the lingering conceits of aesthetic superiority in the West. He called for the intensive study of Mexico's own musical heritage. He accused his predecessors of neglecting the national agenda and, above all, of failing to link the making of art to a social and political agenda. With amazing energy and persistence Chávez came to represent music in modern Mexico from the 1920s to the early 1970s.[24]

Yet, throughout his public career, Chávez retained a curious ambivalence to the nearly authoritarian domination of cultural patronage assumed by the Mexican state. As Claudio Lomnitz has persuasively argued, the patronage of the Mexican state was corrosive and resulted too often—as some have suggested was the case with Rivera—in the superimposition of a constructed "national" Mexican culture over a highly differentiated and complex regional reality. The state sought to control the international perception of modern Mexico by privileging particular artists and writers—Chávez among them. This strategy sought to counteract, within Mexico itself, an "inferiority complex."[25]

However strong Chávez's identity as an "official" artist of the Mexican state and the prophet of Mexican nationalist modernism may have been, in his writing, his music, and above all, his public activity—from a desk or the podium—Chávez was anything but consistent. He preserved his independence. His music reveals a wide range of experimentation, and the rhetoric of rejection toward the Western tradition and the party line of glorification of the national were on numerous occasions directly in conflict with what he actually did and wrote, in notes and words.

Keenly aware of the inconsistencies, contradictions, and ambivalence in his relationship to Mexican revolutionary nationalism—including the engagement of its artists with Marxism—Chávez felt compelled in his 1958–59 Norton Lectures at Harvard (published as *Musical Thoughts* in 1961) to dispel any essentialist image of himself as standard-bearer of a modern Mexican music. In a manner not dissimilar from Tamayo, Chávez by 1958 was already well along in the process of gradually shifting the emphasis in his work from the overtly political and nationalist to the crafting of a personal modernist aesthetic. Art, Chávez argued, must in the end be "an individual expression" in which anything "collective" or national represents a source, often a mirage, but something that is essentially just a defining background. The history of music was not national, properly understood; it was merely the sum of the work of distinct and great individuals, nothing more. Three hundred years of "German music," Chávez concluded, "can be reduced to a few individual names: Bach and Handel, Haydn and Mozart, Beethoven, Wagner and Brahms, and a couple more, if you like."[26]

Chávez's effort to distance himself from his exotic status as representative of the Mexican Revolution and the culture of modern Mexico, and to take refuge in the idea that the aesthetic represents the triumph of an autonomous individualism that can transcend constructs of national identity, was not an act of cowardice or self-serving revisionism. Rather, this stance, given his status as a major composer and a Mexican, elevated his Mexican identity to be equivalent to that of any European. As he once wrote, if Mexico could actually develop its own national style, it could invert a legacy of prejudice and end up marginalizing Western classical musical practice as exotic. Chávez cultivated and exploited the support he received from Edgard Varèse and Aaron Copland in the 1920s; it vindicated his international status as a modernist composer. In 1958 he sought to underscore once more the judgment Henry Cowell made in 1928 that "Carlos Chávez is a composer of music. He is also a Mexican; but although his music may have been somewhat influenced by his nationality, his claim to recognition is not based on his country, but on the actual worth of his music itself."[27]

The irony in Chávez's ideological ambivalences was that he himself exercised tight control over Mexico's burgeoning musical life, first in the late 1920s and then in the 1930s and '40s. But he also rebelled, leaving Mexico for North America and Europe in search of his own voice as a modernist composer. From the start of his public career, Chávez was caught between two revolutionary objectives—the creation of a distinct Mexican modern musical culture and the education of the masses. The latter objective, in music perhaps more than in the visual arts, demanded a program of education that was neither exclusively populist nor sharply rejectionist of European classical concert music.

Discarding entirely the legacy cultivated under Porfirio Díaz—what Chávez termed music of a "French, German, Franco-German flavor"—was too radical a step. That tradition was "natural" for Mexicans, given their historical origins in the twin roots of pre-Columbian civilization and Spain, symbolized by Moctezuma and Cortés; despite its "bourgeois" surface, the Porfirian period also mirrored Molina Enríquez's metaphor of Mexico's sustained historical confrontation between the "Indian anvil" and the "Spanish hammer."[28] For Chávez, the "Mexicanness" that would emerge from the Revolution as an emblem of the national, modern culture, as Lomnitz has characterized it, would have to be a "qualified (but not absolute) critique of Westernization and imperialism."[29]

But in this respect music represented a daunting arena for the creation of a Mexican modernism that could attain world-historical significance. The musical traditions brought by Spain were insufficient and demanded, in the wake of the Revolution, expansion from other European centers. The progress made in importing cosmopolitan musical traditions under Porfirio Díaz could not be just set aside; rather it needed to be enlarged and used differently. For the young Chávez, the key difference between the revolutionary goals in art and culture that took hold in the 1920s and the Porfirian era lay in three vital objectives: the embrace and cultivation of popular idioms; the education of the populace at large; and the support of all things modern and new. Consequently, as conductor, government minister, teacher, and director of the conservatory, Chávez worked to integrate the grand Classical tradition, particularly in its modernist forms. The purpose was not imitation or emulation. That, as the era of Porfirio Díaz demonstrated, had failed in Chávez's view to produce one single great Mexican composer or painter.

But mastery of the grand tradition was an essential tool for realizing the potential of Mexico. Bach and Buxtehude were models of musical thought. Chopin may have been for Chávez a symbol of Romantic resignation and "softness," but he merited study nonetheless. Beethoven was perhaps the most inspiring composer for Chávez, a "rebel" against the elite and convention.[30] Chávez brought music ranging from late Romanticism to Debussy, Honegger, Berg, and Cage into Mexican musical life. He courted serious criticism with his advocacy of John Alden Carpenter's *Skyscrapers*. Advocating the European symphonic tradition was a difficult task. Chávez observed wryly in 1925 that Mexicans did not realize sufficiently what "they are losing for not knowing or not caring about Bach, Stravinsky, Varèse, a symphonic orchestra, or a ballet. The public needs to be educated."[31]

Furthermore, as Leonora Saavedra has argued, Chávez was faced with a dilemma.[32] Though the cultural agenda of the Revolution involved recasting the pre-Conquest civilization of Mexico as central to a modern Mexican identity, there existed no musical analogues to the art and architecture of the pre-Columbian heritage. Artifacts, historical instruments, and depictions of music making existed but no monuments or fragments of pre-Columbian Mexican music. Chávez's compositions that featured the instruments and sounds of pre-Conquest Mexico were inventions, an "imagined" ancient Aztec music, as Chávez himself admitted in the subtitle to his 1940 *Xochipilli*. Chávez's 1936 *Sinfonía india*, like its predecessor, the 1925 ballet *Los cuatro soles*, were extrapolations informed by then widely accepted anthropological assumptions regarding pitch and rhythm. When Chávez claimed that the materials of these indigenously inspired works evoked "the first" music he liked and that spoke to him, he was using his typical politically astute rhetoric, but it was simply untrue.

In writing music that was pointedly Mexican Chávez was forced to utilize, as Ponce had, the rich post-Conquest folkloric traditions in song and dance, the Hispanic Mexican post-Conquest adaptations of Spanish and Cuban influences. But Chávez did so in a non-sentimental, angular manner. As Cowell observed, "Chávez abjures sentimentality and voluptuousness in his music, which is particularly clean-cut, crystalline, straightforward, and with an impelling rhythm."[33] At the core of Chávez's effort to create a national Mexican musical culture was an allegiance to the potential of the modern, the conviction that the various strands of local history could become the basis for a distinctive autonomous new music, both revolutionary and Mexican.

Chávez understood that in its most conventional form, the history of music in the West was, since the sixteenth century, far more dominated by the life and work of master practitioners than art history. The "great" composers and their masterworks defined an international aesthetic practice that transcended political boundaries. The eighteenth-century Mass in D by José Manuel Aldana (discovered in 1940 and revived during that year in the legendary Museum of Modern Art concerts titled "Mexican Music") is evidence of the extensive reach into Mexico of a normative compositional standard at the end of that century.[34]

The challenge facing Chávez and his Mexican contemporaries right after the Revolution was the recognition that with the advent of Romanticism and the attendant rise of modern nationalism the privileging of music as a medium of interiority and subjectivity, the conceit of a shared international normative aesthetic consensus had crumbled. In its place emerged a cult of the artist-composer as hero and, after 1848, a concomitant exclusionary European cultural chauvinism, not accidentally linked to the spread of imperialism. Wagner embodied both trends. From the perspective of the history of music, the map of Europe became segregated over the course of the nineteenth century into a center and a periphery. The Germans, Italians, and the French each assumed the role of the center—as inventors and guardians of the standards of musical form and beauty.

Eastern Europe, from Budapest and Prague to Moscow, found itself at the margins, as did Spain, Scandinavia, and even England (until Elgar) and certainly the United States (until after World War I). This "periphery" reacted with a search for a distinctive local source for art music, even to the extent of constructing criteria of authenticity that foregrounded pre-modern rural traditions threatened by industrialization.

Local musical traditions—rural folk dance and song—became the basis of particularism, innovation, and resistance. Forms of instrumental concert music became imbued with new, fresh, "exotic" materials. Stravinsky's *Sacre* displayed distinctive structures of musical argument—formal procedures, harmonic practices, and novel expectations regarding thematic development drawn from Russian sources—that defied the distinction between center and periphery; folk practices and materials became Stravinsky's means to challenge "German" conceits. His path ran parallel to that charted by Bartók, Janáček, and Szymanowski. The result was a vibrant musical modernism that rejected the superiority of German, French, and Italian late Romanticism.

The early twentieth century witnessed a reaction against a primarily German hegemony of musical and aesthetic standards in the north, south, and east of Europe. Ironically, modernism itself, particularly as defined and realized by Schoenberg—for all its formal radicalism—was seen as furthering and preserving the legitimacy of German superiority in all things musical.

But the triumphant late-Romantic nationalism and early modernism that flourished between 1870 and 1933 was never one of an outright rejection of a shared classical heritage. As the neoclassicism of post–World War I Europe revealed, the periphery sought entrance into the center by appropriating, expanding, and redefining it. From the generation of Dvořák and Tchaikovsky to Sibelius, Enescu, Kodály, and Martinů, the task was to enlarge the scope and range of a European cultural practice that shared a common heritage in the Baroque, the Classical, and early Romanticism.

The chauvinism and invidious distinctions between center and periphery that fueled musical nationalism and modernism during the late nineteenth and early twentieth century still persist, even as analytical categories in historical scholarship. If Russia and Spain continue to be discussed as some sort of "periphery" in the way we represent the dynamics of music history in Europe, how can the historical narrative of European musical culture be useful for understanding and evaluating the history of musical culture in the part of the non-European world that fell under colonial domination in the sixteenth century?

The answer may not be found by relying on appeals to the colonial experience and on generalizations about a post-colonial sensibility. As Paz argued in his pioneering *Labyrinth of Solitude* of 1950, the history of Mexico reveals a unique and multilayered autonomy, derived in part from the complex diversity of pre-Columbian culture, the series of conquests—first by the Aztecs, then the Spanish—and the intrusive and domineering presence of North America.[35] The peculiarities of the Spanish influence, notably in religion, and the bizarre twists in the colonial experience of the nineteenth century suggest that an effort to understand Mexico through the lens of Europe—particularly in terms of a center and a periphery—or through rubrics of the post-colonial may be gratuitous and condescending.

In the 1920s Chávez was a young, internationally minded composer confronting the collapse of international musical norms. The years between the late 1920s and the late 1940s were those of his deepest engagement with the creation of a modern Mexican musical culture. How was he to secure Mexico's uniqueness as its own center and periphery? With Ponce's 1911 foray into a musical nationalism Mexico seemed to follow a path taken by the Russians and the Spanish at the turn of the century. But Chávez was eager to forge a connection between revolutionary nationalism and a radical modernism that was clearly set apart from Romanticism and its notions of expressiveness, musical narration, harmonic consonance, and formal structure based on repetition.[36] Many of Chávez's ideological commitments of the 1920s and '30s are mirror images of comparable modernist credos by Busoni and Schoenberg.

After World War II, it was already evident that Chávez's efforts to found a school of Mexican modernism may not have been successful, even if he had spearheaded the development of a vibrant Mexican musical culture.[37] Chávez's unease in balancing his role in a distinct Mexican musical modernism and his claim to a place in the international artistic scene was further complicated by post–World War II politics. By 1958, the year of the Norton Lectures and during the last phase of Chávez's career, the allure of all things "Mexican" that had so captivated North Americans between 1920 and the outbreak of World War II had worn off. In the context of the Cold War the aesthetic and political demarcations of musical modernism had changed.[38]

The late style in Chávez's large-scale public music was often conservative, as the Sixth Symphony reveals. Even though it was modeled, partly for his students, on Brahms's Fourth, it represents an important commitment to an accessible modernism. Throughout his career, he always displayed a remarkable eclecticism, and therefore a striking variety of styles. There had been an early period of experimentation, which he continued in his later years, writing pieces that share striking similarities with the music of the avant-garde represented by Boulez and Stockhausen. And even in the late period Chávez wrote unabashedly nationalist works. But there was every reason to fear, in 1958, that even as the exotic Mexican aspect was in decline, only the unmistakably Mexican works within his massive output (works like *Sinfonía india*) would survive, not for their virtues as music, but because of their representative status of the Mexican. The Norton Lectures gave Chávez the chance to argue a place for himself as a cosmopolitan composer in the grand tradition, much as Stravinsky and Copland had done with their Norton Lectures, rendering his identity as a Mexican a secondary factor.[39]

Chávez's fear of impending obscurity was prescient. Except for a few works, his music does not hold a secure place in the current repertory. Unlike the muralists and Tamayo, Chávez the composer is largely forgotten. Copland's *El Salón México* has more of a presence in the repertory than any work by Chávez (or any other Mexican composer from the twentieth century). Chávez is remembered most for the institutional and political role he played in developing a vital classical musical life in twentieth-century Mexico. At varying times in his career, he conducted the leading orchestras, led the conservatory, taught, was chief of the arts in the Ministry of Education, a member of the Colegio Nacional, directed the National Institute of Fine Arts, founded the publishing venture Ediciones Mexicanas de Música, and advised several Mexican presidents.[40] In his fine book on musical modernism in Mexico, Alejandro Madrid approvingly quotes José Gorostiza, Chávez's colleague, who admitted to suppressing any interest in Chávez as a composer. Gorostiza confessed, "I believe that Carlos Chávez is above all an agitator. An agitator whose instrument is music as it could have been politics."[41]

José Vasconcelos and the Making of *Mestizaje*

No part of the world can be more challenging to a European perspective, despite its close links to European history with respect to the history of music, than Mexico. The layers of complexity begin with the highly differentiated political and cultural context of the region before the Spanish Conquest. The Spanish rule, the creation of a caste structure, the imposition of Catholicism—the mix of barbaric cruelty and theologically motivated grace—brought Mexico into the nineteenth century with a history as distinct from Europe as from its northern neighbors. The nineteenth-century history of Mexico is framed by the largely violent and oppressive domination of the United States, European intervention in the form of Napoleon III's imposition of a Habsburg prince, and political independence and selective modernization without economic or political reform. One element of this modernization was the cultivation of a European-style cosmopolitan culture, especially in the nation's capital. Justo Sierra (1848–1912), who served as Secretary of Public Instruction under Porfirio Díaz, credited the dictator with creating a "middle class." A vibrant concert and operatic culture flourished—particularly in Mexico City—as did educational institutions and a literary life, all closely connected to Spain, Italy, and France.

But what set Mexico apart was its descent from "two countries and two races," as Sierra put it: the land and culture that thrived before Cortés, and Spanish rule. Mexico owed its capacity to create a nation, and inspire patriotism to a unitary Mexico, both to the native and the European. Writing in 1902, before the Mexican Revolution, Sierra predicted that Mexico and its people needed to "attract immigrants from Europe so as to obtain a cross with the indigenous race, for only European blood can keep the level of civilization that has produced our nationality from sinking."[42] He called on Mexico to sustain the mixture of the European and the "indigenous." Mexico needed to "bring about a complete change in the indigenous mentality through education." Sierra described the task:

> To convert the native into a social asset (and it is the fault of our apathy that he is not one), to make him the principal colonist on intensively cultivated soil, to blend his spirit and ours in a unification of language, of aspirations, of loves and hates, of moral and mental criteria, to place before him the ideal of a strong and happy country belonging to all—to create, in sum, a national soul—is the goal assigned to the future, the program of our national education. Whosoever helps to attain this goal is a patriot.[43]

The most lasting cultural residue from the inwardly directed Mexican Revolution of 1910 has been precisely what Sierra articulated: the creation of a national soul, a comprehensive, unique cultural identity. The triumphant idea of the Mexican Revolution was that Mexico's distinctive history—and by extension that of Iberian America—made possible not only a politics but also a cultural renaissance independent of Europe. The notion emerged of a national identity whose creativity was sustained by the mix of Mexico's two parents: the indigenous and the Spanish. The consequence was the mestizo and the culture of *mestizaje*—cross-fertilization and hybridization, a process that invited a unique pluralism of influence.[44] Among its other virtues, *mestizaje* challenged the distinctions between high and popular art and celebrated the notion of a progressive integration of competing historical influences.

This account of Mexico's history and destiny separates it from any European notion of the "peripheral." In Europe, from the fin de siècle to the mid-1940s, nationalist and essentialist myths of race competed with one another. Purity was prized, not mixture. The "authentic" national was pitted against the corrupt hybrid cosmopolitan (as found in fin-de-siècle Budapest and placed in invidious contrast to the genuine folk traditions by the ethnographic work of Bartók and Kodály). The late nineteenth-century European obsession with racial and national purity flourished at the center, in Germany and France, and radiated outward, finding fertile ground in regions of economic backwardness and weak industrialization. Even such proponents of a unique Eurasian synthesis as Nicholas Roerich, the painter and philosopher who had been Stravinsky's collaborator, did not emphasize creative hybridization or the significance of constituent elements, as the ideology that flourished in revolutionary Mexico did.

The most influential exponent of the ideal of *mestizaje* as the defining element of modern Mexico was José Vasconcelos (1882–1959).[45] He was trained as a lawyer, and during President Madero's tenure turned to educational reform. A prolific and eloquent writer on philosophy and politics, Vasconcelos ended up briefly following in Sierra's footsteps as Minister of Education in 1921, under Álvaro Obregón, until 1924. In Vasconcelos's view, the Mexican mestizo was the representative of the future, a member of a "cosmic," "fifth," "synthetic" race that represented the triumph of human evolution, a superior ethnic and spiritual synthesis of human history. Vasconcelos wrote:

> There is no going back in History, for it is all transformation and novelty. No race returns. Each one states its mission, accomplishes it, and passes away. The truth rules in Biblical times as well as in our times; all the ancient historians have formulated it. The days of the pure whites, the victors of today, are as numbered as were the days of their predecessors. Having fulfilled their destiny of mechanizing the world, they themselves have set, without knowing it, the basis for a new period: The period of the fusion and mixing of all peoples. The Indian has no other door to the future but the door of modern culture, nor any other road but the road already cleared by Latin civilization. The white man, as well, will have to depose his pride and look for progress and ulterior redemption in the souls of his brothers from other castes. He will have to diffuse and perfect himself in each of the superior varieties of the species, in each of the modalities that multiply revelation and make genius more powerful.[46]

Vasconcelos concluded that mestizos were superior to all prior and pure races, particularly the Anglo-Saxon white, since they represented a fusion of all historic racial virtues, from the empathy of the Indian to the intellectual rationality that characterized the white. Within this idiosyncratic race theory of Vasconcelos, fully articulated in *La raza cósmica* of 1925, was a theoretical framework that justified both a new Mexican nationalism and the necessity of advancing the imminent superiority of an Iberian American race, whose most potent exponent was the Mexican. The Mexican Revolution signaled the onset of the final verdict of history. It opened the path to completing the evolution of the mestizo by integrating within the new race European high culture, North American economic and technological rationality, and the indigenous Mexican heritage, which for Vasconcelos was not the Aztec, but rather the prior Mayan and Toltec civilizations. Mexico's potential lay in its "syncretism," as Paz (a Vasconcelos admirer) put in, and in the fact that "Mexico is a nation between two civilizations and two pasts."[47]

The Mexican Revolution was the sharp turn in history that could bring about the golden age of the mestizo. Vasconcelos's adaptation of ideas ranging from antiquity to Hegel and Gobineau might have remained a merely provocative twentieth-century example of Darwinism and German idealism were it not that he was also a politician (who ran for president in 1929 in a highly contested election) and wielded power (until he fell out with President Plutarco Elías Calles) and influence long thereafter. Given his theories, it is not surprising that for Vasconcelos, the task of the Mexican Revolution was to bring to every Mexican access to the great European classics, to the Greco-Roman heritage, and above all, to the aesthetic triumph of Byzantine art and architecture. Vasconcelos, in his role as Minister of Education, proudly announced to his boss, President Obregón, "What this country needs is to sit down and read the *Iliad*. I am going to distribute a hundred thousand Homers in the schools of the nation and in the libraries we are going to set up." Vasconcelos later recalled that, during his ministry, "in a surprise move, the first green cloth copies of Homer, Aeschylus, Euripides, Plato, Dante, Goethe, etc. appeared all over the republic."[48]

Vasconcelos articulated what Octavio Paz called the psychic subsoil of the Mexican Revolution. The Mexican revolutionary project of radical modernization through literacy was designed to permit the Mexican people to redefine themselves, using their past "to return to the source, but it was also a beginning, or more precisely a rebeginning. Mexico turned back to its tradition not in order to repeat itself but to initiate another history."[49]

A myth was created out of a reality—Vasconcelos's fusion of the Indian, the Spanish, and the culture of mechanization of North America. Envisaged was a modernity that drew its substance from "the oldest antiquity," the heritage of Cuauhtémoc and Cuauhnáhuac, as well as from recent history, the era of Chapultepec, i.e. Maximilian and Juárez—subjects not only of painting but of music written by Ponce, Chávez, and Revueltas. Protecting this modern Mexican identity from the radical disfigurement of imperialism and colonialism was its own rediscovery of the great civilizations that preceded the European conquest. The future superiority of the "cosmic" race of the Mexican mestizo rested on the marriage between past and future, the integration of the European with the indigenous, not the mere subordination or displacement of the old by the new.

Ironically, although Vasconcelos is remembered most for his patronage of the muralists (he thought little of traditional canvas painting), music was the art form he most cherished; it cohered with his idiosyncratic sense of an organic structure in history. History was governed by a single unifying theme. It resembled the musical form of a symphony, and specifically that of Vasconcelos's most beloved composer, Beethoven.[50]

Vasconcelos's organic vision of history was not lost on Chávez. It provided the nationalist justification for what otherwise might have been understood as three contradictory positions: the imperative of the modern, the assertion of a national distinction that emanated from an ancient historical heritage, and the integration and dissemination of the European cultural tradition. Chávez—like the famous muralists—was the direct beneficiary of the patronage of José Vasconcelos.

Unlike Rivera, however, Chávez never entirely repudiated Vasconcelos, who actually neglected Mexican composers and favored the conservative European tastes that dominated during the Porfirian era. Chávez acknowledged Vasconcelos in 1925 (shortly after his tenure as minister), observing that "The official initiative (in the times of Vasconcelos) created a new institution, no doubt original and with few precedents, all toward a transcendent idea: to promote features of a national style among the uninitiated, particularly extending to the working classes in the cities. This is an important institution, to be regarded as a powerful muscle. The creation of a Department of Aesthetic Culture signifies a good step."[51] Again in 1936 when Vasconcelos was in exile and in some disrepute, Chávez argued that Vasconcelos was responsible for a "brilliant intervention" that created "much anxiety, much action, much intelligence, but also a bit of confusion."[52]

Chávez shared with his friends the Mexican painters an ambition to invent an aesthetic modernism that was synthetic but novel—representative and symbolic of the nation's mestizo soul. The instrument for realization of this vision was the state, since key to Chávez's modernism was a sustained desire that contemporary Mexican music communicate to the Mexican public.[53] If there was in post-revolutionary Mexican music history a single "patriot," to use Sierra's terms, it was Carlos Chávez. As composer, educator, and representative of the state he remained, to the very end, committed to the realization of Vasconcelos's vision of the unique legacy and aesthetic potential bequeathed to the Mexican mestizo.[54]

Vaconcelos's ideology—and to a lesser extent, Sierra's—explains why Chávez remained determined to bring, as a conductor and organizer, North American and European modernist music to Mexican audiences and why between 1934 and 1940 he embraced the admirable policy of Lázaro Cárdenas of making Mexico a refuge, not only for Trotsky, but for those fleeing fascism in Europe, particularly after the collapse of the Spanish Republic and the dismemberment of Czechoslovakia, the Anschluss of Austria, and the outbreak of World War II.[55] Many émigrés from the European music world became integrated into Mexican musical life (one thinks of Henryk Szeryng, who became a cultural ambassador for Mexico and championed Chávez's Violin Concerto), in part through Chávez's influence. Others, like Marcel Rubin, found work but remained insulated in émigré societies and groups, including anti-fascist and communist associations, and ultimately returned to Europe.[56]

The Proletarians and the Futurists

The Mexican Revolution of 1910 to 1920 bears comparison to the Russian Revolution of 1917, and the decade that immediately followed it. The comparison itself was a lively topic in Mexico after 1917. Beginning in 1920, Mexican intellectuals began to take a close look at the process of state control and institutionalization of the arts in the Soviet Union. The Mexican and Russian revolutions sought to rectify radical economic and social injustice. In Russia the revolution inspired, as it did in Mexico, the euphoric sensibility that a new age had begun, one that was discontinuous with the past. This sensibility encouraged an enthusiasm for a radical break with history, particularly in culture and the arts, and therefore a futuristic aesthetic. The Revolution also highlighted as a central objective the education of the masses, including aesthetic education. The arts were for all people, and not the province of an elite; they were seen as giving a voice to the oppressed. In Russia, the ideological discourse concerning the arts was about class.

The state in Russia was a one-party state, just as it would become in post-revolutionary Mexico—and remain so for all of Chávez's life. The Communist Soviet state created a ministry of "enlightenment" (Narkompros). Within the arts, two competing collectives developed, both including musicians. One faction called for the creation of a new, highly accessible proletarian art, and a second argued on behalf of the futuristic and modernist aesthetic imperative of the Russian Revolution. Initially (and briefly) led by Arthur Lourié, in music this second faction was more eclectic and less ideologically rigid. Lenin himself seemed to favor the second group. It was therefore fitting that his mausoleum should end up being one of the last expressions of a radical modernist architectural style, placed provocatively next to the ancient Kremlin and across from the late nineteenth-century shopping arcade in Red Square.

Part of the ideology of the revolutionary aesthetic futurists was a delight in the mechanistic and industrial uniqueness of modern life, particularly the machine.[57] The rejection of the historicist veneer and substance of pre-revolutionary art was intense. In music, industry and mechanization were celebrated in the music of Alexander Mosolov. Younger composers such as Gavriil Popov embraced newfangled experimental instruments (e.g., the theremin). Under Stalin, radical aesthetic modernism was ultimately suppressed in favor of a reductive construct of proletarian art, an aesthetic augmented by markers of Classicism and traditional nationalism, most visible in the buildings Stalin commissioned for Moscow.

Beginning with the presidency of Obregón, as Mexican artists and intellectuals began to think about the state's role in institutionalizing the educational and cultural principles of the Revolution, they looked to the Soviet Union. The individual they held responsible for the flowering of modernist art in Russia under state patronage was Anatoly Vasilyevich Lunacharsky, who with the support of Lenin's wife, Nadezhda Krupskaya, led the culture ministry from 1917 to 1929. The challenges facing Lunacharsky were vast but comparable, given the extent of illiteracy, to those confronting the Mexicans.[58] Lunacharsky's portfolio included schools, universities, and all the arts. Vasconcelos, writing in 1938, recalled that he was unable to persuade the right or the left of the wisdom of his educational and cultural policies during his term in the government. But what surprised him most was the criticism from the left: "I was not able to convince those who censured me from the left that in Russia, Lunacharsky did the same thing, inspired by Maxim Gorky, the 'maestro' of the proletariat."[59] As early as the 1920s the Spanish writer Eugeni d'Ors directly compared Vasconcelos's strategy in Mexico to Lunacharsky's in Russia.[60]

Vasconcelos, despite his lifelong allegiance to a mystic Christianity and ultimate turn to political conservatism (and a flirtation with fascism), was never loath to credit the model of the Soviet Union under Lenin. By commissioning painters to make a spectacular public art through murals, and by supporting public concerts of classical music—notably Beethoven (including a memorable December 1923 performance of Beethoven's Ninth, with a workers' choir, to over 4,500 people) and to a far lesser extent, new Mexican composers who possessed a national agenda (Chávez among them)—he was emulating the Russian example. Even the publication of classical texts and the spread of classical education to the poor mirrored the Russian model. Vasconcelos was following Gorky in his determination that the great achievements of high culture not remain the privileged domain of the rich but the rightful possessions of all Mexicans.

The goal of the Mexican Revolution was entirely domestic: the creation of a nation committed to social justice with a shared identity. The goal of the Russian Revolution, on the other hand, was seen rather as a harbinger of a forthcoming international economic and social transformation. The Russian Revolution, in contrast to the Mexican, was initially only residually directed at forging an internal national consensus. Notwithstanding this difference, Mexico experienced in the 1920s similar tensions and enthusiasms as a result of the state's patronage of culture and education. Chávez's early modernism, from the 1923 *Tres exágonos*, the *Energía* of 1925 to the 1926 ballet *H.P.,* and finally to *Sinfonía de Antigona* of 1933, reflects the aesthetic futurism of the Revolution in a manner reminiscent of Russian modernism of the Lunacharsky era. The generically modern, rather than the uniquely Mexican, stands out in Chávez's studied attempt to ally himself with an avant-garde; in his music he breaks with conventional form, familiar sonorities, and a reliance on repetition. The abstract titles mirror the Constructivist ideals of the Russian painters of the early 1920s and the music of Nikolai Roslavets, who sought a wholly new system of composition, articulated most powerfully in his 1928 cantata *October*, a work savaged by the proletarian cultural faction.

Chávez explicitly acknowledged the significance of the Soviet example when he published an appreciation of Shostakovich's Symphony No. 1 of 1925 on the occasion of its first Mexican performance in 1937 under his own baton. Chávez recalled that he and his Mexican colleagues had expected that the Soviet regime would produce art "of a fundamentally different nature." "After the Revolution of 1917," he continued, "when in the former Russian empire a new Soviet organization was taking shape, we often wondered what new tendencies, and what new expressions the

Soviet youth would reach in the field of the arts. We were anxious to know how a new political system looking to create a new society would produce a new art, a revolutionary art."[61]

In his account of the Shostakovich symphony Chávez revealed the growing skepticism toward ideologically-driven state patronage he developed during the 1930s. He liked the work but saw it as no more than a fine continuation of Tchaikovsky. Great art, Chávez concluded, would not emerge either out of a "five-year plan" or of obedience to "Stalin's wish." The startling fact in Chávez's view was that the genuine Russian modernists and innovators were still Stravinsky and Prokofiev—whom Chávez, in 1937, did not consider a Soviet composer. Chávez's radical optimism about the creation of an unprecedented revolutionary culture in Mexico may have been tempered, but so too was his youthful dismissal of the pre-revolutionary tradition and the bourgeois obsession with individuality and autonomy from the state. The "last word" regarding Russian modernism still lay, Chávez believed, with "the two great pre-revolutionary musicians."[62]

One of the most significant and ironic aspects of the attempt to engender a new modernist Mexican aesthetic in music involves the sustained enmity between Chávez and composer and conductor Julián Carrillo. Carrillo was born in 1875, more than twenty years before Chávez. The direct beneficiary of Porfirio Díaz's patronage, he was sent to Europe to study and given a violin by the state upon his return in 1904. In Germany Carrillo became invested in exploring music theory and acoustics, and in Mexico he headed the National Conservatory before being forced to flee to the United States in 1914. He returned in 1918 and once again headed the conservatory and conducted the National Symphony. To Chávez, Carrillo represented the old establishment, an individual deaf to revolutionary Mexico and wedded to the conservative concept of compositional practice represented by Salomon Jadassohn—Carrillo's first teacher and an exemplar of the high culture of a regressive era.

However, in 1920 things changed radically. Carrillo had always shown interest in the system of fundamentals and overtones—the physics of pitch. That year, Carrillo presented in Mexico his own microtonal system, Sonido 13—the thirteenth sound. The theory was controversial, as was Carrillo's claim that he had arrived at his own microtonal system independently of others, notably Alois Hába. (Carrillo was justified in asserting his originality, since Hába went public with his microtonal system only in 1923.) Carrillo rapidly found advocates, including Leopold Stokowski, who championed his music as late as the early 1960s.

Carrillo was not only persuaded of the utter originality of his work, but also of its importance to Mexico. He went on to patent and produce microtonal pianos, write several books on music, and travel widely performing and lecturing. He never regained any position of significance in Mexico, however; only a year before his death at age ninety was he awarded a national honor.

In 1924, Chávez and Carrillo came into open conflict over Carrillo's Sonido 13. Somewhat earlier, according to Carrillo's memoirs, the older composer had publicly humiliated his younger colleague, whom he considered insufficiently trained. In fact, the conflict between the two had little to do with Sonido 13 but more with personal enmity and envy on the part of Chávez of Vasconcelos's patronage of Carrillo the conductor in the early 1920s. Vasconcelos's skepticism of musical modernism (he believed music had reached its historical pinnacle in Beethoven) and preference for the European nineteenth-century tradition also played a role. Nonetheless, Chávez took aim at Carrillo's pride in Sonido 13 and published a laconic but sardonic response to a self-serving article of Carrillo's. Chávez continued to be unremittingly contemptuous. In 1937, Carrillo responded to yet another article by Chávez decrying the Porfirian legacy represented by Ponce and Carrillo; Carrillo suggested that Chávez's symphonies were symphonies in name only; he questioned his competence as a composer, and predicted that the nationalist revolutionary enthusiasm of rejecting the "Germanization" of musical culture of the pre-revolutionary era would result in a "regressive low standard for the future" in Mexico.[63]

The ironies in the Chávez-Carrillo conflict are poignant. Chávez intentionally cut Carrillo out of the "authorized" version of Mexican musical modernism. Yet Carrillo put forth Mexico's most radical, discontinuous musical innovation. As Carrillo quipped in 1937, "I call nationalist Mexican music the music that did not exist before Mexico produced it. Does such a thing exist? Is it by chance not Sonido 13?"[64] For all of Chávez's strenuous efforts to secure his own standing as the primary voice of the new and avant-garde, it was Carrillo and not Chávez who went furthest down the path of a revolutionary modernism. Chávez's antipathy was both personal and political. Carrillo came forward with Sonido 13 just at the time when Chávez was experimenting with nonrepetition as a compositional strategy and employing sonority in a manner that would successfully link him to the international avant-garde, an ambition with which he succeeded in large measure through the patronage of Varèse.[65]

Although some scholars detect a moving away from Vasconcelos's ideas on the part of Chávez and his circle, and identify Carrillo as far more tied into Vasconcelos's intellectual orbit, the fact remains that both shared the basic premises of a Mexican revolutionary vision. Carrillo was certainly the polar opposite of Chávez, trained rigorously in the German music tradition, whereas Chávez was largely self-taught. But however defensive Chávez was about Carrillo's talent and privileged career path, in reality he eventually came to share Carrillo's defense of the European heritage as the indispensable basis for musical education. Both men were intensely patriotic, although Chávez was more inclined to the left and issues of social justice—ideals shared by Vasconcelos. Finally, both men believed that the Mexican could also be representative of the modern.[66]

Chávez consistently explored new paths as a composer.[67] He believed, as did many Russian constructivist artists, that the modern involved a reframing of history by rejecting Romanticism and reaching back into a far more distant history, one entirely discontinuous with the eighteenth and nineteenth centuries.[68] The key difference was that Carrillo did not search for the revolutionary in Mexico's own history, recent or distant, but took the political revolution in Mexico as the opportunity to create a Mexican version of the modern as the rational and inevitable historical consequence of the nineteenth century. Carrillo saw microtonal modernism as the fulfillment of the logic implicit in the advanced chromatic harmonic usage and polytonality audible in the most recent European developments. Chávez, in contrast, turned for inspiration to pre-Conquest roots and Hispanic Mexican popular idioms.

The final irony is that Carrillo's early pre-modernist music, notably the D-Major Symphony from 1901, reveals a striking gift. That work is more than an academic exercise. It bears comparison to Dohnányi's D-Minor Symphony No. 1, also written in 1901. These two late-Romantic symphonies display uncommon melodic gifts, a fine sense of drama and lyricism, and an uncanny ear for time and structure. Carrillo's symphony is an exceptional work, even if it is not in some arbitrary sense "original"; it certainly is not worthy of derision as imitative and derivative. Rather, it defies Chávez's youthful but typical modernist and anti-historicist dismissal of the Porfirian era and realizes an ambition dear to the Mexican Revolution: the demonstration of equality with the European. Carrillo, a Mexican from the Porfirian era, wrote a symphony as good as any of its time.

By the same token, the works of Chávez that Carrillo sought to disparage, *Sinfonía de Antigona* and *Sinfonía india*, are two of his masterworks. Concise and explicitly evocative of postwar European neoclassicism, *Sinfonía de Antigona* has an organic pattern of motivic elaboration and skillfully employs modal harmony. Carrillo's brusque dismissal was directed at a work distant from any populist Mexican sensibility and was hardly rejectionist vis-à-vis European models. For all that is obviously Mexican on the surface, *Sinfonía india* displays Chávez's powerful and striking use of rhythm and boasts a harmonic structure deftly aligned with the work's dramatically persuasive formal architecture. There is nothing remotely amateurish about either work. The theorist John Vincent used Chávez's *Sinfonía india* as an example of "white note" technique, a precursor of Chávez's 1937 Ten Preludes for Piano, a "veritable inventory" of a modernist adaptation of modal harmony.[69] The relative brevity of the two symphonies was no doubt shocking in comparison with late-Romantic practice.

Modernism and *Mestizaje*

The Chávez-Carrillo rivalry masks the central dilemma of Carlos Chávez's career. Carrillo was himself not the issue. Despite the patronage of Vasconcelos, Carrillo did not play a major role in Mexican musical life after the mid-1920s, neither as conductor or composer. In contrast, Chávez became Mexican music's central figure, someone who balanced ambition as a composer of high modernism of an international character, with the roles of a supporter of popular Mexican music, a composer of highly accessible national works, and a career as a conductor and administrator. Chávez's career was entirely the beneficiary, if not the invention, of the Mexican Revolution. His reputation as a composer blossomed as a result of it. Unlike Rivera, he was a novice when the institutionalization of revolutionary violence into a one-party state apparatus began in earnest, thereby creating modern Mexico. Chávez's first American biographer, Robert L. Parker, suggested that Chávez's career can be seen as one in which the balance between the national and the cosmopolitan shifted gradually toward the cosmopolitan away from a revolutionary, nationalist, or political agenda, particularly in the post–World War II years.[70] Carrillo, in contrast, was not a beneficiary of the Revolution but a resolute modernist whose Mexican patriotism took a more regressive form, reminiscent of the Porfirian era. He saw himself as contributing to the stature and significance of a modernist Mexico in the world by bringing into Mexico in an intense and accessible manner (as his concert programs under Vasconcelos's tenure reveal), the great achievements of European music, to which the microtonal was a unique Mexican contribution.

The actual shape of Chávez's career as composer and organizer—or "agitator"—tells a different story, however. The key to that story is not biographical but political. The comparison between the Mexican and Russian revolutions holds the key. When Chávez began, the optimism over the Revolution's role in culture inspired by Vasconcelos sparked a flourishing of painting and music marked by a spirit of formal innovation and a generous and democratic appropriation of Mexico's rich history and folk and popular culture. But by the end of Cárdenas's regime—and certainly beginning with Miguel Alemán in the postwar years—the fire of the Revolution had burned out.[71] Although he held no official posts after the Alemán era, Chávez's forays back into Mexican musical and cultural life were increasingly frustrating. The open-ended if chaotic atmosphere of the Obregón years were gradually supplanted by a sclerotic one-party dictatorship marred by corruption, increasing poverty, inequality, and violence. Alemán may have been astonishingly generous as a patron of culture, but the monopoly of state support came at the cost of ceding legitimacy of the political vision of modern Mexico to the party (PRI) and the corrupt reality of the state apparatus.

One historical view is that the Mexican state bought tacit consent, even loyalty, among artists and intellectuals to a hierarchy of patronage and control that had pitifully little to do with the ideals that fueled the struggles and violence of the years between 1910 and 1920, not to speak of the subsequent anti-clerical secularism that sparked armed conflict with supporters of the Church.[72] The opposing view is that in contrast to Russia, particularly under Stalin, where the state and the party held distinct views on what the nature, character, and function of art ought to be (one thinks of the anti-modernist attacks of the later 1930s and the era of Zhdanov in the late 1940s), in Mexico the state had little investment in the character of art itself. Rather than seeing Alemán as dictating to Chávez, the situation was perhaps the other way around, just as Vasconcelos influenced Obregon, and not vice versa. There was no censorship in Mexico of a Soviet character, for example.

But by the same token, the national agenda remained clear as a consequence of the essential role of the state as patron of the arts (something Chávez believed in throughout his entire career). The assertion of the distinctly Mexican and the visible existence of an independent intelligentsia and artistic class, even if that independence was, politically speaking, either impotent or susceptible to self-censorship, were important public symbols for the state.

By leaving Mexico for significant periods of time, first in the 1920s and thereafter throughout his life, mostly to take refuge in New York, Chávez escaped the fate of both living as and being seen exclusively as Mexico's "official" composer. The camouflage of any identifiable "Mexican" elements in the later work, from the Piano Concerto of 1938 and perhaps even *Dark Meadow* (the 1943 Martha Graham ballet score that like *Antigona* was based on ancient Greek material recast in modern form—in this case through the lens of Jungian archetypes) to the Violin Concerto of 1948, reveal Chávez's resistance both to a condescending North American expectation of things "Mexican" (in the sense of Copland's Mexican-inspired works, especially the *Three Latin American Sketches* based on material from 1959), as well as to the tempting patronage of the Mexican state.

In the case of Russia, the ideals of the Bolshevik Revolution, insofar as they flourished in the 1920s (apart from a constant penchant for brutality, even under Lenin) were ultimately crushed by the dictatorship of Stalin, the use of terror, and the stultifying corruption, inefficiency, and mediocrity of the Soviet bureaucracy. The rhetoric that once inspired writers, painters, and composers—of a classless society in which justice and decency prevailed, and in which the arts might flourish with a freedom from demeaning aristocratic patronage or the patronage of private wealth—was replaced with a drab and dark mix of fear and cynicism, audible in the sardonic humor and confessional intensity of Shostakovich's finest music.[73]

Likewise, by the late 1940s in Mexico, the revolutionary rhetoric remained, but little else. Popular post-revolutionary Mexican culture experienced a worldwide commercial success. But that success did little to liberate the international image of the Mexican from the confines of a demeaning exoticism. Only the stunning painting done between the 1920s and the 1960s—and at the end by the resolutely politically radical Siqueiros, a thorn and adornment in the eyes of the state along with the ever more remote Tamayo—seemed to suggest the dormant artistic possibilities of the Mexican Revolution.

In the face of this slow extinguishing of the spirit of the Mexican Revolution, Chávez (who had distanced himself from his engagement with Marxism) continued to compose and to make the case for modernism, both severe and accessible.[74] For Chávez, modernism needed to be true in sound to contemporary existence, without a concession to sentimentality or easy listening. The populist and egalitarian ideals of the Revolution suggested that his music needed to make an impact on first hearing, and not necessarily always require the arcane discernment demanded by the radical modernists of the generation of Boulez. Eclecticism was not a sin. Chávez may not have been always successful but he sought to forge a synthesis between modernism and the public similar to the one cultivated by his close friend and colleague Copland. Chávez, however, ventured further afield, toward Cowell, Cage, and Harrison. Even so, the imprint of the Mexican Revolution never left him. His music is compelling in its originality and syncretic quality. It is an artistic expression of a modernist *mestizaje*.

Above all, Chávez's music shares a consistent moral intent characteristic of the muralists: to reach, as a Mexican, a wider public. And it shares with Tamayo a distinct allegiance to modernism and the power of art to transform reality—which for both men was resolutely Mexican—as the finest expression of the human imagination. Chávez deserves a living place in musical history as both modernist and Mexican. In this sense, he remained true to Vasconcelos's Iberian American dream, and alongside the painters, he realized an artistic legacy equal to the cultural agenda of the Mexican Revolution.

NOTES

1. Octavio Paz, *Essays on Mexican Art*, trans. Helen Lane (New York: Harcourt Brace, 1993), 6. Paz was referring to Erwin Panofsky (1892–1968), arguably the twentieth century's most influential and distinguished art historian whose fame rested, among others, on iconographical interpretation and the capacity to connect art and architecture with culture and history. The 1993 English translation leaves Paz's reference without annotation. Ironically, the 1993 complete edition of the Spanish text, *Los privilegios de la vista I: Arte moderno universal*, in *Obras completas* (Mexico City: Fondo de Cultura Económica), 25, mistakenly identifies Paz's reference as to Wolfgang Panofsky (1919–2007), the distinguished physicist and Erwin's son. This is a cautionary tale about the ephemeral nature of reputation, influence, and fame in scholarship in the humanities. Once synonymous with art history and humanistic scholarship and deserving of a passing reference much as a great writer, painter, or composer might, Panofsky the scholar has been cast into irretrievable obscurity. The author would like to thank Leonora Saavedra for sharing her incomparable expertise in the field and Mariel Fiori and Nicole Caso for their invaluable assistance, particularly on the matter of translation.

2. Ibid., 7.

3. Ibid., 40–41.

4. See the exhibit *Octavio Paz y el Arte*, September 2014–January 2015, Museo del Palacio de Bellas Artes, Mexico City.

5. See Paz, *Essays on Mexican Art*, 119–22. On Orozco in New York, see José Clemente Orozco's *The Artist in New York: Letters to Jean Charlot and Unpublished Writings* (Austin: University of Texas Press, 1974).

6. Among the best accounts of modern Mexican history is still Enrique Krauze's *Mexico: Biography of Power. A History of Modern Mexico, 1810–1996*, trans. Hank Heifetz (New York: Harper, 1997). Also useful is William Weber Johnson's *Heroic Mexico: The Narrative History of a Twentieth-Century Revolution* (Garden City, NY: Doubleday, 1968). For revealing specialized studies on the diverse and complex character of the Revolution, especially cast in contrast with popular and official accounts, see John Womack Jr., *Zapata and the Mexican Revolution* (New York: Vintage Books, 1969); and Claudio Lomnitz, *The Return of Comrade Ricardo Flores Magon* (Brooklyn, NY: Zone Books, 2014).

7. Paz, *Essays on Mexican Art*, 123.

8. See Alejandro L. Madrid's fine introductory ethno-musicological study on the history of popular idioms and traditions in Mexico, *Music in Mexico: Experiencing Music, Expressing Culture* (New York: Oxford University Press, 2013).

9. Paz, "Transfigurations," in *Essays on Mexican Art*, 216–38.

10. The complete catalogue of works by Chávez can be found in *Carlos Chávez: Catalogo completo de sus obras* (Mexico City: Sociedad de Autores y Compositores de Música, 1971).

11. Chávez's public service in the 1930s included oversight over all the arts. He wrote perceptively on the painters. See Carlos Chávez, *Obras: Escritos periodísticos*, ed. Gloria Carmona, 3 vols. (Mexico City: El Colegio Nacional, 1997–2014), 2:543–47, 3:275–78, and 3:309–10.

12. Quoted in Christina Pacheco, *La luz de México: Entrevistas con pintores y fotógrafos*, introduction by Carlos Monsiváis (Mexico City: Fondo de Cultura Económica, 2205), 608.

13. See, for example, Chávez, "Educación intensiva," in *Obras: Escritos periodísticos*, 3:185–93.

14. The two most performed works for orchestra are *Sensemayá* and *Las noche de los Mayas*, a suite, including music he did not write, drawn from a Reveultas film score.

15. See Robert Stevenson, *Music in Mexico: A Historical Survey* (New York: Crowell, 1952).

16. See Paz, *Los privilegios de la vista II: Arte de Mexico*, 60–63, 149–67.

17. On the nineteenth-century musical culture of Mexico, see Otto Mayer-Serra *Panorama de la música mexicana* (Mexico City: El Colegio de Mexico, 1941).

18. See Chávez, "La tesis nacionalista de Ponce," in *Obras: Escritos periodísticos*, 1:299–304; see also Alejandro L. Madrid, *Sounds of the Modern Nation: Music, Culture, and Ideas in Post-Revolutionary Mexico* (Philadelphia: Temple University Press, 2009), 82–110.

19. Chávez, "Artículo prólogo," in *Obras: Escritos periodísticos*, 1:3.

20. See Chávez, "En el octogésimo aniversario de Igor Stravinsky," in *Obras: Escritos periodísticos*, 3:267–74.

21. Chávez, "Importancia actual del florecimiento del la música nacional," in *Obras: Escritos periodísticos*, 1:9.

22. Chávez "La música propria de México," *Obras: Escritos periodísticos*, 1:165

23. Chávez, ibid., 166.

24. It must be acknowledged that there was a "dark" side to Chávez's prominence. There are those who see his prominence as ruthlessly self-engineered. He was so powerful, so often controlling and vindictive that a posthumous animosity against him has developed within Mexican intellectual and scholarly circles. What, however, is beyond question were his energy and his startling success in creating the musical culture of modern Mexico. His historical significance is beyond question. I am indebted to Leonora Saavedra for this perspective.

25. See Claudio Lomnitz-Adler, *Exits from the Labyrinth: Culture and Ideology in the Mexican National Space* (Chicago: Chicago University Press, 1992), 1–4. See also Lomnitz, *Deep Mexico, Silent Mexico: An Anthropology of Nationalism* (Minneapolis: University of Minnesota Press, 201); and *Death and the Idea of Mexico* (New York: Zone Books, 2008).

26. Chávez, *Musical Thought* (Cambridge, MA: Harvard University Press, 1961), 18.

27. Henry Cowell, "Carlos Chávez," *Pro-Musica Quarterly* 7/1 (June 1928): 19.

28. Quoted in Lomnitz-Adler, *Exits from the Labyrinth*, 277.

29. Ibid., 2.

30. Chávez, *Musical Thought*, 7 and 88; see also "Arte proletario," in *Obras: Escritos periodísticos*, 1:261–62.

31. Chávez, "México y la música," in *Obras: Escritos periodísticos*, 1:82.

32. See Leonora Saavedra, "Carlos Chávez's Polysemic Style: Constructing the National, Seeking the Cosmopolitan," *Journal of the American Musicological Society* 68/1 (2015): 99–150.

33. Cowell, "Carlos Chávez," 33.

34. Program pamphlet for "Mexican Music," notes by Herbert Weinstock (New York: Museum of Modern Art, 1940).

35. See the edition that contains Paz's supplements to the original text, *El laberinto de la soledad. Postdata. Vuelta a "El laberinto de la soledad"* (Mexico City: Fondo de Cultura Económica, 2004). For an English translation of the original text, see T*he Labyrinth of Solitude and Other Writings*, trans. Lysander Kemp, Yara Milos, and Rachel Phillips Belash (New York: Grove Press, 1985).

36. Perhaps the most powerful and original chapter in Chávez's Norton Lectures is the chapter "Repetition in Music." See *Musical Thoughts*, 55–84.

37. See the short 1946 pamphlet by Otto Mayer-Serra, "The Present State of Music in Mexico" (Washington, DC: Pan American Union, 1960).

38. See Helen Delpar *The Enormous Vogue of Things Mexican: Cultural Relations between the United States and Mexico, 1920–1935* (Tuscaloosa: University of Alabama Press, 1992). For examples of the North American obsession with Mexico in this period see the classic books of Stuart Chase, *Mexico: A Study of Two Americas*, in collaboration with Marian Tyler (New York: Macmillan, 1931); Frank Tannenbaum, *Peace by Revolution: Mexico after 1910* (New York: Columbia University Press, 1933); and Carleton Beals, *Mexico: An Interpretation* (New York: Huebsch, 1923). A late contribution to this literature is Earl Shorris, *The Life and Times of Mexico* (New York: W. W. Norton, 2004).

39. See Roberto García Morillo, *Carlos Chávez: Vida y obra* (Mexico: Fondo de Cultura Económica, 1960). This extensive biography and analysis of the music brings Chávez up to the late 1950s.

40. See Robert L. Parker, *Carlos Chávez: Mexico's Modern-Day Orpheus* (Boston: Twayne, 1983); and his *Carlos Chávez: Guide to Research* (New York: Garland Press, 1998).

41. Madrid, *Sounds of the Modern Nation*, 51.

42. Justo Sierra, *The Political Evolution of the Mexican People*, trans. Charles Ramsdell, introduction by Edmundo O'Gorman; prologue by Alfonso Reyes (Austin: University of Texas Press, 1969), 368.

43. Ibid.

44. See Chávez's version of this idea in the opening of the Norton Lectures, "A Latin American Composer," in *Musical Thought*, 1–18.

45. Vasconcelos, whom Paz particularly admired, had among the most eclectic and bizarre careers. On Vasconcelos, see Luis A. Marentes, *José Vasconcelos and the Writing of the Mexican Revolution* (New York: Twayne, 2000); Vasconcelos's own *Breve historia de México*, introduction by Luis González y González (Mexico City: Trillas, 1998); and above all, Christopher Domínguez Michael, ed., *Los retornos de Ulises: Una antología de José Vasconcelos* (Mexico City: Secretaría de Educacíon Pública and Fondo de Cultura Económica, 2010). The most penetrating account of Vasconcelos's ideas and their connection to music can be found in the superb dissertation by Leonora Saavedra, "Of Selves and Others: Historiography, Ideology and the Politics of Modern Mexican Music" (PhD diss., University of Pittsburgh, 2001), 51–135.

46. José Vasconcelos, *The Cosmic Race/La raza cósmica*, trans. with an introduction by Didier T. Jaén, afterword by Joseba Gailondo (Baltimore: Johns Hopkins University Press, 1997), 16.

47. Paz, *The Labyrinth of Solitude*, 345, 362; on Vasconcelos, 152–55.

48. José Vasconcelos, *A Mexican Ulysses: An Autobiography*, trans. and abridged by W. Rex Crawford (Bloomington: Indiana University Press, 1963), 158.

49. Octavio Paz, "Re/Visions: Mural Painting," in *Essays on Mexican Art*, 115.

50. Under Vasconcelos's patronage, Jullián Carillo conducted an extraordinary amount of Beethoven. But Chávez was also a Beethoven admirer, as his extensive analysis of several Beethoven symphonies in his 1958 Norton Lectures reveals.

51. Chávez, "México y la música," in *Obras: Escritos periodísticos*, 1:84.

52. Chávez, "Consecuensias del Movimiento de 1911," in *Obras: Escritos periodísticos*, 1:309.

53. See Chávez's chapter "Art as Communication," in *Musical Thought*, 19–34. This emphasis on the wide communicative power of contemporary music was shared by Aaron Copland, the North American colleague with whom Chávez had the most sustained friendship.

54. See Marco Velazquez and Mary Kay Vaughan, "Mestizaje and Musical Nationalism in Mexico," in *The Eagle and the Virgin: National and Cultural Revolution in*

Mexico, 1920–1940, ed. Mary Kay Vaughan and Stephen E. Lewis (Durham, NC: Duke University Press, 2006), 95–118.

55. See Chávez's article "Xenofobia, no" from 1944, in *Obras: Escritos periodísticos*, 2:127–31. The difference between Chávez's repertoire and Julián Carrillo's in the 1920s (see below) as a conductor was Chávez's resolute programming of twentieth-century European and North American composers. See Saavedra, "Of Selves and Others."

56. See Hartmut Krones, "Marcel Rubin und das österreichische Exil in Mexico," in *Geächtet, verboten, vertrieben: Österreichische Musiker, 1934–1938–1945*, ed. Hartmut Krones (Vienna: Böhlau, 2013), 521–50.

57. As suggested below, Chávez's 1926 ballet *H.P.* can be understood in this context.

58. On Lunacharsky, see Sheila Fitzpatrick, *The Commissariat of Enlightenment: Soviet Organization of Education in the Arts Under Lunacharsky* (Cambridge: Cambridge University Press, 1970); Boris Schwartz, *Music and Musical Life in Soviet Russia, 1917–1970* (New York: W. W. Norton, 1972), 10–35; Katerina Clark, *Petersburg: Crucible of Cultural Revolution* (Cambridge, MA: Harvard University Press, 1995); David Haas, *Leningrad's Modernists: Studies in Composition and Musical Thought, 1917–1932* (New York: Peter Lang, 1998); Levon Hakobian, *Music of the Soviet Age, 1917–1987* (Stockholm: Melos Music Literature, 1998); and Frans C. Lemaire, *Le destin russe et la musique: Un siècle d'histoire de la Révolution à nos jours* (Paris: Fayard, 2005).

59. Jose Vasconcelos, "El desastre (Fragmento 1938)," in Domínguez, *Los retornos de Ulises*, 346.

60. Quoted by Xavier Villaurrutia in his article on Vasconcelos, in Domínguez, *Los retornos de Ulises*, 441.

61. Chávez, "Un compositor soviético," in *Obras: Escritos periodísticos*, 1:327.

62. Ibid., 1:328.

63. Quoted in the editorial footnote to Chávez, "La primera etapa nacionalista," in *Obras: Escritos periodísticos*, 1:311.

64. Ibid.

65. See Olga Picún and Consuelo Carredano, "El nacionalismo musical mexicano: Una lectura desde los sonidos y los silencios," in *El arte en tiempos de cambio, 1810–1910–2010*, ed. Fausto Ramírez, Luise Noelle, and Hugo Arciniega (Mexico: Instituto de Investigaciones Estéticas, Universidad Nacional Autónoma de México, 2012).

66. See Madrid, *Sounds of the Modern Nation*, 18–81.

67. See Chávez's essay on the possibilities of electronic music and serialism. "Los instrumentos eléctricos de reproducción musical," from 1932 in *Obras: Escritos periodísticos*, 1:221–27, and "El dodecafonismo en México" from 1955 in *Obras: Escritos periodísticos*, 3:161–64.

68. See Hillel Gregory Kazovsky, "'Long Live Nationality!' Jewish Artists in the Russian Avant-Garde," in *Jewish Artists in the Russian Avant-Garde* (Moscow: Jewish Museum and Center for Tolerance, 2015), 13–24.

69. John Vincent, *The Diatonic Modes in Modern Music* (Hollywood: Curlew Music Publishers, 1974), 375.

70. See Parker, *Carlos Chávez: Mexico's Modern-Day Orpheus*, 15–16; and *Carlos Chávez: A Guide to Research*, 7–8.

71. On Alemán, see Krauze, *Mexico: Biography of Power*, 526–600.

72. See ibid.; Paz, *Essays on Mexican Art*, 141–43 and 147–52; and Lomnitz, *Deep Mexico, Silent Mexico*, 223–27.

73. On the Mexican state and the intellectuals, see Lomnitz-Adler, *Exits from the Labyrinth*.

74. See the fragments collected in volume 3 of *Obras: Escritos periodísticos* that reveal Chávez's attitude at the end of his life (415–21).

Index

Page numbers followed by n indicate notes.
Page numbers in italics indicate figures, tables, or excerpts from works of music.

Index of Carlos Chávez's Compositions

Index of Names and Subjects

Notes on the Contributors

Ana R. Alonso-Minutti is assistant professor of musicology at the University of New Mexico. She holds degrees from the Universidad de las Américas, Puebla (BA) and the University of California, Davis (MA, PhD). Her research interests include contemporary experimental practices, interdisciplinary intersections, and intellectual elites. Some of her essays have been published in *Latin American Music Review*, *Revista Argentina de Musicología*, and *Pauta*, among other journals. Currently she is writing a book tentatively entitled *Mario Lavista and Musical Cosmopolitanism in Late Twentieth-Century Mexico*, to be published by Oxford University Press.

Amy Bauer is associate professor of music at the University of California, Irvine, and received her PhD in music theory from Yale University. She has published articles in *Music Analysis*, *The Journal of Music Theory*, *Contemporary Music Review*, *Indiana Theory Review*, and *Ars Lyrica*, and book chapters on the music of Ligeti, Olivier Messiaen, David Lang, the television musical, and issues in the philosophy and reception of modernist music. She has published a monograph on the music of Ligeti (*Ligeti's Laments: Nostalgia, Exoticism, and the Absolute*, Ashgate, 2011), and has an edited collection forthcoming from Ashgate (*Ligeti's Cultural Identities*, Amy Bauer and Márton Kerékfy, editors).

Leon Botstein is president and Leon Levy Professor in the Arts of Bard College, author of several books, and editor of *The Compleat Brahms* (1999) and *The Musical Quarterly*. The music director of the American Symphony Orchestra and conductor laureate of the Jerusalem Symphony Orchestra, he has recorded works by, among others, Szymanowski, Hartmann, Bruch, Dukas, Foulds, Toch, Dohnányi, Bruckner, Chausson, Richard Strauss, Mendelssohn, Popov, Shostakovich, and Liszt.

David Brodbeck is professor of music at the University of California, Irvine. He has published widely on topics in German musical culture of the nineteenth century, ranging from the dances of Franz Schubert and the sacred music of Felix Mendelssohn to various aspects of Johannes Brahms's life and music and the musical culture of late-nineteenth-century Vienna. His more recent publications include "A Tale of Two Brothers: Behind the Scenes of Goldmark's First Opera," *Musical Quarterly* (2015) and the monograph *Defining Deutschtum: Political Ideology, German Identity, and Music-Critical Discourse in Liberal Vienna* (Oxford University Press, 2014).

Helen Delpar is professor of history emerita in Latin American history at the University of Alabama. Her monograph *The Enormous Vogue of Things Mexican: Cultural Relations Between the United States and Mexico, 1920–1935* (University of Alabama Press, 1992), which received the A. B. Thomas Award, Southeastern Council of Latin American Studies, was groundbreaking in the field of inter-American cultural relations. She has published widely on modern and colonial Latin America, and wrote the chapter on "Mexican Culture, 1920–1945," in the *Oxford History of Mexico*, edited by Michael C. Meyer and William H. Beezley.

Susana González Aktories is professor of comparative literature at the National Autonomous University of Mexico (UNAM). She has a PhD in Spanish philology from the Universidad Complutense de Madrid. Her main fields of research are semiotics and intermediality, mainly the comparison of literature and music. She has particular interest in materiality, notation, and ways of reading and decoding the written text as well as sound documents, focusing on the voice. In recent years she has coedited volumes such as *Reflexiones sobre semiología musical* and *Entre artes/entre actos: Ecfrasis e intermedialidad*.

Roberto Kolb-Neuhaus is professor of music at UNAM, the National University of Mexico. His main research focuses on Silvestre Revueltas. Beyond cataloguing, digitalizing, and recording this composer's work, he has edited and published several books and published articles in prestigious journals in Europe and the Americas. His research on Revueltas involves perspectives such as semiotics, inter- and transmediality, and post-colonial studies, among others.

James Krippner is a professor in the department of history at Haverford College and associate editor and book review editor for *The Americas: A Quarterly Review of Latin American History*. His first book, *Rereading the Conquest: Power, Politics, and the History of Early Colonial Michoacán, Mexico, 1521–1565*, was published in 2001 by the Pennsylvania State University Press. His second book, *Paul Strand in Mexico*, was published by Aperture in 2010. He is currently researching the built environment and religious culture of Rio de Janeiro in the sixteenth and seventeenth centuries.

Rebecca Levi (translator) received her BA from Yale University, where she studied comparative literature and translated several short stories by Italian writer Paolo Zanotti. Since then, she has made a career in music education, working with the El Sistema orchestra program in Venezuela and studying at New England Conservatory in the inaugural class of Abreu Fellows. She has lived in Peru and currently resides in Colombia, where she performs Latin American folk music and teaches with La Red de Música de Medellín.

Ricardo Miranda is professor of musicology at Universidad Veracruzana. His work on Mexican music has appeared in different journals and several books. A specialist on the music of twentieth-century composers Manuel M. Ponce and José Rolón, he has also written on music from the Viceregal and Independence periods. From 2007 to 2010 he was director of the Conservatorio Nacional de Música.

Howard Pollack is John and Rebecca Moores Professor at the University of Houston, and the author of six books, including *Aaron Copland: The Life and Work of an Uncommon Man*, *George Gershwin: His Life and Work*, and most recently, *Marc Blitzstein: His Life, His Work, His World*.

Leonora Saavedra is associate professor of music at the University of California, Riverside. Born in Mexico City, she was director of Mexico's National Center for Music Research (CENIDIM) before moving to the United States. Her research centers upon Mexican music of the late-nineteenth and twentieth centuries, exoticism, nationalism and modernism, music and the state, and the musical relations between Mexico and the United States. Her article "Carlos Chávez's Polysemic Style: Constructing the National, Seeking the Cosmopolitan" appeared recently in the *Journal of the American Musicological Society*, and she is currently writing a book on Mexican music for Oxford University Press.

Antonio Saborit is the director of the Museo Nacional de Antropología at the Instituto Nacional de Antropología e Historia (INAH) of Mexico. A researcher at the Dirección de Estudios Históricos at INAH, he holds degrees in modern languages, history, and ethnohistory from Universidad Nacional Autónoma de México (UNAM) and the Escuela Nacional de Antropología e Historia (ENAH). He is the author of numerous works on art, anthropology, and history, including "Marius de Zayas: Transatlantic Visionary of Art" (in Deborah Cullen, ed., *Nexus New York*, 2009).

Stephanie N. Stallings graduated with a PhD in musicology from the Florida State University in 2009. Her research interests include Pan-Americanism, international cultural exchange, Mexican modernism, and arts in diplomacy. She works for the Los Angeles County Arts Commission as a researcher and evaluator of public arts engagement programs.

Christina Taylor Gibson teaches at the Catholic University of America in Washington, D.C. She studies musical modernism in the Americas during the first half of the twentieth century, with particular interest in identity creation, reception, and cultural exchange—particularly between the United States and Mexico. Recent publications include "Manuel M. Ponce's *canciones* in New York: Mexican Musical Identity and the Mexico Vogue," in *Music, Longing, and Belonging* edited by Magdalena Waligórska (2013) and "The Reception of Carlos Chávez's *Horsepower:* A Pan-American Communication Failure," *American Music* (Summer 2012) .

Luisa Vilar-Payá is a professor of musicology at Universidad de las Américas, Puebla, México, where she also served as dean of arts, humanities, and social sciences for twelve years, until 2011. Her research focuses on twentieth-century music and beyond, with an emphasis on music analysis as a key factor of historical reception. Her publications in Argentina, Mexico, Spain, and the United States have focused on contemporary composers, with an emphasis on women. She has also published on Carlos Chávez, Silvestre Revueltas, and the American analytical reception of Arnold Schoenberg. She holds degrees from Columbia University and UC Berkeley.

OTHER PRINCETON UNIVERSITY PRESS VOLUMES PUBLISHED IN CONJUNCTION WITH THE BARD MUSIC FESTIVAL

Brahms and His World
edited by Walter Frisch (1990)

Mendelssohn and His World
edited by R. Larry Todd (1991)

Richard Strauss and His World
edited by Bryan Gilliam (1992)

Dvořák and His World
edited by Michael Beckerman (1993)

Schumann and His World
edited by R. Larry Todd (1994)

Bartók and His World
edited by Peter Laki (1995)

Charles Ives and His World
edited by J. Peter Burkholder (1996)

Haydn and His World
edited by Elaine R. Sisman (1997)

Tchaikovsky and His World
edited by Leslie Kearney (1998)

Schoenberg and His World
edited by Walter Frisch (1999)

Beethoven and His World
edited by Scott Burnham and Michael P. Steinberg (2000)

Debussy and His World
edited by Jane F. Fulcher (2001)

Mahler and His World
edited by Karen Painter (2002)

Janáček and His World
edited by Michael Beckerman (2003)

Shostakovich and His World
edited by Laurel E. Fay (2004)

Aaron Copland and His World
edited by Carol J. Oja and Judith Tick (2005)

Franz Liszt and His World
edited by Christopher H. Gibbs and Dana Gooley (2006)

Edward Elgar and His World
edited by Byron Adams (2008)

Sergey Prokofiev and His World
edited by Simon Morrison (2008)

Brahms and His World (revised edition)
edited by Walter Frisch and Kevin C. Karnes (2009)

Richard Wagner and His World
edited by Thomas S. Grey (2009)

Alban Berg and His World
edited by Christopher Hailey (2010)

Jean Sibelius and His World
edited by Daniel M. Grimley (2011)

Camille Saint-Saëns and His World
edited by Jann Pasler (2012)

Stravinsky and His World
edited by Tamara Levitz (2013)

Franz Schubert and His World
edited by Christopher H. Gibbs and Morten Solvik (2014)